Winner, Numismatic Literary Guild "Extraordinary Merit" Award
(Cherrypickers' Guide, 5th edition, volume II)

Cherrypickers' Guide
Celebrating 30-plus years!
Since 1990

Reader Comments

What People are Saying About the *Cherrypickers' Guide*

"The *Cherrypickers' Guide* represents one-stop shopping for anyone interested in the most important varieties among U.S. coins. With this single volume, the eagle-eyed collector will be prepared to identify valuable coins that many others have missed."

Leonard Augsburger
President, Liberty Seated Collectors Club
Coauthor, **The Secret History of the First U.S. Mint**

"The *Cherrypickers' Guide* is the ultimate reference for variety collectors. As a cataloger, I keep a copy of the book on my desk and refer to it constantly. When I travel to conventions, I never leave home without it."

Mark Borckardt
Numismatic researcher

"I cannot imagine collecting U.S. coins without a copy of the *Cherrypickers' Guide* near at hand. In this latest volume, editor Larry Briggs adds his expertise to the rock-solid foundation built by J.T. Stanton, Bill Fivaz, and other specialists."

Q. David Bowers
Chairman Emeritus, Stack's Bowers Galleries
Research Editor, **A Guide Book of United States Coins**

"The *Cherrypickers' Guide* is entertaining, educational, and useful in a thousand ways."

Kenneth Bressett
Past president, American Numismatic Association
Editor Emeritus, **A Guide Book of United States Coins**

"Numismatics should always be a voyage of discovery, of learning new facts and having fun in the process. I can think of no single, better resource for discovery, facts, and fun than the *Cherrypickers' Guide.*"

Richard Doty (1942–2013)
Senior Curator of Numismatics, Smithsonian Institution

"No numismatic reference grabs me the way the *Cherrypickers' Guide* does each and every time a new volume is published. I immediately devour the whole book as fast as I can. I love my numismatic library and this book is easily the most often used of them all!"

Mike Ellis
Governor, American Numismatic Association
Past president, CONECA

"One of the great thrills of numismatics is to discover an unattributed rarity. The *Cherrypickers' Guide* provides the tools for anyone to make such a discovery. A great book for beginners or advanced collectors!"

Jeff Garrett
Past president, American Numismatic Association
***Senior Editor,* A Guide Book of United States Coins**

"The *Cherrypickers' Guide* helps identify that rare 'needle-in-a-haystack' variety with easy-to-use attribution guides and excellent close-up images. It's handy to carry, easy to navigate, and gives you the knowledge that was once available only to advanced collectors and specialists."

Ron Guth
Chief Investigator, Numismatic Detective Agency
***Coauthor,* 100 Greatest U.S. Coins**

"The *Cherrypickers' Guide* continues to be the standard bearer for popular variety collecting. Professionally, I use it on an almost daily basis, and it's always within arm's reach."

David W. Lange (1958–2023)
Research Director, NGC
***Author,* A Guide Book of Modern United States Proof Coin Sets**

"The *Cherrypickers' Guide* is an awesome treasure map with great pictures and information, loaded with education for the novice and the advanced collector, including how to tell the good from the spurious."

Brian Raines
Die-variety specialist

"The *Cherrypickers' Guide* remains a book that both the die-hard specialist and the novice collector can enjoy, being what may be the best compilation of significant and popular die varieties."

Tanner Scott
Coeditor, doubleddie.com

"I wish I had an off-center cent for every time I referred a caller to check in the *Cherrypickers' Guide* for a die variety they just found. It's the best reference guide to the most important die varieties. The close-up photos make it easy for anyone—novice or advanced collector—to compare and identify their coins. The *Cherrypickers' Guide* is an absolute must for your numismatic library."

Fred Weinberg
Numismatic researcher and coin dealer
***Coauthor,* 100 Greatest U.S. Error Coins**

CHERRYPICKERS' GUIDE

to Rare Die Varieties of United States Coins

Sixth Edition • Volume II
Half Dimes Through Quarter Dollars

Normal 1966 Dime.

Regular dimes from the Special Mint Sets of 1966 are worth a couple dollars. But look closer. . . .

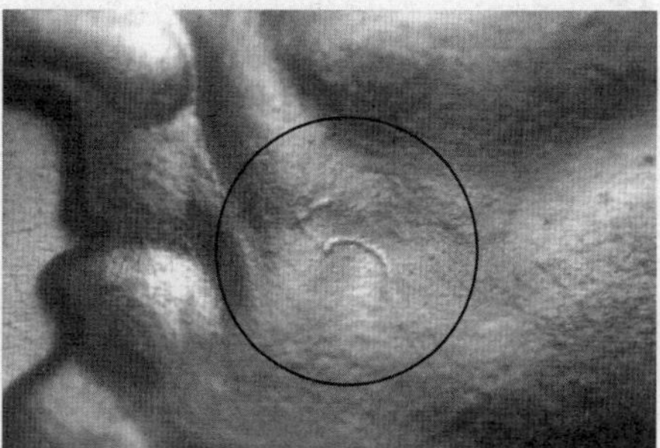

Rare 1966 "5 on Cheek" Variety.

If you see a mark that resembles a numeral 5 on President Roosevelt's cheek, you have a rare die variety worth $200 or more!

Bill Fivaz · J.T. Stanton

Volume Editor: Larry Briggs

Forewords by Q. David Bowers and Kenneth Bressett

CHERRYPICKERS' GUIDE

to Rare Die Varieties of United States Coins

Sixth Edition • Volume II

Second Printing

SINCE 1934

©2026 Whitman®

4001 Helton Dr., Florence, AL 35630

whitman.com

The Cherrypickers' Guide is a registered trademark of Whitman.

All rights reserved, including duplication of any kind and storage in electronic or visual retrieval systems. Permission is granted for writers to use a reasonable number of brief excerpts and quotations in printed reviews and articles, provided credit is given to the title of the work and to the authors. Written permission from the publisher is required for other uses of text, illustrations, and other content, including in books and electronic or other media.

Correspondence concerning this book may be directed to the publisher, Attn: Cherrypickers, at the mailing address above, or by emailing Cherrypickers@whitman.com.

ISBN: 978-07948-50111 / ZT2135-03/26 / Ebook ISBN: 978-07948-51965

Printed in China

Disclaimer: Expert opinion should be sought in any significant numismatic purchase. This book is presented as a guide only. No warranty or representation of any kind is made concerning the completeness of the information presented. The authors and editor are professional numismatists who regularly buy, trade, and sometimes hold certain of the items discussed in this book.

Caveat: The price estimates given are subject to variation and differences of opinion. Before making a decision to buy or sell, consult the latest information. Past performance of the rare-coin market or any coin or series within that market is not necessarily an indication of future performance, as the future is unknown. Such factors as changing demand, popularity, grading interpretations, strength of the overall coin market, and economic conditions will continue to be influences.

Advertisements within this book: Whitman does not endorse, warrant, or guarantee any of the products or services of its advertisers. All warranties and guarantees are the sole responsibility of the advertiser.

About the Cover: The central featured coin is the 1919 Mercury dime with a doubled-die obverse (cataloged as FS-10-1919-101), a variety discovered fairly recently. At an American Numismatic Association World's Fair of Money presentation in Atlanta, Bill Fivaz and Whitman publisher Dennis Tucker used this coin as a case study in how visually dramatic die varieties can remain undiscovered for generations—just waiting to be found by a keen-eyed cherrypicker!

For a complete catalog of numismatic reference books, supplies, and storage products, visit Whitman online at Whitman.com.

CONTENTS

DEDICATION

J.T. Stanton.

This volume of the *Cherrypickers' Guide* is dedicated to researcher, writer, coin dealer, teacher, and constant hobby ambassador J.T. Stanton.

J.T., one-half of the creative team (along with coauthor Bill Fivaz) behind the *Cherrypickers' Guide to Rare Die Varieties of United States Coins,* died October 19, 2018, following a brief illness, at the age of 66. He was surrounded by his family at the time of his passing.

If you asked J.T. what his initials stood for, he would reply, "Just Terrific!" (Actually, it's Jeffery Thomas.) He was born in Macon, in the heart of Georgia, about 85 miles south of Atlanta. J.T.'s career was in retail management and printing, but the hobby community knew him best as a professional numismatist and educator who helped popularize "cherrypicking"—the art and science of closely examining what appear to be normal coins, looking for doubled dates and other die anomalies that reveal them to be rare and valuable varieties.

J.T. Stanton, CONECA past president Mike Ellis, and Bill Fivaz pose with the *Cherrypickers' Guide* at the American Numismatic Association World's Fair of Money, Denver, Colorado, August 2006.

J.T. and Bill debuted the first edition of the *Cherrypickers' Guide* at the January 1990 Florida United Numismatists convention in Tampa. Collectors bought the 500 copies the authors carried to the show and they gathered a backlog of orders to be mailed later. The first print run of 3,000 books sold out in less than 10 months. Word-of-mouth publicity and excitement in the numismatic press convinced J.T. and Bill to create a second edition, with more listings, the addition of retail values, and other improvements. It took collectors about six months to snap up the second edition's print run of 5,000 books.

The third edition featured about five times as many varieties as the first. It went into six printings totaling more than 28,000 copies—a best-seller in the antiques-and-collectibles market.

By the fourth edition the *Cherrypickers' Guide* was so large it had to be divided into two volumes. Volume I covered half cents through nickels. Whitman Publishing acquired rights to the book and published volume II, with half dimes through silver dollars, gold, and commemoratives, in 2006.

"I first met J.T. Stanton in December 2005, in Atlanta, after Whitman bought the *Cherrypickers' Guide*," recalled publisher Dennis Tucker. "He was 15 years into his journey as one of the most famous popular names in the hobby—but he was as humble, down-to-earth, and good-natured as anyone I've met. He insisted that we put him up at 'the cheapest hotel you can find,' and not make a fuss. We had breakfast at the local waffle place."

J.T. was always forward-thinking, upbeat, and optimistic. He cared deeply about the hobby and coin collectors. "Above all," he and Bill have said, "always use courtesy and respect in all your dealings, be honest, and always act in a professional manner. You'll make some friends along the way, and we guarantee you'll come out ahead in the long run."

"The last time I talked with J.T.," said Dennis, "was a few months before he passed, when we had several conversations about coins and life in general. He and Susan, his wife of 38 years, had recently moved from their longtime home city of Savannah to a town about an hour south and slightly inland. 'I love it here,' he told me. 'I feed the deer twice each day, and the freshwater lake is 75 feet from my back door. Every day Susan and I are down here we enjoy it more and more.' He talked about having privacy but also the advantages of a community. 'And I've always loved nature,' he said, 'so this really is a slice of Heaven.'

"Our last acts of collaboration as publisher and author/researcher illustrate J.T.'s generosity to the hobby. When I told him Whitman needed some photographs of modern Lincoln cents, Roosevelt dimes, and Washington quarters, he threw open his entire image library of coins. He said if there was anything he hadn't photographed yet, to just let him know. And if one of the large groups of photos wasn't in the style or format we needed, he could reshoot everything in three weeks."

When J.T. passed away, he had been happily selling coins on eBay (with more than 17,000 positive transactions), was active in ongoing discussion and analysis of die varieties, and had recently pitched a new book idea. He was a numismatist to the end.

With a grateful hobby's thanks, this volume of the *Cherrypickers' Guide* is dedicated to J.T. Stanton.

FOREWORD

Q. David Bowers

Time was when relatively few interesting die varieties were known to the coin-collecting fraternity. The *Guide Book of United States Coins* (the hobby's popular "Red Book," first issued in 1946) listed certain of these, after which ensuing editions listed more. Today the *Red Book* offers a few hundred, mostly devoted to early coinage issues, and the 1,504-page *Mega Red* includes even more. Examples include the 1794 copper cent with 94 five-pointed stars on the reverse, one of the most curious varieties of all time; and the cent of 1801 with the reverse having three errors—II and ITED instead of UNITED, one stem missing from the wreath, and the fraction expressed as the mathematically meaningless 1/000. A variety of 1800 silver dollar is called the AMERICAI, because of the extraneous I at the end of the word. Then we have various doubled-die coins, led by the famous 1955 doubled-die Lincoln cent, and joined by the 1916 doubled-die Buffalo nickel and others. With few exceptions, these varieties listed in the *Red Book* are at once relatively scarce and very expensive.

As interesting as these *Red Book*–listed coins may be, they are only the tip of the iceberg!

A great change came to the hobby in 1962 when Frank G. Spadone published his *Major Variety & Oddity Guide of United States Coins.* This popular book was, for lack of a better expression, for the "common man"—listing many varieties not found in the *Red Book*, but interesting to collect, and dating mainly from the modern era. Today, Spadone's pioneering work is little remembered, but it remains important as a foundation.

Enter Bill Fivaz and J.T. Stanton and their *Cherrypickers' Guide to Rare Die Varieties.* Greatly expanding the field of opportunity, the authors studied coins mainly from the twentieth century and compiled a veritable encyclopedia of interesting repunchings, misplaced dates, and the like. Armed with a copy of this book a collector, with magnifying glass in hand, could review a dealer's stock of seemingly ordinary Washington quarters or Mercury dimes and find curious and interesting varieties—mintmarks misaligned or punched over each other, oddities in the lettering, and more. A very nice collection could be formed at modest cost, all the while offering the thrill of the chase.

Today the sixth edition, volume II, of the *Cherrypickers' Guide,* now with well-known expert Larry Briggs building upon the work of Fivaz and Stanton, is the latest and most extensive passport to finding treasures. Coin conventions, shops, Internet listings, and even pocket change are the hunting fields for varieties that in all instances are fascinating to own, and, in some cases, are very valuable. Recently a 1975 No S Proof Roosevelt dime traded hands for $516,000! You might not find a coin that will buy you a new house, but with the *Cherrypickers' Guide* the chances are very good that you will capture many different coin varieties and enjoy them all.

The treasure map is now in your hands. Good luck!

Q. David Bowers
Wolfeboro, New Hampshire

Since 1953, Q. David Bowers—the "Dean of American Numismatics"—has been active in the hobby as an award-winning author, coin dealer, auctioneer, and researcher. He is chairman emeritus of Stack's Bowers Galleries and numismatic director of Whitman Publishing, and serves as senior editor of Mega Red, *the expanded version of the* Red Book.

FOREWORD

Kenneth Bressett

There are many different ways to enjoy the hobby of numismatics. Nearly every collector has some uniquely personal motivation as to what is important or how to achieve their goals. The number of different coins available to hobbyists seems endless. The reasons for wanting to acquire, preserve, and classify these coins are equally numerous and complex.

For some collectors it is the thrill of the hunt, for others the pride of ownership or the satisfaction of completing a set or series. For most there is an underlying pleasure in knowing that acquiring a special coin was not only prudent but also profitable. Even the most altruistic collector takes pleasure in seeing that an investment of time and money has paid dividends.

When it comes to selecting coins to fit any collecting agenda, *saber es poder*—knowledge is power. Whatever your objectives are it is vitally important to know that each coin is genuine and to correctly interpret what you are seeing when you examine it. With that thought in mind, the *Cherrypickers' Guide* was written. This book is a gateway to understanding, classifying, and appreciating the many unusual—albeit sometimes minuscule—varieties of United States coins that are often misunderstood or ignored by a vast majority of collectors.

What began as a basic listing of valuable varieties that might be disregarded by the casual or traditional collector has, in the latest expanded volume of this book, grown into a new sphere of specialization that is of interest to thousands of collectors. Taking a more careful look at *all coins is* no longer something reserved for specialists, but a necessity for anyone interested in learning about how coins are made, what can go wrong in the minting process, and why some seemingly unimportant variations can make a difference of hundreds of dollars in value.

Selecting which varieties belong in a specialized book like this is no easy task. Some of the pieces listed here are included to illustrate abnormal coins even though they have little or no premium value. Most listings, however, show which varieties have a numismatic premium that might otherwise go unnoticed by the casual observer. Learning to identify the kinds of variations that are included in this catalog will arm even the most novice hobbyist with a knowledge of what to look for in discovering similar valuable varieties and perhaps open a whole new world of collectible coins.

We are fortunate to have this extensive listing by some of the country's leading experts to guide us through this exciting field of collecting. People frequently asked why certain of these coins are not listed in the *Guide Book of United States Coins* (the "Red Book"). Or why some are there while others are not. The reason is there would never be enough room to include them all in the *Red Book*. This specialized catalog meets the demand. I am sure you will find it entertaining, educational, and useful in a thousand ways.

Kenneth Bressett
Colorado Springs, Colorado

Kenneth Bressett, editor emeritus of the best-selling Guide Book of United States Coins *(the "Red Book"), has been active in numismatics since the 1940s. His accomplishments—research, writing, and serving in hobby organizations, including as president of the American Numismatic Association—have earned him nearly every important award in the hobby.*

PREFACE

This sixth edition, volume II, of the *Cherrypickers' Guide* celebrates more than 30 years of die variety–hunting, one of the most popular movements in numismatics. It all started with two collectors from Georgia.

Numismatist Bill Fivaz, by mid-1989, was well known for his curious habit of searching collections and dealers' inventories for neat coin varieties. Around June of that year, J. Woodside of Scotsman Coins in St. Louis, Missouri, suggested to Bill that he should write a book telling other collectors about his interest. Bill called a friend and fellow variety enthusiast, printer J.T. Stanton, to talk about the idea, and they agreed that such a reference was needed by the hobby community.

Bill and J.T. were very experienced in numismatics, but both were novices when it came to publishing—and certainly not prepared for the monumental project they were about to undertake. Their first thought was to include about 100 of the most significant coinage varieties—the ones that any collector would want. Those 100 varieties quickly grew into more than 160. With that, the two collectors worked out a format for the book, and the first *Cherrypickers' Guide* blossomed.

J.T. was well established in the printing business, so he handled the book's production. The U.S. Postal Service was kept busy as copy was shuttled back and forth between Bill, in Dunwoody, Georgia, and J.T., 275 miles away in Savannah. They sent the final laid-out pages to press in November 1989, hoping to have the book printed, bound, and ready for distribution in time for the Florida United Numismatists (FUN) convention the first weekend of January 1990. On his way to that show in Tampa, J.T. stopped by the bindery in Jacksonville, Florida. His plan was to pick up about 500 copies—a sufficient quantity for the show, they felt, not quite sure how well the book would be received and how brisk its sales would be.

When they left Tampa that Sunday, they had sold all 500 copies, and had a roster of additional orders to be mailed as soon as possible.

That first edition of the *Cherrypickers' Guide* was a great learning experience for Bill and J.T. both. They didn't expect to sell the entire initial print run of 3,000 copies, and actually felt lucky when they sold out in less than 10 months. Before long they planned a second edition, with more listings and the addition of retail values, along with other improvements. Thanks to coverage in the numismatic press and word-of-mouth publicity among variety enthusiasts, excitement grew for the second edition. Dealers and wholesalers wanted the book to offer to their customers. The new edition's print run of 5,000 copies sold out in about six months.

Bill and J.T. were very pleased with the hobby's acceptance of the *Cherrypickers' Guide*—and the fact that grading services were using the Fivaz-Stanton (FS) attribution numbers on their slabs. (To the best of the authors' knowledge, ANACS was the first to recognize a coin with a Fivaz-Stanton designation.) It seemed that Bill and J.T. had luckily stumbled onto a book with the right topic at the right time.

The second edition was made in both regular and spiral-bound formats. "The *Cherrypickers' Guide* might well have been the first mainstream numismatic book to be offered with the spiral or coil binding," said J.T. This format is perfect for collectors: they can lay the book open to a particular variety without struggling to keep the book flat, leaving their hands free to hold a coin and magnifying glass.

For the third edition, the entire print run was published in the spiral format.

When it was time for that third edition, the authors had a big hurdle to overcome: J.T. simply didn't have time to handle the production. So they set out to find a willing publisher. Several were contacted, and several were interested, with Bowers and Merena being the authors' ultimate choice. They worked to provide the hobby community what became their best effort yet. The third edition featured about five times as many varieties as the first; it went to six printings and more than 28,000 copies before the fourth edition finally came out.

Since J.T. was in the business of printing (and by this time some publishing), he and Bill asked famous numismatist Q. David Bowers (a principal of Bowers and Merena) if they could produce the fourth edition themselves. "Being the gentleman everyone knows, Bowers immediately agreed," J.T. recalled later. "If that's what we wanted, that's what he wanted."

The fourth edition became by far the duo's largest effort to that date, so large in fact that it had to be divided into two volumes to accommodate the spiral binding. Volume I included half cents through nickels. Volume II (later published by Whitman Publishing, in 2006) picked up with half dimes and bigger denominations. The division was a natural one. Volume I contained all minor coinage, and there are a lot of people who collect only cents and nickels. Volume II included other popular series comprising silver half dimes through dollars (including Bust and Liberty Seated series), federal gold coinage, and commemoratives. For collectors' convenience, volume II introduced a newly simplified Fivaz/Stanton numbering system.

The fifth edition, volume I, was published in 2009. It carried on the *Cherrypickers'* tradition, with updated market information, new varieties, a new appendix on the minting process, and other improvements. It continued the new Fivaz-Stanton numbering system introduced in the previous volume. An appendix cross-referenced the old numbering system, allowing collectors and dealers to bring their listings up to date.

With the fifth edition, volume II, published in 2012, Bill Fivaz and J.T. Stanton remained involved in the book's production while passing the torch to a new volume editor, Ken Potter. Well known in the hobby as a coin dealer, a published researcher, and the consummate die-variety specialist, Potter has his finger constantly on the pulse of the variety-collecting segment of numismatics. Thanks to Ken's coordination and management, the fifth edition, volume II, included dozens of upgraded photographs, more than 100 new listings, updated content, and even a whole new section on silver, gold, and platinum bullion-coin varieties. Ken brought together a team of pricing experts and analysts to provide the most accurate market pricing on the coins listed. The book was 32 pages longer than the fourth edition's volume II, and it featured nearly 800 unique varieties—about five times the coverage of the first edition published twenty-some years earlier.

A new cycle started with the sixth edition, volume I, in 2015. Longtime die-variety specialist, hobby educator, writer, and CONECA Hall of Famer Michael Ellis was brought on as the volume editor. For die-variety collectors, Mike needed no introduction; he'd edited the fourth edition, volume I, of the *Guide,* which earned him a 2001 "Extraordinary Merit" award from the Numismatic Literary Guild. Mike grabbed the baton carried by Fivaz, Stanton, and Potter, and ran with it, upgrading photos, conferencing with series specialists to bring the old listings up to date and add more than 140 new varieties, and making sure hobbyists got all the information they needed to build a great collection. Thanks to his coordination and the work of a team of experts, with Bill Fivaz providing constant support, 48 pages were added to the new volume.

Coauthor J.T. Stanton passed away in late 2018, so he never saw the rest of the sixth edition come to fruition. He would be proud of the effort put in by Bill and by new volume editor Larry Briggs, another award-winning numismatist well-known in the hobby community as a longtime dealer, author, and educator. Larry had served the American Numismatic Association as president of its Authentication Committee. A student of history and archaeology, his specialties include error coins and die varieties, Liberty Seated coinage, and early American coppers. Larry brought great depth and breadth to the rest of the sixth edition, drawing on his own encyclopedic knowledge and consulting specialists around the country to add more than 200 new varieties, including many completely new sections.

While the fifth edition covered half cents through bullion in two volumes, the sixth edition separates that broad (and expanding) coverage into three volumes. The sixth edition, volume II, catalogs half dimes, dimes, twenty-cent pieces, and quarter dollars from the early 1800s to date. This includes many of the most popular U.S. coin series, including Mercury and Roosevelt dimes, Washington quarters, and Liberty Seated and Barber coinage. Volume III is a study of half dollars and silver dollars, trade dollars, modern dollar coins, gold coins from $1 to $20, classic commemoratives, bullion, and U.S./Philippine coins.

Volume II, which you now hold, includes updated, revised, and in some cases completely new research for each of the book's nearly 450 coins. Among its coverage are almost 80 new half dimes, dimes, twenty-cent pieces, and quarters. More than half of these new additions are among the Roosevelt dimes, Liberty Seated quarters, and Washington quarters, but there are significant Mercury dimes and Standing Liberty quarters, and even new Capped Bust quarters, among other additions.

"The *Cherrypickers' Guide* proves that there are times when someone can get lucky, and tackle the right subject at the right time," Bill and J.T. have said. "We enjoyed the experience of creating the book, and hope our readers have learned a lot from the contributions of all the people who have made it possible—those who have provided varieties and information, and who have made other contributions, including values, rarity data, and other vital details."

The year 2020 marked the thirtieth anniversary of their creation. If collector enthusiasm is a good measuring stick, the *Cherrypickers' Guide* will continue to serve the hobby for generations to come.

CREDITS AND ACKNOWLEDGMENTS

Kenneth Bressett, editor emeritus of the *Guide Book of United States Coins*, has said this about the hobby's most famous publication: "The *Red Book* is not the work of any single person. It comes from the efforts of coin dealers, collectors, and readers worldwide who share their knowledge and experience."

Truer words have never been spoken, and the sentiment applies to the *Cherrypickers' Guide*, as well.

Bill Fivaz and J.T. Stanton are the authors of the *Cherrypickers' Guide*—and now long-time advisor Larry Briggs has joined the team as editor of the sixth edition, volume II—but the backbone of the book is the contributions, over many years, of hundreds of coin collectors, dealers, auction firms, hobby organizations, and specialists. Because of their generosity, the *Cherrypickers' Guide* has grown into the popular and indispensable reference it is today. In this section we give a tip of the hat to those who have shared their knowledge.

Membership organizations are vitally important to the hobby. Thanks to them, numismatics is a living, breathing science (in addition to being an art), with new discoveries constantly being made. Fresh understanding comes from active research and diligent study and the sharing of knowledge. This advances everyone's enjoyment of the hobby.

For the sixth edition, volume II, of the *Cherrypickers' Guide*, we give thanks to the memberships of two very active hobby groups that lead the way in research in their respective fields. Members of the **Barber Coin Collectors Society** (online at barbercoins.org) and the **Liberty Seated Collectors Club** (lsccweb.org) generously advised on die varieties within their specialties and shared information, photographs, and ideas. Their expertise was very important to the half dime, dime, twenty-cent piece, and quarter dollar sections. Special acknowledgment goes to **John Frost** (president, BCCS, and director of education, LSCC) for his coordination of the group effort, for providing his own considerable insight, and for reviewing manuscript drafts and page proofs.

Membership information for these groups is given in the introductions to relevant coin series. We encourage collectors and dealers, and anyone interested in American history of the early 1800s to late 1900s, to jump into the Barber Coin Collectors Society and the Liberty Seated Collectors Club.

Many individuals have shared information, descriptions, rarity data, market values (updated on a constant basis), and keen-eyed observations of a coin series or even a particular variety. We'd like to acknowledge several whose work was especially important for the sixth edition, volume II, of the *Cherrypickers' Guide*.

Grateful thanks are due to **Jon Potts** for sharing his knowledge of Mercury and Roosevelt dimes. Jon's expertise, and his review of page layouts, in these popular coin series was especially helpful.

José M. Gallego's knowledge of Washington quarters was a tremendous resource, especially drawing from his research on the reverse types in this series. José's images and charts enable collectors to sort through this important information with ease.

Washington quarter specialist **José Cortez** also shared research and guidance on varieties, including his studies of obverse and reverse design alterations.

Accurate and timely analysis of pricing in the coin market is very important to hobbyists. In addition to the extensive real-world knowledge of volume editor Larry Briggs, we were fortunate to rely on the expertise of specialists in compiling values for this volume. To that end, **Robert Lawson** and **Chris Welch** contributed greatly.

As he has in past volumes, **James Wiles** shared a great deal of information, including advice and high-resolution photographs (by way of Variety Vista) for many sections.

Good photography is a very important resource for understanding and identifying die varieties. **Heritage Auctions**, **NGC**, **PCGS**, and **Stack's Bowers Galleries** were generous in sharing their professional photographs, among the best in the world of rare coins.

Numerous other collectors, dealers, and specialists have contributed to the *Cherrypickers' Guide* since the first edition. We wish to thank all those variety enthusiasts who have been willing to generously share their coins, photographs, knowledge, and experience. Those who have contributed to this and earlier volumes are noted here. If we have missed anyone, it is with our most sincere apologies.

Bill Affanato
Leonard Albrecht
Roger Alexander
Brian Alford
Brian Allen
Matt Allman
Gary Alt
ANACS
Walter Anderson
Guy Araby
Richard Austin
Chuck Avery
Saverio Barbieri
Richard Bateson
Frank Baumann*
Joe Beaupied
Ed Becker
Roger Beckner
Steve Bernatowicz
Jack Beymer
David Biglow
Dick Bland
Al Blythe*
Cliff Bolling
Don Bonser
John Bordner*
Q. David Bowers
Charlie Boyd*
Mike Bozovich
Dan Brady
Jym Braun
Kenneth Bressett
Larry Briggs
David Brody
Robert Bruce*
Gene Bruder
Mike Bruggeman
Paul Bucerel
Bill Bugert
B. Buholtz
Vincent Burke
Ty Buxton
Cameo Coin Gallery
David J. Camire
Will Camp
Terry Campbell*
Donald Cantrell
Rick Carpenter
Jennifer Casazza
Charles Cataldo Jr.*
Ken Chylinski
Nicholas Ciancio*
Ted Clark*
Clem Clement
Mark Clewell
Tim Clough
Blaine Coffey
Coin World
Lou Coles
Frank J. Colletti
CONECA
Jim Conrad*
Edward Cook
Bert Corkhill
José Cortez*
Sean Craig
Billy Crawford*
David Crawford
Whaden Curtis
Charles Daughtrey
Dave's DCW Collection
Ray Davis
Lee Day
Tom DeLorey
George Derwart
Rick DeSanctis
DM Rare Coins
Daniel Dodge
J.T. Donahue
David Druzisky
Justin Duane
Elliott Durann
Edgewood Coin Co.
Brian Edwards
Harry Ellis*
Mike Ellis
Larry Emard
Bill Erdokos
Richard Evans
Rob Ezerman
Anthony Fanger
Michael "Skip" Fazzari
Joe Feld
Steven Feltner
Ron Fern
Michael S. Fey
Gerald Fishman
Jason Fishman
Ed Fletcher
Gerry Fortin
John Frost
Geoffrey Fults
Paul Funaiole
José Gallego
Bill Gase
Paul Geiserbach
Sam Gelberd
Ray Gelewski
Jack Gorby*
Don Gordon*
Rudy Gos
Mike Gourley
Peter Goydos
Jane Gray
Marlon Green
David Greenfelder
Brian Greer
Bob Grellman
Robert Griffiths
Linda Hagopian
Richard Hana
Joe Haney
Rob Hanks Jr.
Lloyd Hanson*
B.D. Harding
Tim Hargis

*** deceased**

Linda Harp
Ash Harrison
Tom Hart
Donald Hauser
James W. Hay
Dennis Heard
Doug Heisler
Richard Helbig
John Hemphill
Alan Herbert*
Heritage Auctions
Ronald Hickman*
Lee Hiemke
Doug Hill
Ken Hill
Mike Holstein
ICG
The Ike Group
Adrian Jellinek
Jim Jones
Martin Jordan
Matt Juppo
Mike Jurek
Carl Kanoff
Gary Kelly
Jerry Kennison
Jonathan Kern
Jeff Kierstead
Derry King
Joe Kirchgessner
Keith Klopfenstein*
Robert Knauss
Gerald Kochel
Bud Kolanda
Martin Krashoc
James Kropp
Harold Kuykendall
L&C Coins
Jim Lafferty
Rick Lajoie
David W. Lange*
Robert Lawson
Frank Leone
Akio Lis
Fred Lindsey
Don Lommler
Mark Lowers
Carl R. Loyd
Lee Lydston
Lee Maples
Aimee McCabe
Steve McCabe
John McCurdy
Mark McWherter*
Roy Maines
Ross Manning
Arnold Margolis*
J.P. Martin
Kip Mecum
R.A. Medina
Alan Meghrig
Tom Mendonca
Anthony Mesaros*
Michael Mesaros
Michael Michel
Ed Miller
Joe Miller
John Miller
Tom Miller
Ward Miller
Warren Mills
Mike Mizak*
MMNS
Michael Morris
David Moss
Wali Motorwalla
Allan C. Murphy
Dan Murray
BJ Neff
NGC
Gene Nichols
Neil Niederman
P. Nilson
John Nogosek
Charlie Nowack
Numismatic News
Numismedia.com
Jim O'Donnell*
Old Pueblo Coin Exchange
Dick Osborne
Lynn Ourso
Jeff Oxman
Dick Painter
Mike Paradis
Brett Parrish
Dennis Paulsen
George Pauwells
Richard Pawley
Daniel Pazsint
PCGS
PCI
Ben Peters
Sandy Peters
Karen Peterson*
Larry Philbrick*
Bob Piazza
Chris Pilliod
Denny Polly
Ron Pope*
Ken Potter
Colleen Prebish
Andrew Prechtl*
Al Raddi
Brian Raines
Wayne Rattray
RCNH
Roger Reiner
Paul Reitmeir
Doug Riley
Mike Ringo*
Joe Rizdy
John Roberts
Emory Robinson*
Rogers' Coins
Del Romines*
Lee Roschen
Gary Rosner
P. Scott Rubin
Tony Russo
Bob Ryan
Rick Rybicki
Jerry Sajbel
Steve Santangelo
Charles Schaefer
George Schaetzle
Steve Schmidt
Tanner Scott
Terry Searcy*
SEGS
Mark Serafine
Gary Shaffstall
Blaise Sidor
Rich Sisti
Sue Sisti
E.O. Smith
Jim Smith
Les Leroy Smith
Ruben Smith
Richard Snow
Art Snyder
Terry Souder
Max Spiegel
Howard Spindel
Stack's Bowers Galleries
Jeff Stahl
J.T. Stanton*
John Starr
Larry Steve
Suzanne Stewart
Bob Stimax
Tom Stott
Jim Stoutjesdyk
Eric Striegel
Dave Stutzman
Andrew Suchan
Kevin Swan
Norm Talbert*
Sol Taylor
David Thacker
Dave Thomas
Jeff Thomas
Carson Torpey
Lee Tucker
Andy Turnbull
Leroy Van Allen
Marilyn Van Allen*
John L. Veach
Kyle Vick
Michael Volz
Gary Wagnon
Dan Walker
W.O. Walker

*** deceased**

Mike Wallace
J.R. Walters*
Jonathan Warren
Troy Watkins
Richard Watts
Val Webb
Charity Welch
Chris Welch
David Welch
John Wells
Dave Welsh
Michael Werda
Vic West
John Wexler
Paul Wheeler
Bill White
Bob White
C.C. Whitaker
John Whitworth
James Wiles
Dave Wilson
Al Windholtz
Chuck Wishon
Tim Wissert
Andy Wong
Jay Woodside
Hank Woods
James Wooldridge
C.L. Wyatt
Jerry Wysong
Vicken Yegparian
Keith Zaner*
Dan Zaporra
Frank M. Zapushek
Anthony Zito

If you discover a new die variety and would like to have it considered for a future volume of the *Cherrypickers' Guide*, or if you have additional information to share on a variety already listed in the book, please write to:

Whitman
Attn: Cherrypickers' Guide
4001 Helton Drive
Florence AL 35630

Don't mail coins to this address, but good, clear photographs are always helpful.

You can also email cherrypickers@whitman.com.

Please include as much information as possible when writing. Happy cherrypicking, and we hope to hear from you soon!

*** deceased**

HOW TO USE THIS BOOK

As do most technical reference books (especially those involving numismatics), the *Cherrypickers' Guide* frequently uses abbreviations, acronyms, and numbering systems to identify and attribute its listings as clearly as possible. This section explains the symbols and concepts involved.

Symbols Used in This Book

The *Pocket Change* symbol indicates a variety that may reasonably be expected to be found in circulation today. Pocket Change varieties typically are cents dated after 1958, Jefferson nickels (other than silver wartime issues), dimes and quarters minted after 1964, half dollars minted after 1970, and some circulation-strike modern dollars.

The *Red Book* symbol indicates a variety that is listed in the most recent edition of the *Guide Book of United States Coins* (popularly known as the "Red Book"), the best-selling annual price guide of U.S. coins.

The *Mega Red* symbol indicates a variety that is listed in the most recent edition of the *Guide Book of United States Coins, Deluxe Edition* (a greatly expanded 1,504-page version of the *Red Book*), also known as *Mega Red*.

The *Young Numismatists* symbol indicates a variety that young and/or emerging collectors might want to focus on. Many of these fall into the Pocket Change category as well. In most cases, coins marked with the YN symbol are varieties of coins that are very inexpensive when found in their "normal" format, either in Mint State or high circulated grades. They usually can be sold for significant premiums through private sale or through auctions. Finding these varieties can help finance the collection of a numismatist with modest funds.

The *New Listing* symbol indicates that a variety is newly listed in this volume of the *Cherrypickers' Guide*. It also appears when some, but not all, of the entries in a new Group Variety Listing are new to this edition.

Abbreviations Used in This Book

DDO	doubled-die obverse	PF	Proof
DDR	doubled-die reverse	PUP	Pick-Up Point
I	Interest Factor	R	rarity
L	Liquidity Factor	RPD	repunched date
LD	Large Date	RPM	repunched mintmark
MPD	misplaced date	SD	Small Date
n/a	not available	SMS	Special Mint Set
NA	No Arrows	TDO	tripled-die obverse
ND	No Drapery	TDR	tripled-die reverse
N/L	not listed	URS	Universal Rarity Scale
OMM	over mintmark	WD	With Drapery

PICK-UP POINTS (PUPs)

A variety's *Pick-Up Point* is its area most prone to exhibit whatever characteristic(s) makes the variety unique, and is the specific area of the coin to zero in on when looking for a variety. In most cases, this will be the date, the mintmark, or legends. Other PUPs include denticles, stars, designer's initials, and various design elements.

VARIETY VALUE AND NORMAL VALUE

Throughout the guide we offer values for varieties in several grades of preservation. (For more information on grading, refer to guides such as the *Official American Numismatic Association Grading Standards for United States Coins* and *Grading Coins by Photographs: An Action Guide for the Collector and Investor*.)

Sources for the values of varieties include:

- actual sales (retail or auction) reported to us, with the most recent sales bearing the most weight;
- our assessments comparing one variety to another similar in rarity, collectibility, interest, and other factors; and
- recommendations from dealers and collectors who specialize in particular series or denominations.

Note that cells left blank within pricing charts indicate that the variety is not known to exist in that grade; cells containing a dash (—) indicate that the variety is so rare in that grade that sales records are rarely found; and cells with italicized figures indicate that the market for that variety in that grade is unsettled.

Also included in this volume are fair-market values for each variety's *normal*-version coin. In most cases, these values are derived from the *Guide Book of United States Coins* (the "Red Book") and *Mega Red* (the deluxe expanded edition of the *Red Book*). They reflect actual retail sales from more than a hundred of the most respected dealers across the country. These "normal coin" values provide an easy comparison for the amount or percentage of premium each variety can command.

As with any price guide, the values listed here should be used mainly as reference points. Although the editors take great pains to ensure as much accuracy as possible, values can and do change over time, especially among normal coins and varieties that trade frequently.

Factors Affecting Value

Always keep in mind the two major factors affecting the value of any item: supply and demand. If 10 people want a particular variety and only 6 examples are available, the value will be far greater than a similar variety desired by 10 people with 20 examples available.

With numismatic varieties especially, add to those two economic forces a very important aesthetic factor: *eye appeal*! As a general rule (there may be very few exceptions), the more visually dramatic a variety, the greater its value. For instance, compare two different repunched dates, with similar rarity and in similar grade, on two 1868 Shield nickels—one with a wide degree of separation and one with a very close separation. The variety with the wide separation usually commands a greater price.

Values are subject to change whenever a variety becomes more readily available, or if it becomes more desirable. Variety values certainly change with the normal fluctuations of the numismatic market. Remember that, generally speaking, **the higher the numismatic value of a particular coin, the lower the premium associated with its varieties**. For example, a nice doubled die on an Uncirculated Liberty Head $20 gold coin will (generally) command little, if any, premium from a non-specialist.

A variety's die state (or stage) can also play an important part in pricing. Those of earlier die states typically sell for higher prices because they show sharper features than those of later die states (where the features may be subdued or nearly gone). Exceptions exist where a later die state may actually be visibly stronger, or where other variations to the die may create greater demand, but as a general rule, the earlier the die state, the more the coin is worth to a specialist.

Market Values for Actively Traded Varieties

The values for some popular varieties, such as the 1955 doubled-die obverse Lincoln cent, fluctuate often with market trends. Given this, we highly recommend that you refer to other *current* price guides to obtain an up-to-date value for the variety. (Some of the varieties listed in the *Cherrypickers' Guide* are also noted in other hobby price guides that are updated on a regular basis.) Values for varieties are included in the *Cherrypickers' Guide* for reference only. Collectors and dealers can compare the prices noted with current prices and use the difference as a guide for possibly adjusting other similar varieties.

The Registry Set Phenomenon

In recent years the formation of registry sets has become a popular pursuit. This collecting concept was pioneered by PCGS and picked up by NGC. Registry sets offer hobbyists the challenge of building the highest-grade collection of coins certified in a particular series. For top-grade and very rare varieties, the spirit of competition sometimes leads to abnormal auction-bidding activity. This can result in prices that otherwise would seem unbelievably high. Collectors should be aware that unusually high prices paid at auction might reflect the "registry set phenomenon"—an effect caused when two bidders compete strongly for a particular rare variety—rather than a repeatable market scenario.

The Fivaz-Stanton (FS) Numbering System

The Fivaz-Stanton (FS) numbering system changed dramatically in the fourth edition, volume II (published in 2006).

In the older system, before that change, adding new listings was problematic. The older system simply left no room for additions. In many instances, additional decimal places were required. Also, an attribution number such as FS-05-003.752, or even FS-10c-0.008, was complicated, and disconnected from the normal thought processes of most collectors.

The current system allows for additions to the listings on an ongoing basis, and *without any limitation*! Also, it can be quickly interpreted to know what coin and type of variety it represents.

Reading the Fivaz-Stanton Number

With the Fivaz-Stanton numbering system, the complete listing number includes

- the **denomination**, followed by
- the **date** and **mintmark** (if there is a mintmark), and finally
- the sequential **"identifier" number**.

The identifier number essentially denotes the type of variety, and/or the location of its point of interest. This number is usually three digits, but can be four digits.

Example: *FS-10-1919-101* represents a dime (*-10-*) dated 1919 (*-1919-*), with a doubled-die obverse (*-101*).

There is one major exception in the identifier number system. The Morgan and Peace dollar series use their Van Allen–Mallis (VAM) numbers (when available) as the identifier. This is more convenient for VAM enthusiasts and for the grading services. For instance, with an 1878 VAM-44, the FS number is FS-S1-1878-044.

Most third-party professional grading services will gladly change an existing slab with the old FS number for a new slab with the newer FS numbering system. You can expect a fee for this service, but it will usually be lower than for a normal submission.

Identifiers for Fivaz-Stanton Numbers

The following are the identifiers for the Fivaz-Stanton numbers and their related meanings. Any coin with both an obverse and a reverse variety will be identified with two ID numbers separated with a slash.

101–299	obverse doubled die
301–399	obverse date variety
401–499	obverse variety, miscellaneous
501–699	mintmark variety
701–799	miscellaneous variety
801–899	reverse doubled die
901–999	reverse variety, miscellaneous

A four-digit identifier is used for dates that include two or more major types. For instance, a date variety on an 1867 With Rays Shield nickel might be FS-05-1867-301, yet a date variety on an 1867 No Rays Shield nickel might be FS-05-1867-1301. There are a few instances when there are three or more distinct types, such as the 1864 Indian Head cent (copper-nickel; bronze No L; and bronze With L). In these cases the first type will be three digits, while the second and third types will be four digits, such as 1301 and 2301.

With two major types, such as the 1867 With Rays and 1867 No Rays nickels, the With Rays varieties would have three digits, such as 301. The No Rays varieties would have four digits, such as 1301. The 1 at the beginning of the No Rays varieties differentiates the second type from the first.

Old Fivaz-Stanton Numbers Previously Included in the Listings

In earlier volumes, old-style Fivaz-Stanton numbers were sometimes included as a cross-reference, in parentheses. Because the new FS numbering system has taken hold within the collecting community, we no longer include the old numbers within the coin-by-coin listings. (However, you can find them in the cross-reference appendix.)

Abbreviations for Denominations

HC	half cent	G2.5	$2.50 gold piece
LC	large cent	G5	$5 gold piece
01	small cent	G10	$10 gold piece
02	two-cent piece	G20	$20 gold piece
3S	three-cent piece (silver)	C50	commemorative half dollar
3N	three-cent piece (nickel)	P25	$25 American Platinum Eagle
05	nickel five-cent piece	P100	$100 American Platinum Eagle
H10	half dime	SE	$1 American Silver Eagle
10	dime	FHC	Philippines half centavo
20	twenty-cent piece	F01	Philippines centavo
25	quarter dollar	F05	Philippines five centavos
50	half dollar	F10	Philippines ten centavos
S1	silver dollar	F20	Philippines twenty centavos
T1	trade dollar	F50	Philippines fifty centavos
C1	clad dollar / golden dollar	FP	Philippines peso
G1	gold dollar		

In the sixth edition, volume III, longtime cherrypickers will note the addition, for the first time, of U.S./Philippine die varieties, which are identified by an *F* before the denomination.

Rarity Factor

The rarity ratings used in the *Cherrypickers' Guide* are based upon the Universal Rarity Scale developed by Q. David Bowers. This is the only rarity scale available that is reasonably accurate for die varieties of the late-nineteenth, twentieth, and twenty-first centuries. Following you will find a background of the older Sheldon rarity scale, and details of Bowers's Universal Rarity Scale.

The Sheldon Scale

For many years, the only method of reasonably identifying numismatic rarity was with the use of the Sheldon scale, designed in 1949 by author Dr. William H. Sheldon to identify the rarity of large cent varieties. The Sheldon scale was simply a progression of eight levels into which the populations of all large-cent varieties were to fall. Each level was prefaced with the letter R, for Rarity:

R-1	common
R-2	not so common
R-3	scarce
R-4	very scarce (estimated 76–200 pieces in existence)
R-5	rare (31–75 pieces)
R-6	very rare (13–30 pieces)
R-7	extremely rare (4–12 pieces)
R-8	unique, or nearly so (1–3 pieces)

Put to its original use, the Sheldon scale worked very well, as most varieties of large cents ranged from scarce to very rare. Other numismatic writers adapted it for use with grading and rarity of many other coin series and denominations, as it was the only common scale in existence. However, it was not quite appropriate for most series, most varieties, or most errors, especially for coin types of the late-nineteenth, twentieth, and twenty-first centuries, with their high mintages. For instance, using this scale, the 1955 doubled-die Lincoln cent would be considered "common" or "not so common." Yet we know it is in fact scarce.

Bowers's Universal Rarity Scale (URS)

Clearly, another scale was needed by the hobby community for indicating rarity of all coins. Leave it to numismatic historian Q. David Bowers to recognize the need and develop a system that could be used for any series, and any rarity. (In fact, it can be used not only for coins, but for virtually anything whose rarity, scarcity, or availability is important.) Bowers developed the Universal Rarity Scale (URS), which, as its name implies, is universal for any coin or item. He outlined this scale in the June 1992 issue of *The Numismatist*. It has been adopted by many writers and catalogers and is used throughout the *Cherrypickers' Guide*.

The URS is simple and reasonable in its mathematical progression:

URS-0	none known	URS-12	1,001 to 2,000
URS-1	1 known; unique	URS-13	2,001–4,000
URS-2	2	URS-14	4,001–8,000
URS-3	3 or 4	URS-15	8,001–16,000
URS-4	5–8	URS-16	16,001–32,000
URS-5	9–16	URS-17	32,001–65,000
URS-6	17–32	URS-18	65,001–125,000
URS-7	33–64	URS-19	125,001–250,000
URS-8	65–125	URS-20	250,001–500,000
URS-9	126–250	URS-21	500,001–1,000,000
URS-10	251–500	URS-22	1,000,001–2,000,000
URS-11	501–1,000	(et seq.)	

When using rarity numbers with coins, there are a couple important factors to remember:

1. **Rarity generally differs from one grade to another.** If a coin is listed as URS-13 (2,001 to 4,000 known) it might be relatively common. However, if there are only 2 pieces known in grades above About Uncirculated, it would be a true rarity (URS-2) in MS-63. Such is the case with the 1888-O Morgan dollar, Hot Lips variety. These are fairly common in Very Good and Fine, but virtually unknown above About Uncirculated. Such a coin is often referred to as a *condition rarity*.
2. **Rarity and value are not always as closely related as one might expect.** If there are 10 known examples of a particular variety, but only 7 or 8 collectors are interested in it, the coin would certainly be rare, but because of a relatively low Interest Factor (low demand), it would not command much of a premium. Conversely, there could be 10,000 pieces known of a variety, but if 20,000 collectors are interested in obtaining one, the premium over the normal value of the coin would be much greater, due to the high Interest Factor (high demand). This brings us back to the age-old economic law of supply and demand.

Interest Factor

Interest Factor is a term we use to indicate, in our opinion, just how much demand a particular coin or variety has.

- A variety with a very high Interest Factor is in high demand, with several thousands of collectors desiring it.
- A medium Interest Factor may indicate that the variety is desired by hundreds or a few thousand people.
- A low Interest Factor might indicate that the coin is sought by just a handful of collectors.

In the *Cherrypickers' Guide*, we rate each variety's Interest Factor as follows:

I-5 very high interest (most general collectors interested)
I-4 high interest (most variety collectors interested)
I-3 moderate interest (most series collectors interested)
I-2 minimal interest (some collectors interested)
I-1 very low interest (only very specialized collectors interested)

The Interest Factor, combined with the rarity, influences the value of a variety or error. However, eye appeal is also a very important factor and must be considered in the final evaluation. A critical part of eye appeal for a variety or error is the relative strength or visibility of its defining characteristic—how easily can it be seen?

As a variety receives more publicity within the numismatic press, its Interest Factor might rise as demand increases. This can cause the retail/auction price or value to increase without any change in the estimated quantity available.

Liquidity Factor

The Liquidity Factor indicates how quickly or how easily a coin or variety *should* sell, given normal market conditions.

- A coin with a high Liquidity Factor would be expected to sell right away, generally commanding full or even inflated values.
- A coin with a low Liquidity Factor would not normally sell very easily or quickly, and then usually at a discount from suggested values.

Hot or highly active market conditions can inflate the Liquidity Factor of any coin, with a cold market having the opposite effect.

Our Liquidity Factor scale is as follows:

L-5 will sell easily, and often above listed value
L-4 will usually sell quickly at listed value (for variety enthusiasts)
L-3 will often sell in a reasonable time period, often to specialists
L-2 might sell in time, maybe at a discounted price
L-1 might sell provided the right buyer is available, but at a discount

OTHER NUMBERS AND ABBREVIATIONS

Identification numbers and abbreviations appear more frequently in the study of mint errors (and especially die varieties) than within the regular segment of the hobby. Some are easy methods of precisely identifying different varieties. Others are used to describe rarity, or even a certain class or type of variety. The important fact is with the use of these numbers, most specialists will know right away exactly which variety is being discussed. At the very least, a dealer or collector can consult a reference and find the corresponding number along with photos or detailed descriptions, for easy and accurate identification.

Most of these identification systems are simply numbers listed after the date, mintmark, and denomination. Some are more complex identification listings and include letters or symbols to further identify the variety or error.

CONECA Abbreviations

The CONECA die-variety files originated in the 1970s as an independent effort under the leadership of Alan Herbert and John Wexler. When Wexler retired from the hobby in the mid-1980s, he sold the doubled-die portion to CONECA. The RPM files went into private hands, where they stayed until 1997, when they too were sold to CONECA. Since then CONECA has maintained and expanded the files under the leadership of Dr. James Wiles, who has developed them into the most comprehensive set of die-variety files available, with almost 10,000 listings and more than 60,000 published photos. The club's ownership of the files guarantees their perpetual existence. Therefore, the *Cherrypickers' Guide* has chosen to cross-reference to the CONECA files for all twentieth- and twenty-first–century die varieties, whenever possible.

These three-letter acronyms have been adopted by CONECA to indicate the various variety types. They are followed by a number to indicate listing sequence (e.g., DDO-001). Additional information about the CONECA numbering system can be found at www.varietyvista.com.

Note that a variety listed as 001 is not necessarily the strongest, the most desirable, or the most valuable (although this is often the case). Note also that some previous editions of the *Cherrypickers' Guide* (the third edition, and volume I of the fourth and fifth editions) incorporated different CONECA numbers for doubled-die varieties which included the class and spread of the doubling; this information can also be found on www.varietyvista.com.

DDO Doubled-Die Obverse
DDR Doubled-Die Reverse
IMM Inverted Mintmark
MAD Misaligned Die Clash
MDO Master Die Doubled Obverse
MDR Master Die Doubled Reverse
MMO Mintmark Omission
MMS Mintmark Style
MPD Misplaced Date
ODV Obverse Design Variety
OMM Over Mintmark
RDV Reverse Design Variety
RED Re-Engraved Design
RPD Repunched Date
RPM Repunched Mintmark
WDC Wrong Denominational Clash

Numbering Systems from Other Publications

Other numbers are used from time to time in the *Cherrypickers' Guide* to indicate how a variety is cataloged in another reference book. The list below might not be comprehensive, as new books and reference works are being produced constantly:

Ahwash	Ahwash, Kamal M., *Encyclopedia of United States Liberty Seated Dimes 1837–1891* (1977).
Fortin	Fortin, Gerry, *Liberty Seated Dimes Web-Book*. www.seateddimevarieties.com.
Greer	Greer, Brian, *Complete Guide to Liberty Seated Dimes* (2005).
JR	John Reich Society
Lawrence	Lawrence, David, *Complete Guide* books on Barber coinage (dimes, 1991; quarters, 1989; half dollars, 1991).
LM	Logan, Russell, and John McCloskey, *Federal Half Dimes 1792–1837* (1998).
Valentine	Valentine, D.W., *The United States Half Dimes* (1931, reprinted 1975).

Average Die Life

The list below indicates the average number of strikes measured for dies of recent coin designs. These figures, which are for circulation-strike dies, are presented as a range, as there is considerable variance. Dies can and do last longer, and some may be retired earlier due to damage.

Dies can be repaired depending on the severity of the damage, but in the end, most dies are retired for cracks or die chips due to metal fatigue. The number of strikes needed to produce a metal-fatigue failure vary widely from 50,000 to more than 2 million strikes. Retirement can also occur if an abnormality—such as doubling—is discovered on a die.

Lincoln cent, 1996–2008 (Memorial reverse)	800,000–2,000,000
Lincoln cent, 2009 (four Bicentennial reverses)	250,000–550,000
Lincoln cent, 2010–date (Shield reverse)	400,000–600,000
Jefferson nickel, 2011–2014	400,000–700,000
Roosevelt dime, 2011–date	400,000–800,000
Washington quarter, 1932–1998 (Eagle reverse)	350,000
Washington quarter, 1999–2009 (56 State and Territory reverses)	150,000–350,000
Washington quarter, 2010–2021 (America the Beautiful reverses)	250,000–1,200,000
Kennedy half dollar, 1964–2006*	160,000
Sacagawea and Native American dollars, 2000–2011**	250,000
Presidential dollars, 2007–2011** (20 designs)	250,000–800,000

* From 2002 to 2020, Kennedy half dollars were not distributed directly into circulation. Starting in 2021, in response to national coin shortages, the coins were again released for circulation.

** The Mint has not produced circulating dollar coins since 2011.

Historically, a coin's redesign negatively affected the expected life of its dies by some 30 to 70 percent. The average would improve slightly over time, as technicians analyzed problems from the preceding year and "tweaked" dies to address cracking issues. Once a new design was in operation for three to five years, Mint personnel would have improved die life to its maximum.

Also note that from 2010 through 2011, the mint facilities changed how the stamping process was lubricated. Lubrication is now added during the blank-washing process instead of using stamping oil at the press. This caused die life to increase for the nickel, dime, and quarter.

The Philadelphia and Denver Mints produce billions of coins every year. Mint technology and processes are constantly improving, changing, and advancing. We will update this section with new information as it is made public.

Whitman Publishing would like to thank Thomas Jurkowsky, Director of Corporate Communications for the United States Mint, and the Mint's manufacturing technicians, for their contributions to this section.

Treatment of New Variety Listings

We understand—and want our readers to understand—that the very act of listing a new variety in the *Cherrypickers' Guide* can increase collector demand and, therefore, its liquidity and market value. This can have the effect of temporarily bringing some volatility to the market. Still, in most cases volume editor Larry Briggs, with input from specialist dealers and collectors and review by author Bill Fivaz, has provided rarity, interest, liquidity, and valuations for nearly every newly listed variety. Readers should note that this information is considered reliable at the time of publication, and it may vary over time—sometimes dramatically, and sometimes very soon after publication.

Each section features a chart of all newly listed varieties within that denomination or coin type, and also a chart of any low-interest and/or debunked varieties removed since the fifth edition (see below). This information can be found directly after the introductory text.

Treatment of Low-Interest and Debunked Varieties

As in other recent volumes, we have identified certain varieties that have proven over time to be of low collector interest. We have removed these from the coin-by-coin listings in order to make room for other, more significant, varieties. These removed coins remain *Cherrypickers' Guide* varieties (rather than being considered "deleted"); for example, they continue to be cross-referenced and summarized in the appendix.

Varieties debunked as counterfeit, and classifications that later research revealed to be erroneous, are removed entirely, with a note of explanation in the text.

Grouped Variety Listings

Varieties that are very similar and occur either on a single-date issue or several dates of a series are compiled in one entry that covers all the variety as a group—for example, the "Long Nock" Morgan silver dollars, which are studied in volume III.

Capped Bust Half Dimes, 1829–1837

Bust coinage varieties may be slightly different from what many of us are accustomed to encountering in late-nineteenth-century and later coinage. During the Bust era the die-making process differed somewhat from that of later years. Often a template and punches were used to place many of the design elements, letters, and numbers into the working die, rather than in the hub (as was the custom for later coinage). Therefore, it is not uncommon to see slight differences in positioning of these elements. In some cases, individual letter or number punches were used, which can account for one or more letters or numbers appearing over another.

One of the most active and educational numismatic specialty clubs in the United States is the John Reich Collectors Society. Bust half dimes, dimes, quarters, half dollars, and dollars are all within the focus of this excellent group. At the time of this publication, membership dues are $25 annually. Members receive three issue of the award-winning *John Reich Journal* every year. (To request a free sample issue of the *Journal,* visit the Society's website, download the membership application, provide the requested information, and send it as your request.) The Society also has an official weekly e-magazine, the *JR Newsletter.* No dues or fees are required to receive the newsletter, though subscribers are encouraged to join the JRCS. The *Newsletter* is archived online.

Take a tip from us—membership in any numismatic specialty club is always highly educational and worth the modest annual dues.

Visit the JRCS website at www.jrcs.org to find a membership application, club details, a list of events and contacts, and educational information. Contact the Society by mail at

John Reich Collectors Society
Attn: W. David Perkins, Treasurer
PO Box 3039
Centennial CO 80161-3039

Capped Bust Half Dimes Removed From the Fifth Edition, Volume II

Date, Variety	Fivaz-Stanton number	PUP	Notes
1829, Repunched Date	FS-H10-1829-301	9 of date	Not a rare die variety.

Note: Varieties removed are still considered *Cherrypickers' Guide* varieties (as opposed to being "delisted"); for example, they will continue to be cross-referenced and summarized in appendix H. (Exceptions include varieties debunked as counterfeits, or those which later research revealed to be erroneously classified. Those will be delisted completely.)

1834, 3 Over Inverted 3 — FS-H10-1834-301

VARIETY: Repunched Date
PUP: 3 of date
URS-9+ · I-3 · L-3

LM-1; VALENTINE-5, -5A
"Blundered Date" Variety

Description: The 3 of the date was first punched into the die in an inverted position, then corrected without any attempt to remove the initial punching.

Comments: This variety has been known for decades. Collector interest started to increase around 1997. The metal in the lower loop of the 8 is a die chip.

	VG-8	F-12	VF-20	EF-40	AU-50	MS-63	MS-65
VARIETY	$70	$80	$110	$225	$400	$1,100	$3,000
NORMAL	$65	$75	$105	$200	$250	$925	$2,500

1836, 3 Over Inverted 3 — FS-H10-1836-301

VARIETY: Repunched Date
PUP: 3 of date
URS-9 · I-3 · L-3

LM-3; VALENTINE-4
"Blundered Date" Variety

Description: The date shows a repunched 3 over an inverted 3.

Comments: Collector interest has grown for this variety (as it has for the 1834 half dime with a blundered date). It first reached *Cherrypickers' Guide* status in the fifth edition.

	VG-8	F-12	VF-20	EF-40	AU-50	MS-63	MS-65
VARIETY	$80	$100	$120	$190	$300	$900	$3,000
NORMAL	$75	$95	$105	$180	$250	$890	$2,500

Liberty Seated Half Dimes, 1837–1873

To quote the late Al Blythe, a good friend and a specialist in these coins, "The Liberty Seated half dime series is rich in varieties, overdates, repunched dates, and blundered dies. This provides a fertile ground for collectors who enjoy this facet of numismatics." Truer words could not be spoken.

Typically, specialists who collect any one of the Liberty Seated denominations will collect them all. The design is arguably one of the most interesting in American numismatics. During the many years the basic motif was in use, there were several changes in its details, giving collectors more to study and contemplate.

Liberty Seated half dimes contain numerous die varieties, including some that are considered very rare by specialists. Many of the varieties in the series are in great demand, and almost always easy to sell.

For collectors seriously interested in these coins, we strongly recommend membership in the Liberty Seated Collectors Club, one of the best specialized clubs in numismatics. The LSCC attends more than twenty regional events each year, providing educational programs, exhibits at club tables, and meetings.

The award-winning *Gobrecht Journal*, the official publication of the club, is issued to members three times annually (in March, July, and November), in full color. This extensive publication is loaded with excellent educational articles. The *Gobrecht Journal* is research-orientated and contains articles on all Liberty Seated coinage denominations, from half dimes to trade dollars. You can preview sample articles online at https://nnp.wustl.edu/library/publisherdetail/2096

The Club also publishes *The E-Gobrecht*, a monthly email-based publication, distributed to club members and interested non-members at no cost. *The E-Gobrecht* contains information of a timely nature, such as recent auction sales, LSCC regional meeting or event announcements, and feature articles on new variety discoveries. You can download all back issues of *The E-Gobrecht* from the LSCC website's "E-Gobrecht Archives" page.

At the time of this publication, Liberty Seated Collectors Club membership dues are $30 per year. For membership information, visit the Club website at www.lsccweb.org, or write to

Liberty Seated Collectors Club
Leonard Augsburger, President
Email: leonard.augsburger@wustl.edu

LIBERTY SEATED HALF DIMES REMOVED FROM THE FIFTH EDITION, VOLUME II

DATE, VARIETY	FIVAZ-STANTON NUMBER	PUP	NOTES
1842-O, Repunched Date	FS-H10-1842o-301	Date	Removed for lack of collector interest.
1853, Arrows, Dot Below 5 of Date	FS-H10-1853-401	5 of date	Variety not confirmed.
1855, DDO, Clashed Dies	FS-H10-1855-101	Lower skirt	Removed for lack of collector interest.
1871, Misplaced Date	FS-H10-1871-301	Rock	Removed for lack of collector interest.

Note: Varieties removed are still considered *Cherrypickers' Guide* varieties (as opposed to being "delisted"); for example, they will continue to be cross-referenced and summarized in appendix H. (Exceptions include varieties debunked as counterfeits, or those which later research revealed to be erroneously classified. Those will be delisted completely.)

NEW LIBERTY SEATED HALF DIMES IN THE SIXTH EDITION, VOLUME II

DATE, VARIETY	FIVAZ-STANTON NUMBER	PUP
1840-O, No Drapery, Large O	FS-H10-1840o-501	Mintmark
1849, "9 Over So-Called 8"	FS-H10-1849-303	Date
1863-S, Misplaced Date	FS-H10-1863S-301	Base of rock

1838 — FS-H10-1838-901

VARIETY: Rusted Reverse Die — **VALENTINE-10**
PUP: Reverse around AMERICA
URS-8 · I-3 · L-2

Description: The reverse exhibits a rough, pebbly appearance. This variety occurs on the Large Stars coin.

Comments: Generally speaking, evidence of rust on working dies is very rare. Only a very few examples are known to exist for any reverse dies. Very little information is available for this variety. Its value is subjective at this point. Collectors of Liberty Seated coinage consider this one of the more desirable varieties.

	G-4	VG-8	F-12	VF-20	EF-40	AU-50	MS-60
VARIETY	$25	$40	$55	$110	$160	$225	$375
NORMAL	$20	$35	$50	$65	$125	$200	$300

1839-O — FS-H10-1839o-501

Variety: Reverse of 1838 **Valentine-1**
PUP: Mintmark
URS: G/VG, URS-5; F/VF, URS-6; EF/AU, URS-6; MS, Unknown

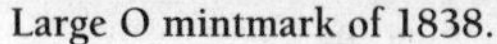
Large O mintmark of 1838.

Normal O, used on majority of 1839 mintage.

Description: This variety has the large O mintmark on the reverse (type of 1838).

Comments: About 55 to 65 pieces are known in all grades, with most being AG. No more than 10 are known in EF or finer. Larry Briggs notes the finest grades he's seen is an AU+ (pictured in Breen's *Encyclopedia*). Early-die-state, high-grade specimens also show a repunched 9.

	G-4	VG-8	F-12	VF-20	EF-40	AU-50	MS-60
Variety	$1,000	$1,750	$2,250	$2,750	$3,500	$4,500	n/a
Normal	$94	$100	$148	$225	$499	$686	$1,971

1840-O, No Drapery — FS-H10-1840o-501

Variety: Huge O, No Drapery **Valentine-1, -8; CONECA: N/L**
PUP: Mintmark; drapery area
URS-7 · I-5 · L-5

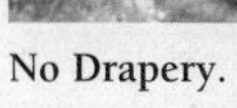
No Drapery.

Description: The Huge O mintmark measures 1.2 mm in width.

Comments: There are two different Large O, No Drapery dies: V-1 (very scarce) and V-8 (very rare). Few sales have been publicized. Larry Briggs estimates 50 to 75 examples exist in all grades. Those finer than EF are seldom seen. Values shown here are for V-1. The rarer V-8 is valued at $525 in Very Fine.

	G-4	VG-8	F-12	VF-20	EF-40	AU-50
Variety	$75	$100	$165	$250	$375	–
Normal	$70	$95	$155	$245	$365	$795

1840-O, No Drapery — FS-H10-1840o-901

VARIETY: Transitional Reverse **VALENTINE-6**

PUP: Reverse letters, split buds, and leaf clusters by DIME

URS-8 · I-4 · L-3

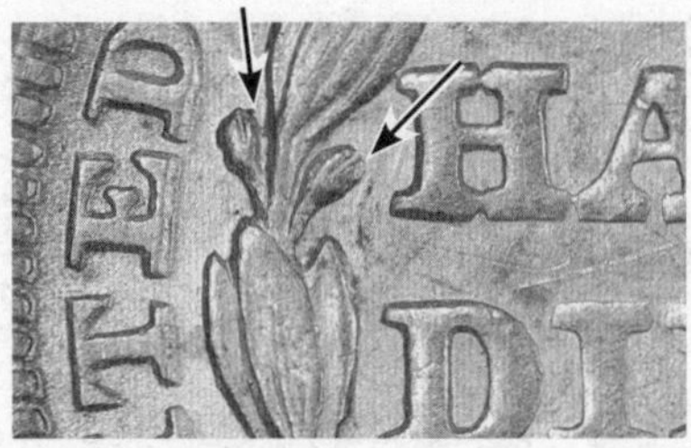

Transitional reverse die with open buds and three-leaf cluster.

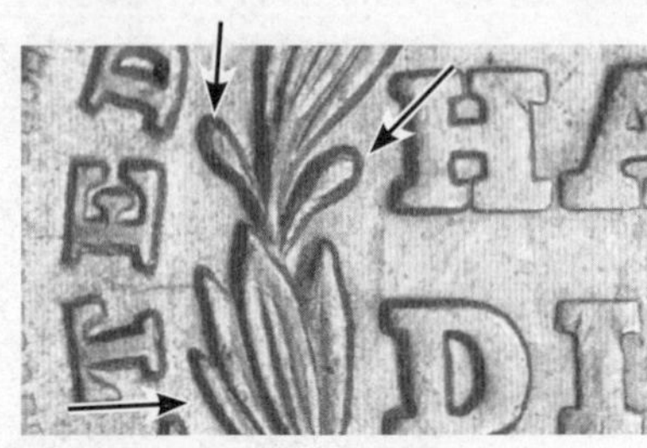

Regular reverse die with closed buds and four-leaf cluster.

Description: This very scarce transitional variety exhibits large letters and open or split buds on the reverse die, along with a small O mintmark. The key diagnostic of the variety is three-leaf clusters on either side of the word DIME (the common reverse has four-leaf clusters).

Comments: In all, the 1840-O No Drapery half dimes total eight different varieties. Only one die, however, is transitional — Valentine 6. Key diagnostics are simple: this rare variety has only three leaves and has split buds instead of the single bud.

	G-4	VG-8	F-12	VF-20	EF-40	AU-50	MS-60
VARIETY	$150	$200	$350	$475	$650	$1,000	$1,500
NORMAL	$70	$95	$155	$245	$365	$795	$1,400

1843 — FS-H10-1843-301

VARIETY: Repunched Date **VALENTINE-6A**

PUP: Date

URS-9 · I-3 · L-2

Description: This is a very nice repunched date, most evident with secondary numerals 1, 8, and 4 south of the primary date.

Comments: High-grade examples are always in demand. This is a very well-known RPD, and very popular among Liberty Seated specialists.

	G-4	VG-8	F-12	VF-20	EF-40	AU-50	MS-60	MS-63
VARIETY	$25	$40	$60	$110	$175	$245	$325	$525
NORMAL	$20	$35	$40	$45	$75	$160	$225	$400

1844 — FS-H10-1844-301

Variety: Repunched Date **Valentine-3C**
PUP: Date
URS-9 · I-3 · L-2

Description: This is a wonderful RPD, with secondary images evident north and south of the primary 1 and 8, and secondary images evident south of the first 4. Overlapping images are also evident on the last 4 of the date.

Comments: This variety is always popular among Liberty Seated specialists. Note: The variety is much more common than the very scarce Plain Date.

	G-4	VG-8	F-12	VF-20	EF-40	AU-50	MS-60	MS-63
Variety	$23	$30	$40	$60	$110	$190	$300	$425
Normal	$20	$25	$35	$55	$105	$180	$290	$415

1845 — FS-H10-1845-301

Variety: Misplaced Date
PUP: Date
URS-2 · I-5 · L-5

Description: This variety exhibits an 8 and a 4 clearly protruding from the rock above the date.

Comments: Discovered in 1997 by Bill Fivaz, this variety should be considered very rare due to the length of time it remained unknown. More than 20 years after its discovery, still very few examples have emerged!

	G-4	VG-8	F-12	VF-20	EF-40	AU-50	MS-60	MS-63
Variety	$100	$150	$200	$250	$300	$400	$500	$700
Normal	$30	$35	$40	$45	$60	$145	$225	$375

1845 — FS-H10-1845-302

VARIETY: Repunched Date — **VALENTINE-5**
PUP: Date
URS-8 · I-3 · L-2

Description: All four digit of the date are repunched, with the secondary image slightly northwest of the primary date.

Comments: This variety is another well-known repunched date. Note: The shallow "doubling" around the numbers is probably the result of the shoulder of the date punch(es) hitting the die.

	VG-8	F-12	VF-20	EF-40	AU-50	MS-60	MS-63
VARIETY	$35	$50	$100	$175	$240	$345	$475
NORMAL	$30	$40	$45	$60	$145	$225	$375

1848 — FS-H10-1848-301

VARIETY: Large Date — **VALENTINE-1A**
PUP: Date
URS-9 · I-5 · L-4

Description: The digits of the date are much larger than normal. It is very obvious a 4-digit logotype punch intended for a dime was used. The digits protrude well into the rock. A secondary 8 is evident between the 4 and the second 8.

Comments: Beware of coins listed as the Large Date that are not! The "Normal" values listed below are for the Medium Date.

	VG-8	F-12	VF-20	EF-40	AU-50	MS-60	MS-63
VARIETY	$40	$60	$125	$245	$325	$575	$1,150
NORMAL	$30	$40	$60	$95	$180	$300	$490

1848 — FS-H10-1848-302

Variety: Possible Overdate
PUP: Date
URS-8 · I-4 · L-3

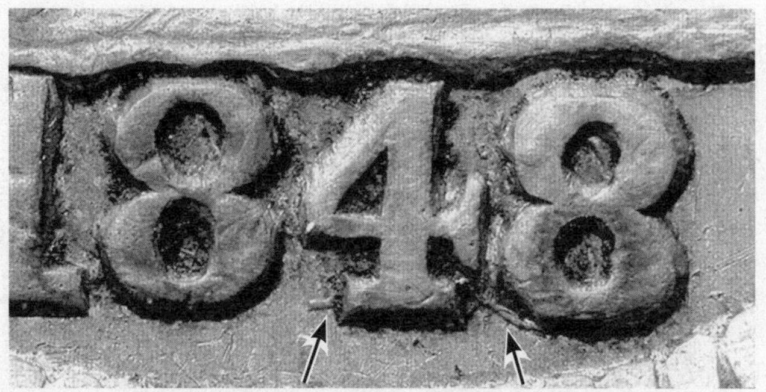

Description: Many specialists believe this to be a tripled overdate, 8 Over 7 Over 6. Further study may prove it to be a normal RPD, as the "spike" believed to be that of the 7 appears very much like a portion of an underlying 8, partially polished off.

Comments: The lower portion of a repunched 4 is evident left of the primary 4. Note: The "Normal" values listed below are for the Medium Date.

	VG-8	F-12	VF-20	EF-40	AU-50	MS-60	MS-63
Variety	$35	$50	$75	$125	$225	$375	$500
Normal	$30	$40	$60	$95	$180	$300	$490

1849, 9 Over 6 — FS-H10-1849-301

Variety: Overdate (Near 6, Close Date) — **Valentine-4**
PUP: Date
URS-8 · I-5 · L-5

Description: The diagonal angles on the 4 in the date match those on the 1846 date, not the 1848.

Comments: Formerly listed as a 9 Over 8 overdate, this variety has been reidentified as a 9 Over 6 and features a compact date that is virtually centered between the rock and the denticles.

	F-12	VF-20	EF-40	AU-50	MS-60	MS-63
Variety	$95	$140	$225	$325	$585	$1,000
Normal	$40	$58	$100	$175	$265	$750

1849, 9 Over 6 FS-H10-1849-302

VARIETY: Overdate (Far 6, Wide Date) **VALENTINE-2**
PUP: Date
URS-7 · I-5 · L-5

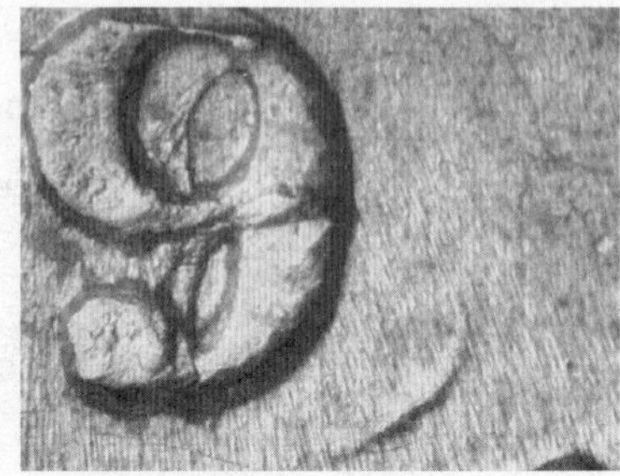

Description: The diagonal angles on the 4 in the date match those on the 1846 date—not the 1848.

Comments: Debate among specialists centered on whether this overdate is a 9 Over 6, or, as formerly listed, a 9 Over 8 (suggested by the inward curve of the underlying digit, midway up on the left side). The *Guide Book of United States Coins* (the "Red Book") lists it as "9 Over Widely Placed 6." This is a very popular variety, with Liberty Seated specialists being especially interested. *Note:* Early die states show repunching on all four digits.

	F-12	VF-20	EF-40	AU-50	MS-60	MS-63
VARIETY	$115	$175	$295	$375	$700	$1,250
NORMAL	$40	$58	$100	$175	$265	$750

1849, "9 Over So-Called 8" FS-H10-1849-303

VARIETY: Overdate, Very High Date **VALENTINE-1**
PUP: Date position; last digit of date
URS-7 · I-5 · L-5

Description: This overdate virtually touches the rock. On worn specimens, all digits of the date appear to do so. The date is compact, but extremely high compared to its two 1849 sisters, FS-301 and FS-302.

Comments: Contrasting this variety to the two other overdates of this year is easy. The 1 and 8 virtually touch the rock, while the right top of the 4 seems to touch as well. The 9 has very little separation from the rock. The figure of the "so-called" 8 is seen clearly within the 9. This is scarcer than FS-302 and even more so than FS-301.

	F-12	VF-20	EF-40	AU-50	MS-60	MS-63
VARIETY	$125	$195	$325	$425	$775	$1,500
NORMAL	$40	$58	$100	$175	$265	$750

1853, With Arrows — FS-H10-1853-301

Variety: Misplaced Date
PUP: Date
URS-4 · I-5 · L-4

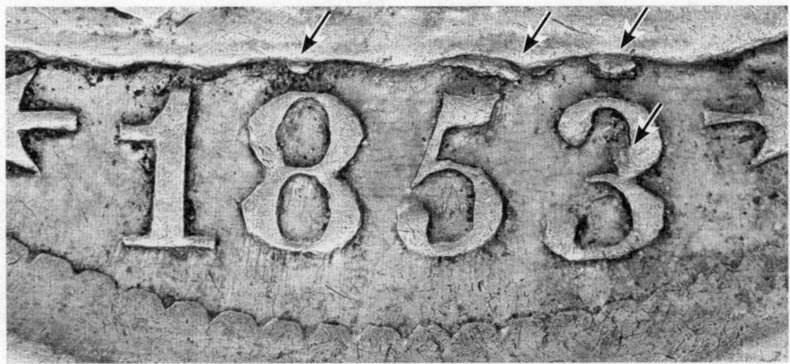

Description: The lower portions of numerals 8, 5, and 3 are visible protruding from the lower portion of the rock, above the primary date. Half dime specialist Al Blythe, who discovered this variety in 1990, said that remains of a 2 can be seen behind the upper portion of the 3.

Comments: This variety—certainly a nice MPD—may prove to be an overdate.

	VG-8	F-12	VF-20	EF-40	AU-50	MS-60	MS-63
Variety	n/a	n/a	n/a	n/a	n/a	n/a	n/a
Normal	$35	$40	$45	$75	$150	$200	$350

1856 — FS-H10-1856-301

Variety: Misplaced Date
PUP: Rock above date
URS-7 · I-4 · L-2

Description: A portion of an 8 is quite evident in the rock just above the primary 8.

Comments: This is one of the many nice varieties discovered by Joe Miller. In the fifth edition of the *Cherrypickers' Guide* (2012), valuations ranged from $30 to $370. However, Larry Briggs observes, "I don't know of any sales of this variety"—and for that reason, any values have to be speculative.

	VG-8	F-12	VF-20	EF-40	AU-50	MS-60	MS-63
Variety	n/a	n/a	n/a	n/a	n/a	n/a	n/a
Normal	$35	$40	$45	$70	$125	$185	$300

1858 FS-H10-1858-301

Variety: Repunched Date **Valentine-10**
PUP: Date
URS-8 · I-5 · L-5

Description: The date was first punched into the die very high, then corrected and punched in the normal location. The original high-date punch remains very evident within the upper portions of the primary date.

Comments: This is considered one of the scarcest varieties amongst the Liberty Seated half dimes—easily 10 to 15 times scarcer than its inverted-date counterpart (next entry)! The Liberty Seated Collectors Club has assigned Valentine-10 to this variety.

	VG-8	F-12	VF-20	EF-40	AU-50	MS-60	MS-63
Variety	$95	$115	$195	$325	$525	$975	$1,750
Normal	$35	$40	$45	$75	$150	$200	$350

1858 FS-H10-1858-302

Variety: Inverted Date **Valentine-9**
PUP: Date
URS-10 · I-5 · L-4

Description: The first date was punched into the die in an inverted orientation, then corrected. The bases of the secondary digits are visible between the primary digits.

Comments: Discovered by Jess Patrick in 1963. This variety, although one of the most well-known of the Liberty Seated half dime series, and very spectacular, can still be cherrypicked. It is scarce—but much less so than the 1858 repunched date (preceding). The Liberty Seated Collectors Club has assigned Valentine-9 to this variety.

	VG-8	F-12	VF-20	EF-40	AU-50	MS-60	MS-63
Variety	$55	$85	$165	$275	$400	$800	$1,400
Normal	$35	$40	$45	$75	$150	$200	$350

1861, "1 Over 0" FS-H10-1861-301

Variety: Possible Overdate **Valentine-5**
PUP: Date
URS-9 · I-4 · L-3

Description: An 1860 date was first punched into the die, after which an 1861 date was punched into the die over the 0.

Comments: This variety is readily available (it can be cherrypicked with relative ease) but very popular. Some specialists feel it is not an overdate. Two "Plain" 1 Over 0 varieties exist with minor date-position differences. There also exists a rare 1 Over 0 with a DDO (on UNITED STATES OF AMERICA), discovered by Larry Briggs at the Norweb Collection preview in 1987.

	VG-8	F-12	VF-20	EF-40	AU-50	MS-60	MS-63
Variety	$35	$55	$125	$225	$340	$450	$600
Normal	$30	$40	$45	$70	$120	$175	$300

1863-S FS-H10-1863S-301

Variety: Misplaced Date **Valentine: N/L; CONECA: N/L**
PUP: Base of rock
URS-6 · I-5 · L-4

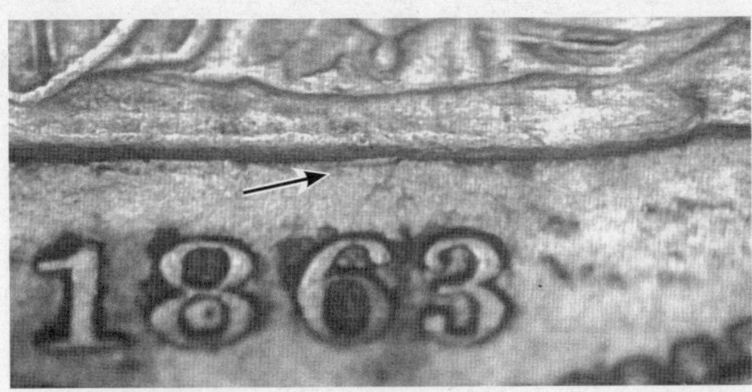

Description: The bottom loop of an extra digit protrudes from the rock, above the 6.

Comments: The 1863-S half dime in general is very scarce; with the MPD it is borderline rare. Five pieces were confirmed as of 2022. Values shown here are based on actual sales.

	VG-8	F-12	VF-20	EF-40	AU-50	MS-60	MS-63
Variety	$200	n/a	n/a	n/a	$675	n/a	n/a
Normal	$65	$105	$200	$300	$425	$800	$1,175

1865-S — FS-H10-1865S-301

VARIETY: Repunched Date — **VALENTINE-1 AND -4**
PUP: Date
URS-9 · I-4 · L-3

Description: The RPD is evident with a secondary 5 south of the primary 5, and secondary 1 and 6 north of those numerals.

Comments: The RPD represents probably 50 percent of all 1865-S half dimes. Two varieties exist (Valentine-4 is pictured here); both are scarce and they command a small premium over "Plain Date" 1865-S coins.

	VG-8	F-12	VF-20	EF-40	AU-50	MS-60	MS-63
VARIETY	$95	$145	$225	$350	$625	$1,000	$2,200
NORMAL	$80	$125	$200	$345	$550	$990	$2,190

1872 — FS-H10-1872-101

VARIETY: Doubled-Die Obverse — **VALENTINE-6**
PUP: AMERICA
URS-9 · I-4 · L-3

Description: Doubling is evident on UNITED STATES OF AMERICA (especially on AMERICA) and on most elements of Miss Liberty. The strongest is on the shield and the drapery area to the right of the shield.

Comments: This is one of the more popular varieties in the series—readily available in all grades AG through VF; scarce in EF; rare in AU; and very rare in Mint State. With patience this can still be cherrypicked. A minor secondary DDO exists with doubling only on the shield stripes.

	VG-8	F-12	VF-20	EF-40	AU-50	MS-60	MS-63
VARIETY	$55	$75	$145	$275	$375	$650	$1,000
NORMAL	$35	$40	$45	$55	$85	$165	$300

1872-S, Mintmark Below Bow — FS-H10-1872S-301

Variety: Misplaced Date, and Repunched Date — **Valentine-6; CONECA: N/L**
PUP: Pendant and above date
URS-6 · I-5 · L-4

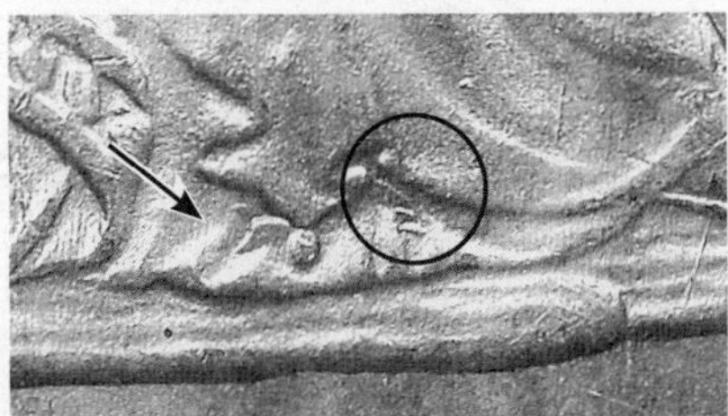

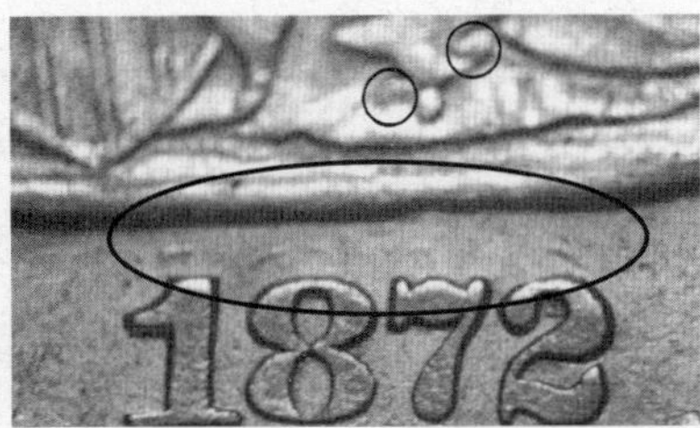

Description: The top of a numeral 1 is embedded to the left side of the pendant. Just to the right side of the pendant ball is the top-right portion of an 8. Below the rock and above the date is the top remnant of another entire date (1872).

Comments: Although known since the late 1980s, very few pieces have surfaced. The entire date portion probably fades with strike. Early-die-state pieces showing this entire punching are rare, and bring a substantial premium. Values listed here are for early-die-state pieces. This is one of the most dramatic date repunchings of any Liberty Seated coin, in any series. It is similar to (but not the same as) Valentine-5. Very few examples are known in any grade.

	VG-8	F-12	VF-20	EF-40	AU-50	MS-60	MS-63
Variety	$75	$100	$165	$275	$375	$575	$750
Normal	$35	$40	$45	$55	$100	$180	$300

1872-S, Mintmark Below Bow — FS-H10-1872S-302

Variety: Misplaced Date — **Valentine-5**
PUP: Left of pendant; below skirt
URS-8 · I-4 · L-3

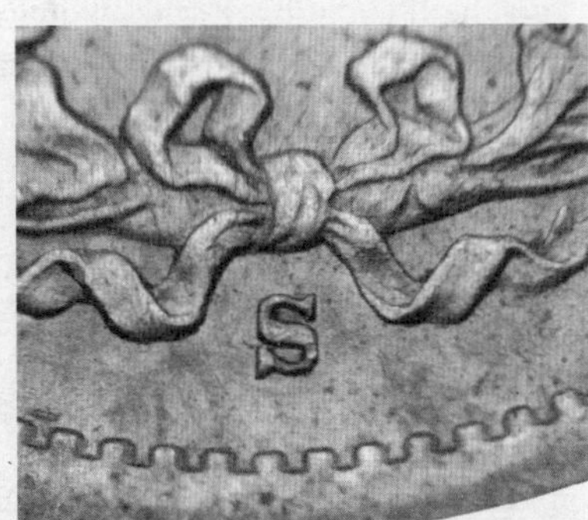

Mintmark location.

Description: Bottom remnants of 7's appear to the left of the pendant and below the skirt, on the rock.

Comments: This variety, first listed in the fifth edition of the *Cherrypickers' Guide* (2012), has turned out to be very scarce. With patience and persistence, you can cherrypick it for a nominal price.

	VG-8	F-12	VF-20	EF-40	AU-50	MS-60	MS-63
Variety	$45	$65	$95	$145	$185	$245	$365
Normal	$35	$40	$45	$55	$120	$165	$300

Capped Bust Dimes, 1809–1837

Bust coinage varieties may be slightly different from what many of us are accustomed to encountering in late-nineteenth-century and later coinage. During the Bust era the die-making process differed somewhat from that of later years. Often a template and punches were used to place many of the design elements, letters, and numbers into the working die, rather than in the hub (as was the custom for later coinage). Therefore, it is not uncommon to see slight differences in positioning of these elements. In some cases individual letter or number punches were used, which can account for one or more letters or numbers appearing over another.

One of the most active and educational numismatic specialty clubs in the United States is the John Reich Collectors Society. Bust half dimes, dimes, quarters, half dollars, and dollars are all within the focus of this excellent group. At the time of this publication, membership dues are $25 annually. Members receive three issues of the award-winning *John Reich Journal* every year. (To request a free sample issue of the *Journal,* visit the Society's website, download the membership application, provide the requested information, and send it as your request.) The Society also has an official weekly e-magazine, the *JR Newsletter.* No dues or fees are required to receive the newsletter, though subscribers are encouraged to join the JRCS. The *Newsletter* is archived online.

Take a tip from us—membership in any numismatic specialty club is always highly educational and worth the modest annual dues.

Visit the JRCS website at www.jrcs.org to find a membership application, club details, a list of events and contacts, and educational information. Contact the Society by mail at

John Reich Collectors Society
Attn: W. David Perkins, Treasurer
PO Box 3039
Centennial CO 80161-3039

New Capped Bust Dime Varieties in the Sixth Edition, Volume II

Date, Variety	Fivaz-Stanton number	PUP
1814, Close STATES OF	FS-10-1814-901	Legend
1820, Close STATES OF	FS-10-1820-901	Legend
1829, Extra Large 10C	FS-10-1829-902	Denomination

1814 FS-10-1814-901

Variety: Close STATESOFAMERICA **CONECA: N/L; JR-5**
PUP: STATES OF
URS-8 · I-5 · L-5

FS-10-1814-901.

Regular 1814 dime.

Description: The words STATES OF AMERICA are so crowded that they appear to be one word.

Comments: This variety is very popular amongst Bust coinage and *Red Book* dime variety collectors. It has greatly increased in popularity and value over the past decade. Usually found in low grades and with problems. Choice, problem-free examples are truly scarce and they command substantial premiums.

	G-4	VG-8	F-12	VF-20	EF-40	AU-50
Variety	$300	$475	$850	$1,275	$2,000	$3,000
Normal	$95	$150	$225	$350	$800	$1,400

1820 FS-10-1820-901

Variety: Close STATESOFAMERICA **CONECA: N/L; JR-1**
PUP: STATES OF
URS-9 · I-5 · L-5

FS-10-1820-901.

Regular 1820 dime.

Description: STATES OF AMERICA appears as one word. A die bulge is usually seen on the obverse from 7 o'clock to 9 o'clock.

Comments: This is the same reverse die from the 1814 STATESOF variety, once again employed for coinage. It's very scarce, but not as rare as the 1814. Usually found in low grades and with problems, this variety is in demand from Bust dime and *Red Book* variety collectors.

	G-4	VG-8	F-12	VF-20	EF-40	AU-50
Variety	$225	$350	$525	$850	$1,450	$2,250
Normal	$80	$125	$165	$300	$650	$875

1829 FS-10-1829-301

Variety: Curl-Base 2 **JR-10**
PUP: 2 of date
URS-7 · I-5 · L-5

FS-10-1829-301.

Regular 1829 date.

Description: This rare variety exhibits a wavy or "curled" base on the 2. (The base of a typical 2 for this date is flat, with a serif.)

Comments: Only one working die had the curl-base 2, and it obviously was used for a short press run. Almost all specimens are low-grade, i.e., Fine or below. A small quantity is known in VF. Finer examples (EF and above) might not exist. Demand is very high for any grade and the variety sells virtually immediately when offered.

	G-4	VG-8	F-12	VF-20	EF-40	AU-50	MS-60
Variety	$4,500	$7,000	$13,500	$16,500	n/a	n/a	n/a
Normal	$50	$60	$80	$140	$375	$550	$1,400

1829 FS-10-1829-901

Variety: Small Over Large 10 C **JR-9**
PUP: Denomination 10 C
URS-9 · I-4 · L-4

Description: The denomination, 10 C, on the reverse die was punched first with a large 10 C, then again with a smaller 10 C. The large 10 C is clearly evident north of the primary small 10 C.

Comments: This variety has been known for some time. Interest in it has increased since the late 1990s.

	G-4	VG-8	F-12	VF-20	EF-40	AU-50	MS-60	MS-63
Variety	$40	$60	$90	$145	$375	$500	$1,200	$2,200
Normal	$35	$55	$80	$140	$365	$490	$1,190	$1,500

1829 — FS-10-1829-902

VARIETY: Extra Large 10 C. **CONECA: N/L; JR-1**
PUP: Denomination
URS-8 · I-5 · L-4

FS-10-1829-902. Extra Large 10-cent.

Medium 10 C.

Description: The denomination, 10 C., is visibly larger than on other dimes of this date.

Comments: Although the *Red Book* and *Coin Dealer Newsletter* list three sizes of 10 C. dies, there are actually four: Small 10 C.; Medium 10 C.; Large 10 C.; and Extra Large 10 C. The Extra Large commands the biggest premium. Usually found in AG to VG, it becomes progressively rarer as its grade escalates, and is quite rare in Mint State.

	VG-8	F-12	VF-20	EF-40	AU-50	MS-60	MS-63
VARIETY	$65	$110	$175	$475	$925	$1,750	$4,250
NORMAL	$60	$80	$140	$375	$550	$1,400	$1,600

1830, 30 Over 29 — FS-10-1830-301

VARIETY: Overdate **JR-4, -5**
PUP: Date
URS-10 · I-3 · L-3

Description: Portions of the underlying 2 and 9 are evident behind the 3 and 0 in the date. The tail of the 2 is evident to the right of the lower curve of the 3. The very top of the 9 is evident above the 0. Surface doubling from the initial 1829 punch is also evident on the 8.

Comments: New research indicates there were only two dies for this variety (two different reverse dies sharing the same obverse die). When first published in the 1971 *Scott's Comprehensive Catalogue and Encyclopedia of U.S. Coins,* this overdate was considered exceedingly rare. In fact, it is common; its popularity explains the premium it commands. Neither die is scarcer than the other. With diligence they can be cherrypicked quite easily!

	G-4	VG-8	F-12	VF-20	EF-40	AU-50	MS-60	MS-63
VARIETY	$40	$55	$75	$125	$300	$500	$1,250	$2,500
NORMAL	$35	$50	$70	$115	$285	$490	$1,240	$1,500

Liberty Seated Dimes, 1837–1891

Liberty Seated dimes are a paradise for variety enthusiasts. Significant varieties are known and can be found for virtually every date and mint. From minor repunched mintmarks to major doubled dies, and even major design changes, the varieties are abundant.

Virtually all of the varieties within the series are in high demand by the large number of Liberty Seated specialists. In general, values for the varieties have been increasing at an even faster rate than for the normal coins. An eagle-eyed cherrypicker can easily earn a significant income by picking varieties that go unnoticed by most non-specialist dealers.

For collectors seriously interested in these coins, we strongly recommend membership in the Liberty Seated Collectors Club, one of the best specialized clubs in numismatics. The LSCC attends more than twenty regional events each year, providing educational programs, exhibits at club tables, and meetings.

The award-winning *Gobrecht Journal*, the official publication of the club, is issued to members three times annually (in March, July, and November), in full color. This extensive publication is loaded with excellent educational articles. The *Gobrecht Journal* is research-orientated and contains articles on all Liberty Seated coinage denominations, from half dimes to trade dollars. You can preview sample articles online at https://nnp.wustl.edu/library/publisherdetail/2096

The Club also publishes *The E-Gobrecht*, a monthly email-based publication, distributed to club members and interested non-members at no cost. The *E-Gobrecht* contains information of a timely nature, such as recent auction sales, LSCC regional meeting or event announcements, and feature articles on new variety discoveries. You can download all back issues of *The E-Gobrecht* from the LSCC website's "E-Gobrecht Archives" page.

At the time of this publication, Liberty Seated Collectors Club membership dues are $30 per year—a bargain, considering the amount of resources available. If you join the LSCC, you will be connecting with the most serious and knowledgeable collectors and dealers in the hobby. For membership information, visit www.lsccweb.org, or write to

Liberty Seated Collectors Club
Leonard Augsburger, President
Email: leonard.augsburger@wustl.edu

Liberty Seated Dimes Removed From the Fifth Edition, Volume II

Date, Variety	Fivaz-Stanton number	PUP	Notes
1872, Doubled-Die Obverse	–	–	This was listed in error.
1872, Repunched Date	FS-10-1872-301	Date	Removed for lack of collector interest.
1890-S, Repunched Mintmark	FS-10-1890S-502	Mintmark	Removed for lack of collector interest.

Note: Varieties removed are still considered *Cherrypickers' Guide* varieties (as opposed to being "delisted"); for example, they will continue to be cross-referenced and summarized in appendix H. (Exceptions include varieties debunked as counterfeits, or those which later research revealed to be erroneously classified. Those will be delisted completely.)

New Liberty Seated Dimes in the Sixth Edition, Volume II

Date, Variety	Fivaz-Stanton number	PUP
1839-O, Huge O	FS-10-1839o-502	Mintmark
1855, Doubled-Die Obverse	FS-10-1855-101	Shield
1876-CC, Doubled-Die Reverse	FS-10-1876CC-801	ONE DIME

1838, Small Stars — FS-10-1838-801

Variety: Small Stars and Doubled-Die Reverse — **Greer-101; Fortin-101/101A**
PUP: Bow on reverse, D in dime
URS-9 · I-4 · L-3

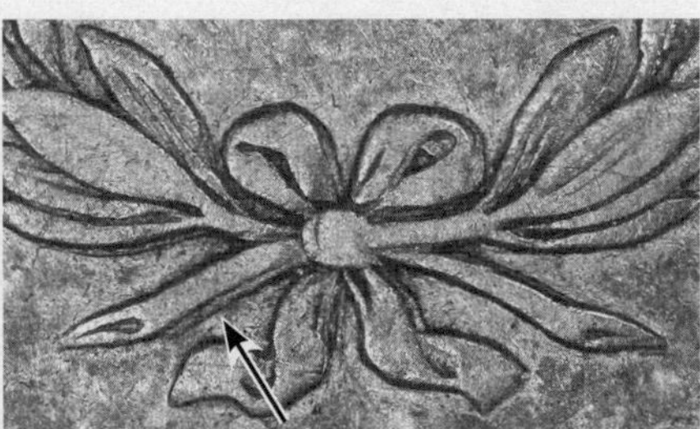

Description: Small stars on obverse. Always found with a die crack through the first six stars on the left. Doubling on the lower-left portion of the stem and bow, the leaves, and the D of DIME.

Comments: Apparently a half dime punch was used and then discarded (hence the small stars). This variety seems to be more readily available than its mintage of ~30,000 suggests. It can still be cherrypicked, with patience. It's scarcer than its Large Stars counterpart and brings more money, as well. All Small Stars coins have the DDR—no exceptions. However, not all DDRs are Small Stars.

	G-4	VG-8	F-12	VF-20	EF-40	AU-50	MS-60
Variety	$35	$50	$75	$175	$250	$450	$550
Normal	$30	$40	$70	$125	$200	$425	$540

1838, Large Stars — FS-10-1838-802

Variety: Doubled-Die Reverse — **Greer-101; Fortin-102**
PUP: Bow on reverse, D in dime
URS-8 · I-4 · L-4

Description: Doubling is evident on the D of DIME, and the bow and lower-left portions of the leaves.

Comments: The same die was used for the 1838, Small Stars, DDR. The Large Stars variety, while scarce, commands a smaller premium than its Small Stars DDR sister.

	G-4	VG-8	F-12	VF-20	EF-40	AU-50	MS-60
Variety	$30	$45	$60	$145	$200	$325	$500
Normal	$25	$35	$40	$65	$180	$300	$490

1839-O — FS-10-1839o-501

Variety: Repunched Mintmark — **Greer-102; Fortin-104/104A**
PUP: Mintmark
URS-9 · I-4 · L-3

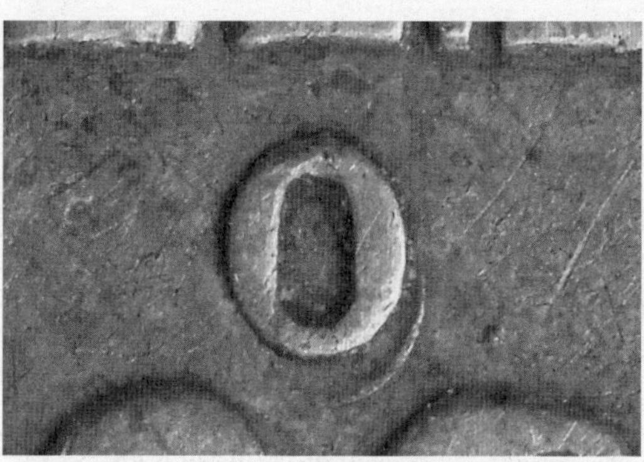

Description: On the Large O variety, the secondary O mintmark is evident southeast of the primary O. This O mintmark variety has a very slight tilt to the right. Note: There is also a Huge O variety (see next listing).

Comments: Scarce but not rare, this very strong RPM can be cherrypicked with patience and diligence.

	G-4	VG-8	F-12	VF-20	EF-40	AU-50	MS-60
Variety	$35	$55	$80	$175	$325	$450	$750
Normal	$30	$45	$75	$150	$250	$440	$740

1839-O — FS-10-1839o-502

VARIETY: Huge O — **CONECA: N/L; GREER: HUGE O, REV. 38-O;**
PUP: Mintmark — **FORTIN-108/108A; AHWASH-7**
URS-7 · I-5 · L-5

Description: This variety has the "Huge O" mintmark, tilted to the right, and the reverse of 1838-O. The obverse usually shows weakness in 18 (of the date) and the first three stars on the left. Only one die.

Comments: Three different sizes of mintmark occur for this year: the Small O, the Large O, and the Huge O. Usually found in low grades and with problems, this variety is rare in any grade, and especially so in EF and AU. No true Uncs are known. This is a prize for the cherrypicker!

	G-4	VG-8	F-12	VF-20	EF-40	AU-50
VARIETY	$145	$245	$345	$650	$1,000	n/a
NORMAL	$30	$50	$85	$150	$250	$450

1841-O — FS-10-1841o-901

VARIETY: Transitional Reverse (Small O) — **GREER-101; FORTIN-102**
PUP: Reverse, closed buds and leaf by U of UNITED; mintmark
URS-7 · I-5 · L-4

Description: Note the closed buds and the second leaf from the left in the group of four to the left of the bow knot. The leaf on the Closed Bud reverse reaches only halfway across the bottom of the U in UNITED.

Comments: This die pair was struck with a reverse die that was to have been discontinued in 1840, but saw limited use into 1841. This is a very rare and important variety in this series. It has the Small O mintmark (compare it to the next listing). With due diligence and a lot of luck, it can occasionally be cherrypicked. Usually found in low grades and with problems.

	G-4	VG-8	F-12	VF-20	EF-40	AU-50	MS-60
VARIETY	$650	$1,100	$1,750	$2,850	$6,250	n/a	n/a
NORMAL	$30	$40	$50	$100	$150	$325	$850

1841-O — FS-10-1841o-902

VARIETY: Transitional Reverse (Large O) **GREER-102; FORTIN-101**
PUP: Reverse, closed buds; mintmark
URS-8 · I-5 · L-4

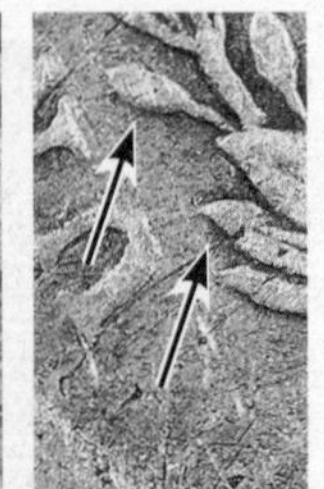

Description: Note the closed buds and the second leaf from the left in the group of four to the left of the bow knot. The leaf on the Closed Bud reverse reaches only halfway across the bottom of the U in UNITED.

Comments: This die pair was struck with a reverse die that was to have been discontinued in 1840, but saw limited use into 1841. This is a very rare and important variety in this series. It has the Large (or Normal) O mintmark (compare it to the preceding listing). Usually found in low grades and with problems.

	G-4	VG-8	F-12	VF-20	EF-40	AU-50	MS-60
VARIETY	$450	$650	$1,400	$2,500	$5,250	n/a	n/a
NORMAL	$30	$40	$50	$100	$150	$325	$850

1843 — FS-10-1843-301

VARIETY: Repunched Date **GREER-101; FORTIN-102**
PUP: Date
URS-8 · I-4 · L-3

Description: This is a nice repunched date, with a secondary 1 and 8 evident north, and a secondary 4 and 3 evident north of the primary numerals.

Comments: The regular 1843 dime, although not a rare date, is fairly scarce, making this double-date variety a little tougher to cherrypick than one might think! This is one of the nicest double-date varieties in the series.

	G-4	VG-8	F-12	VF-20	EF-40	AU-50	MS-60
VARIETY	$25	$35	$45	$75	$125	$275	$500
NORMAL	$20	$25	$30	$40	$70	$150	$475

1853, With Arrows — FS-10-1853-301

Variety: Repunched Date **Greer-103; Fortin-107**
PUP: Date
URS-7 · I-4 · L-3

Description: The secondary image of the date is evident on all four digits, to the east.

Comments: This is the most evident RPD for this date of Liberty Seated dime and for the 1853–1855 With Arrows type.

	VG-8	F-12	VF-20	EF-40	AU-50	MS-60
Variety	$75	$125	$175	$300	n/a	n/a
Normal	$15	$25	$35	$55	$165	$350

1855, With Arrows — FS-10-1855-101

Variety: Doubled Die Obverse **Greer-101, Fortin-101a/103**
PUP: Shield
URS-6 · I-3 · L-3

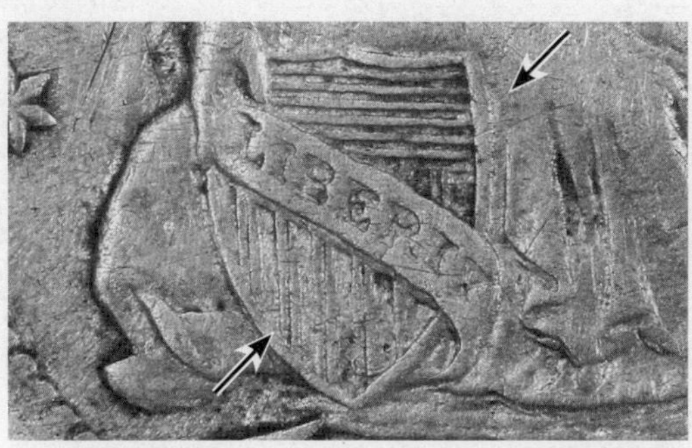

Description: As with the doubled-die obverse on the 1855 half dime and quarter dollar, the doubling is on the vertical shield stripes and the right edge of the shield.

Comments: This is a very scarce variety that, outside of Liberty Seated specialists, has been virtually unknown to the mainstream hobby. Two different dies exist, nearly identical in doubling, and of about equal rarity.

	VG-8	F-12	VF-20	EF-40	AU-50	MS-60
Variety	$30	$45	$75	$125	$275	$450
Normal	$20	$25	$35	$65	$185	$350

1856, Small Date — FS-10-1856-101

VARIETY: Doubled-Die Obverse — **GREER-101; FORTIN-108**
PUP: Shield
URS-9 · I-2 · L-2

1856, Small Date.

1856, Large Date.

Description: Doubling is evident with a close spread on the right side and top of the shield; on the banner across the shield; and as a doubled pole.

Comments: This doubled die is difficult to notice on lower-grade coins. There is also a Proof doubled die that is very similar, but it commands little or no premium over normal market values.

	VG-8	F-12	VF-20	EF-40	AU-50	MS-60
VARIETY	$25	$40	$65	$110	$195	$350
NORMAL	$15	$20	$30	$60	$150	$325

1856-O, Large O — FS-10-1856o-301

VARIETY: Repunched Date, Large O — **GREER-101; FORTIN-105**
PUP: Date, mintmark
URS-8 · I-3 · L-3

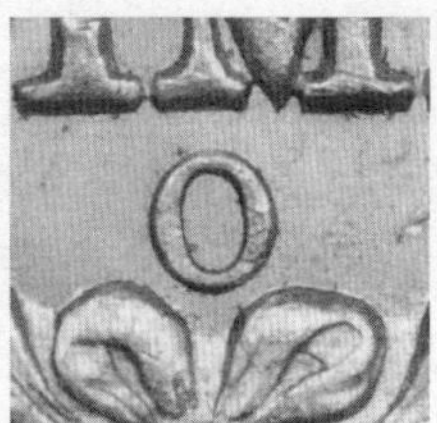
Large O.

Medium O.

Description: This variety exhibits a strong repunched date. The obverse is paired with a die exhibiting the Large O mintmark.

Comments: (Erroneously listed in the fifth edition as FS-10-1856o-2301.) This is one of the stronger repunched dates in the Liberty Seated dime series. It can be located easily in lower grades, but very tough above VF.

	VG-8	F-12	VF-20	EF-40	AU-50	MS-60
VARIETY	$40	$65	$110	$200	$400	$750
NORMAL	$35	$60	$100	$155	$390	$740

1872 FS-10-1872-302

Variety: Misplaced Date **Greer-104; Fortin: 109a**
PUP: Rock area above 7 in the date
URS-7 · I-3 · L-2

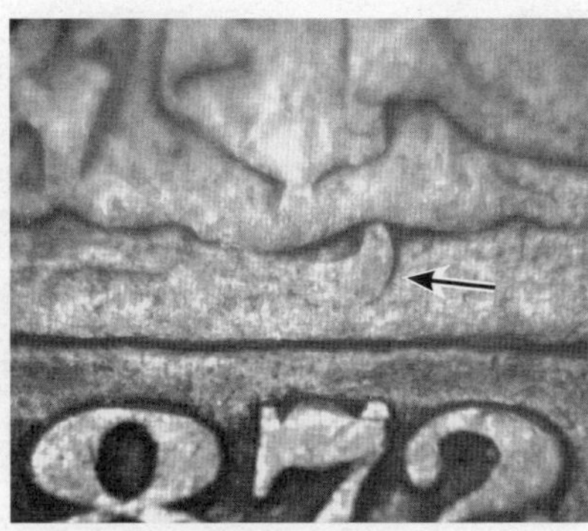

Description: The outer curve of a numeral 2 shows in the rock above the 7 of the date.

Comments: This is one of the nicer misplaced dates known in the Liberty Seated dime series.

	VG-8	F-12	VF-20	EF-40	AU-50	MS-60
Variety	$30	$50	$100	$140	$195	$325
Normal	$20	$25	$30	$40	$90	$175

The Cherrypickers' Guide HELPFUL HINTS

Don't get hung up on just the die varieties listed in this book. There are many nice, yet-to-be-discovered treasures out there waiting for you to cherrypick!

If you can't discern a variety with a 7x loupe, it probably isn't significant enough to earn the attention of other collectors.

Values provided in this book for die varieties are for raw (unslabbed) coins. Varieties correctly attributed, certified, and graded by a third-party grading service may command higher premiums—but not necessarily. Ultimately, the marketplace of collectors determines a variety's value.

1872 FS-10-1872-801

VARIETY: Doubled-Die Reverse **GREER: N/L; FORTIN-105**
PUP: Entire reverse
URS-7 · I-4 · L-3

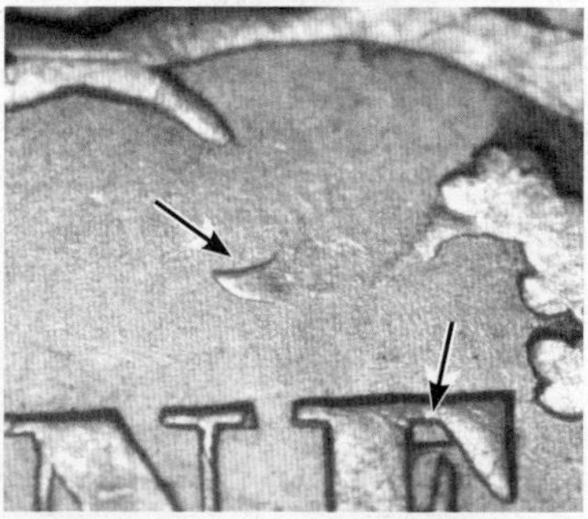

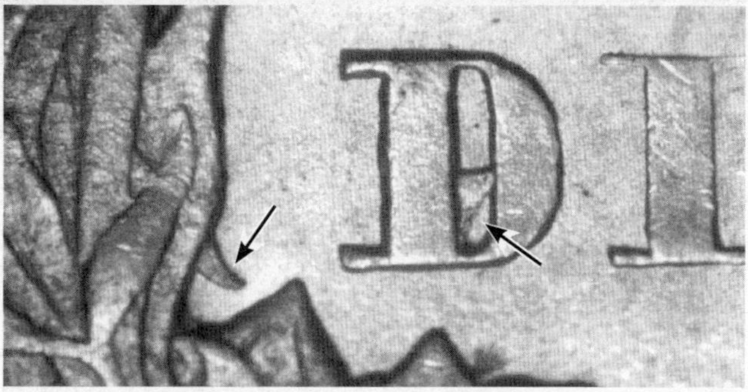

Description: On this variety, the first hubbing was almost totally obliterated by the second, which was rotated about 170° from the first. The key diagnostics are inside the opening of the D and the center arm of the E of ONE. The tip of the weaker lower-left leaf is evident above the primary E of ONE. Other elements are also clearly visible.

Comments: This is one of the most dramatic doubled dies ever discovered. Lee Day reported it to J.T. Stanton in 1997, and Tom DeLorey confirmed that the variety is a doubled die. Since publication in the *Cherrypickers' Guide* several more finds have been reported.

	VG-8	F-12	VF-20	EF-40	AU-50	MS-60
VARIETY	$50	$75	$150	$250	$375	$750
NORMAL	$15	$25	$30	$40	$90	$175

1873, No Arrows, Close 3 — FS-10-1873-301

Variety: Repunched Date — **Greer-101; Fortin-103**

PUP: Date

URS-7 · I-3 · L-3

Description: A strongly repunched date shows secondary digits west of the primary digits.

Comments: The normal 1873, Close 3, while not a rare date, still is fairly scarce. The Repunched Date variety is *very* scarce!

	VG-8	F-12	VF-20	EF-40	AU-50	MS-60
Variety	$25	$45	$75	$145	$235	$400
Normal	$20	$35	$50	$75	$125	$250

1873, With Arrows — FS-10-1873-101

Variety: Doubled-Die Obverse — **Greer-101; Fortin-103**

PUP: Shield

URS-6 · I-5 · L-5

Description: Strong doubling is evident on the shield and on the banner across the shield.

Comments: This is an extremely rare—and very dramatic—doubled die. Although well known for decades, very few specimens have been reported (28 verified as of 2022). The highest-graded example known is an AU.

	VG-8	F-12	VF-20	EF-40	AU-50	MS-60
Variety	$700	$1,000	$1,750	$2.750	n/a	n/a
Normal	$20	$30	$60	$155	$325	$550

1875 FS-10-1875-301

VARIETY: Misplaced Date **GREER-104; FORTIN-107**
PUP: Denticles below 8 in date
URS-6 · I-4 · L-3

Description: The top of a numeral 1 is clearly evident protruding from the denticles below the date.

Comments: Chris Pilliod discovered this variety in January 1991. Since that time just a few more examples have been found.

	VG-8	F-12	VF-20	EF-40	AU-50	MS-60
VARIETY	$35	$50	$100	$225	$350	$475
NORMAL	$15	$20	$25	$35	$85	$155

THE CHERRYPICKERS' GUIDE HELPFUL HINTS

Please be sure to read the information in the front of this book. It sets the tone for the material that follows and makes it easier to interpret the information for each listing.

The die varieties listed in this book are only the tip of the iceberg. Even more are yet to be discovered. Always examine closely any coin you obtain. You might discover a great variety that soon every collector wants! (Be sure to let us know when you do.)

Note: When you study auction results, especially for high-grade rarities, be aware of the "registry set effect." Two eager collectors who both want the #1-rated set can drive prices up and up—but their frenzy isn't necessarily a snapshot of the broader market.

1876-CC FS-10-1876CC-101, 102, 103

Variety: Doubled-Die Obverse **Greer-101A, -101B, -101C; Fortin-105, -106, -107**
PUP: OF AMERICA
URS-9 · I-4 · L-4

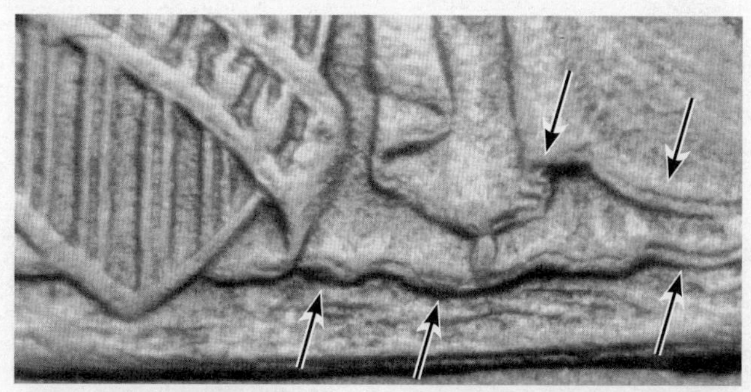

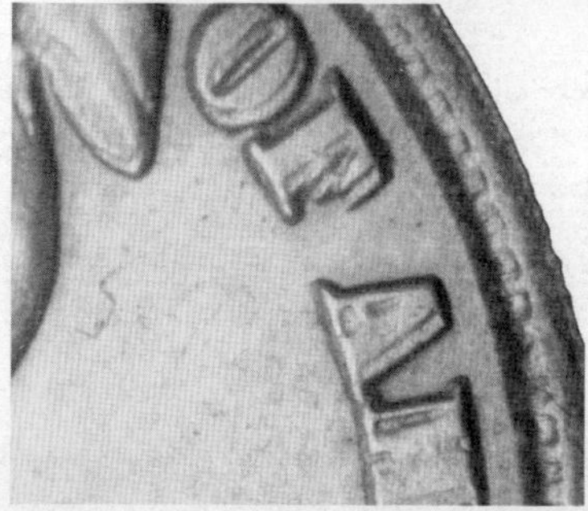

FS-10-1876CC-101 (Level CC).

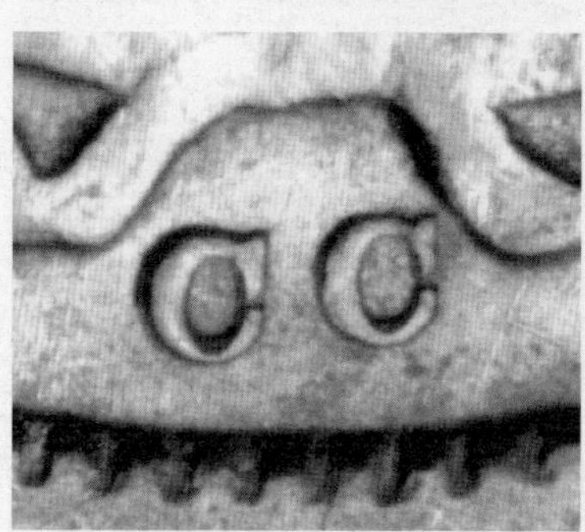

FS-10-1876CC-102 (Right C High).

FS-10-1876CC-103 (Right C Low) (rarest).

Description: Doubling with a very strong spread is evident on OF AMERICA. Doubling is also visible on the lower folds of the gown and on the lower portion of the rock.

Comments: There is only one obverse paired with three different reverses (as shown). This variety is very common in AG to VG; scarce in Fine to VF; very scarce in EF; and starts becoming rare in AU and better. There is virtually no difference in value amongst the three different DDO varieties.

	VG-8	F-12	VF-20	EF-40	AU-50	MS-60
Variety	$35	$55	$115	$195	$325	$475
Normal	$30	$50	$70	$110	$180	$375

1876-CC — FS-10-1876CC-301

VARIETY: Misplaced Date — **GREER-104; FORTIN-111**
PUP: Gown by shield
URS-7 · I-4 · L-3

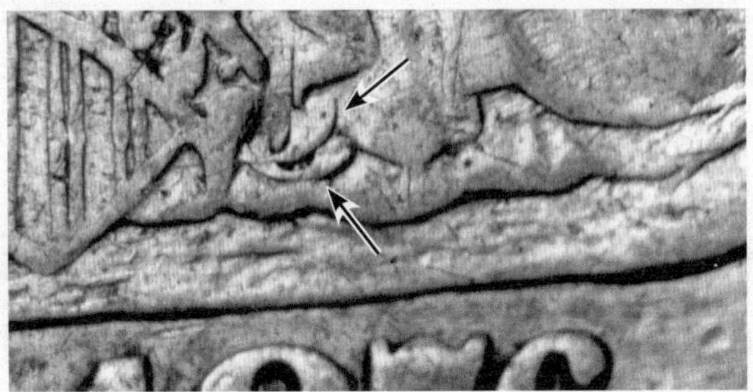

Description: The bases of two 6s are evident in the gown by the shield, overlapping one another.

Comments: This variety shows another very massive misplaced date. Though very scarce, with diligence it can still be cherrypicked.

	VG-8	F-12	VF-20	EF-40	AU-50	MS-60
VARIETY	$50	$75	$125	$175	$295	$445
NORMAL	$30	$50	$70	$110	$180	$375

1876-CC — FS-10-1876CC-801

VARIETY: Doubled-Die Reverse — **CONECA DDR-001; FORTIN-116**
PUP: E of ONE, ME of DIME
URS-7 · I-4 · L-3

Description: Very strong doubling is evident, especially on the E of ONE and the ME of DIME.

Comments: This variety is nearly always found from a rusted reverse die. It is a Type I reverse.

	VG-8	F-12	VF-20	EF-40	AU-50	MS-60
VARIETY	$70	$90	$140	$200	n/a	n/a
NORMAL	$30	$50	$70	$110	$180	$375

1876-CC — FS-10-1876CC-901

Variety: Type II Reverse — **Greer-101; Fortin-101**
PUP: Left reverse ribbon
URS-7 · I-5 · L-4

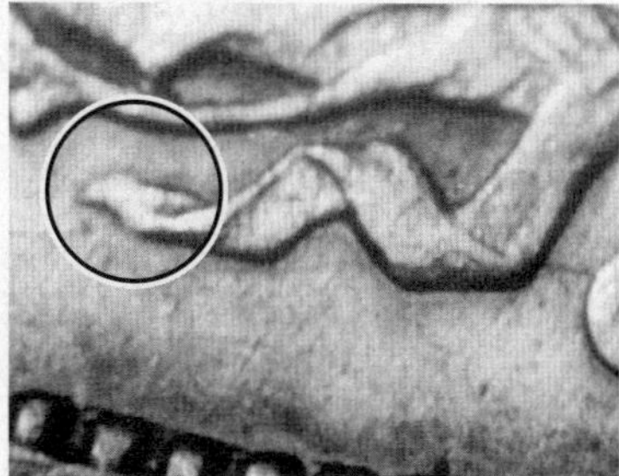

Type II reverse. Note the single-point ribbon end.

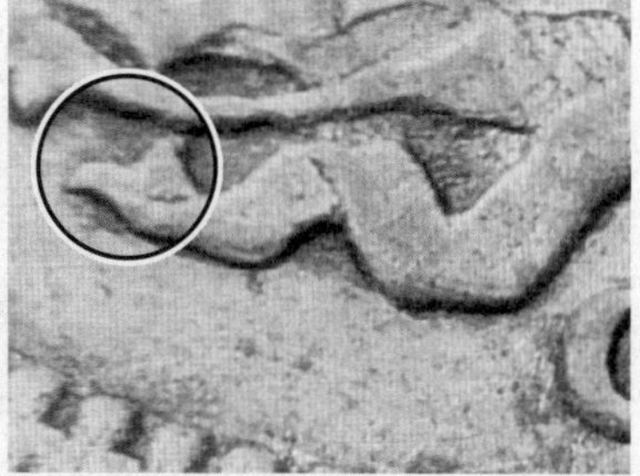

Type I reverse. Note the split ribbon end.

Description: On the Type II reverse, there is a single point to the end of the left ribbon. (The common Type I reverse shows a split ribbon end.)

Comments: This very scarce variety has become highly collectible. It is usually found in low grades (AG to VG). Any examples grading EF or finer can be considered rare.

	VG-8	F-12	VF-20	EF-40	AU-50	MS-60
Variety	$50	$100	$175	$275	$425	$650
Normal	$20	$40	$70	$110	$165	$270

1876-S — FS-10-1876S-301

Variety: Repunched Date — **Greer-N/L; Fortin-122**
PUP: 18 of date
URS-6 · I-3 · L-2

Description: Repunching is strongly apparent on the 18 of the date, and possibly a bit on the lower 7.

Comments: This variety made its first *Cherrypickers' Guide* appearance in the fifth edition (2012). Although not rare as a normal date, the 1876-S is fairly scarce if you need it. Throw in the repunched date, and you have a very scarce variety.

	VG-8	F-12	VF-20	EF-40	AU-50	MS-60
Variety	$30	$45	$75	$120	$175	$275
Normal	$15	$20	$25	$40	$80	$165

1877-CC — FS-10-1877CC-301

VARIETY: Overdate — **GREER-N/L; FORTIN-107, -108**

PUP: Date, shield

URS-7 · I-4 · L-3

Description: Surface doubling of the upper curve of a 6 is apparent on the horizontal bar of the second 7. Also visible are a 1/1 and doubling and tripling of the lower 7s. Surface doubling fades in lower grades and weaker strikes. The die gouge in the shield is the key to realizing you have this overdate.

Comments: This variety was discovered by Rick DeSanctis, and made its *Cherrypickers' Guide* debut in the fifth edition (2012). One obverse die is paired with two different reverses. Values listed here are for early-die-state coins showing the 7 Over 6 surface doubling.

	VG-8	F-12	VF-20	EF-40	AU-50	MS-60
VARIETY	n/a	n/a	$95	$175	$275	n/a
NORMAL	$30	$45	$75	$150	$200	$325

1887-S — FS-10-1887S-501

VARIETY: Repunched Mintmark — **GREER-N/L; FORTIN-102**

PUP: Mintmark

URS-8 · I-3 · L-3

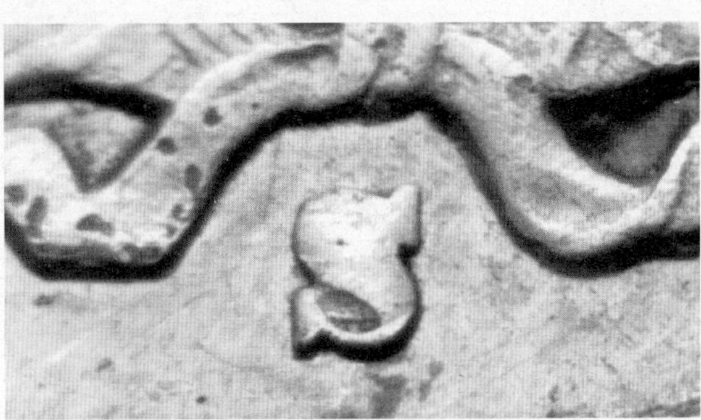

Description: A secondary S mintmark is evident within the lower loop of the primary S.

Comments: This variety does not appear to match the photographs of CONECA RPM-2, which is also listed as Greer-102.

	VG-8	F-12	VF-20	EF-40	AU-50	MS-60
VARIETY	$25	$35	$50	$75	$135	$225
NORMAL	$15	$20	$25	$35	$85	$165

1888-S — FS-10-1888S-501

Variety: Repunched Mintmark — **Greer-101; Fortin-105**
PUP: Mintmark
URS-7 · I-4 · L-3

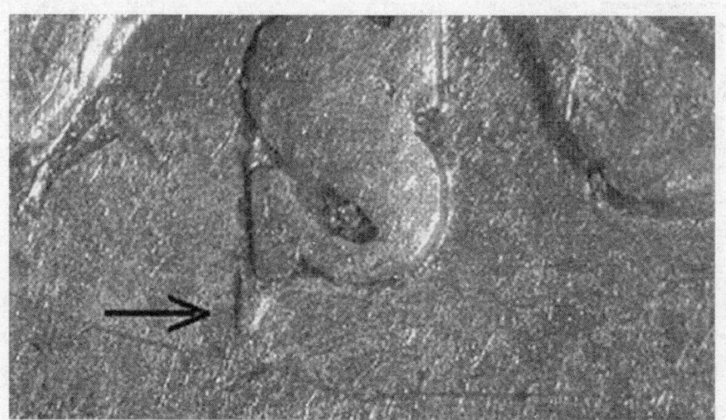

Description: A secondary S mintmark is evident just below the primary S, showing only the lower serif. The left curve of the secondary S is also visible in the lower opening of the primary S.

Comments: Greer lists this variety as very scarce. The normal 1888-S Liberty Seated dime is fairly common, but the variety is seldom seen. When you need this date for your collection, it can feel rare—and the variety, rarer still!

	VG-8	F-12	VF-20	EF-40	AU-50	MS-60
Variety	$45	$65	$105	$175	$245	$375
Normal	$20	$25	$30	$55	$100	$300

1889 — FS-10-1889-801

Variety: Doubled-Die Reverse / Repunched Date — **Greer-101; Fortin-105**
PUP: Left wreath (reverse); date
URS-9 · I-3 · L-2

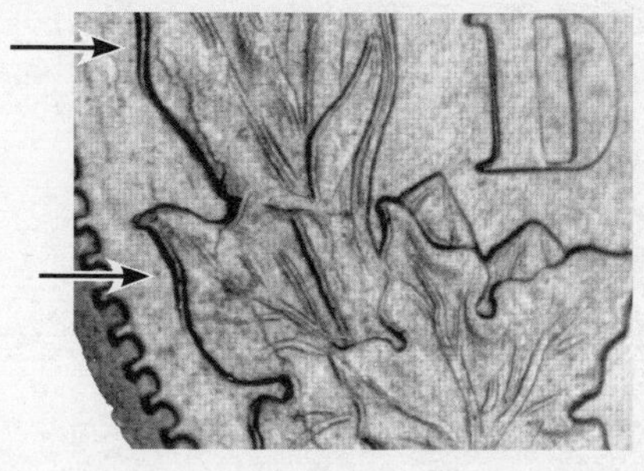

Description: Doubling is evident on the left side of the wreath, from 7 o'clock to 11 o'clock. The second 8 of the date is doubled.

Comments: This variety is fairly easy to cherrypick, usually in low grades. The second 8 of the date is lightly recut north. The key pickup point for the reverse doubled die is a long die crack on the left outer leaves.

	VG-8	F-12	VF-20	EF-40	AU-50	MS-60
Variety	$30	$45	$85	$125	$195	$325
Normal	$15	$20	$30	$45	$95	$135

1890 FS-10-1890-301

VARIETY: Misplaced Date **GREER-101; FORTIN-105**
PUP: Gown by shield
URS-8 · I-3 · L-2

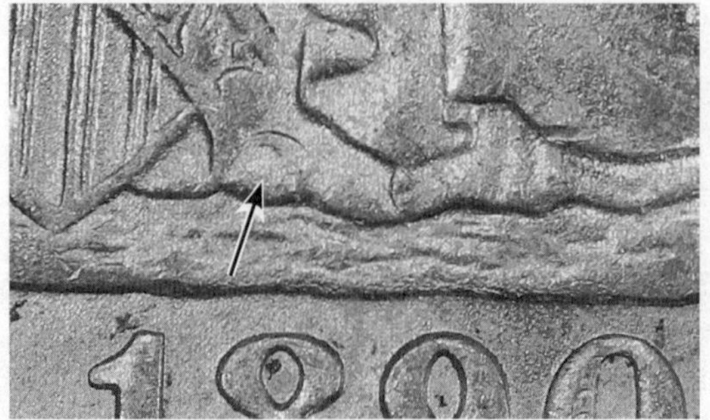

Description: The top of a digit—probably a 9—is evident in the gown just to the right of the banner across the shield.

Comments: This is another variety with a nice misplaced date next to the Y of LIBERTY, in the gown. The area by the right of the shield is recessed, which protects the MPD and allows it to be visible even on low-grade coins.

	VG-8	F-12	VF-20	EF-40	AU-50	MS-60
VARIETY	$30	$45	$75	$110	$165	$245
NORMAL	$15	$20	$25	$35	$85	$165

1890 FS-10-1890-302

VARIETY: Misplaced Date **GREER-102; FORTIN-106**
PUP: Gown by shield
URS-6 · I-4 · L-3

Description: The tops of four digits are evident in the gown.

Comments: Two digits are in the lower gown to the left of the pendant, and two digits are in the lower gown to the right of the pendant. Fortin considers this variety to be the key to the misplaced dates, as well as the top 100 of Liberty Seated dimes. EF or finer coins are a real prize!

	VG-8	F-12	VF-20	EF-40	AU-50	MS-60
VARIETY	$45	$75	$125	$175	$245	$375
NORMAL	$15	$20	$25	$35	$85	$165

1890-S — FS-10-1890S-501

Variety: Repunched Mintmark — **Greer: NL; Fortin-111**
PUP: Mintmark
URS-7 · I-4 · L-3

Description: The primary S mintmark is larger and centered over the initial smaller S, which is visible within and to the right of the upper loop of the primary S.

Comments: This Medium S Over S repunched mintmark was discovered by Todd Stickel. The normal 1890-S Liberty Seated dime is scarce; the die variety is *very* scarce. (Note: This variety was wrongly cross-referenced as Greer-101 in the fifth edition. It is actually Fortin-111.)

	VG-8	F-12	VF-20	EF-40	AU-50	MS-60
Variety	$40	$65	$100	$175	$275	$425
Normal	$20	$25	$55	$85	$150	$350

1891 — FS-10-1891-301

Variety: Misplaced Date — **Greer-101**
PUP: Denticles below date
URS-7 · I-3 · L-3

Description: The top of a digit is directly below and between the 8 and 9 of the date.

Comments: The misplaced date is very evident, even in lower grades. With diligence this variety can be cherrypicked.

	VG-8	F-12	VF-20	EF-40	AU-50	MS-60
Variety	$25	$45	$75	$125	$175	$275
Normal	$15	$20	$30	$45	$95	$150

1891-O — FS-10-1891o-501

VARIETY: Repunched Mintmark — **GREER-101; FORTIN-109; AHWASH-7**
PUP: Mintmark
URS-8 · I-4 · L-3

Description: The primary O mintmark was punched over a previously punched horizontal O.

Comments: Although very scarce, this die variety can still be cherrypicked. It is popular and in demand.

	VG-8	F-12	VF-20	EF-40	AU-50	MS-60
VARIETY	$50	$75	$125	$200	$300	$450
NORMAL	$20	$30	$35	$50	$100	$185

1891-S — FS-10-1891S-501

VARIETY: Repunched Mintmark — **GREER-101; FORTIN-105; AHWASH-5**
PUP: Mintmark
URS-8 · I-4 · L-3

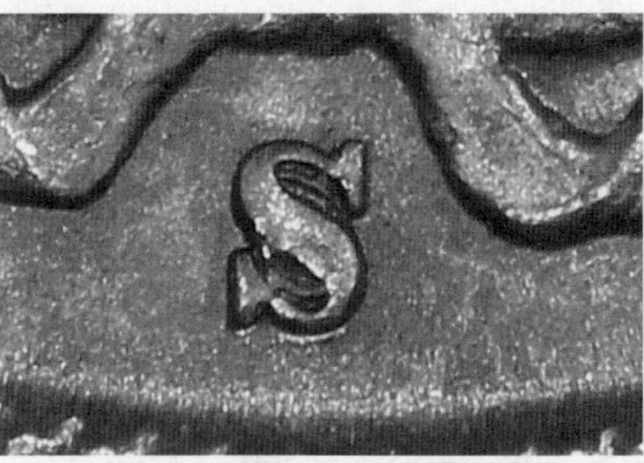

Description: As on the 1890-S Repunched Mintmark, the larger primary S mintmark (known as the Medium S) was punched squarely over the smaller initial S, and is evident within both loops of the primary S.

Comments: This Medium S Over Small S repunched mintmark is scarce and very popular among Liberty Seated dime specialists.

	VG-8	F-12	VF-20	EF-40	AU-50	MS-60
VARIETY	$30	$50	$125	$175	$275	$350
NORMAL	$15	$20	$25	$35	$85	$185

Barber Dimes, 1892–1916

When the third edition of the *Cherrypickers' Guide* went to press, only a limited number of die varieties had been reported in the Barber series. Some were known but were not included in that edition. Since that time a significant number of new varieties have come to light, and there are undoubtedly many more yet to be discovered. Even anomalies such as die chips, found in particular on some 1892 Barber dimes, can be interesting (the 1912-S dime with die chips is a new listing in this volume of the *Cherrypickers' Guide*). For these reasons we encourage close inspection of all Barber coins.

To build your knowledge of Barber coins in general and Barber die varieties in particular, we heartily recommend membership in the Barber Coin Collectors' Society. The BCCS is a group of hundreds of collectors and dealers dedicated to the study of the American coinage of Charles E. Barber, chief engraver of the United States Mint from 1880 to 1917. Social interactions at regional meeting venues nationwide are a key element of the "BCCS Experience." Members receive four issues annually of the award-winning *Journal of the Barber Coin Collectors' Society*. In addition, the BCCS attends more than 20 regional events each year, providing educational programs, exhibits at club tables, and meetings.

The BCCS is online at www.barbercoins.org. There, you'll find educational articles; population censuses and rarity surveys; membership information; and general information about Charles Barber, the three Barber silver series, and Liberty Head nickels.

Annual membership dues are a bargain at $20. For more information, contact

BCCS
John Frost, President
PO Box 1723
Decatur IL 62525
E-mail: bccs@BarberCoins.org

Barber Dimes Removed From the Fifth Edition, Volume II

Date, Variety	Fivaz-Stanton number	PUP	Notes
1892, Repunched Date	FS-10-1892-301	Date	Removed for lack of collector interest.
1892, Repunched Date	FS-10-1892-302	Date	
1892-O, Repunched Date	FS-10-1892o-301	Date	
1895-S, Repunched Date	FS-10-1895S-301	Date	
1896, Repunched Date	FS-10-1896-301	Date	
1897, Repunched Date	FS-10-1897-301	Date	
1897, Repunched Date	FS-10-1897-302	Date	
1897, Repunched Date	FS-10-1897-303	Date	

Barber Dimes Removed From the Fifth Edition, Volume II

Continued from previous page.

Date, Variety	Fivaz-Stanton number	PUP	Notes
1899-O, Repunched Date	FS-10-1899o-301	Date	Removed for lack of collector interest.
1899-O, Repunched Mintmark	FS-10-1899o-501	Mintmark	
1903, Repunched Date	FS-10-1903-301	Date	
1903-O, Repunched Date	FS-10-1903o-301	Date	
1906, Repunched Date	FS-10-1906-301	Date	
1906-D, Repunched Date, Repunched Mintmark	FS-10-1906D-302	Date	
1906-D, Repunched Date, Misplaced Date	FS-10-1906D-303	Date	
1907-D, Repunched Date	FS-10-1907D-301	Date	
1908, Repunched Date	FS-10-1908-301	Date	
1908, Repunched Date	FS-10-1908-302	Date	
1908, Repunched Date	FS-10-1908-303	Date	
1908-D, Repunched Date	FS-10-1908D-301	Date	
1908-D, Repunched Date	FS-10-1908D-302	Date	
1908-D, Repunched Date	FS-10-1908D-304	Date	
1908-D, Repunched Date	FS-10-1908D-305	Date	
1908-D, Repunched Date	FS-10-1908D-306	Date	
1908-D, Repunched Date	FS-10-1908D-307	Date	
1908-O, Repunched Date	FS-10-1908o-301	Date	
1908-O, Repunched Date	FS-10-1908o-302	Date	

Note: Varieties removed are still considered *Cherrypickers' Guide* varieties (as opposed to being "delisted"); for example, they will continue to be cross-referenced and summarized in appendix H. (Exceptions include varieties debunked as counterfeits, or those which later research revealed to be erroneously classified. Those will be delisted completely.)

New Barber Dimes in the Sixth Edition, Volume II

Date, Variety	Fivaz-Stanton number	PUP
1893, 3 Over 2	FS-10-1893-301	Date
1905-O, Micro O	FS-10-1905o-501	Mintmark
1906, Repunched Date	FS-10-1906-302	Date
1906-D, D Over O	FS-10-1906D-501	Mintmark
1906-O, Repunched Date, Repunched Mintmark	FS-10-1906o-301 / 501	Date, Mintmark
1912-D, Repunched Mintmark	FS-10-1912D-501	Mintmark
1912-S, Die Chips	FS-10-1912S-401	Lip and jaw

1893 — FS-10-1893-301

Variety: So-Called 3 Over 2 — **Lawrence-101**
PUP: 3 of date
Circulation strike: URS-8 · I-4 · L-4
Proof: URS-6 · I-4 · L-4

Description: What appears to be remnants of a numeral 2 (a faint line) is within the lower loop of the 3.

Comments: This controversial variety (whether it is or isn't an overdate) is in demand by Barber dime collectors. Known for years, and highly desirable, it is found in both circulation-strike and Proof formats. The variety can be seen only on coins grading Fine or better. It is scarce in any grade, but can be cherrypicked with patience. Good luck! Values shown are for circulation strikes.

	VF-20	EF-40	AU-50	AU-55	MS-60	MS-63
Variety	$450	$750	$1,500	$2,000	$3,000	$4,500
Normal	$35	$55	$85	$100	$170	$275

1893-S — FS-10-1893S-501

Variety: Repunched Mintmark — **Lawrence-101; CONECA: RPM-001**
PUP: Mintmark
URS-8 · I-4 · L-3

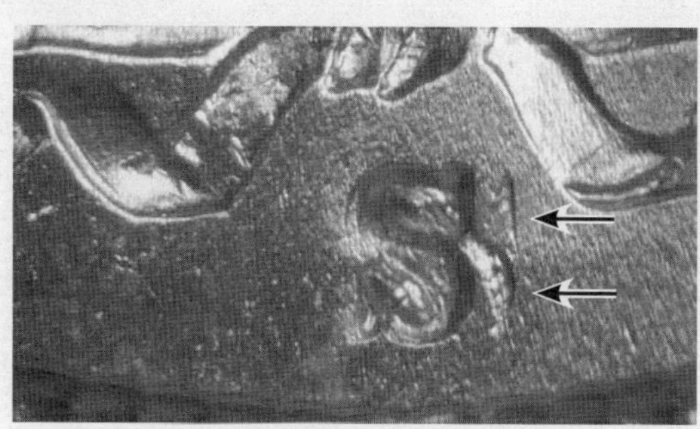

Description: The secondary S is evident east of the primary S.

Comments: This repunched mintmark is well known among variety collectors and Barber specialists. There are two other interesting RPMs known for this date. This variety is frequently found with strike or shelf doubling to the left of the primary S, resulting in what looks like a tripled mintmark. Many Barber dime collectors try to locate one of these so-called 1893-S/S/S coins, and they are occasionally found.

	F-12	VF-20	EF-40	AU-50	AU-55	MS-60	MS-63
Variety	$50	$75	$125	$200	$275	$375	$750
Normal	$45	$65	$100	$165	$185	$365	$740

1901-O — FS-10-1901o-501

VARIETY: Repunched Mintmark — **LAWRENCE-103; CONECA: RPM-001**
PUP: Mintmark
URS-7 · I-4 · L-4

Description: This variety exhibits an O mintmark over a horizontal O.

Comments: This can be found with some cherrypicking diligence and hard work! Usually seen in AG to VG. Anything Fine or better is a prize, and EF or better grades are quite rare.

	G-4	VG-8	F-12	VF-20	EF-40	AU-50	AU-55	MS-60
VARIETY	$25	$45	$85	$175	$350	$450	$575	$825
NORMAL	$9	$12	$25	$45	$95	$200	$300	$750

1905-O — FS-10-1905o-501

VARIETY: Micro O — **LAWRENCE: 101**
PUP: Mintmark
URS-10 · I-5 · L-4

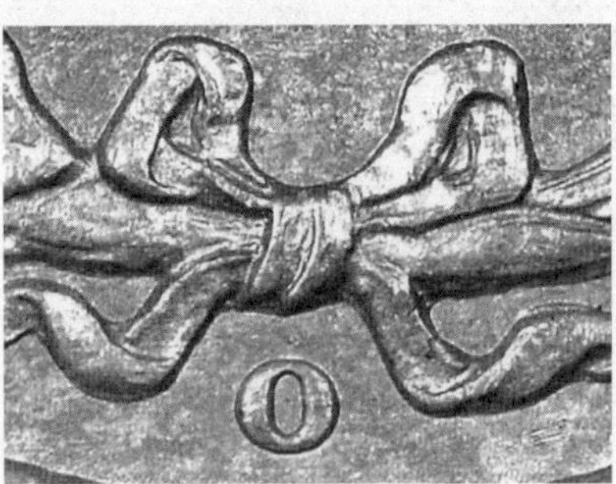

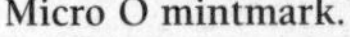

Micro O mintmark.

Regular O mintmark.

Description: A Barber quarter mintmark was used on this Barber dime date, about half the size of the normal New Orleans Barber dime mintmark.

Comments: This is easily found in grades of AG to VG. Fine and VF grades are scarce, while EF and better are rare. Any AU or MS example is a true prize!

	G-4	VG-8	F-12	VF-20	EF-40	AU-50	AU-55	MS-60
VARIETY	$50	$75	$125	$250	$600	$850	$1,500	$2,500
NORMAL	$10	$18	$45	$65	$125	$150	$200	$325

1906 — FS-10-1906-302

VARIETY: Repunched Date **CONECA: N/L**
PUP: Date

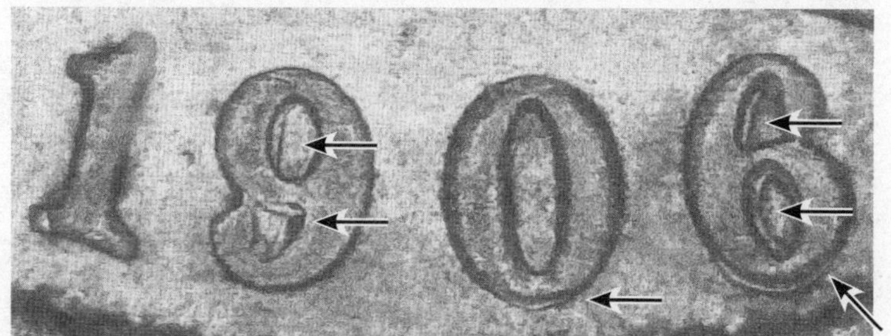

Description: Strong repunching is evident on the 9 and 0 of the date, and especially on the 6.

Comments: This is a nice new RPD that is very clearly visible. Its rarity, popularity, and liquidity remain to be established; in the meantime, be on the lookout!

	EF-45	AU-55	MS-60	MS-63	MS-64	MS-65
VARIETY	n/a	n/a	n/a	n/a	n/a	n/a
NORMAL	$35	$75	$135	$200	$300	$400

1906-D, D Over O — FS-10-1906D-501

VARIETY: Overmintmark **CONECA: N/L**
PUP: Mintmark
URS-1 · I-5 · L-5

Description: The original New Orleans mintmark was overpunched by a Denver mintmark.

Comments: Discovered by Roger Beckner in 2009, this low-grade example is the only one reported to date. At present there is no reliable sales information to report. John Frost notes: "The discovery coin is an AG-3, demonstrating that the overmintmark is visible in all grades. Any higher-grade piece would have been found by now, so I expect this will always be an extremely rare variety, and any new discoveries will be in low grade."

	G-4	VG-8	F-12	VF-20	EF-40	MS-60
VARIETY	n/a	n/a	n/a	n/a	n/a	n/a
NORMAL	$9	$12	$15	$20	$55	$175

1906-O — FS-10-1906o-301

VARIETY: Repunched Date, Misplaced Date — **LAWRENCE: N/L**
PUP: Date
URS-3 · I-3 · L-2

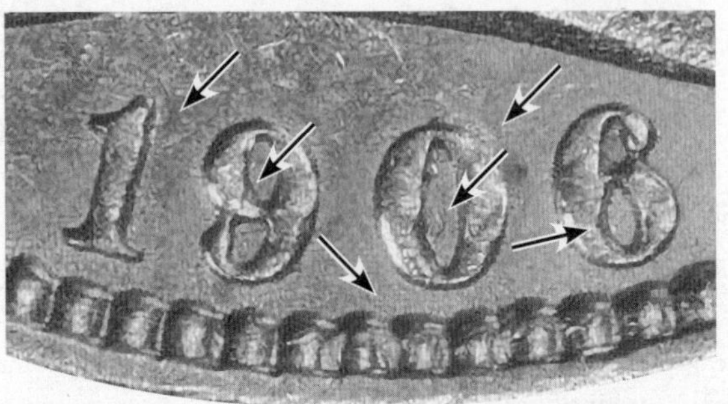

Description: All four digits are repunched, with the secondary 1 and 9 east, the secondary 0 northeast, and the secondary 6 evident within the loop of the primary 6. Another digit, possibly a 0, is visible within the denticles between the 9 and the 0.

Comments: Auction data are unknown for this variety.

	VG-8	F-12	VF-20	EF-40	AU-50	AU-55	MS-60
VARIETY	n/a	n/a	n/a	n/a	n/a	n/a	n/a
NORMAL	$10	$25	$55	$100	$135	$170	$250

1906-S — FS-10-1906S-301 / 501

VARIETY: Repunched Date, Repunched Mintmark — **LAWRENCE: N/L**
PUP: Date, mintmark
URS-6 · I-4 · L-3

Description: A secondary digit is evident within the lower loop of the 9 and within the upper loop of the 6. The earlier die states show a secondary S mintmark north of the primary S, indicating there may have been more than one repunched S.

Comments: This is an impressive combination of die characteristics—a nice repunched date with a nice S Over S repunched mintmark. The normal coin itself is scarce, and the variety is very scarce. Definitely worth looking for; happy hunting!

	VG-8	F-12	VF-20	EF-40	AU-50	AU-55	MS-60
VARIETY	$25	$35	$75	$100	$175	$250	$375
NORMAL	$13	$16	$35	$75	$145	$200	$275

1907 — FS-10-1907-301

Variety: Repunched Date — **Lawrence:** 103
PUP: Date
URS-6 · I-3 · L-3

Description: Dramatically repunched numerals 1 and 9 are visible north of the primary numbers of the date.

Comments: At present this is a very scarce variety. Occurring on a common-date Barber dime, it affords the sharp-eyed collector opportunities to cherrypick a nice (and valuable) repunched date.

	VG-8	F-12	VF-20	EF-40	AU-50	AU-55	MS-60
Variety	$25	$35	$50	$75	$100	$135	$200
Normal	$9	$12	$15	$35	$75	$105	$135

1907-O — FS-10-1907o-501

Variety: Repunched Mintmark — **Lawrence:** N/L
PUP: Mintmark
URS-6 · I-4 · L-3

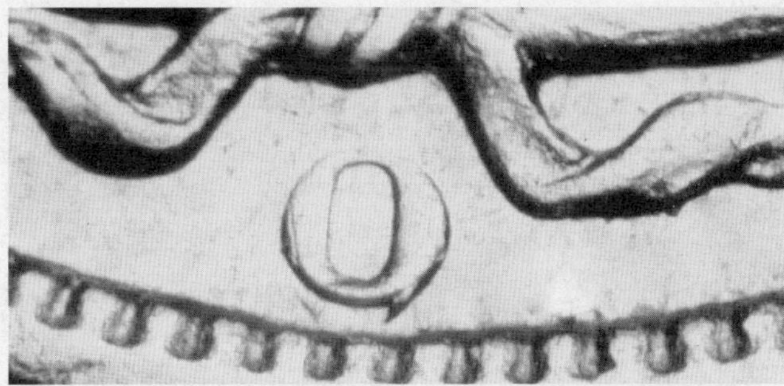

Description: A very clear secondary O mintmark is visible south of the primary mintmark.

Comments: This is one of the nicer RPMs in the Barber dime series—a very sharp, clear variety, and scarce. As a normal coin the 1907-O is a fairly common date, so you have an excellent chance of cherrypicking this scarce variety.

	VG-8	F-12	VF-20	EF-40	AU-50	AU-55	MS-60
Variety	$30	$50	$70	$100	$145	$200	$275
Normal	$20	$40	$55	$80	$110	$150	$225

1908-D — FS-10-1908D-303

Variety: Overdate — **Lawrence-104**
PUP: Date
URS-7 · I-4 · L-3

Description: Multiple punchings are visible within the numerals 9, 0, and 8 of the date.

Comments: Very unusual and rare, this neat overdate has had few examples found so far. It's a nice, collectible variety that can be found with due diligence (and great luck). Happy hunting!

	VG-8	F-12	VF-20	EF-40	AU-50	AU-55	MS-60
Variety	n/a	n/a	n/a	n/a	n/a	n/a	n/a
Normal	$9	$12	$15	$35	$75	n/a	$135

1912-D — FS-10-1912D-501

Variety: Repunched Mintmark — **Lawrence: N/L**
CONECA: RPM-001
PUP: Mintmark
URS-8 · I-4 · L-3

Description: A boldly repunched D mintmark is visible to the north.

Comments: This is a strong repunched mintmark, plainly evident.

	VG-8	F-12	VF-20	EF-40	AU-50	AU-55	MS-60
Variety	n/a	n/a	n/a	n/a	n/a	n/a	n/a
Normal	$8	$10	$15	$35	$75	$100	$130

1912-S — FS-10-1912S-101

Variety: Doubled-Die Obverse — **Lawrence: N/L**
PUP: UNITED
URS-6 · I-4 · L-3

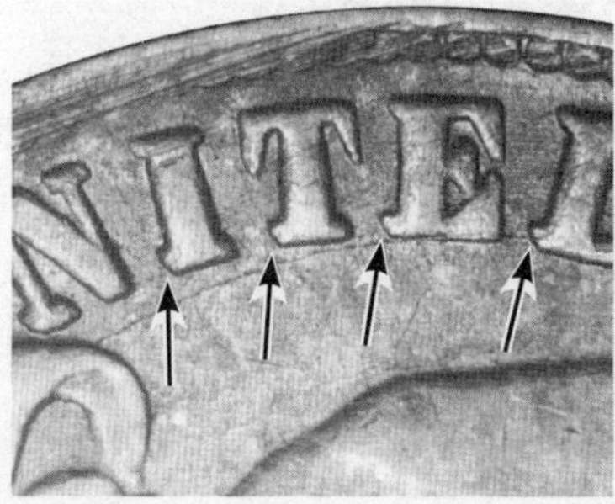

Description: Doubling is evident on all lettering of UNITED STATES OF AMERICA, and most notably on UNITED.

Comments: With this being one of the few doubled dies in the Barber dime series, interest has far outgrown supply in recent years. As knowledge of the variety has increased, so have market values. Since its first publication, few examples have come to light. This is a great find for the sharp-eyed (and lucky!) cherrypicker.

	VG-8	F-12	VF-20	EF-40	AU-50	AU-55	MS-60
Variety	$100	$145	$265	$375	$525	$675	$950
Normal	$13	$15	$25	$50	$90	$110	$185

1912-S — FS-10-1912S-401

Variety: Die chips — **CONECA: N/L**
PUP: Lip and jaw
URS-TBD · I-5 · L-5

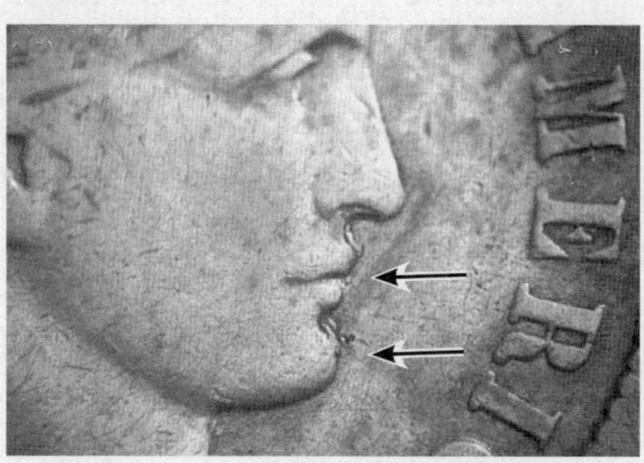

Description: There are prominent die chips at the lips and jaw of Miss Liberty.

Comments: With growing interest in the Barber dime series, this variety is sure to attract attention and perhaps lead to more discoveries. The discovery coin is unique as of publication of this volume, and it's too early to establish reliable market values.

	VG-8	F-12	VF-20	EF-40	AU-50	MS-60
Variety	n/a	n/a	n/a	n/a	n/a	n/a
Normal	$13	$15	$25	$50	$90	$185

Mercury Dimes, 1916–1945

Mercury dimes are one of the most widely collected series of the twentieth century. Collector interest is perennial, thanks to their artistic design. The coins were still in circulation during the collecting boom of the 1950s and 1960s—another factor that has strengthened modern interest.

Unlike Jefferson nickels, Roosevelt dimes, and Lincoln cents, there are relatively few die varieties among Mercury dimes. Several of them, however, are quite dramatic and in very high demand. Serious collectors are interested in the scarce and rare dates, as well as nicely struck coins that exhibit "full split bands" on the reverse.

The most remarkable and well-known varieties are certainly the overdates of 1942 and 1942-D, though other significant varieties exist. The 1945-D, D Over Horizontal D, and the 1945-S, S Over Horizontal S, are highly prized finds. Other varieties include repunched mintmarks, doubled dies, and a very likely S Over D variety from 1945. One significant recent discovery is the 1919 Doubled Die Obverse, featured on the front cover of this volume. How this variety went undiscovered for nearly 100 years is a mystery of numismatics!

As of this publication there are no clubs devoted exclusively to the study of the Mercury dime. However, for collectors interested primarily in the varieties within the series, we suggest membership in CONECA, the national error and variety club. Each issue of their bi-monthly publication, *The ErrorScope,* contains articles on errors and die varieties of all types, and even from other countries. CONECA also offers a lending library, and examination, listing, and attribution services. It holds annual meetings (referred to as Errorama) at major conventions around the country.

Information on a number of individual membership levels, ranging from $7.50 to $37.50, can be found at the CONECA website, https://conecaonline.org, or by writing to

CONECA Membership
PO Box 223
Armada MI 48005-0223
Email: maria@conecaonline.org

Mercury Dimes Removed From the Fifth Edition, Volume II

Date, Variety	Fivaz-Stanton number	PUP	Notes
1937, Doubled-Die Obverse	FS-10-1937-101	IN GOD WE TRUST	Removed for lack of collector interest.
1939, Doubled-Die Obverse	FS-10-1939-101	Date	
1941-S, Doubled-Die Reverse	FS-10-1941S-801	E PLURIBUS UNUM	

1945, Doubled-Die Obverse	FS-10-1945-901	Date	Listed erroneously as FS-901; should have been FS-101
1945-S, Possible Overmintmark	FS-10-1945S-511	Mintmark	Removed for lack of collector interest.

Note: Varieties removed are still considered *Cherrypickers' Guide* varieties (as opposed to being "delisted"); for example, they will continue to be cross-referenced and summarized in appendix H. (Exceptions include varieties debunked as counterfeits, or those which later research revealed to be erroneously classified. Those will be delisted completely.)

New Mercury Dimes in the Sixth Edition, Volume II

Date, Variety	Fivaz-Stanton number	PUP
1919, Doubled-Die Obverse	FS-10-1919-101	IN GOD WE TRUST
1926, Doubled-Die Obverse	FS-10-1926-101	R in LIBERTY
1935, Doubled-Die Obverse	FS-10-1935-101	Date
1936-D, Repunched Mintmark	FS-10-1936D-501	Mintmark
1942-S, Repunched Mintmark	FS-10-1942S-502	Mintmark
1943-D, Repunched Mintmark	FS-10-1943D-501	Mintmark
1945-D, Repunched Mintmark	FS-10-1945D-503	Mintmark
1945-S, Inverted S	FS-10-1945S-504	Mintmark

1919 — FS-10-1919-101

Variety: Doubled-Die Obverse — **CONECA: DDO-001**
PUP: IN GOD WE TRUST
URS-5 · I-5 · L-5

Description: There is strong doubling on the motto IN GOD WE TRUST, visible even in lower grades.

Comments: This variety is a recent discovery, with very few examples. At a "Money Talks" presentation at the February 2020 American Numismatic Association National Money Show in Atlanta, Bill Fivaz used this as a case study in how visually dramatic die varieties can remain undiscovered for generations—just waiting to be found by a keen-eyed cherrypicker! The value below is based on one actual sale; check recent market activity.

	VG-8	F-12	VF-20	EF-40	AU-50	MS-63
Variety	$2,500	n/a	n/a	n/a	n/a	n/a
Normal	$4	$5	$7	$12	$35	$165

1926 FS-10-1926-101

VARIETY: Doubled-Die Obverse **CONECA: DDO-001**
PUP: R in LIBERTY
URS-5 · I-5 · L-5

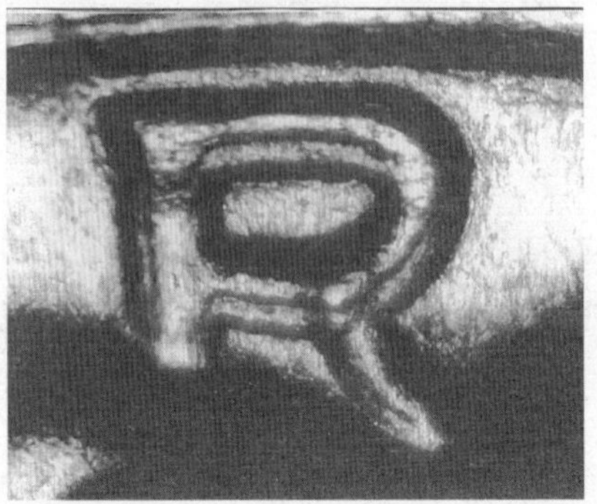

Description: There is strong doubling on the R of LIBERTY.

Comments: This is a fairly recent (2018) discovery and a very rare variety. Its interest and liquidity are high. Market values, as of yet unstable, will be reported in the next edition of the *Cherrypickers' Guide.*

	VG-8	F-12	VF-20	EF-40	AU-50	MS-63
VARIETY	n/a	n/a	n/a	n/a	n/a	n/a
NORMAL	$4	$5	$6	$8	$16	$70

1928-S FS-10-1928S-501

VARIETY: Large S Mintmark **CONECA: MMS-003**
PUP: Mintmark
URS-8 · I-4 · L-4

Large S (scarce).

Small S (common).

Description: This variety exhibits a large-sized S mintmark almost twice the size of its Small S sister.

Comments: This is a very scarce variety in all grades, with rarity escalating as grade increases. Finding an example in Mint State would make your day—or, for that matter, your year! Very few Uncirculated pieces are known. Full Band coins will command a premium.

	VF-20	EF-40	AU-50	MS-60	MS-63
VARIETY	$125	$250	$425	$575	$750
NORMAL	$7	$20	$45	$155	$325

1929-S — FS-10-1929S-101

Variety: Doubled-Die Obverse **CONECA: DDO-001**
PUP: Date. IN GOD WE TRUST
URS-7 · I-3 · L-3

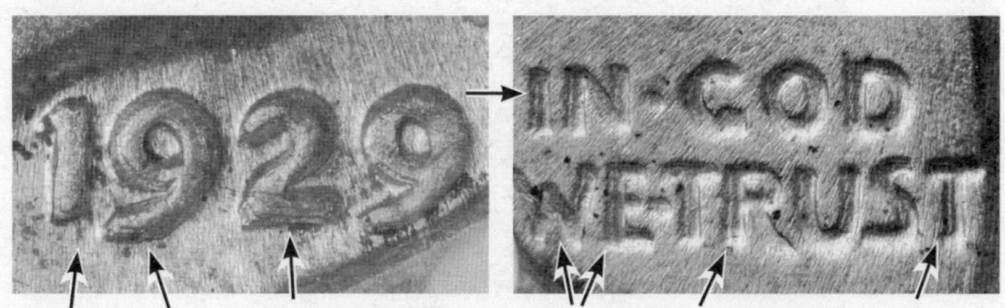

Description: This variety shows nice doubling on the date, and very nice doubling on IN GOD WE TRUST.

Comments: With the recent discoveries of the 1919 and 1926 doubled dies, interest in doubled dies (including this one) in the Mercury dime series has dramatically increased! This appears to be a very scarce or rare variety, as very few examples have come to light. Note that Full Band coins will command higher prices.

	VF-20	EF-40	AU-50	MS-60	MS-63
Variety	$30	$45	$65	$95	$165
Normal	$6	$10	$22	$35	$50

1931-D — FS-10-1931D-101

Variety: Doubled-Die Obverse **CONECA: DDO-001**
PUP: Date
URS-8 · I-3 · L-3

Description: Light doubling is evident on the date

Comments: (When this variety was first listed in the *Cherrypickers' Guide,* in the fourth edition, its correct FS attribution was omitted.) Note that Full Band coins will command a premium.

	VF-20	EF-40	AU-50	MS-60	MS-63
Variety	$40	$60	$90	$140	$190
Normal	$25	$45	$65	$105	$145

1931-S FS-10-1931S-101

VARIETY: Tripled-Die Obverse **CONECA: DDO-001**
PUP: Date, IN GOD WE TRUST
URS-7 · I-3 · L-3

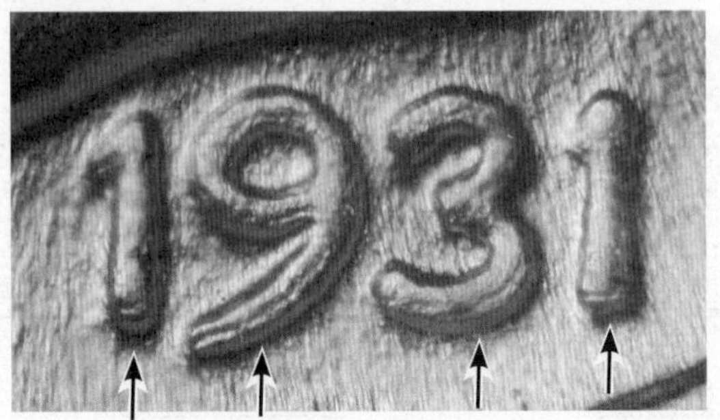

Description: There is moderate tripling on the date and on IN GOD WE TRUST.

Comments: With the growing collector interest in doubled dies, this date's popularity has dramatically increased. Note how many new varieties have been added to this volume of the *Cherrypickers' Guide*; with the attention they bring, more will surely be discovered in the future! Full Band coins will command premiums above those listed below.

	VF-20	EF-40	AU-50	MS-60	MS-63
VARIETY	$28	$45	$75	$130	$175
NORMAL	$12	$25	$50	$120	$155

1934-D FS-10-1934D-501

VARIETY: Repunched Mintmark **CONECA: RPM-001**
PUP: Mintmark
URS-7 · I-5 · L-4

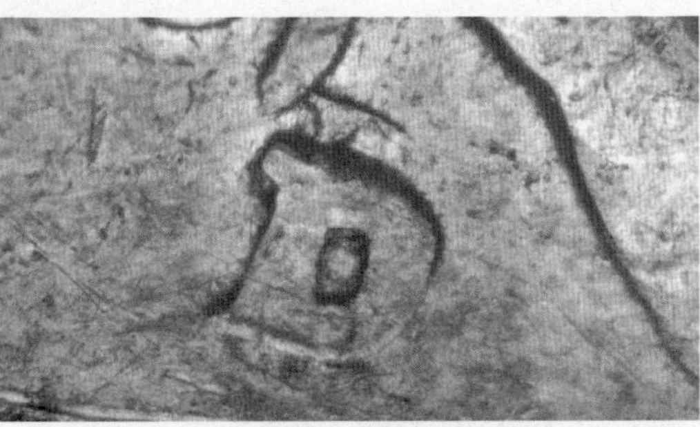

Description: A secondary D mintmark is visible north of the primary D, touching the olive leaf.

Comments: Many hobbyists feel this is a Large D Over Small D overmintmark, but that is unproven. Whatever its true nature, the coin is quite rare. Larry Briggs states he has seen only three pieces over the past 25 years (two VG and one VF). This is a great variety and in high demand! Full Band coins will command a premium . . . if any exist!

	VG-8	F-12	VF-20	EF-40	AU-50	MS-60	MS-63
VARIETY	$30	$40	$50	$95	$165	$245	$375
NORMAL	$2	$3	$4	$9	$35	$65	$75

1935 — FS-10-1935-101

Variety: Doubled-Die Obverse **CONECA: DDO-002**
PUP: Date
URS-6 · I-3 · L-3

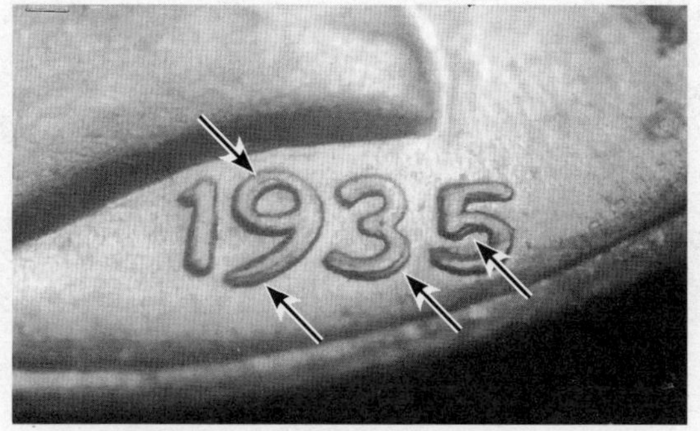

Description: The doubling is nice and clear on the entire date.

Comments: This is a very nice recently discovered DDO. With interest increasing in the Mercury dime series, this is sure to be added to variety collectors' want lists. Values will stabilize and will be reported in future editions.

	EF-40	AU-50	MS-60	MS-63	MS-65	MS-66
Variety	n/a	n/a	n/a	n/a	n/a	n/a
Normal	$4	$8	$11	$17	$37	$65

1935-S — FS-10-1935S-501

Variety: Repunched Mintmark **CONECA: RPM-001**
PUP: Mintmark
URS-9 · I-3 · L-3

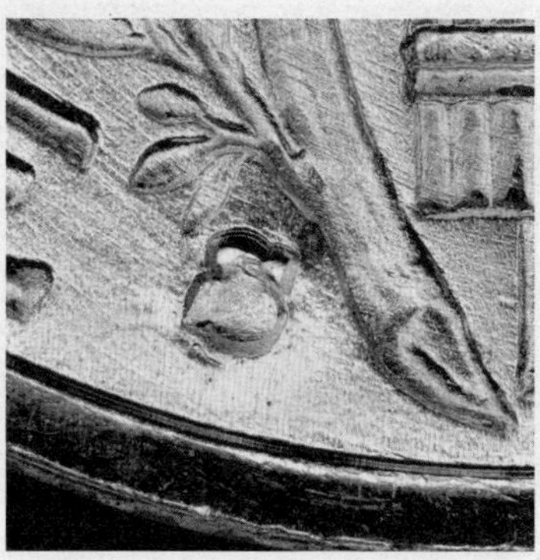

Description: A secondary S mintmark is evident south of the primary S.

Comments: This is a scarce RPM. On the coin examined by the editors, strike doubling was also evident on the north side of the primary mintmark. Full Band coins will command premium prices.

	VF-20	EF-40	AU-50	MS-60	MS-63
Variety	$10	$20	$30	$45	$75
Normal	$4	$6	$18	$25	$35

1936 FS-10-1936-101

VARIETY: Doubled-Die Obverse **CONECA: DDO-001**
PUP: Date, IN GOD WE TRUST
URS-9 · I-3 · L-3

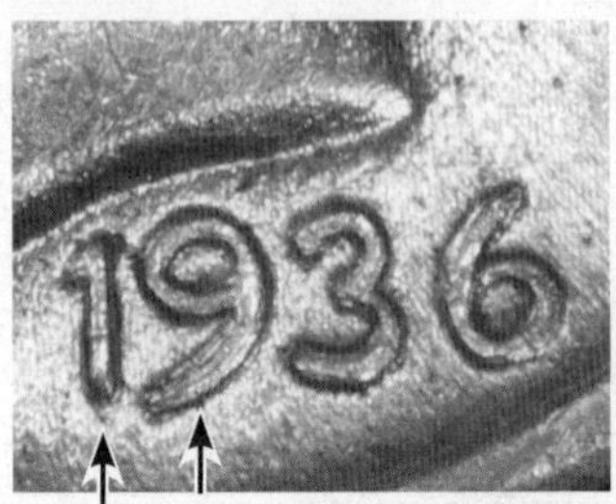

Description: Moderate doubling is seen on the date and on IN GOD WE TRUST. Lesser doubling is evident on LIBERTY.

Comments: As far as doubling goes, this is one of the nicer varieties in the Mercury dime series. Publication of new doubled dies in the series has opened wide the door of collector interest! With increased demand have come higher prices. (Full Band coins will command even higher premiums.) This is a nice variety to cherrypick.

	VF-20	EF-40	AU-50	MS-60	MS-63
VARIETY	$15	$20	$40	$90	$125
NORMAL	$3	$4	$8	$12	$20

1936-D FS-10-1936D-501

VARIETY: Repunched Mintmark **CONECA: RPM-001**
PUP: Mintmark
URS-6 · I-4 · L-3

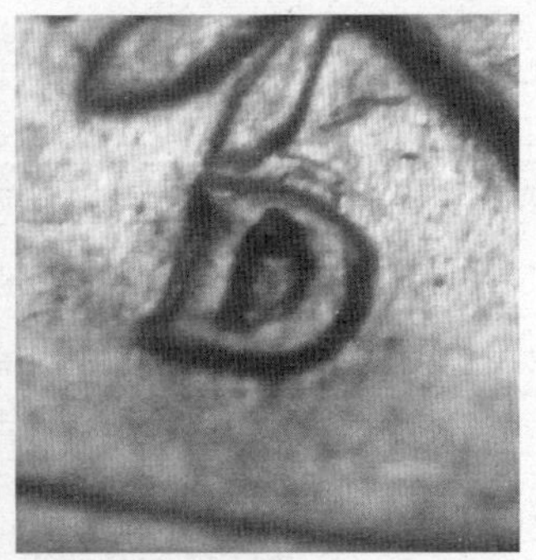

Description: This repunched mintmark is very nice and very clear.

Comments: With the growing popularity of RPMs, this new listing is likely to bring enthusiasm among variety collectors. The regular 1936-D is already a scarce dime, and the presence of the RPM should make this die variety *very* scarce.

	EF-40	AU-50	MS-60	MS-63	MS-65	MS-66
VARIETY	n/a	n/a	n/a	n/a	n/a	n/a
NORMAL	$7	$17	$30	$42	$60	$85

1936-S — FS-10-1936S-110

Variety: Possible Overdate — **CONECA: N/L**
PUP: Date
URS-1 · I-4 · L-5

YN

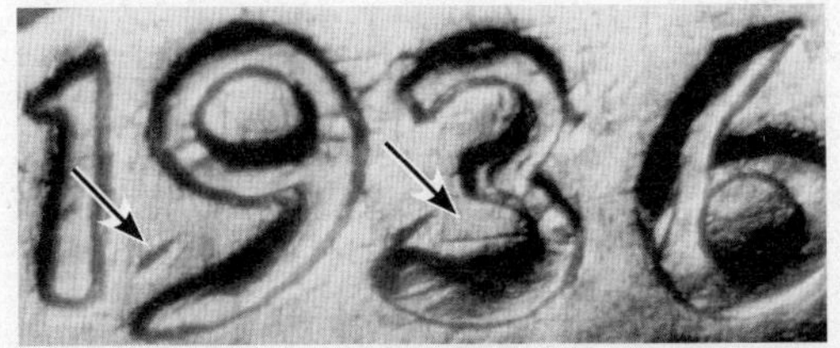

Description: The secondary image of a 2 is evident beneath the 3 of the date. Most evident is the flat portion of the base of the underlying 2. Remains of what may be a secondary 9 are evident to the left of the primary 9. Many die-polish marks are also evident throughout the surface of the obverse. No doubling is evident on other elements.

Comments: Overlays seem to confirm this to be a 1936-S Over 1929-S! The shapes match the 2 on 1929-dated dimes. Stranger things have happened. Keep in mind that 1936 was during the Great Depression, when Mint personnel wanted to save money whenever possible. Recorded sales between 2013 and 2018: $3,500 (MS-65), $1,500 (MS-64), and $600 (MS-63). Regardless of any disagreements between specialists (some say it's not an overdate), this coin is rare!

	EF-40	AU-50	AU-55	MS-60	MS-63	MS-64	MS-65
Variety	$150	$250	$375	$750	$1,000	$2,500	n/a
Normal	$4	$14	$18	$25	$32	$36	$40

1937-S — FS-10-1937S-101

Variety: Doubled-Die Obverse — **CONECA: DDO-001**
PUP: Date, IN GOD WE TRUST
URS-8 · I-3 · L-3

Description: Doubling is evident on the date and on IN GOD WE TRUST, as well as on designer Adolph Weinman's initials (AW).

Comments: Interest in doubled dies has grown immensely over the past five years, with the advent of discoveries like the major 1919 and 1926 Mercury dimes. Collectors are well advised to look at as many Mercuries as possible!

	EF-40	AU-50	AU-55	MS-60	MS-63	MS-65
Variety	$10	$15	$20	$35	$50	$85
Normal	$4	$13	$16	$21	$32	$42

1939-D — FS-10-1939D-501

VARIETY: Repunched Mintmark **CONECA: RPM-001**
PUP: Mintmark
URS-8 · I-4 · L-3

Description: The secondary D mintmark is evident south of the primary D.

Comments: This is a scarce variety that has grown in popularity along with the entire series. Mercury dime RPMs are highly collectible. Note that Full Band examples will command a premium.

	EF-40	AU-50	AU-55	MS-60	MS-63	MS-65
VARIETY	$8	$12	$20	$30	$45	$75
NORMAL	$4	$7	$8	$9	$14	$35

1940-S — FS-10-1940S-501

VARIETY: Repunched Mintmark **CONECA: RPM-001**
PUP: Mintmark
URS-9 · I-3 · L-3

Description: This S Over S Over S Over S mintmark is quadruple-punched, with secondary images evident to the west and with several split serifs.

Comments: This is one of the nicest RPMs for the entire Mercury dime series. It's very scarce and in high demand. Full Band coins will command a premium.

	EF-40	AU-50	AU-55	MS-60	MS-63	MS-65
VARIETY	$20	$35	$50	$70	$95	$125
NORMAL	$4	$7	$8	$9	$17	$35

1940-S — FS-10-1940S-101 / 801

Variety: Doubled-Die Obverse, Doubled-Die Reverse **CONECA: DDO-002, DDR-001; PUP:** Date **Wexler: WDDO-001, WDDR-001**
URS-7 · I-4 · L-3

Description: Obverse doubling shows clearly on the date, designer Adolph Weinman's initials, and IN GOD WE TRUST. Reverse doubling is on the upper portion of the entire reverse.

Comments: (Erroneously listed as FS-10-1940S-901 in the fifth edition.) This is a nice, and very scarce, dual DDO/DDR in the Mercury dime series. All seen have weakness on the lower portion of 40 in the date. Full Band coins will command a premium.

	EF-40	AU-50	AU-55	MS-60	MS-63	MS-65
Variety	$35	$50	$75	$100	$125	$175
Normal	$4	$7	$8	$9	$17	$35

1941 — FS-10-1941-101

Variety: Doubled-Die Obverse **CONECA: DDO-002**
PUP: TRUST
URS-6 · I-4 · L-3

Description: Strong doubling is visible on RUS of TRUST. Other doubling is evident on the nose, the truncation of the bust, and the base of the 1 in the date. Strong die-polish lines show through IN GOD WE TRUST, as well.

Comments: This is a very scarce doubled die that commands a nice premium and is in great demand. Full Band coins bring higher prices.

	EF-40	AU-50	AU-55	MS-60	MS-63	MS-65
Variety	$25	$45	$70	$100	$125	$175
Normal	$4	$6	$7	$8	$14	$32

1941-D — FS-10-1941D-101 / 801

VARIETY: Doubled-Die Obverse, Doubled-Die Reverse **CONECA: DDO-001, DDR-001**
PUP: Date, IN GOD WE TRUST; OF AMERICA
URS-8 · I-4 · L-3

Description: Obverse doubling is most evident on the date and IN GOD WE TRUST. On the reverse, OF AMERICA is most visibly doubled.

Comments: (Erroneously listed as only a DDO, FS-10-1941D-101, in the fifth edition.) This is another decent dual variety, showing doubling on both obverse and reverse. To date, no high-grade example has been reported to examine for an early die state. This coin is scarce and popular, with demand having increased over the past five years. Full Band coins will command a premium.

	EF-40	AU-50	AU-55	MS-60	MS-63	MS-65
VARIETY	$15	$25	$35	$48	$75	$125
NORMAL	$4	$7	$8	$9	$15	$27

1941-S — FS-10-1941S-501

VARIETY: Small S (Repunched Mintmark) **CONECA: RPM-001**
PUP: Mintmark
URS-8 · I-4 · L-3

Description: The secondary S mintmark is evident north of the primary S.

Comments: RPMs in the Mercury dime series have become increasingly popular, and this is one of the nicer ones. Note this is *not* a Large S Over Small S mintmark; rather, it is a Small S repunched mintmark. Full Band coins will command premium prices.

	EF-40	AU-50	AU-55	MS-60	MS-63	MS-65
VARIETY	$20	$35	$45	$65	$100	$165
NORMAL	$4	$6	$7	$8	$14	$32

1941-S — FS-10-1941S-502

Variety: Small S (Repunched Mintmark) **CONECA: RPM-005**
PUP: Mintmark
URS-7 · I-3 · L-2

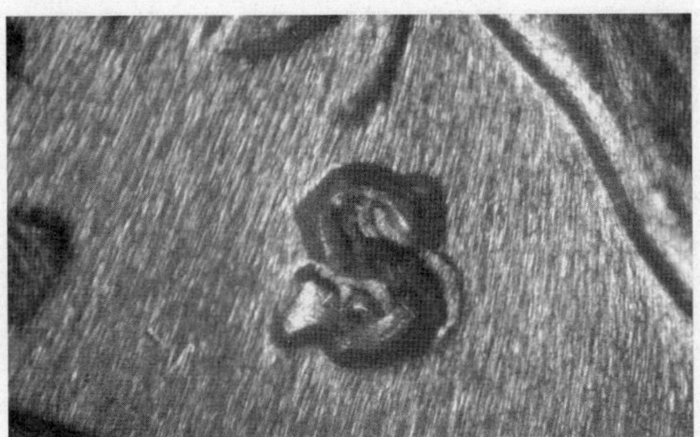

Description: A slightly tilted secondary S mintmark is evident east of the primary S.

Comments: This is a nice, collectible RPM in the Mercury dime series. While it is actually scarcer than its "sister" coin (see preceding), its visual appeal is not as strong, which results in lower popularity. Full Band coins will command higher prices.

	EF-40	AU-50	AU-55	MS-60	MS-63	MS-65
Variety	$10	$15	$20	$30	$45	$70
Normal	$4	$6	$7	$8	$14	$32

1941-S — FS-10-1941S-511

Variety: Large S **CONECA: MMS-004**
PUP: Mintmark
URS-9 · I-5 · L-5

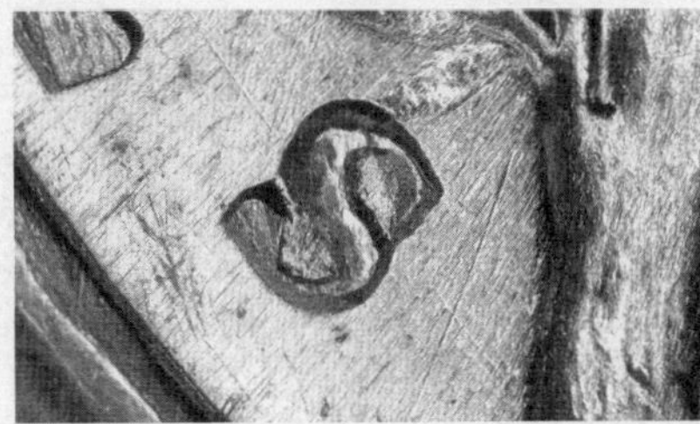

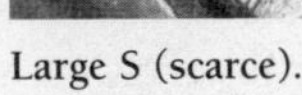

Large S (scarce).

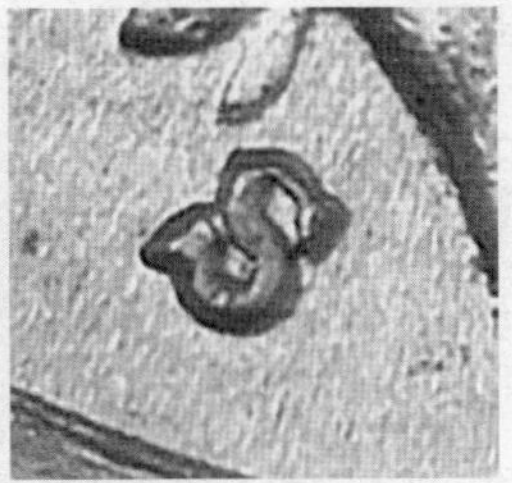

Small S (common).

Description: The Large S mintmark is about 50 percent larger in size than the Small S. Its upper serif points downward, while its lower serif is rounded like the bell of a trumpet.

Comments: The so-called Trumpet Tail S mintmark is rare for this date. While long overlooked by collectors, the variety is well known now, and has been growing in popularity and demand. As grade increases, so does rarity—and value. Full Band coins command a premium.

	EF-40	AU-50	AU-55	MS-60	MS-63	MS-65
Variety	$40	$75	$100	$150	$250	$475
Normal	$4	$6	$7	$8	$14	$32

1942, 42 Over 41 — FS-10-1942-101/502

VARIETY: Doubled-Die Obverse, Overdate — **CONECA: DDO-001**
PUP: Date, IN GOD WE TRUST
URS-12 · I-5 · L-5

Description: Very clear doubling is evident on the 42 Over 41 overdate, with light doubling on the motto, as well. The 4 is doubled to the East.

Comments: This variety is easily spotted by the double-tailed 4 and the clear 2 Over 1. All genuine pieces—no exceptions!—show a diagonal die scratch on the reverse, between the stem and the left vertical sticks. Because this variety sells so frequently and market values fluctuate, check the most recent market listings and auctions to evaluate prices. Full Band coins command a premium.

	EF-40	AU-50	AU-55	MS-60	MS-63	MS-65
VARIETY	*2023 prices for this popular variety range from $500 to $15,000 or considerably more.*					
NORMAL	$4	$5	$6	$7	$14	$32

1942-D, 42 Over 41 — FS-10-1942D-101

VARIETY: Doubled-Die Obverse, Overdate, Repunched Mintmark — **CONECA: 001, RPM-004**
PUP: Date, mintmark, motto
URS-10 · I-5 · L-5

Description: Note the strong 4 Over 4 west, and the weak 2 Over 1. Light doubling is seen on IN GOD WE TRUST, as well as a D mintmark repunched west of the primary D.

Comments: This Denver Mint variety is much rarer than its Philadelphia counterpart! Inexperienced collectors think it should look like the Philly coin and should be as clear, when in fact its 2 Over 1 is weak in comparison. This variety was basically unknown (except to a savvy few specialists) until publicized in 1974. It wasn't shown in price guides until the mid-1970s. Since pricing fluctuates, check current market values and auctions. Full Band coins command a premium.

	EF-40	AU-50	AU-55	MS-60	MS-63	MS-65
VARIETY	*2023 prices for this popular variety range from $450 to $10,000 or considerably more.*					
NORMAL	$4	$5	$6	$7	$14	$30

1942-D

FS-10-1942D-501

VARIETY: Repunched Mintmark **CONECA: RPM-005**
PUP: Mintmark
URS-9 · I-4 · L-3

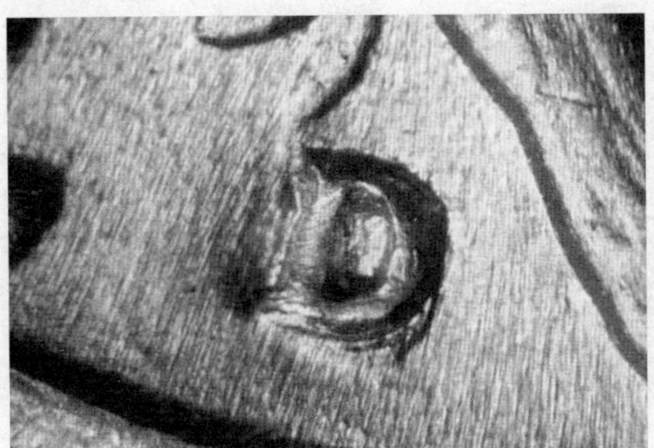

Description: The repunched D mintmark is evident south of the primary D.

Comments: The strength of this RPM makes the variety much in demand. This is easily one of the nicest RPMs in the Mercury dime series. Full Band coins command premium prices.

	EF-40	AU-50	AU-55	MS-60	MS-63	MS-65
VARIETY	$10	$15	$20	$30	$45	$75
NORMAL	$4	$5	$6	$7	$14	$30

1942-S

FS-10-1942S-501

VARIETY: Inverted Mintmark **WEXLER: WIMM-001; POTTER: VCR-001, IMM-001**
PUP: Mintmark
URS-8 · I-4 · L-3

Inverted S.

Description: The S mintmark of this variety is inverted.

Comments: Only a handful of these have been reported, in spite of much publicity. At first glance the mintmark appears symmetrical. However, it has a more oval center within the upper loop of the S—a diagnostic normally found at the lower loop—and the serifs are angled slightly different from each other. On high-grade, early-die-state coins, these characteristics make it possible to conclusively identify this as an Inverted S. The variety is not recognized by CONECA. Presently, no reliable sales information is available.

	EF-40	AU-50	AU-55	MS-60	MS-63	MS-65
VARIETY	n/a	n/a	n/a	n/a	n/a	n/a
NORMAL	$4	$7	$8	$9	$22	$32

1942-S — FS-10-1942S-502

VARIETY: Repunched Mintmark **CONECA: RPM-003**
PUP: Mintmark
URS-6 · I-3 · L-3

Description: The secondary mintmark is visible to the southeast of the primary S.

Comments: This is a nice strong RPM. All but a few remnants of the first S were removed, leaving the large spur. This will be a popular variety due to its easy visibility. Market values will stabilize with time and will be reported in future editions of the *Cherrypickers' Guide*.

	EF-40	AU-50	AU-55	MS-60	MS-63	MS-65
VARIETY	n/a	n/a	n/a	n/a	n/a	n/a
NORMAL	$4	$7	$8	$9	$22	$32

1943-D — FS-10-1943D-501

VARIETY: D Over Inverted D **CONECA: RPM-005**
PUP: Mintmark
URS-5 · I-4 · L-3

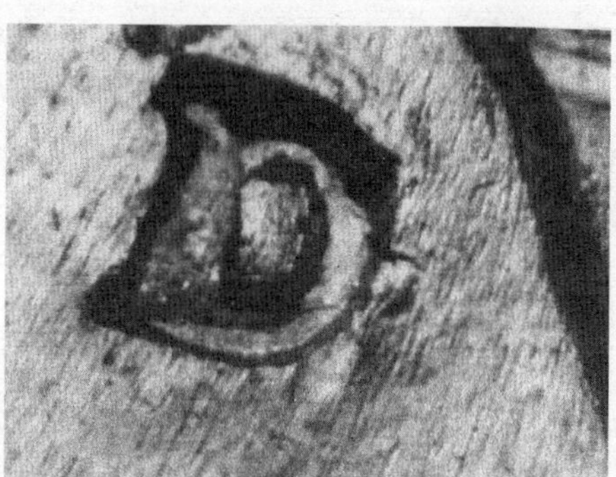

Description: The D mintmark was punched over an inverted initial D. The vertical stem of the original D is seen to the right of the second punch.

Comments: This is a neat new variety worth looking for. Market values will take some time to stabilize enough for reliable reporting.

	EF-40	AU-50	MS-60	MS-63	MS-64	MS-65
VARIETY	n/a	n/a	n/a	n/a	n/a	n/a
NORMAL	$4	$5	$6	$7	$17	$30

1943-S FS-10-1943S-501

Variety: Repunched Mintmark **CONECA: RPM-001**
PUP: Mintmark
URS-7 · I-4 · L-4

Description: A strong quadruple-punched S mintmark is visible north, northeast, and southwest of the primary S.

Comments: This is the nicest repunched mintmark among 1943-S Mercury dimes, as well as one of the nicest in the entire series. It is very scarce and popular. Full Band coins command a premium.

	EF-40	AU-50	AU-55	MS-60	MS-63	MS-65
Variety	$10	$15	$20	$30	$50	$95
Normal	$4	$5	$6	$8	$17	$30

1943-S FS-10-1943S-511

Variety: Trumpet Tail Mintmark **CONECA: MMS-004**
PUP: Mintmark
URS-7 · I-4 · L-4

Description: The top serif of the Trumpet Tail S points downward, with the lower serif rounded, much like the bell of a trumpet.

Comments: This variety is considerably rarer than the 1941-S, Large S. It is extremely rare in Mint State. Examples with Full Bands command a significant premium.

	EF-40	AU-50	AU-55	MS-60	MS-63	MS-65
Variety	$40	$50	$65	$100	$175	$325
Normal	$4	$5	$6	$8	$17	$30

1944-D FS-10-1944D-501

Variety: Repunched Mintmark **CONECA: RPM-003**
PUP: Mintmark
URS-8 · I-4 · L-4

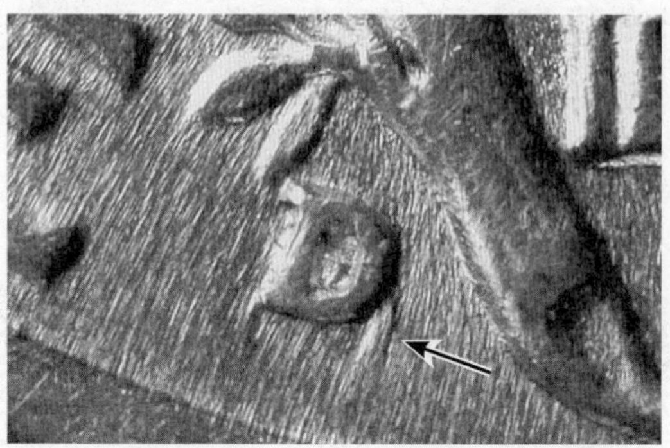

Description: The secondary D mintmark is evident (and major) southeast of the primary D.

Comments: This RPM displays one the most major separations of any in the Mercury dime series. This is a very nice and popular variety. Full Band coins command higher prices.

	EF-40	AU-50	AU-55	MS-60	MS-63	MS-65
Variety	$10	$15	$20	$30	$50	$75
Normal	$4	$5	$6	$8	$17	$30

1945-D FS-10-1945D-101 / 501

Variety: Doubled-Die Obverse, Repunched Mintmark **CONECA: RPM-001, DDO-N/L**
PUP: Mintmark, LIBERTY
URS-8 · I-4 · L-3

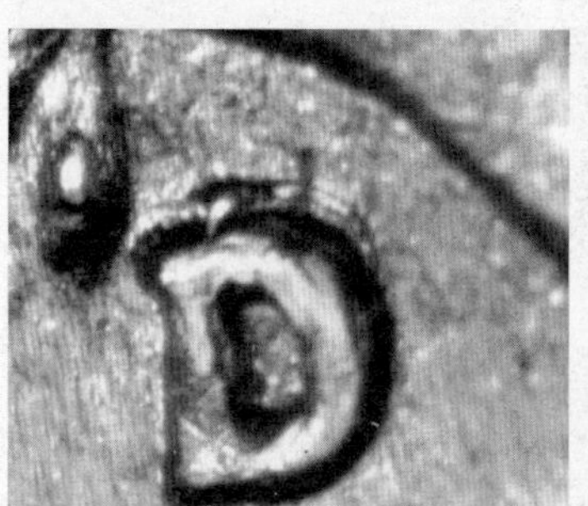

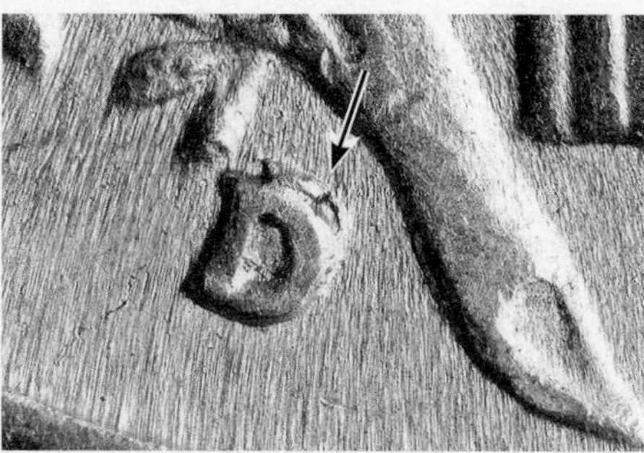

Description: A nice secondary D mintmark is evident northeast of the primary D. Minor doubling is seen on LI of LIBERTY—this is not mentioned by CONECA or the Variety Vista site as of our printing.

Comments: This is a very nice RPM that actually appears to be tripled! The obverse comes with minor doubling on LIBERTY (presently unlisted elsewhere). Full Band coins command a premium.

	EF-40	AU-50	AU-55	MS-60	MS-63	MS-65
Variety	$10	$15	$20	$45	$65	$110
Normal	$4	$5	$6	$7	$14	$26

1945-D — FS-10-1945D-502

Variety: RD Over Horizontal D **CONECA: RPM-006**
PUP: Mintmark
URS-6 · I-5 · L-5

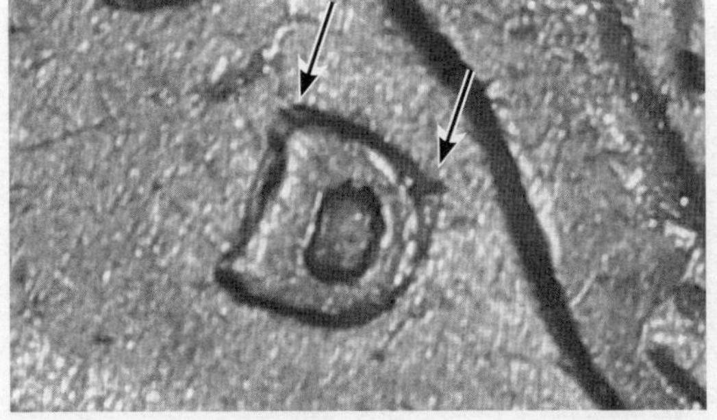

Description: The first D mintmark was punched erroneously into the die horizontally, and then corrected.

Comments: (Erroneously listed as FS-10-1945D-506 in the fifth edition.) This variety was discovered in the late 1990s. Only a few examples have surfaced since then! It is very scarce, popular, and in demand. Full Band coins will command a premium.

	EF-40	AU-50	AU-55	MS-60	MS-63	MS-65
Variety	$250	$350	$450	$575	$725	$1,000
Normal	$4	$5	$6	$7	$14	$26

1945-D — FS-10-1945D-503

Variety: Repunched Mintmark **CONECA: RPM-009**
PUP: Mintmark
URS-5 · I-3 · L-3

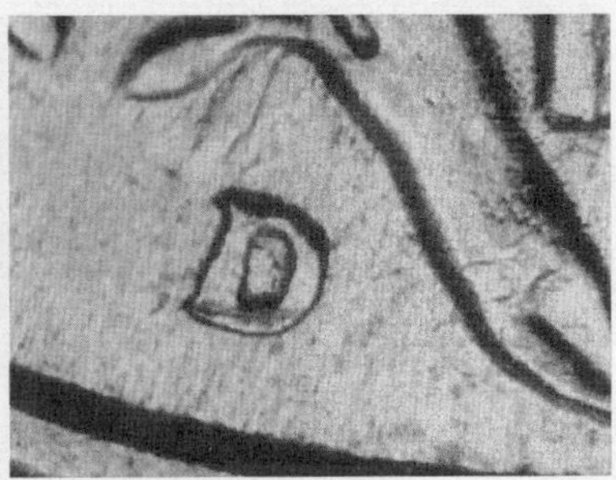

Description: The secondary D mintmark is evident as an arc inside the primary D.

Comments: This variety is a recent discovery, and one collectors should be on the lookout for.

	EF-40	AU-50	MS-60	MS-63	MS-65	MS-66
Variety	$5	$10	$15	$20	$33	$50
Normal	$4	$5	$7	$14	$26	$30

1945-S — FS-10-1945S-503

Variety: Inverted S Over Horizontal S — **CONECA: RPM-003**
PUP: Mintmark
URS-6 · I-5 · L-5

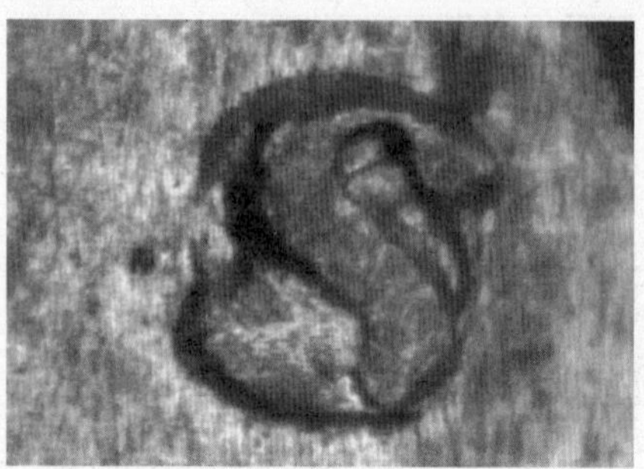

Description: The first S was punched into the die horizontally and then corrected. This has been confirmed by studying overlaid images.

Comments: This variety was discovered prior to the 1945-D, D Over Horizontal D. The 1945-S variety should be considered rare in all grades. Examples with Full Bands command premium prices.

	EF-40	AU-50	AU-55	MS-60	MS-63	MS-65
Variety	$200	$300	$375	$500	$700	$1,000
Normal	$4	$5	$6	$7	$14	$30

1945-S — FS-10-1945S-504

Variety: Inverted Mintmark — **CONECA: IMM-001**
PUP: Mintmark
URS-6 · I-4 · L-4

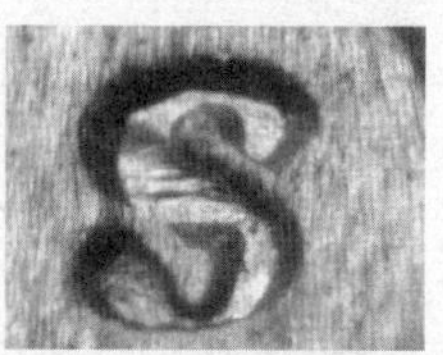

Description: The S mintmark was punched into the die in an inverted position.

Comments: This is an interesting variety, and somewhat difficult to find. It joins many other significant varieties from the World War II era. As market values stabilize, we'll report them in future editions of the *Cherrypickers' Guide*.

	EF-40	AU-50	AU-55	MS-60	MS-63	MS-65
Variety	n/a	n/a	n/a	n/a	n/a	n/a
Normal	$4	$5	$6	$7	$14	$30

1945-S — FS-10-1945S-512

Variety: Micro S — **CONECA: MMS-007**
PUP: Mintmark
URS-11 · I-5 · L-5

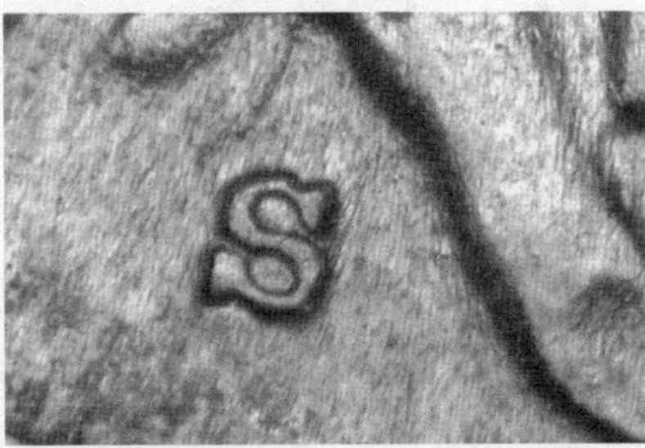

Micro S (scarce).

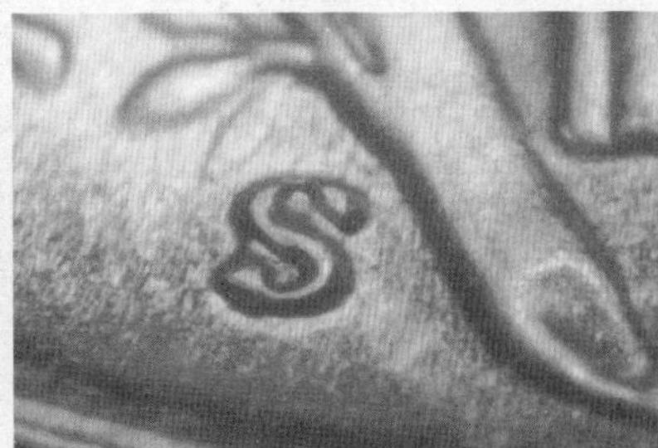

Knob Tail S (common).

Description: In this variety, the S mintmark is significantly smaller than the S of a normal mintmark punch.

Comments: While only scarce, not rare, this variety is very popular amongst Mercury dime specialists. It has the only mintmark size and shape known to have been used in the 1940s. It was probably the same-size S as was used on the Philippine coinage minted in San Francisco in 1944 and 1945. Full Band examples command a hefty premium.

	EF-40	AU-50	AU-55	MS-60	MS-63	MS-65
Variety	$6	$7	$10	$21	$35	$75
Normal	$4	$5	$6	$7	$14	$30

For best cherrypicking results, make sure you read "How to Use This Book," in the front. It will help you interpret the information for each listing.

And remember, the die varieties in this book aren't the only ones in the series. Even more are waiting to be discovered. Always closely examine your coins, even the ones you get in pocket change. You might make an important discovery! (Be sure to let us know when you do.)

Be aware of the "registry set effect" when you study auction results, especially for high-grade rarities. If two collectors both aspire to the #1-rated set, and they both need a rare coin that's come up for bid, and they both have fat wallets, their bidding war might set a record. This momentary competition doesn't necessarily illustrate the rest of the market.

Roosevelt Dimes, 1946 to Date

As of our publication date, there are no numismatic clubs devoted strictly to the study of the Roosevelt dime. However, with growing interest in the series, a Roosevelt dime club can't be far off. The coins are widely collected, both as a series and for die varieties. If you're interested in varieties, this is certainly an area that can yield a pot of gold.

Roosevelt dime varieties include visually attractive doubled dies, repunched mintmarks, overmintmarks, and even missing mintmarks. In fact, the CONECA DieVariety Master Listing shows hundreds each of doubled dies and repunched mintmarks for this series. Some of the most attractive and desirable doubled dies include a 1950-D reverse, several 1960 Proof obverses, and a 1968-S Proof obverse. The overmintmarks include the 1947-S, S Over D, and a possible 1950-D over S. Also included are a really attractive and scarce 1953-D Over Horizontal D; a 1959-D, D Over Inverted D; and a 1962-D, D Over Horizontal D. Most valuable varieties in the series are illustrated in this volume.

Repunched mintmarks are abundant, and RPM collectors are constantly joining the ranks of Roosevelt dime enthusiasts. With numerous examples being discovered, and with the growth of the collector base, RPMs in this and other series are becoming more popular—and valuable!

An important note on Full Bands Roosevelt dimes: Many otherwise common coins in this series are genuinely rare when they have Full Bands (FB). (Note: The descriptor "Full Torch" is used by NGC, and "Full Bands" by PCGS. They are synonymous. In the *Cherrypickers' Guide* we generally use Full Bands.)

There are two pairs of horizontal bands on the reverse—one pair at the top of the torch and the other at the bottom. While in many cases the two bands at the top are full, in most cases the lower two are not. The problem arises at the rightmost side of these bands, near the side of the torch. To qualify as Full Bands, there should be full separation of the bands, with no nicks or other interruptions. A solid incuse line should be evident all the way across from the left to the right, on both pairs of bands.

Please consult the various professional grading services' websites for more detailed descriptions.

Values given in this chapter are for Roosevelt dimes without Full Bands. Value differences can be considerable. For example, a dime without Full Bands worth $40 in MS-67 might be worth $1,600 in MS-67FB.

A Roosevelt dime torch with Full Bands.

This rarity issue is not confined to die varieties, but applies to regular Roosevelt dimes, as well. It illustrates the value in cherrypicking for uncommon strike quality, as well as for uncommon die characteristics.

Note also: For some varieties, very high prices have been observed for ultra-high grades, especially those with Cameo designations (on Proofs) and those certified with Full Bands (PCGS) and Full Torch (NGC). **Extraordinarily high prices are largely due to competitive auction bidding for Registry Set coins.**

For collectors interested primarily in the varieties within the Roosevelt dime series, we strongly recommend membership in CONECA, the national error and variety club. Each issue of their bi-monthly publication, The *ErrorScope*, contains articles on errors and varieties of all U.S. coin types, and even from other countries. CONECA also offers a lending library, and examination, listing, and attribution services. It holds annual meetings (referred to as Errorama) at major conventions around the country.

Information on a number of individual membership levels, ranging from $7.50 to $37.50, can be found at the CONECA website, https://conecaonline.org, or by writing to:

CONECA Membership
PO Box 223
Armada MI 48005-0223
Email: maria@conecaonline.org

Roosevelt Dimes Removed From the Fifth Edition, Volume II

Date, Variety	Fivaz-Stanton number	PUP	Notes
1947-D, Doubled-Die Obverse	FS-10-1947D-102	LIBERTY	Removed for lack of collector interest.
1948, Doubled-Die Reverse	FS-10-1948-801	UNITED STATES OF AMERICA, flame	
1950, Proof, Doubled-Die Reverse	FS-10-1950-801	AMERICA	
1953-S, Repunched Mintmark	FS-10-1953S-501	Mintmark	
1959-D, Repunched Mintmark	FS-10-1959D-503	Mintmark	
1960, Proof, Doubled-Die Obverse	FS-10-1960-104	TRUST	
1960, Proof, Doubled-Die Obverse	FS-10-1960-105	TRUST	
1964-D, Repunched Mintmark	FS-10-1964D-503	Mintmark	
1964-D, Repunched Mintmark	FS-10-1964D-504	Mintmark	
1964-D, Repunched Mintmark	FS-10-1964D-505	Mintmark	
1964-D, Repunched Mintmark	FS-10-1964D-506	Mintmark	
1964-D, Doubled-Die Reverse	FS-10-1964D-803	AMERICA, ONE DIME	This was a misattributed FS-801.
1968-S, Proof, Doubled-Die Reverse	FS-10-1968S-802	UNITED	Removed for lack of collector interest.

Note: Varieties removed are still considered *Cherrypickers' Guide* varieties (as opposed to being "delisted"); for example, they will continue to be cross-referenced and summarized in appendix H. (Exceptions include varieties debunked as counterfeits, or those which later research revealed to be erroneously classified. Those will be delisted completely.)

NEW ROOSEVELT DIMES IN THE SIXTH EDITION, VOLUME II

DATE, VARIETY	FIVAZ-STANTON NUMBER	PUP
1946-S, Repunched Mintmark	FS-10-1946S-505	Mintmark
1949-S, "Bugs Bunny"	FS-10-1949S-401	Lip
1950-D, Repunched Mintmark	FS-10-1950D-502	Mintmark
1953-S, "Bugs Bunny"	FS-10-1953S-401	Lip
1953-S, Acorn Variety	FS-10-1953S-901	Olive on left; M in DIME
1955-S, "Bugs Bunny"	FS-10-1955S-401	Lip
1957, Proof, Doubled-Die Obverse	FS-10-1957-101	Motto, designer's initials, date
1966, "5" on Cheek	FS-10-1966-401	Cheek
1970-S, Proof, No S	FS-10-1970S-501	Mintmark area
1971-D, Repunched Mintmark	FS-10-1971D-501	Mintmark
1975-S, Proof, No S	FS-10-1975S-502	Mintmark area
1983-S, Proof, No S	FS-10-1983S-501	Mintmark area
2015, Doubled-Die Reverse	FS-10-2015-801	Leaf overlapping torch

1946 — FS-10-1946-101 / 803

VARIETY: Doubled-Die Obverse, Doubled-Die Reverse **CONECA: DDO-004, DDR-003**
PUP: Date, LIBERTY, IN GOD WE TRUST, ONE DIME
URS-5 · I-4 · L-3

Description: Strong doubling is evident on all obverse lettering, on the date, and on designer John Sinnock's initials, JS. Doubling on the reverse is seen on OF AMERICA, ONE DIME, UNUM, and the dot to the right of UNUM.

Comments: This is one of the more popular varieties of the 1946 dime. In stage A there is no reverse doubling. The reverse die was changed, and in stage B there is nice doubling as described above. Very few coins have been slabbed for registry sets! Full Band coins bring premiums substantially higher than those listed here.

	EF-40	AU-50	MS-60	MS-63	MS-65	MS-66
VARIETY	$10	$15	$30	$45	$95	$145
NORMAL	$3.25	$4	$5	$6	$12	$25

1946 — FS-10-1946-102 / 804

Variety: Doubled-Die Obverse, Doubled-Die Reverse **CONECA: DDO-004, DDR-004**
PUP: Date, IN GOD WE TRUST, LIBERTY, initials; UNITED, ON, E PLUR
URS-8 · I-4 · L-3

Description: Strong doubling is evident on all obverse lettering, on the date, and on designer John Sinnock's initials (JS). The reverse has minor doubling on UNITED, ON of ONE, and E PLUR.

Comments: This variety is struck from the same obverse die as FS-10-1946-101, but with a different minor doubled-die reverse. It is much more readily available than FS-101.

	EF-40	AU-50	MS-60	MS-63	MS-65	MS-66
Variety	$7	$15	$20	$40	$70	$145
Normal	$3.25	$4	$5	$6	$12	$25

1946 — FS-10-1946-103 / 805

Variety: Doubled-Die Obverse, Doubled-Die Reverse **CONECA: DDO-026, DDR-009**
PUP: Date, IN GOD WE TRUST, UNITED STATES OF AMERICA, E PLURIBUS UNUM, ONE DIME
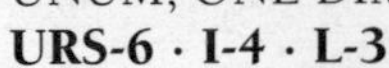
URS-6 · I-4 · L-3

Description: Strong doubling is evident on all obverse lettering, including the initials (JS) of designer John Sinnock, and on the date.

Comments: Several other doubled dies for this date are very similar. Doubling is strong on the obverse and light on the reverse. Very few varieties for this die have emerged since its discovery. Prices have been unstable; Full Bands coins have sold for as little as $122 and as much as $1,000! Values shown here are for coins without Full Bands.

	EF-40	AU-50	MS-60	MS-63	MS-65	MS-66
Variety	$20	$30	$50	$95	$135	$225
Normal	$3.25	$4	$5	$6	$12	$25

1946 FS-10-1946-104

VARIETY: Doubled-Die Obverse **CONECA: DDO-008**
PUP: Date, IN GOD WE TRUST, designer's initials
URS-5 · I-5 · L-4

Description: Strong doubling is evident on IN GOD WE TRUST, the date, and the initials (JS) of designer John Sinnock. A medium counterclockwise spread is evident on LIBERTY.

Comments: Of the many 1946 Roosevelt dime varieties, this one brings the largest premium. It is very scarce, and growing in popularity, as shown by recent sales.

	EF-40	AU-50	MS-60	MS-63	MS-65	MS-66
VARIETY	$45	$75	$115	$175	$375	$525
NORMAL	$3.25	$4	$5	$6	$12	$25

1946 FS-10-1946-801

VARIETY: Doubled-Die Reverse **CONECA: DDR-006**
PUP: UNITED
URS-6 · I-4 · L-3

Description: Strong doubling is evident on UNITED, the olive branches, and the leaves.

Comments: A strong die crack is visible through the T of STATES and the oak leaf. Very few traceable sales have occurred since this very scarce variety's initial listing. Full Bands coins seem to bring large premiums over those without Full Bands.

	EF-40	AU-50	MS-60	MS-63	MS-65	MS-66
VARIETY	$7	$15	$40	$65	$145	$210
NORMAL	$3.25	$4	$5	$6	$12	$25

1946 — FS-10-1946-802

Variety: Doubled-Die Reverse **CONECA: DDR-007**
PUP: Olive stem
URS-2 · I-5 · L-4

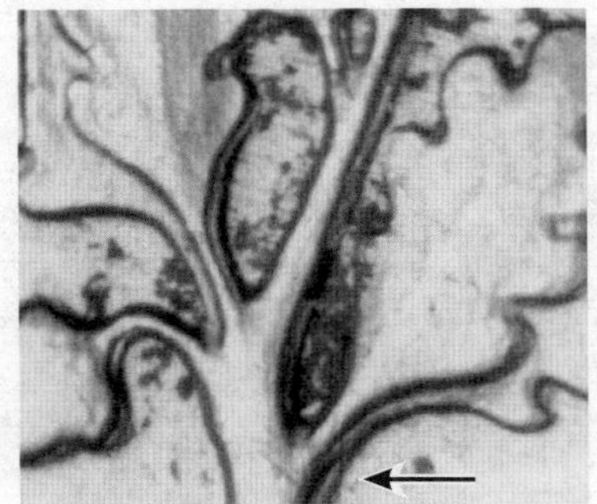

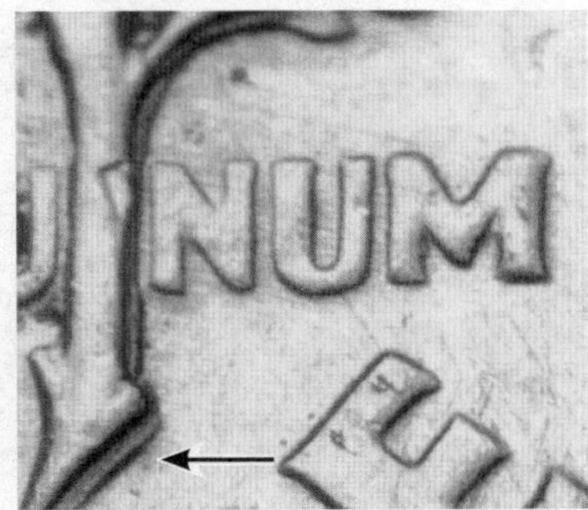

Description: Very strong doubling is visible on the olive stem, branches, and leaves. Very close doubling is evident on UNUM.

Comments: This variety is unusual in that the very strong doubling is evident only in the areas described. Since its discovery, this coin has proven to be quite rare, with very few examples verified and only one certified (PCGS, AU). No sales are recorded.

	EF-40	AU-50	MS-60	MS-63	MS-65	MS-66
Variety	n/a	n/a	n/a	*$250*	n/a	n/a
Normal	$3.25	$4	$5	$6	$12	$25

1946-D — FS-10-1946D-501

Variety: Repunched Mintmark **CONECA: RPM-025**
PUP: Mintmark
URS-7 · I-4 · L-3

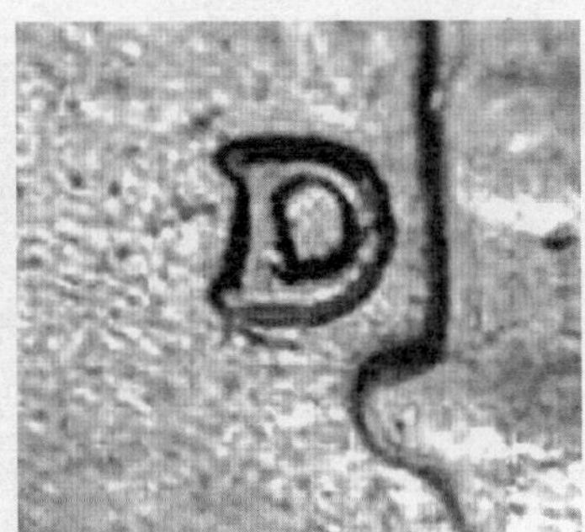

Description: A strong repunched mintmark is evident south of the primary D mintmark. There is a die crack from the flame to the rim.

Comments: Since the first listing of this variety, very few examples have come to light. The coin has so far proven to be rare in all grades. At present only two sales have been verified, both for Full Bands coins.

	EF-40	AU-50	MS-60	MS-63	MS-65	MS-66
Variety	$100	$150	$190	$250	$450	$600
Normal	$3.25	$4	$5	$6	$15	$30

1946-D — FS-10-1946D-502

Variety: Repunched Mintmark — **CONECA: RPM-015**
PUP: Mintmark
URS-7 · I-4 · L-3

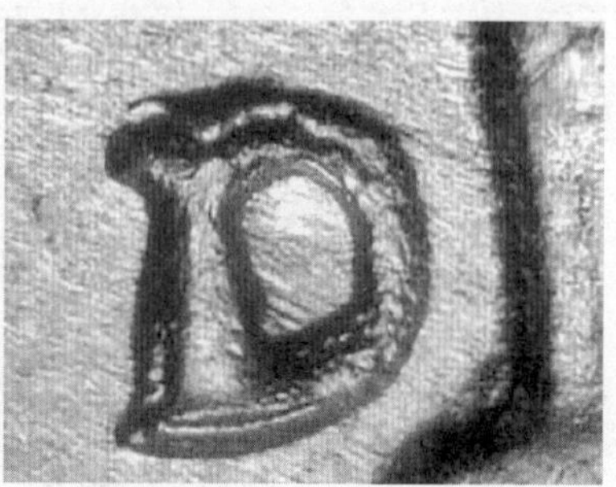

Description: A secondary D mintmark is evident north of the primary D.

Comments: This repunched mintmark was not listed in the RPM book by Tom Miller and John Wexler. The variety is scarce, one of the nicer RPMs for the date, and growing in popularity. More non–Full Bands coins exist than those with Full Bands, by a wide margin.

	EF-40	AU-50	MS-60	MS-63	MS-65	MS-66
Variety	$10	$20	$30	$45	$125	$175
Normal	$3.25	$4	$5	$6	$15	$30

1946-D — FS-10-1946D-503

Variety: Repunched Mintmark — **CONECA: Resembles RPM-011**
PUP: Mintmark
URS-4 · I-4 · L-3

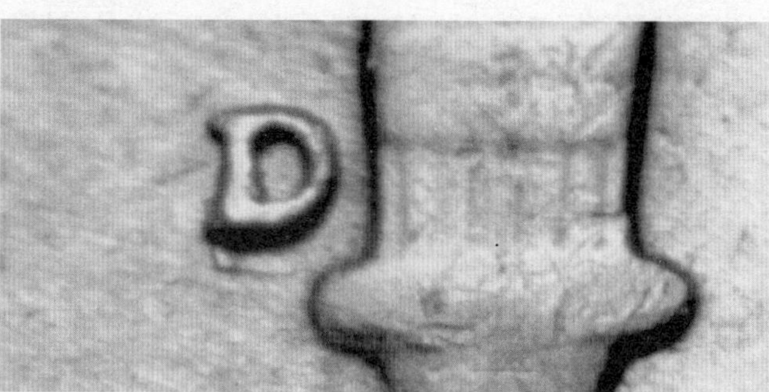

Description: This variety has a very strong repunched mintmark, with the secondary D south of the primary D.

Comments: A review of CONECA's listings leads us to believe RPM-011 is the best match for this repunched mintmark. However, this RPM seems to be very rare; no sales have been confirmed.

	EF-40	AU-50	MS-60	MS-63	MS-65	MS-66
Variety	n/a	n/a	n/a	*$250*	n/a	n/a
Normal	$3.25	$4	$5	$6	$15	$30

1946-S — FS-10-1946S-501 / 801

Variety: Repunched Mintmark / Doubled-Die Reverse **CONECA: DDR-001, RPM-001**
PUP: Mintmark, UNUM
URS-8 · I-4 · L-3

Description: The doubled die is most evident on AMERICA, the right olive branch, the leaves, UNUM, and DIME. The mintmark is quadrupled, with remnants of three secondary S mintmarks north of the primary.

Comments: Most of the value for this variety is for the significant RPM. Although not rare, it is popular because of the quadrupled S (Trumpet Tail style) and a nice doubled die. This variety is available up to grades of MS-68, as well as premium Full Bands coins. Values shown here are for non–Full Bands.

	EF-40	AU-50	MS-60	MS-63	MS-65	MS-66
Variety	$7	$15	$30	$45	$75	$125
Normal	$3.25	$4	$4.50	$5	$20	$35

1946-S — FS-10-1946S-502 / 802

Variety: Repunched Mintmark, Doubled-Die Reverse **CONECA: DDR-002, RPM-002**
PUP: UNITED STATES, mintmark
URS-9 · I-4 · L-3

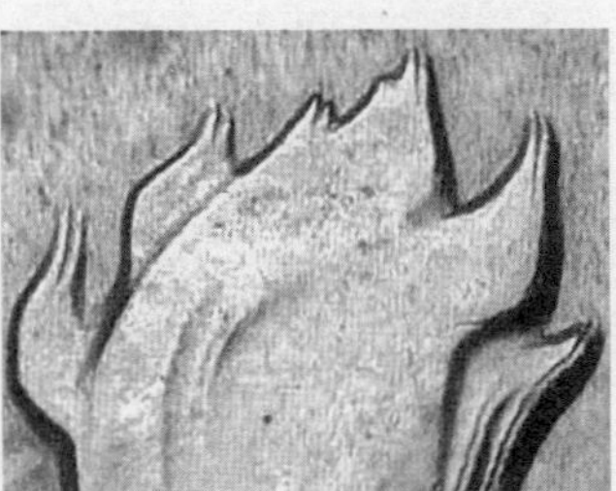

Description: The secondary S mintmark is evident southeast of the primary S. Doubling is most noticeable on UNITED STATES and E PLURIBUS. Nice doubling is visible at the top of the torch and on the left leaves.

Comments: This coin has a nice repunched mintmark (a Trumpet Tail S) and decent doubling. It's not rare, but is very popular because of its dual-variety status. Full Bands coins bring substantially higher prices than the values shown here, which are for coins without those features.

	EF-40	AU-50	MS-60	MS-63	MS-65	MS-66
Variety	$7	$15	$30	$40	$70	$100
Normal	$3.25	$4	$4.50	$5	$20	$35

1946-S — FS-10-1946S-503

VARIETY: Repunched Mintmark — **CONECA: RPM-013**
PUP: Mintmark
URS-6 · I-4 · L-3

Description: This is a very strong repunched mintmark—actually triple-punched, with both secondary S mintmarks visible north of the primary S.

Comments: This variety has, surprisingly, stayed very scarce since its original listing in the *Cherrypickers' Guide*. It is scarcer *without* Full Bands than *with*. Note the Trumpet Tail style of the S mintmark.

	EF-40	AU-50	MS-60	MS-63	MS-65	MS-66
VARIETY	$10	$15	$35	$75	$150	$300
NORMAL	$3.25	$4	$4.50	$5	$20	$35

1946-S — FS-10-1946S-504

VARIETY: Sans-Serif Mintmark — **CONECA: MMS-003**
PUP: Mintmark
URS-6 · I-5 · L-4

Description: The mintmark on this one die is of the sans-serif type (lacking the slight projections finishing the strokes of the S).

Comments: This variety is rare in any grade—including circulated! In 2007 the only Mint State coin known at the time sold for $750. Since, an EF has sold for $258, an AU-58 for $450, and an MS-66FB for more than $1,250 (in November 2019). Cherrypicking this coin will make your day!

	EF-40	AU-50	MS-60	MS-63	MS-65	MS-66
VARIETY	$250	$400	$550	$750	$1,250	$1,500
NORMAL	$3.25	$4	$4.50	$5	$20	$35

1946-S

FS-10-1946S-505

Variety: Repunched Mintmark
CONECA: RPM-005
PUP: Mintmark
URS-9 · I-5 · L-4

Description: This variety exhibits a strongly repunched S mintmark to the west.

Comments: This is one of the nicer repunched mintmarks for this date. The secondary S shows to the south and west and inside both loops of the primary S.

	AU-50	MS-60	MS-63	MS-65	MS-66
Variety	$5	$10	$15	$35	$75
Normal	$4	$4.50	$5	$20	$35

1947

FS-10-1947-101

Variety: Doubled-Die Obverse
CONECA: DDO-002
PUP: IN GOD WE TRUST, date
URS-5 · I-5 · L-4

Description: Very strong doubling is evident on the date, IN GOD WE TRUST, the JS initials of designer John Sinnock, and LIBERTY.

Comments: This is a very strong DDO, especially when compared to others in the series. Since its addition to the *Cherrypickers' Guide*, very few examples have come to light. Fewer than a dozen Mint State coins are known, none with Full Bands. This is a huge sleeper in the Roosevelt dime series!

	EF-40	AU-50	MS-60	MS-63	MS-65	MS-66
Variety	$200	$300	$400	$600	$1,200	$1,500
Normal	$3.25	$4	$5	$6	$13	$25

1947-D — FS-10-1947D-101

Variety: Doubled-Die Obverse — **CONECA: DDO-003**
PUP: Date
URS-3 · I-5 · L-4

Description: Strong doubling is evident on the date and the JS initials of designer John Sinnock. There is extreme thickening of IN GOD WE TRUST that would probably show strong separation lines on earlier die states.

Comments: We'd like to see an early die state of this DDO. The variety has remained quite rare despite publicity from being included in the *Cherrypickers' Guide* since 2012. In Mint State, no examples with Full Bands, and only one or two without, have been verified. This is a cherrypicker's dream coin!

	EF-40	AU-50	MS-60	MS-63	MS-65	MS-66
Variety	n/a	n/a	n/a	*$400*	n/a	n/a
Normal	$3.25	$4	$5	$7	$12	$30

1947-S, So-Called S Over D — FS-10-1947S-501

Variety: So-Called Overmintmark — **CONECA: OMM-001**
PUP: Mintmark
URS-9 · I-5 · L-4

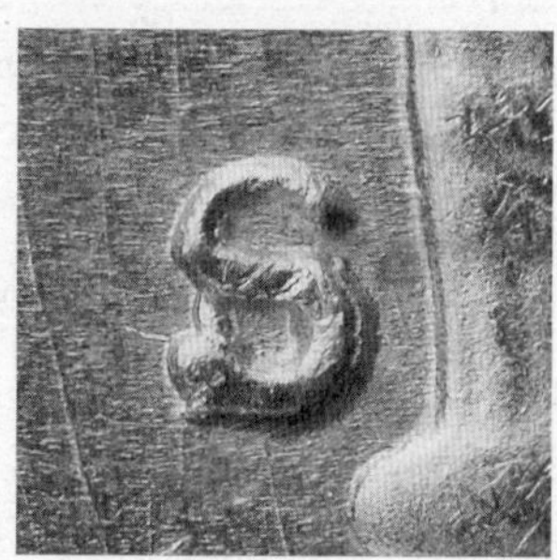

Description: The S mintmark may have been punched over a D mintmark. Remnants of the initial D mintmark are evident only across the opening of the lower loop, and slightly right of the lower loop.

Comments: This variety and the next are very similar. Note that FS-10-1947S-501 has the sans-serif S mintmark, and FS-502 has the Trumpet Tail S. This variety is very rare with Full Bands, but easily acquired without. It is more common than FS-502.

	EF-40	AU-50	MS-60	MS-63	MS-65	MS-66
Variety	$35	$45	$60	$80	$145	$185
Normal	$3.25	$4	$5	$7	$15	$30

1947-S, So-Called S Over D

FS-10-1947S-502

Variety: Overmintmark **CONECA: OMM-002**
PUP: Mintmark
URS-7 · I-5 · L-4

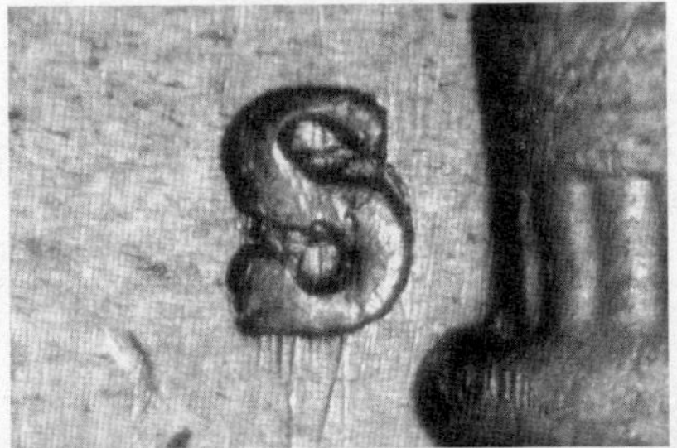

Description: The S mintmark was punched over a D mintmark. Remnants of the initial D mintmark are evident within the upper loop of the S, and across the opening of the lower loop.

Comments: This variety and the preceding are very similar. FS-10-1947S-501 has the sans-serif S mintmark. FS-10-1947S-502 has the Trumpet Tail S, and is much scarcer. Very few Full Bands examples exist. Very few Gem Uncirculated non–Full Bands coins have been reported.

	EF-40	AU-50	MS-60	MS-63	MS-65	MS-66
Variety	$40	$55	$95	$175	$325	$500
Normal	$3.25	$4	$5	$7	$15	$30

1947-S

FS-10-1947S-503

Variety: Repunched Mintmark **CONECA: RPM-002**
PUP: Mintmark
URS-8 · I-4 · L-3

Description: The secondary S mintmark is evident protruding north of the primary S.

Comments: This is one of several nice Roosevelt dime repunched mintmarks for 1946 and 1947. It has turned out to be much scarcer than originally thought. No Full Bands coins have been verified. Be on the lookout!

	EF-40	AU-50	MS-60	MS-63	MS-65	MS-66
Variety	$10	$20	$35	$55	$100	$145
Normal	$3.25	$4	$5	$7	$15	$30

1947-S FS-10-1947S-504

VARIETY: Repunched Mintmark **CONECA: RPM-004**
PUP: Mintmark
URS-6 · I-4 · L-3

Description: The secondary S mintmark is somewhat centered under the primary S, with a rotation clockwise, showing east of the primary upper loop and west of the primary second loop.

Comments: CONECA lists six RPMs for the 1947-S dime. There probably are others. Try to locate them all! This variety is borderline rare, and prices have fluctuated in high grades. Recorded sales include an MS-66FB selling in 2014 for $512, and again in 2016 for $110.

	EF-40	AU-50	MS-60	MS-63	MS-65	MS-66
VARIETY	$15	$20	$35	$50	$95	$125
NORMAL	$3.25	$4	$5	$7	$15	$30

1947-S FS-10-1947S-801

VARIETY: Doubled-Die Reverse **CONECA: DDR-001**
PUP: E PLURIBUS UNUM
URS-7 · I-4 · L-3

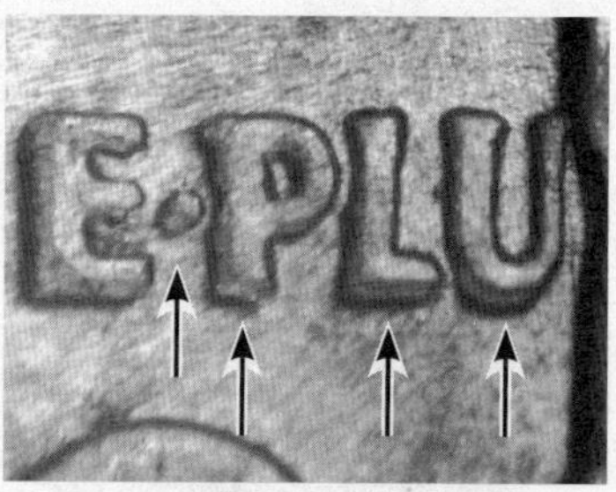

Description: Very strong doubling is evident on all reverse lettering, on E PLURIBUS UNUM, and on almost all leaves and branches.

Comments: On the few specimens we have examined, there is a spike protruding from the top of the R in PLURIBUS. Early-die-state coins should command a higher premium. This is a very scarce coin in all grades, with but one Full Bands example verified. A very nice doubled die that at present is very reasonably priced.

	EF-40	AU-50	MS-60	MS-63	MS-65	MS-66
VARIETY	$10	$20	$35	$50	$95	$155
NORMAL	$3.25	$4	$5	$7	$15	$30

1948-S FS-10-1948S-501

Variety: Repunched Mintmark **CONECA: RPM-001**
PUP: Mintmark
URS-5 · I-4 · L-4

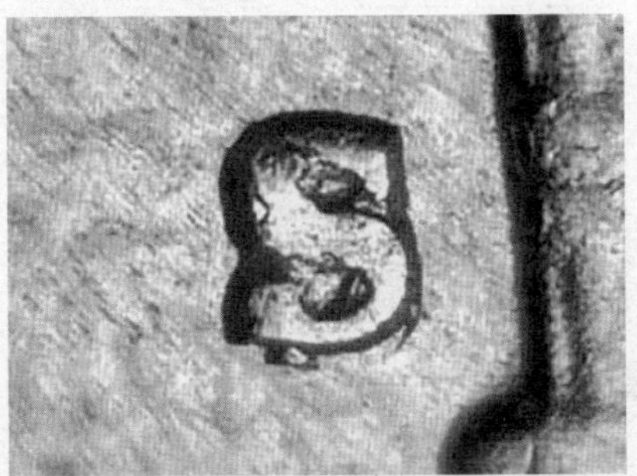

Description: An underlying S mintmark appears southeast of the primary mintmark.

Comments: This is one of the more dramatic repunched mintmarks for the Roosevelt dime series—and apparently a rare variety that's fallen under the radar! Sales have ranged from $46 for a Very Fine to as much as $705 for an MS-66 regular strike. Finding a happy medium is sometimes a challenge.

	EF-40	AU-50	MS-60	MS-63	MS-65	MS-66
Variety	$45	$65	$100	$160	$225	$300
Normal	$3.25	$4	$5	$7	$15	$25

1949-S FS-10-1949S-401

Variety: "Bugs Bunny" **CONECA: N/L**
PUP: Lip
URS-5 · I-3 · L-3

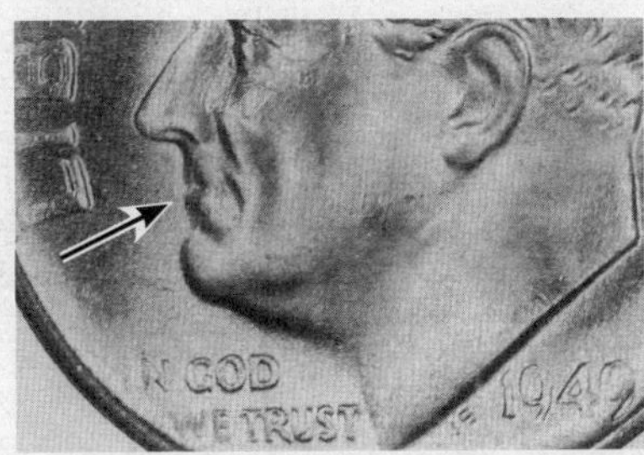

Description: Clash marks on the upper lip of President Franklin Roosevelt create a "Bugs Bunny" variety.

Comments: This is one of several Bugs Bunny varieties in the Roosevelt dime series. As with the similar Bugs Bunny varieties in the Franklin half dollars, they are becoming quite collectible.

	EF-40	AU-50	MS-60	MS-63	MS-65	MS-66
Variety	n/a	n/a	n/a	*$50*	n/a	n/a
Normal	$5	$15	$25	$45	$65	$75

1950-D

FS-10-1950D-501

Variety: Repunched Mintmark or Possible Overmintmark **CONECA: N/L**
PUP: Mintmark
URS-1 · I-5 · L-5

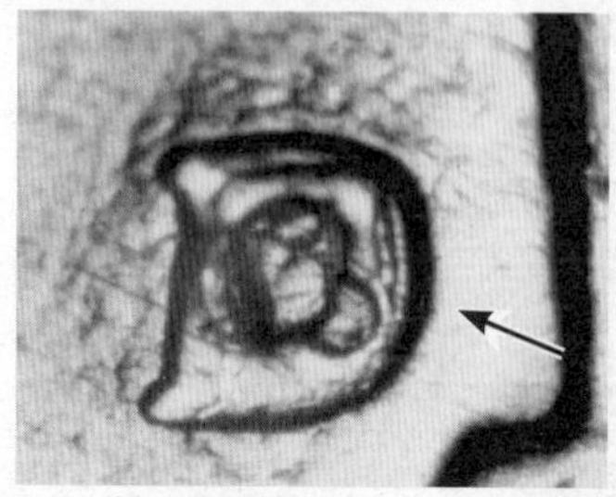

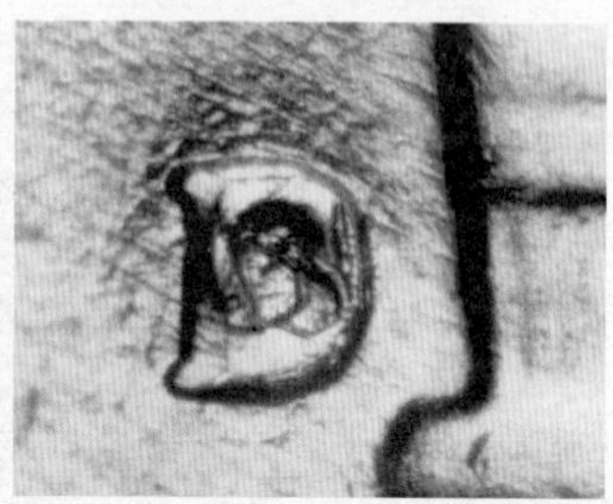

Description: The diagonal stroke of the initially punched S mintmark is visible within the opening of the primary D mintmark. The lower curve of an S is apparent on the lower right curve of the D.

Comments: It's remarkable that this variety escaped notice for so long. One would think the late discovery is a clear indication of rarity. Because there is some question as to whether this might actually be die damage rather than a variety, we would like to see another example to confirm. CONECA declines to recognize this variety. To date, PCGS has certified only one coin—graded MS-65!

	EF-40	AU-50	MS-60	MS-63	MS-65	MS-66
Variety	n/a	n/a	n/a	n/a	$750	n/a
Normal	$3.25	$4	$5	$7	$12	$30

1950-D

FS-10-1950D-502

Variety: Repunched Mintmark **CONECA: RPM-001**
PUP: Mintmark
URS-6 · I-4 · L-3

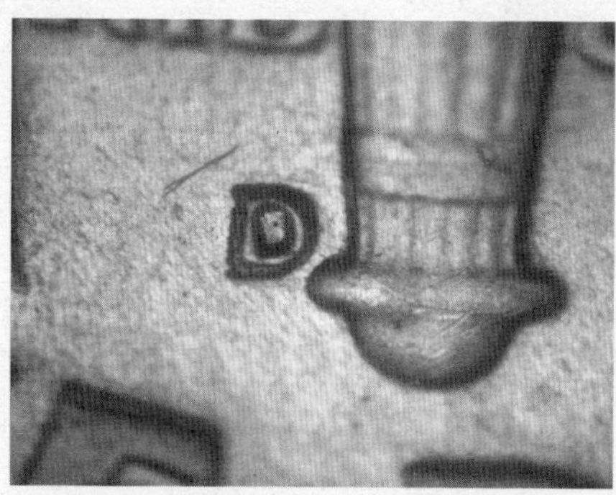

Description: This variety shows good doubling southwest of the primary D mintmark.

Comments: This is a very nice recent discovery, and, with its sharply separated repunching, a great example for RPM collectors to chase after! As of publication, it's very scarce or even rare—but surely more examples will come to light.

	EF-40	AU-50	MS-60	MS-63	MS-65	MS-66
Variety	n/a	n/a	n/a	n/a	n/a	n/a
Normal	$3.25	$4	$5	$7	$12	$30

1950-D — FS-10-1950D-801

Variety: Doubled-Die Reverse **CONECA: DDR-001**
PUP: E PLURIBUS UNUM
URS-7 · I-4 · L-4

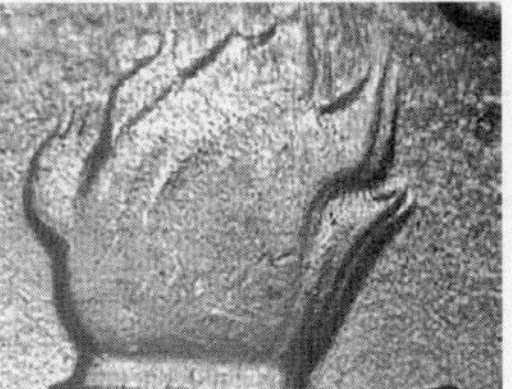

Description: Strong doubling is evident on E PLURIBUS UNUM, the lower portions of the oak and olive branches, and the lower left portion of the torch.

Comments: This variety has been known for a long time, and is readily available at a reasonable cost. It is found in regular strike and with Full Bands.

	EF-40	AU-50	MS-60	MS-63	MS-65	MS-66
Variety	$20	$30	$50	$75	$150	$250
Normal	$3.25	$4	$5	$7	$12	$30

1950-S — FS-10-1950S-501

Variety: S Over Inverted S **CONECA: RPM-005**
PUP: Mintmark
URS-8 · I-5 · L-4

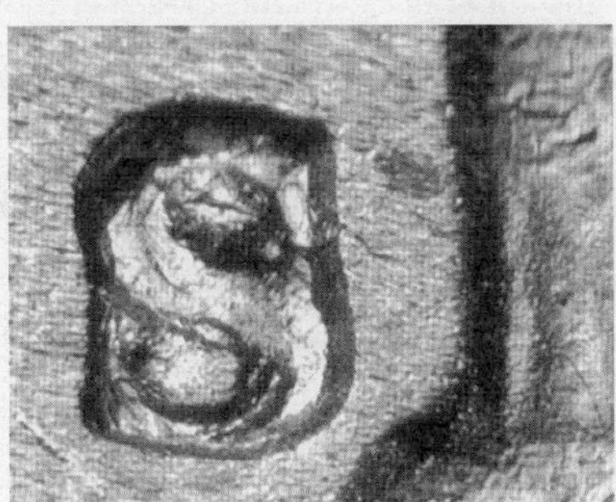

Description: An S mintmark is visible punched squared over a previously punched S.

Comments: In earlier editions, this was listed as an overmintmark (S Over D). CONECA lists it as S Over Inverted S, indicating that the line enclosing the lower loop is that of the long upper serif on an inverted S. We are inclined to agree. Note that no Full Bands coins have been verified.

	EF-40	AU-50	MS-60	MS-63	MS-65	MS-66
Variety	$25	$35	$50	$85	$150	$250
Normal	$5	$15	$25	$38	$55	$75

1951-D FS-10-1951D-501

VARIETY: Repunched Mintmark **CONECA: RPM-001**
PUP: Mintmark
URS-9 · I-3 · L-3

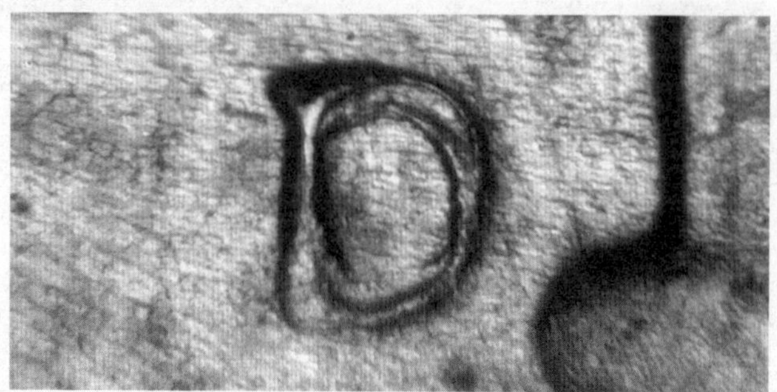

Description: An underlying D mintmark is evident north of the primary mintmark.

Comments: This nice RPM was first listed as a *Cherrypickers' Guide* variety in the fifth edition. It's found in grades MS-64 and finer, including with and without Full Bands. To date none have been graded less than MS-64!

	EF-40	AU-50	MS-60	MS-63	MS-64	MS-65	MS-66
VARIETY	n/a	n/a	n/a	$35	$50	$65	$100
NORMAL	$3.25	$4	$5	$7	$10	$28	$25

1952-S FS-10-1952S-501

VARIETY: Repunched Mintmark **CONECA: RPM-001**
PUP: Mintmark
URS-6 · I-5 · L-4

Description: An underlying S mintmark is visible north of the mintmark.

Comments: This is one of the more visually dramatic RPMs for the Roosevelt dime series. Note that no Full Bands coins have been certified as of yet. This seems to be a scarce variety on an already fairly scarce date.

	EF-40	AU-50	MS-60	MS-63	MS-65	MS-66
VARIETY	$25	$35	$45	$60	$125	$200
NORMAL	$4	$6	$8	$10	$12	$35

A note of caution while you're studying auction results: Always be aware of the "Registry Set Effect." This happens when two strong bidders, competing to build the best registry set, push an auction price into the stratosphere. For some Roosevelt dime die varieties, you might see very high prices for coins in ultra-high grades, especially those with Cameo designations (on Proofs) and those certified with Full Bands (PCGS) or Full Torch (NGC) details.

Keep in mind that an auction is a moment in time, and competition for the same coin variety might be completely different next time around.

This aggressive bidding, driven by registry set competition, is seen in other coin series, too, not just with Roosevelt dimes.

1953-D — FS-10-1953D-501

Variety: Repunched Mintmark — **CONECA: RPM-003**
PUP: Mintmark
URS-6 · I-5 · L-4

Description: The first D mintmark was punched horizontally, with the primary mintmark punched in the correct (vertical) orientation. The variety can easily be identified by the upper serif of the underlying D, which appears as a spike protruding from the upper part of the curve.

Comments: This variety apparently is rare, with few coming to light since its discovery and publication. To date, all slabbed by PCGS and NGC have been Full Bands (Full Torch). Finding one of these in the wild will be great cherrypicking.

	EF-40	AU-50	MS-60	MS-63	MS-65	MS-66
Variety	$50	$75	$150	$250	$300	$400
Normal	$3.25	$4	$5	$7	$10	$20

1953-S FS-10-1953S-401

VARIETY: "Bugs Bunny" **CONECA: N/L**
PUP: Roosevelt's lip
URS-6 · I-3 · L-3

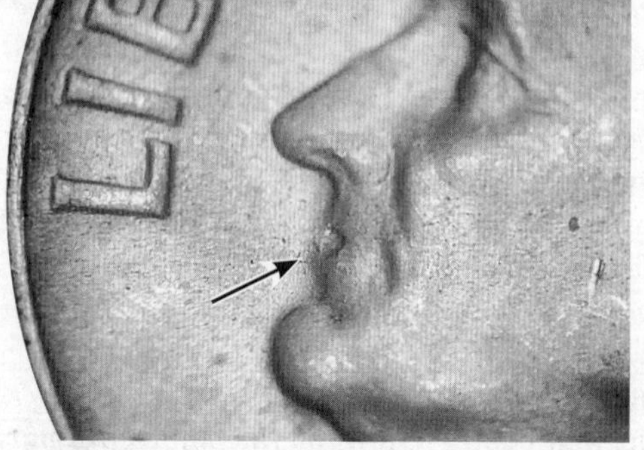

Description: Clash marks on the upper lip of President Franklin Roosevelt create the appearance of rabbit teeth—a "Bugs Bunny" variety.

Comments: The photo above shows a late die state. It illustrates that perseverance and hard work still pay off with new discoveries! Note that a similar 1953-D variety has also been found.

	EF-40	AU-50	MS-60	MS-63	MS-65	MS-66
VARIETY	$5	$7	$10	$15	$25	$40
NORMAL	$4	$5	$6	$7	$11	$25

1953-S FS-10-1953S-501

VARIETY: Repunched Mintmark **CONECA: RPM-002**
PUP: Mintmark
URS-6 · I-4 · L-3

Description: An underlying S appears north of the mintmark.

Comments: This is one of the more dramatic repunched mintmarks for the series. Earlier die states show more of the upper curve. This coin has turned out to be quite rare, with very few pieces surfacing since its discovery! Few regular and no Full Band / Torch coins have been verified. A common date—a rare variety!

	EF-40	AU-50	MS-60	MS-63	MS-65	MS-66
VARIETY	$45	$75	$150	$225	$350	$500
NORMAL	$4	$5	$6	$7	$11	$25

1953-S FS-10-1953S-901

VARIETY: "Acorn" Variety **CONECA: N/L**
PUP: Olive on left; M in DIME
URS-9 · I-3 · L-3

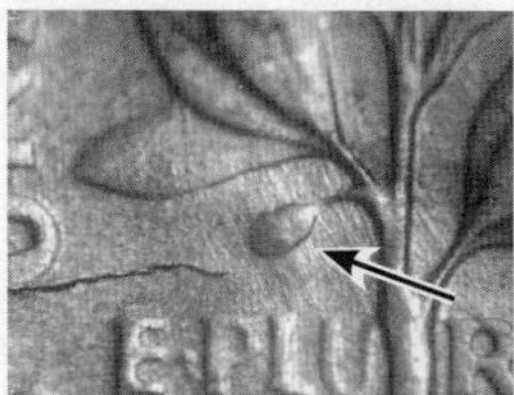

Description: The olive on the left branch resembles an acorn due to severe die polishing and a clashed die. There are several heavy reverse die cracks.

Comments: Heavy die polishing is evident throughout the reverse, especially in the right field, where an oak leaf is nearly gone and the bottoms of some letters in PLURIBUS are missing. Note the heavy die gouges on the M and at the top left of the E of DIME. Heavy die cracks run from the rim through the M of DIME, and from the left rim through the U of UNITED to the "acorn." Earlier die states do not show all of these features and would not qualify as the FS 901.

	VF-20	EF-40	AU-50	MS-60	MS-63	MS-65
VARIETY	$10	$20	$35	$50	$75	$150
NORMAL	$3.50	$4	$5	$6	$7	$11

1954, Proof FS-10-1954-101

VARIETY: Doubled-Die Obverse **CONECA: DDO-001**
PUP: Date
URS-8 · I-4 · L-3

Description: Doubling is evident as extreme extra thickness on all obverse lettering and numerals, especially on the 9 and 4 of the date.

Comments: This is popular as a "naked eye" variety. It can be easily detected by the die chip at the base of the 4. It can be found with regular Proof fields, and in Cameo and Deep Cameo. The values shown here are for regular Proof coins.

	PF-63	PF-64	PF-65	PF-66
VARIETY	$60	$80	$100	$150
NORMAL	$12	$15	$18	$25

1954 FS-10-1954-801

Variety: Doubled-Die Reverse **CONECA: DDR-002**
PUP: Right side of torch base and oak stem
URS-5 · I-5 · L-5

Description: Doubling is slightly evident at the bottom of the torch and on the oak stem, rotated slightly in a counterclockwise direction.

Comments: This is a really neat and exciting variety. A gem example has been provided for better photos for this volume of the *Cherrypickers' Guide*. To date, no Full Bands coins have been certified. Examples submitted for certification have graded from VF-35 to MS-66.

	EF-40	AU-50	MS-60	MS-63	MS-65	MS-66
Variety	$50	$75	$125	$175	$250	$400
Normal	$3.25	$4	$4.50	$5	$10	$20

1954-S FS-10-1954S-501

Variety: Repunched Mintmark **CONECA: RPM-001**
PUP: Mintmark
URS-8 · I-4 · L-3

Description: Secondary S mintmarks are evident northwest of the primary S and very slightly south of the primary S.

Comments: This is one of the nicer RPMs of the Roosevelt dime series. While it is not rare, it's very collectible. To date, no Full Bands coins have been certified.

	VF-20	EF-40	AU-50	MS-60	MS-63	MS-65
Variety	$8	$15	$20	$30	$50	$100
Normal	$3.25	$4	$5	$6	$10	$16

1954-S FS-10-1954S-401

VARIETY: Missing Designer's Initials **CONECA: N/L**
PUP: Below bust, to left of date
URS-7 · I-4 · L-3

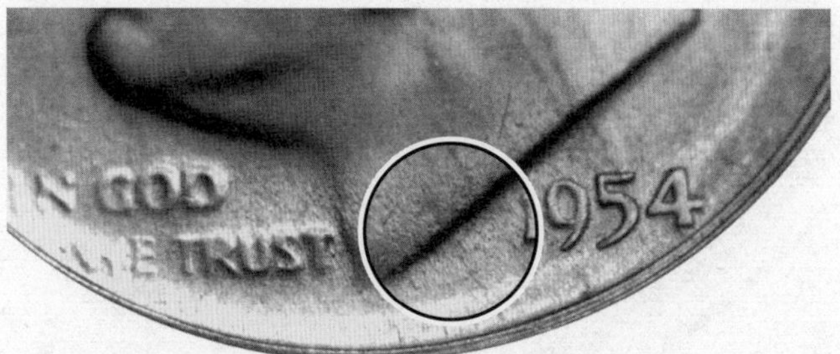

Description: Designer John Sinnock's initials (JS) are missing from their normal location below the bust and to the left of the date.

Comments: (This variety was first published in the fifth edition of the *Cherrypickers' Guide*, where it was accidentally cataloged as FS-1954S-901 instead of FS-401.) For an abraded obverse die, the reverse die is found well struck, with several Full Band coins having been graded. It's a good cherrypicking day if you can find one of these! Happy hunting.

	EF-40	AU-50	MS-60	MS-63	MS-65	MS-66
VARIETY	$20	$35	$50	$75	$145	$200
NORMAL	$3.25	$4	$5	$6	$10	$16

1955-S FS-10-1955S-401

VARIETY: "Bugs Bunny" **CONECA: N/L**
PUP: Lip
URS-6 · I-3 · L-3

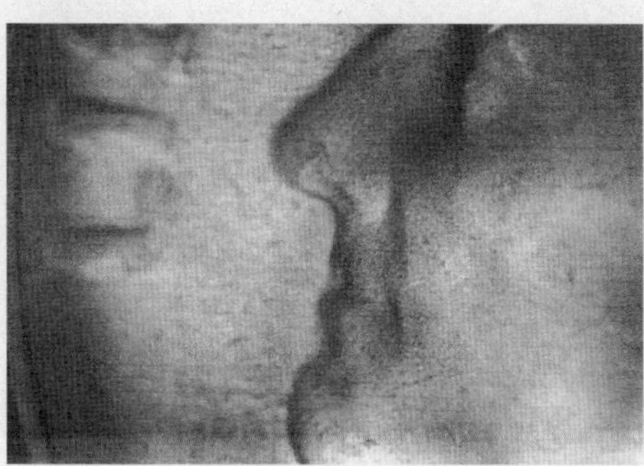

Description: Clash marks at the mouth of President Franklin Roosevelt give the appearance of rabbit teeth—hence, a "Bugs Bunny" variety.

Comments: The clash marks at the mouth are from the leaves on the reverse. Be sure to check other dates in the Roosevelt dime series for similar clash marks. Note the die abrasion on the nose, in the photograph above.

	EF-40	AU-50	MS-60	MS-63	MS-65	MS-66
VARIETY	$5	$7	$10	$15	$25	$40
NORMAL	$3.25	$4	$5	$6	$8	$15

1956, Proof FS-10-1956-101

Variety: Doubled-Die Obverse **CONECA: DDO-002**
PUP: IN GOD WE TRUST, date
URS-7 · I-3 · L-3

Description: Extreme extra thickness, typical of Class VI doubled dies, is evident on IN GOD WE TRUST, LIBERTY, the date, and designer John Sinnock's initials (JS).

Comments: This variety has seen high prices from 2016 to 2021. Coins sold have been graded from PF-64 up to PF-68 Deep Cameo! Values listed here are for Deep Cameo coins.

	PF-63DC	PF-64DC	PF-65DC	PF-66DC	PF-67DC
Variety	$50	$75	$125	$150	$175
Normal	$6	$7	$8	$10	$20

1957, Proof FS-10-1957-101

Variety: Doubled-Die Obverse **CONECA: DDO-001**
PUP: IN GOD WE TRUST, designer's initials, date
URS-7 · I-4 · L-3

Description: Doubling is evident on designer John Sinnock's initials (JS), on the motto IN GOD WE TRUST, and on the date.

Comments: This variety isn't visually spectacular, but doubling is rather scarce on Proof coinage, which contributes to its interest.

	PF-60	PF-63	PF-64	PF-65	PF-66	PF-67
Variety	$10	$15	$17	$25	$32	$45
Normal	$4.00	$4.50	$4.75	$5	$8	$25

1959-D FS-10-1959D-501

Variety: D Over Inverted Mintmark **CONECA: RPM-002**
PUP: Mintmark
URS-9 · I-4 · L-4

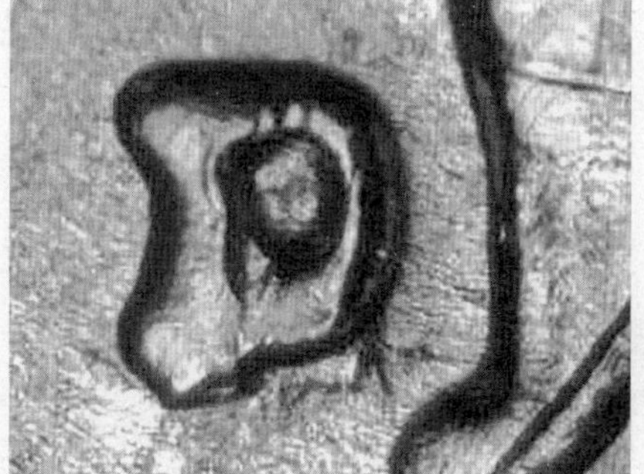

Description: The D mintmark was punched into the die inverted, and then punched with the D correct.

Comments: This is a very nice variety that can be located with little difficulty. (Note: In the fourth edition of the *Cherrypickers' Guide*, it was incorrectly listed as FS-10-1959D-511. That was corrected in the fifth edition.)

	EF-40	AU-50	MS-60	MS-63	MS-65	MS-66
Variety	$7	$15	$25	$40	$65	$100
Normal	$3.25	$3.50	$3.75	$4	$7	$14

1959-D FS-10-1959D-502

Variety: Repunched Mintmark **CONECA: RPM-004**
PUP: Mintmark
URS-4 · I-4 · L-4

Description: A secondary curve to the west is evident within the primary loop of the D mintmark. Portions of the secondary vertical are to the left of the primary.

Comments: The primary D mintmark exhibits strike doubling on the right. This is apparently a very scarce variety. Very few pieces have been certified, with no verified sales.

	EF-40	AU-50	MS-60	MS-63	MS-65	MS-66
Variety	n/a	n/a	n/a	*$75*	n/a	n/a
Normal	$3.25	$3.50	$3.75	$4	$7	$14

1959-D — FS-10-1959D-504

VARIETY: Repunched Mintmark **CONECA: RPM-001**
PUP: Mintmark
URS-6 · I-4 · L-3

Description: A very strong underlying D appears north of the mintmark.

Comments: This is one of the strongest RPMs known for the Roosevelt dime series. It was first listed as a *Cherrypickers' Guide* variety in the fifth edition, and has proven very scarce with very low certified-population reports. It has had a diverse sales history. In July 2013 an MS-66 Full Bands sold at $836. The same exact coin resold in November 2016 for $97!

	EF-40	AU-50	MS-60	MS-63	MS-65	MS-66
VARIETY	$10	$20	$30	$45	$100	$150
NORMAL	$3.25	$3.50	$3.75	$4	$7	$14

1960, Proof — FS-10-1960-101

VARIETY: Doubled-Die Obverse **CONECA: DDO-001**
PUP: TRUST, eye
URS-6 · I-4 · L-3

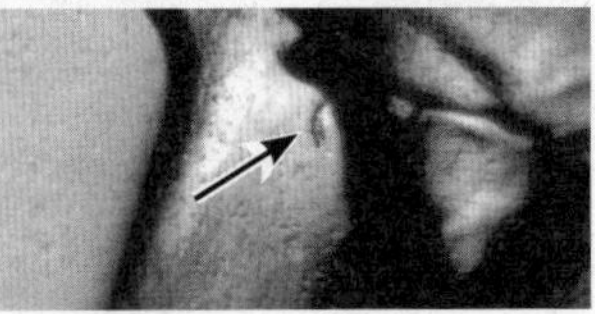

Die gouge at eye is diagnostic on all stages.

Description: Doubling is strongly evident on IN GOD WE TRUST, and moderately so on LIB of LIBERTY, on designer John Sinnock's initials (JS), and on the date.

Comments: This variety was first listed in the *Cherrypickers' Guide* in the fifth edition. It has enjoyed fantastic sales for a seemingly minor DDO! Examples are certified in regular Proof, Cameo, and Deep Cameo—the finest being PF-68+ DC (sold for $1,650 in 2016, and $871 in 2019). This appears to be a real sleeper, and a potentially exciting cherrypicker find. Note it is easily confused with FS-104; see the comparison of doubling on the I of IN at that entry. Early die states show doubling on the date, which is virtually absent on later die states.

	PF-63	PF-64	PF-65	PF-66	PF-67
VARIETY	$100	$150	$175	$250	$350
NORMAL	$4	$4.50	$5	$10	$18

1960, Proof FS-10-1960-102a

Variety: Double-Die Obverse, Early Die State **CONECA: DDO-005**
PUP: Date, IN GOD WE TRUST
URS-9 · I-4 · L-4

Description: Extremely strong doubling is evident on all obverse lettering and on the date.

Comments: Because it has been well known for years, several examples of this variety have come to light. Early-die-state coins are rarer than late-die-state coins (see FS-102b). Availability has made prices wane in recent years, but this variety is still popular and sellable.

	PF-63	PF-64	PF-65	PF-66	PF-67
Variety	$35	$50	$75	$100	$125
Normal	$4	$4.50	$5	$10	$18

1960, Proof FS-10-1960-102b

Variety: Doubled-Die Obverse, Late Die State **CONECA: DDO-005**
PUP: Date, IN GOD WE TRUST
URS-8 · I-4 · L-3

Description: Extremely strong doubling is evident on all obverse lettering and on the date. Late-die-state examples exhibit a very weak date.

Comments: Values shown here are for late-die-state coins (and are usually lower than for early-die-state examples). Note that much of the 19 of the date has been polished away. Intermediate die states exist between the extremes shown here and for FS-102a.

	PF-63	PF-64	PF-65	PF-66	PF-67
Variety	$30	$45	$65	$90	$110
Normal	$4	$4.50	$5	$10	$18

1960, Proof — FS-10-1960-103

Variety: Doubled-Die Obverse — **CONECA: DDO-004**
PUP: Designer's initials, TRUST, date
URS-6 · I-5 · L-4

Description: Medium to strong doubling is evident on IN GOD WE TRUST, on designer John Sinnock's initials (JS), and on the date.

Comments: This variety was first listed as a *Cherrypickers' Guide* variety in the fifth edition. It remains underrated, but high grades have seen huge sales in recent years. In 2019 a PF-69 DC sold for $1,920. In 2021 another (same grade) sold for $2,436. Values shown here are for lesser grades, and for regular Proofs (not Deep Cameo).

	PF-63	PF-64	PF-65	PF-66	PF-67
Variety	$30	$45	$65	$90	$110
Normal	$4	$4.50	$5	$10	$18

1960, Proof — FS-10-1960-801

Variety: Doubled-Die Reverse — **CONECA: DDR-001**
PUP: UNITED
URS-7 · I-4 · L-3

Description: Moderate doubling is evident on all reverse lettering, with the strongest spread on UNITED, ONE, and E PLU.

Comments: Relatively few examples of this die variety have been reported to date. While regular Proofs and cameo Proofs exist of this variety, no deep cameo examples are yet known.

	PF-63	PF-65	PF-66
Variety	$35	$60	$100
Normal	$4	$5	$10

1960-D

FS-10-1960D-501

Variety: Repunched Mintmark
CONECA: RPM-003
PUP: Mintmark
URS-7 · I-4 · L-3

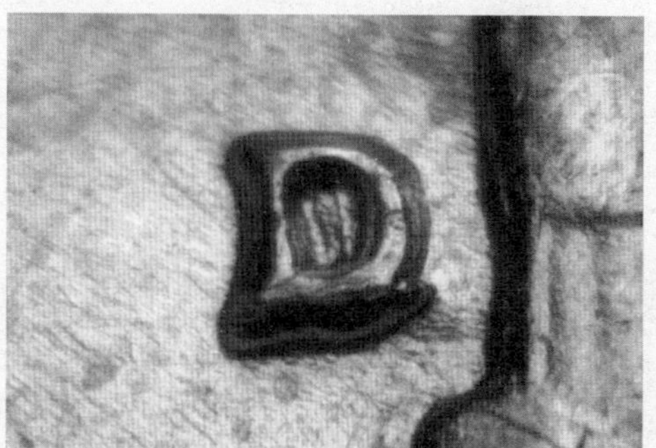

Description: This repunched mintmark is visible as two secondary vertical lines within the opening of the primary D, and a spike to the right of the primary D.

Comments: Over the period of time this die variety has been known, just enough pieces have been discovered to supply demand.

	EF-40	AU-50	AU-55	MS-60	MS-63	MS-65	MS-66
Variety	$20	$30	$40	$45	$100	$275	$375
Normal	$3.25	$3.50	$3.60	$3.75	$4	$6	$15

1961-D

FS-10-1961D-801

Variety: Doubled-Die Reverse
CONECA: DDR-001
PUP: UNITED
URS-6 · I-4 · L-3

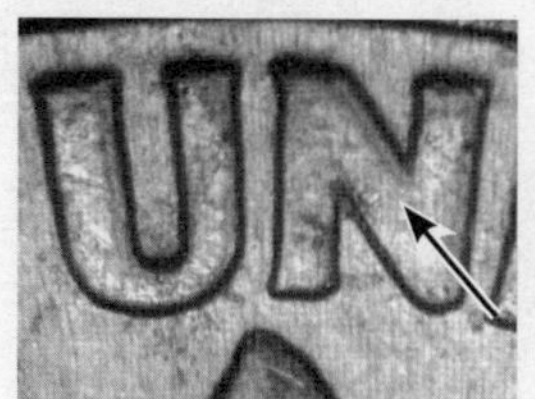

Description: Moderate doubling is visible on UNITED and on ONE DIME, with a lighter spread on STATES OF AMERICA and E PLURIBUS UNUM.

Comments: To date, relatively few examples have been reported of this variety. Since the fifth edition of the *Cherrypickers' Guide* (2012), almost no additional pieces have surfaced. Also, very few sales have been reported. Within the hobby community, little demand has led to low values for those that have been sold. Only one Full Bands coin has been verified so far.

	EF-40	AU-50	AU-55	MS-60	MS-63	MS-65	MS-66
Variety	n/a	n/a	n/a	$35	$60	$125	$250
Normal	$3.25	$3.50	$3.60	$3.75	$4	$6	$12

1962-D FS-10-1962D-501

VARIETY: Repunched Mintmark **CONECA: RPM-005**
PUP: Mintmark
URS-6 · I-4 · L-4

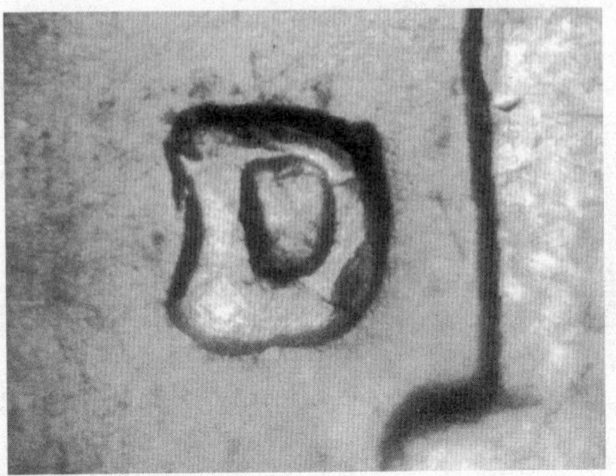

Description: The D mintmark was first punched into the die horizontally, and then corrected.

Comments: Few examples have been reported for this variety, and, strangely, no auction records have been verified for it.

	EF-40	AU-50	AU-55	MS-60	MS-63	MS-65	MS-66
VARIETY	n/a	n/a	n/a	n/a	*$75*	n/a	n/a
NORMAL	$3.25	$3.50	$3.60	$3.75	$4	$6	$12

1963 FS-10-1963-101

VARIETY: Doubled-Die Obverse **CONECA: DDO-101**
PUP: Date **"FORKED TAIL" VARIETY**
URS-7 · I-4 · L-3

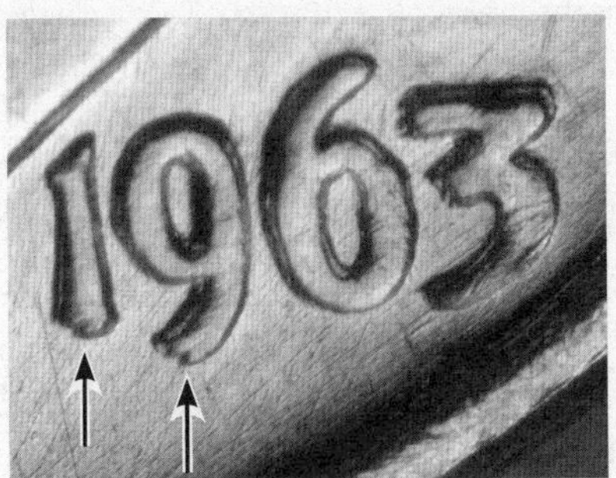

Description: The doubling is evident on the date, LIBERTY, and IN GOD WE TRUST.

Comments: This Roosevelt dime variety (known as the "Forked Tail") can be found in Uncirculated Mint Sets. It appears to be a very scarce variety, although it can be found with persistence and luck.

	EF-40	AU-50	MS-60	MS-63	MS-65	MS-66
VARIETY	n/a	n/a	n/a	$75	$115	$175
NORMAL	$3.25	$3.50	$3.75	$4	$6	$12

1963, Proof — FS-10-1963-801

Variety: Doubled-Die Reverse — **CONECA: DDR-001**
PUP: UNITED, E PLURIBUS UNUM
URS-9 · I-5 · L-4

Description: Doubling is evident with a strong spread on UNITED, and, to a lesser degree, on STATES OF AMERICA, E PLURIBUS UNUM, the leaves, and ONE DIME.

Comments: Collectors are advised to check all early-1960s Proof sets for die varieties. This particular DDR is very popular, and readily found with due diligence. It is found in regular Proof, cameo Proof, and deep cameo Proof, suggesting a fairly large run for this die. Certified population reports substantiate that this variety—though popular—is not rare.

	PF-63	PF-64	PF-65	PF-66	PF-67
Variety	$50	$65	$85	$125	$165
Normal	$4.50	$4.75	$5	$8	$10

1963, Proof — FS-10-1963-802

Variety: Doubled-Die Reverse — **CONECA: DDR-009**
PUP: UNITED, ONE DIME
URS-8 · I-4 · L-3

Description: Very strong doubling is evident on all obverse lettering, but strongest on UNITED and ONE DIME.

Comments: This is likely the most impressive reverse doubled die for the 1963 Roosevelt dime in Proof. It also seems to be the scarcest of all the series' Proof reverse die varieties. Most examples are known in normal Proof state, with very few in cameo and none verified in deep cameo as of early 2023. Values listed here are for regular Proof coins.

	PF-63	PF-64	PF-65	PF-66	PF-67
Variety	$50	$75	$100	$150	$250
Normal	$4.50	$4.75	$5	$8	$10

1963, Proof — FS-10-1963-803

VARIETY: Doubled-Die Reverse — **CONECA: DDR-012**
PUP: UNITED STATES
URS-9 · I-4 · L-3

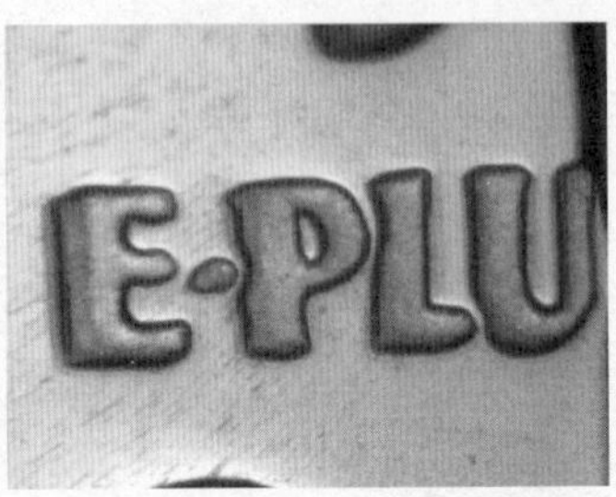

Description: Doubling is evident on UNITED STATES and E PLU, with weaker doubling visible on OF AMERICA, ONE DIME, and other elements.

Comments: There are 21 different doubled dies listed by CONECA for the 1963 Roosevelt dime reverse. Of those, 18 are on Proof coinage. This variety is popular among specialists, with enough supply to meet demand. Cameo coins are rare and deep cameo coins very rare (and, when available, bring substantial premiums over the values listed here, which are for regular Proofs).

	PF-63	PF-64	PF-65	PF-66	PF-67
VARIETY	$40	$65	$90	$110	$160
NORMAL	$4.50	$4.75	$5	$8	$10

1963, Proof — FS-10-1963-804

VARIETY: Doubled-Die Reverse — **CONECA: DDR-004**
PUP: UNITED
URS-8 · I-4 · L-3

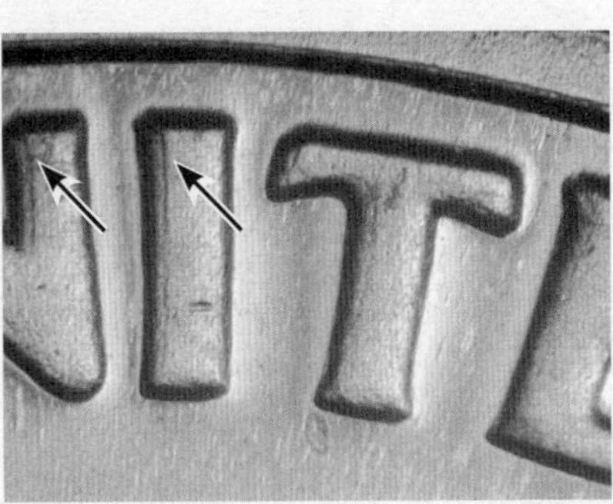

Description: Doubling is very strong on UNITED, with split serifs on most other letters on the reverse.

Comments: This variety is similar to FS-10-1963-801, but rarer and with fewer examples verified. Also, this variety almost always comes as a normal Proof, with just a few cameo coins and no deep cameos verified so far. Lower demand has brought lower market values.

	PF-63	PF-64	PF-65	PF-66	PF-67
VARIETY	$40	$50	$60	$90	$125
NORMAL	$4.50	$4.75	$5	$8	$10

1963 — FS-10-1963-805

Variety: Doubled-Die Reverse — **CONECA: DDR-014**
PUP: UNITED
URS-8 · I-4 · L-3

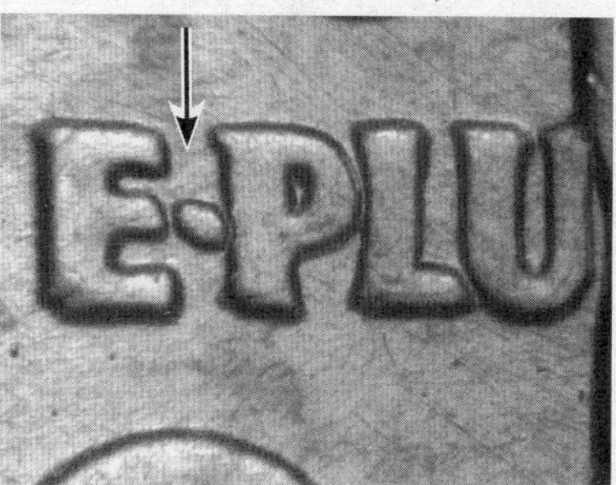

Description: Doubling is evident on UNITED, E PLURIBUS, the olive branch, and the stem. Lesser doubling is visible on ONE DIME.

Comments: Reminder: This is not a Proof coin! This DDR is fairly scarce and its value, as would be expected, escalates with grade. No Full Bands or Full Torch coins have been verified as of publication.

	AU-50	AU-55	MS-60	MS-63	MS-64	MS-65	MS-66
Variety	$25	$30	$40	$65	$115	$200	$350
Normal	$3.25	$3.50	$3.75	$4	n/a	$6	$12

1963-D — FS-10-1963D-801

Variety: Doubled-Die Reverse — **CONECA: DDR-001**
PUP: AMERICA
URS-7 · I-4 · L-3

Description: Doubling is evident on all reverse lettering, with the most obvious doubling on AMERICA and the top of the flame.

Comments: Most known examples grade MS-64 to MS-66. Since this variety was first reported in the *Cherrypickers' Guide*, few new examples have come to light. No Full Bands or Full Torch coins have been confirmed.

	AU-50	AU-55	MS-60	MS-63	MS-64	MS-65	MS-66
Variety	n/a	$20	$25	$50	$100	$125	$200
Normal	$3	$3.10	$3.15	$3.25	n/a	$6	$12

1964, Proof — FS-10-1964-101

VARIETY: Doubled-Die Obverse **CONECA: DDO-005**
PUP: IN GOD WE TRUST, LIBERTY
URS-3 · I-4 · L-4

Description: Strong doubling is evident on IN GOD WE TRUST, on LIBERTY, and on designer John Sinnock's initials (JS, at the truncation of Roosevelt's neck).

Comments: Note there are at least four weaker obverse doubled dies for Proof 1964 Roosevelt dimes. This one is apparently much rarer than earlier thought, as very few pieces have been reported. No cameos or deep cameos have been confirmed.

	PF-66	PF-67	PF-68
VARIETY	$350	$550	$1,000
NORMAL	$8	$10	n/a

1964 — FS-10-1964-801

VARIETY: Doubled-Die Reverse **CONECA: DDR-006**
PUP: DIME, AMERICA
URS-5 · I-4 · L-3

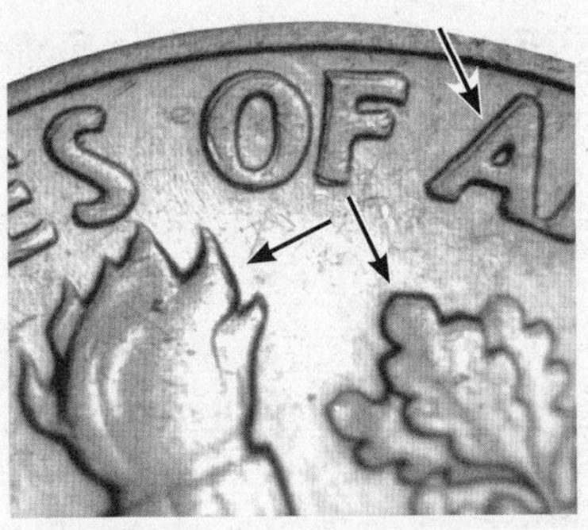

Description: Doubling is evident on all lettering on the reverse, the oak stems and leaves, and the flame. Doubling is strongest on DIME and AMERICA.

Comments: This Roosevelt dime variety and the next (FS-802) are similar, but the doubling is in different directions. While this is a very scarce variety, low demand has suppressed prices. No Full Bands or Full Torch coins have been verified.

	AU-55	AU-58	MS-60	MS-63	MS-64	MS-65	MS-66
VARIETY	$110	$125	$140	$200	$250	$350	n/a
NORMAL	$3.25	$3.50	$3.75	$4	$5	$6	$12

1964 FS-10-1964-802

Variety: Doubled-Die Reverse **CONECA: DDR-008**
PUP: DIME, AMERICA
URS-7 · I-4 · L-3

Description: Doubling is visible on all lettering on the reverse, the oak stems, and the flame. The doubling is strongest in AMERICA.

Comments: Compare the direction of the doubling with that of the previous 1964 Roosevelt dime listing, FS-801. This is a scarce variety. It is found with and without Full Bands. The values shown here are for coins without Full Bands.

	AU-50	AU-58	MS-60	MS-63	MS-64	MS-65	MS-66
Variety	$45	$65	$100	$170	$250	$300	$400
Normal	$3.25	$3.50	$3.75	$4	$5	$6	$12

1964-D FS-10-1964D-501

Variety: Repunched Mintmark **CONECA: RPM-003**
PUP: Mintmark
URS-7 · I-4 · L-4

Description: The secondary D mintmark is visible with a wide spread toward the northeast. Also evident are the left upright and lower right curve of the weaker D.

Comments: This variety is very scarce in all grades, and very rare with Full Bands or Full Torch details. Coins above MS-65 are virtually nonexistent.

	EF-40	AU-50	MS-60	MS-63	MS-64	MS-65	MS-66
Variety	n/a	n/a	$75	$100	$125	$200	$275
Normal	$3	$3.25	$4	$5	$6	$12	$30

1964-D — FS-10-1964D-502

VARIETY: Repunched Mintmark **CONECA: RPM-006**
PUP: Mintmark, torch area
URS-6 · I-5 · L-4

YN

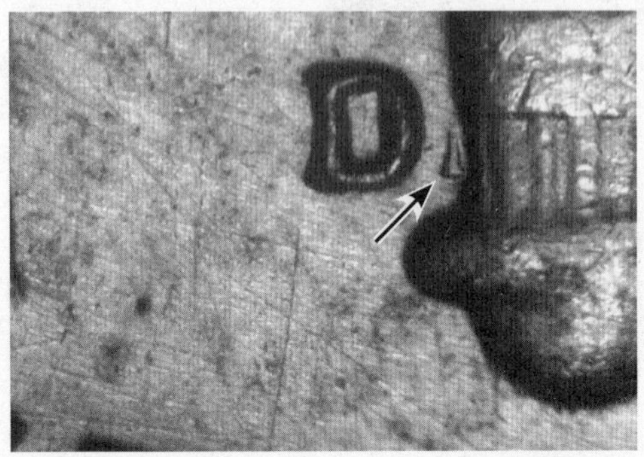

Description: A trace of a secondary D mintmark is evident protruding from the left side of the torch.

Comments: This variety was discovered in 1996 by Joe Miller. It's one of the most dramatic RPMs ever found! Since its discovery, very few examples have come to light. No Full Bands or Full Torch coins have been verified, and no recent sales have been reported.

	EF-40	AU-50	MS-60	MS-63	MS-64	MS-65
VARIETY	n/a	$40	$65	$100	$165	$300
NORMAL	$3	$3.25	$4	$5	$6	$12

1964-D — FS-10-1964D-801

VARIETY: Doubled-Die Reverse **CONECA: DDR-001**
PUP: UNITED STATES OF AMERICA, ONE DIME
URS-8 · I-4 · L-3

Description: Doubling is evident on all lettering on the reverse, on the top of the flame, and on the tips of the leaves on higher-grade pieces.

Comments: This is a very nice and popular DDR. No Full Bands or Full Torch coins are known, and to date none have graded higher than MS-65.

	AU-50	AU-55	AU-58	MS-60	MS-63	MS-64	MS-65
VARIETY	$40	$50	$60	$70	$150	$200	$325
NORMAL	$3.25	$3.50	$3.75	$4	$5	$6	$12

1964-D — FS-10-1964D-802

CONECA: DDR-003

Variety: Doubled-Die Reverse
PUP: ONE, E PLU
URS-7 · I-4 · L-3

Description: Doubling is most evident on ONE DIME, UNITED, E PLU, and the oak stems. Lesser doubling is visible on RIBUS UNUM and AMERICA.

Comments: This is a very scarce variety whose demand is apparent in pricing and market activity. Full Bands and Full Torch coins are quite rare and bring substantial premiums when available (example: an MS-65 Full Bands that sold for $1,375).

	AU-50	AU-58	MS-60	MS-63	MS-64	MS-65	MS-66
Variety	n/a	$60	$70	$150	$225	$325	$450
Normal	$3.25	$3.75	$4	$5	$6	$12	$30

1966, Special Mint Set — FS-10-1966-401

CONECA: N/L

Variety: "5" on Cheek
PUP: Cheek
URS-5 · I-5 · L-5

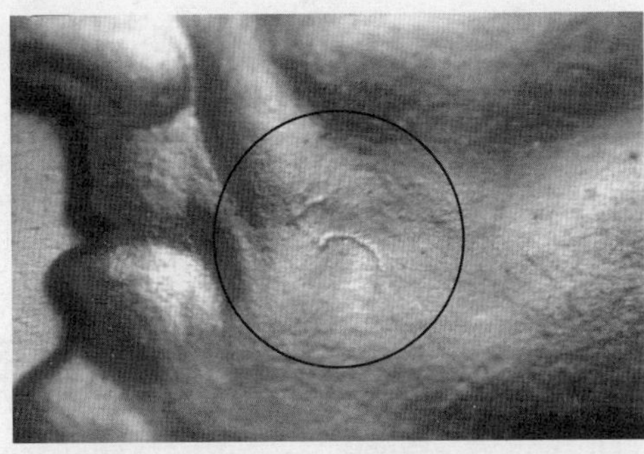

Description: A mark that resembles a numeral 5 is visible on President Roosevelt's cheek.

Comments: Overlays confirm that this variety is similar to the 1952 "Superbird" Proof Washington quarter. It was discovered in 2015 by Robert Lawson, and is presently considered rare, with only 12 to 15 examples found in recent years. Note that it's found in Special Mint Sets only, and only on "frosted face" coins. Values shown below are based on actual sales.

	MS-60	MS-63	MS-65	MS-66	MS-67
Variety	n/a	$200	n/a	$500	$750
Normal	$2	$2.10	$2.25	$3	$10

1967 — FS-10-1967-101

VARIETY: Doubled-Die Obverse **CONECA: DDO-001**
PUP: IN GOD WE TRUST, date, designer's initials
URS-4 · I-5 · L-5

Description: Doubling is evident on IN GOD WE TRUST, the date, and designer John Sinnock's initials (JS) at the base of Roosevelt's bust.

Comments: Although this doubled die has been known for years, it remains very rare. To date, no verified examples have shown up to be graded through the major grading services—and there have been no verified sales.

	AU-58	MS-60	MS-63	MS-64	MS-65	MS-66
VARIETY	n/a	n/a	*$300*	n/a	n/a	n/a
NORMAL					$2	$5

1968 — FS-10-1968-101

VARIETY: Doubled-Die Obverse **CONECA: DDO-001**
PUP: Date, LIBERTY, designer's initials
URS-8 · I-4 · L-3

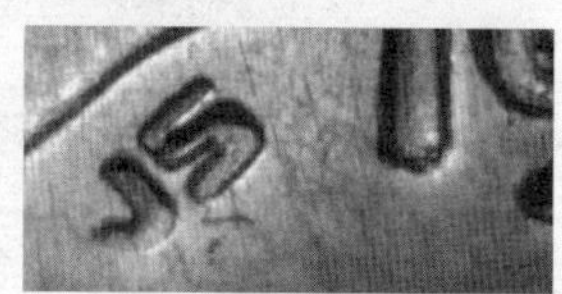

Description: Doubling is evident on LIBERTY, IN GOD WE TRUST, the date, and designer John Sinnock's initials (JS) at the base of Roosevelt's bust.

Comments: This variety, discovered by James Wiles, can be found in some Uncirculated Mint sets. To date, no Full Bands or Full Torch coins have been verified.

	EF-40	AU-50	MS-60	MS-63	MS-65	MS-66
VARIETY	$25	$40	$55	$75	$125	$225
NORMAL					$2	$5

1968-S, Proof — FS-10-1968S-101

Variety: Doubled-Die Obverse — **CONECA: DDO-002**
PUP: LIBERTY, IN GOD WE TRUST
URS-6 · I-4 · L-3

Description: Doubling is evident on LIBERTY and IN GOD WE TRUST, and slightly visible on the date.

Comments: Although this variety has been known for years, it remains very rare. No cameo or deep cameo coins have been verified.

	PF-63	PF-65	PF-66	PF-67	PF-68
Variety	$95	$175	$275	$425	$600
Normal		$2	$4	$6	

1968-S, Proof — FS-10-1968S-102

Variety: Doubled-Die Obverse — **CONECA: DDO-008**
PUP: IN GOD WE TRUST, Date
URS-8 · I-4 · L-3

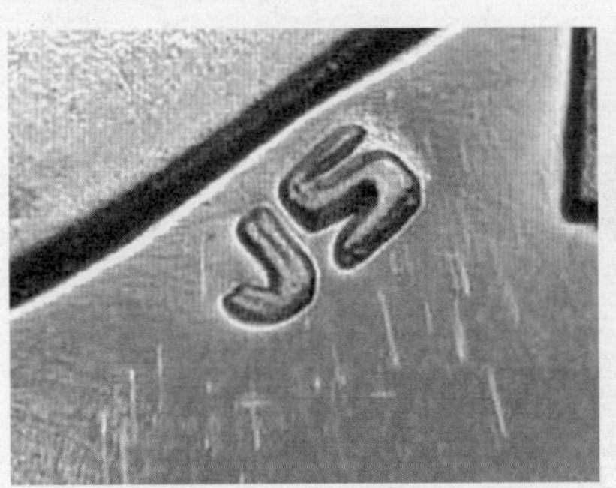

Description: There is moderate doubling on IN GOD WE TRUST, on designer John Sinnock's initials (JS, at the truncation of Roosevelt's bust), and on the date, with a light spread on LIBERTY.

Comments: Several examples of this variety have been found in recent years, changing its status from very rare to very scarce. Only one cameo has been verified, and no deep cameos.

	PF-63	PF-64	PF-65	PF-66	PF-67	PF-68
Variety	$50	$65	$85	$100	$170	$275
Normal			$2	$4	$6	

1968, Proof, No S — FS-10-1968S-501

VARIETY: Missing Mintmark — **CONECA: MMO-001**
PUP: Mintmark area near date
URS-8 · I-5 · L-5

Description: The S mintmark was inadvertently omitted from the die.

Comments: The defective die was probably discovered before the end of the die's life. This is a popular variety with high liquidity. Other San Francisco dimes lacking the mintmark were minted in 1970, 1975, and 1983. Values fluctuate.

	PF-63	PF-64	PF-65	PF-66	PF-67	PF-68
VARIETY	*See current pricing resources for the latest values.*					
NORMAL			$2	$4	$6	

1968-S, Proof — FS-10-1968S-502

VARIETY: Repunched Mintmark — **CONECA: RPM-001**
PUP: Mintmark
URS-4 · I-3 · L-3

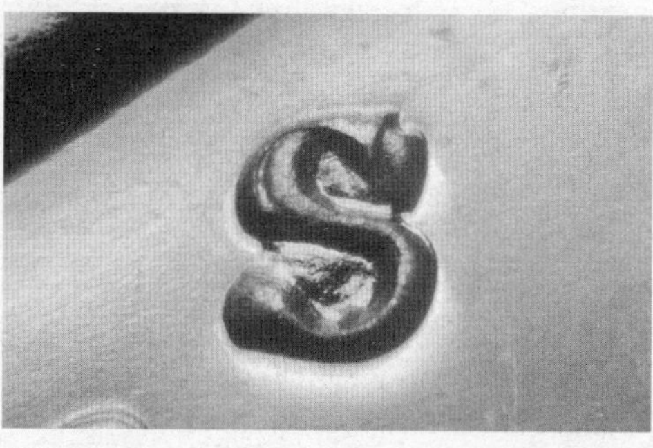

Description: The secondary S mintmark is very close to and west of the primary S.

Comments: The obverse is also a very minor doubled die, but that does not increase the coin's value. Since first reported, surprisingly very few pieces have come to light. Also, no cameo or deep cameo coins have been reported. This is a sleeper that could make your day if cherrypicked! Happy hunting.

	PF-63	PF-64	PF-65	PF-66	PF-67
VARIETY	$75	$100	$150	$250	$450
NORMAL			$2	$4	$6

1968-S, Proof

FS-10-1968S-801

CONECA: DDR-001

Variety: Doubled-Die Reverse
PUP: UNITED, E PLURIBUS UNUM, DIME
URS-7 · I-4 · L-3

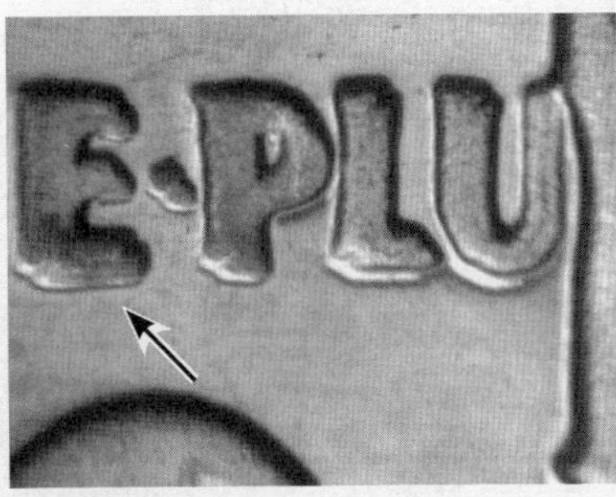

Description: Doubling is evident on UNITED STATES, ONE DIME, and E PLURIBUS UNUM. Weaker doubling is evident on AMERICA and on the olive stems.

Comments: This variety is still considered rare, even though a few more pieces have been found since the fifth edition of the *Cherrypickers' Guide* was published (2012). It is found in regular Proof and Cameo, but no Deep Cameo Proofs have been verified.

	PF-64	PF-65	PF-66	PF-67	PF-68	PF-69
Variety	$50	$75	$110	$225	$325	$425
Normal		$2	$4	$6		

1969

FS-10-1969-901

CONECA: RDV-002

Variety: Reverse of 1968
PUP: Flames of torch
URS-6 · I-4 · L-3

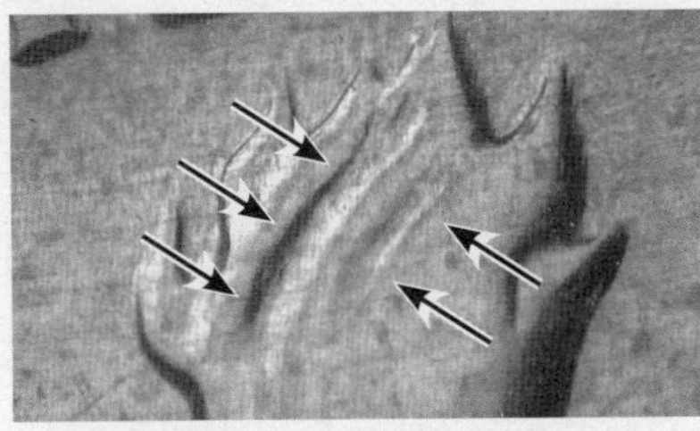

Variety style: a deep valley in a high-relief flame.

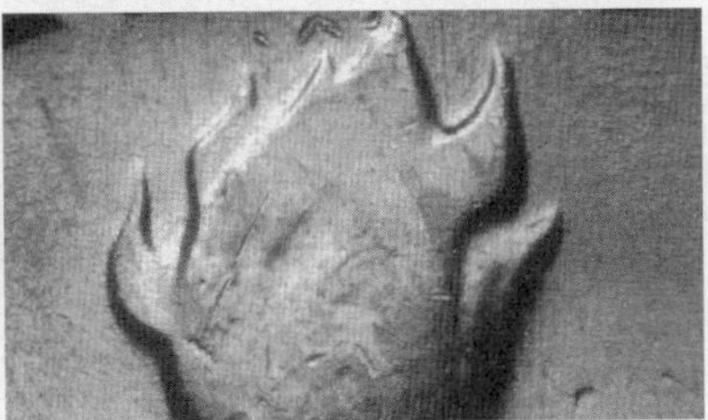

Common circulation-strike style: a shallow valley in a low-relief flame.

Description: Two deep valleys are evident within the flame, which is struck in high relief.

Comments: This reverse die was first used for 1968 Proof dimes. Its design style (with a high-relief torch) also appears on just a few 1969, 1970, and 1970-D circulation strikes. (After 1970 this reverse style became standard for all Roosevelt dimes from all mints, through 1980.) The 1969 is the rarest of the three Reverse of 1968 varieties. Full Bands coins are extremely rare.

	AU-50	MS-60	MS-63	MS-64	MS-65
Variety	$50	$100	$165	$325	n/a
Normal					$3

1969-D FS-10-1969D-501

VARIETY: Repunched Mintmark **CONECA: RPM-001**
PUP: Mintmark
URS-9 · I-4 · L-3

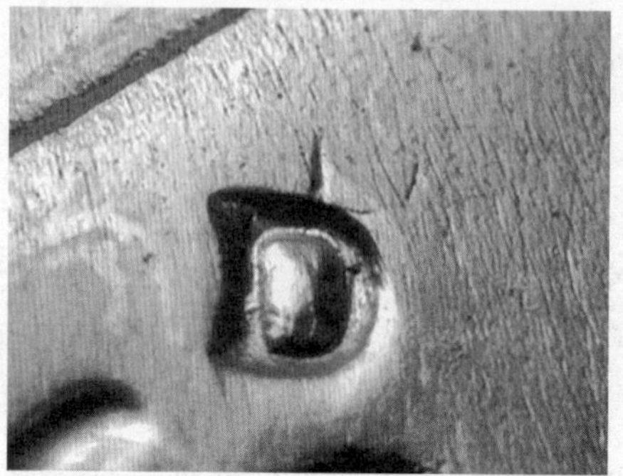

Description: This RPM has a very wide spread to the northeast.

Comments: This variety is found only in Uncirculated Mint sets! Scarce in any condition, it is extremely rare with Full Bands details; such coins bring substantial premiums over the values listed here.

	EF-40	AU-50	MS-60	MS-63	MS-65	MS-66
VARIETY	n/a	n/a	$30	$45	$75	$125
NORMAL					$2	$6

1970 FS-10-1970-801

VARIETY: Doubled-Die Reverse **CONECA: DDR-001**
PUP: UNITED STATES OF AMERICA
URS-4 · I-4 · L-3

Description: Doubling is evident on all reverse lettering, especially on UNITED STATES OF AMERICA, with slightly weaker doubling on ONE DIME.

Comments: This variety is extremely rare. No verified sales have been confirmed—but it's clear there is short supply to meet the demand.

	EF-40	AU-50	MS-60	MS-63	MS-64	MS-65	MS-66
VARIETY	n/a	n/a	n/a	n/a	n/a	n/a	n/a
NORMAL						$2	$6

1970 — FS-10-1970-901

VARIETY: Reverse of 1968 — **CONECA: RDV-002**
PUP: Flames of torch
URS-7 · I-4 · L-3

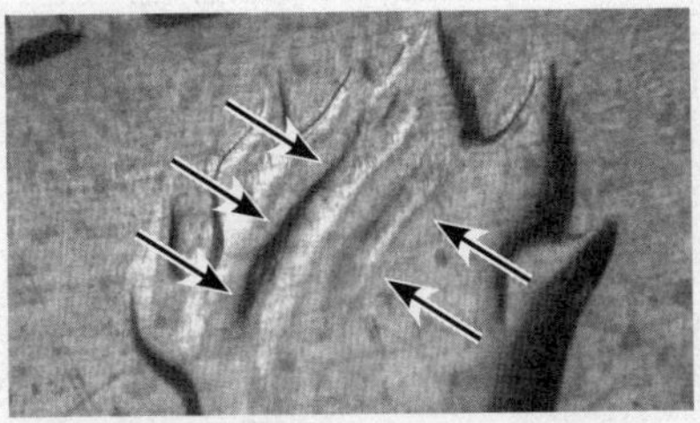
Variety style: a deep valley in a high-relief flame.

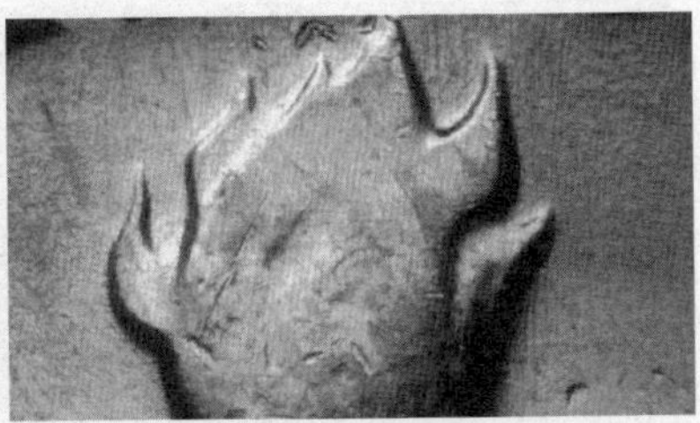
Common circulation-strike style: a shallow valley in a low-relief flame.

Description: Two deep valleys are evident within the flame, which is struck in high relief.

Comments: This reverse die was used almost entirely on 1968–1970 Proof dimes, but is also known for three circulation-strike dates (1969, 1970, and 1970-D). The 1970 is the second-scarcest of the three. Examples have been graded in a wide range of conditions, from Choice VF to Uncirculated, but no Full Bands coins have been verified. So far, few sales have been reported.

	VF-30	EF-40	AU-50	MS-60	MS-63	MS-65	MS-66
VARIETY	$35	$40	$45	$55	$90	$145	$275
NORMAL						$2	$6

1970-D — FS-10-1970D-801

VARIETY: Doubled-Die Reverse — **CONECA: DDR-001**
PUP: UNITED STATES OF AMERICA, E PLURIBUS UNUM
URS-4 · I-4 · L-3

Description: Doubling is evident on UNITED STATES OF AMERICA, on the flame, on the tops of the oak leaves, and (very slightly) on UNUM.

Comments: This is one of three very different reverse doubled dies that have been found in Uncirculated Mint sets. While scarce, enough coins seem to be available to meet demand. Coins without Full Bands are the norm; those with Full Bands are very rare and bring substantial premiums over the values listed here.

	EF-40	AU-50	MS-60	MS-63	MS-65	MS-66
VARIETY	$10	$20	$45	$70	$150	$175
NORMAL					$2	$5

1970-D — FS-10-1970D-802

Variety: Doubled-Die Reverse — **CONECA: DDR-004**
PUP: UNITED STATES OF AMERICA
URS-9 · I-4 · L-3

Description: Moderate doubling is evident on all reverse lettering, the flame, and the tops of the oak leaves.

Comments: This is arguably the nicest of all 1970-D reverse doubled dies. It can be cherrypicked in circulation or from Uncirculated Mint sets. No Full Bands coins have been confirmed.

	AU-50	MS-60	MS-63	MS-64	MS-65	MS-66
Variety	$30	$60	$90	$110	$160	$200
Normal					$2	$5

1970-D — FS-10-1970D-901

Variety: Reverse of 1968 — **CONECA: RDV-002**
PUP: Flames of torch
URS-8 · I-4 · L-3

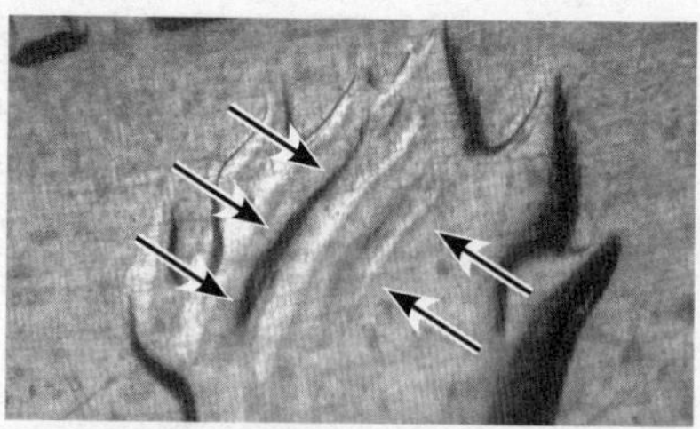

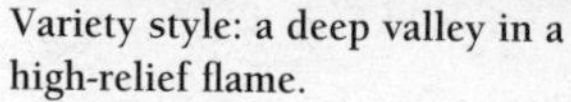

Variety style: a deep valley in a high-relief flame.

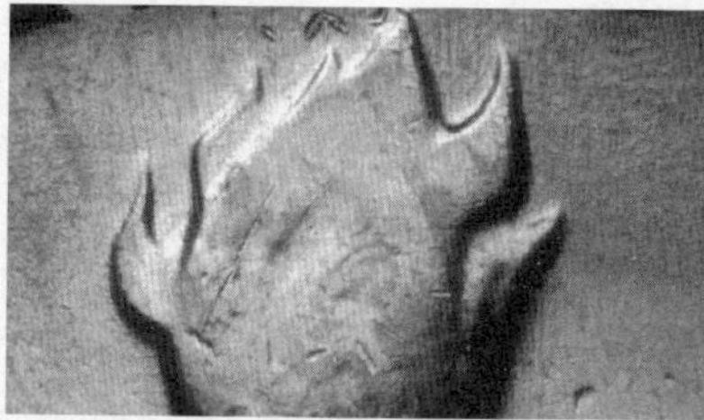

Common circulation-strike style: a shallow valley in a low-relief flame.

Description: Two deep valleys are evident within the flame, which is struck in high relief.

Comments: See the related 1969 and 1970 entries. This style of reverse die was used mostly on 1968–1970 Proof dimes, but is also known for a small quantity of three circulation-strike dates. Of the three, the 1970-D is the most common. Sales activity and market values show that demand is strong. The 1970-D variety is known both with and without Full Bands details.

	EF-40	AU-50	MS-60	MS-63	MS-64	MS-65	MS-66
Variety	$25	$35	$50	$75	$95	$135	$275
Normal						$2	$5

1970-S, Proof, No S

FS-10-1970S-501

Variety: Missing Mintmark

CONECA: MMO-001

PUP: Mintmark area near date

URS-8 · I-5 · L-5

Description: The S mintmark, normally located above the date, is missing.

Comments: San Francisco began minting U.S. Proof coins in 1968, with an S mintmark indicating their origin. In some cases Proof dies were shipped from the Philadelphia Mint to San Francisco without the mintmark, and these dies were accidentally used to strike some coins that made their way past the Mint's inspectors. All No S Proof coins are rare. The anomaly is known among 1968, 1970, 1975, and 1983 dimes (among other coins, such as 1971 nickels.) This rare variety can still be cherrypicked in unsearched 1970 Proof sets.

	PF-63	PF-64	PF-65	PF-66	PF-67	PF-68
Variety	*See current pricing resources for the latest values.*					
Normal			$2	$4	$6	

1971-D

FS-10-1971D-501

Variety: Repunched Mintmark

CONECA: RPM-001

PUP: Mintmark

URS-4 · I-5 · L-5

Description: There is a strongly repunched D mintmark south of the primary mintmark.

Comments: To date there have been no confirmed sales of this very rare variety (only five certified as of our press date). Publication in the *Cherrypickers' Guide* will surely bring more to light.

	EF-40	AU-50	MS-60	MS-63	MS-64	MS-65	MS-66
Variety	n/a	n/a	n/a	n/a	n/a	n/a	n/a
Normal						$2.50	$6

1975-S, Proof — FS-10-1975S-501

VARIETY: Repunched Mintmark — **CONECA: RPM-001**
PUP: Mintmark
URS-6 · I-4 · L-3

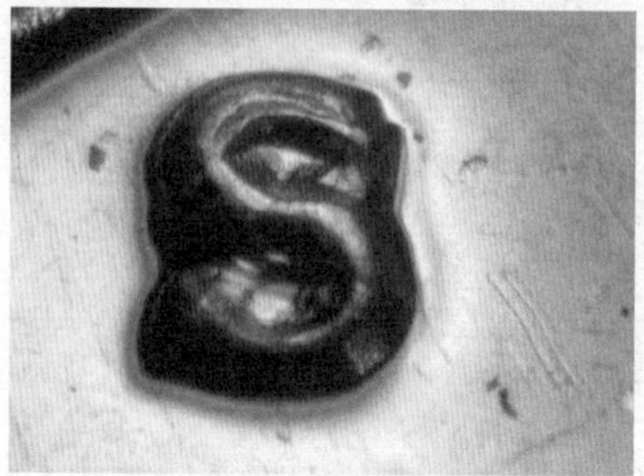

Description: The secondary S mintmark north is very close, visible at the top of the primary S.

Comments: There are at least two different RPMs for this date and mint. Surprisingly few examples of this one have turned up since its first *Cherrypickers' Guide* publication. It can be found with regular, Cameo, and Deep Cameo surfaces. Higher-grade coins bring substantial premiums. Values shown here are for normal (not Cameo or Deep Cameo) coins.

	PF-63	PF-65	PF-66	PF-67	PF-68
VARIETY	$20	$35	$50	$150	$250
NORMAL		$2.50	$4	$6	

1975-S, Proof, No S — FS-10-1975S-502

VARIETY: Missing Mintmark — **CONECA: MMO-001**
PUP: Mintmark area near date
URS-2 · I-5 · L-5

Description: The S mintmark, normally located above the date, is missing.

Comments: In 1975 an anonymous California collector purchased five Proof sets from the Mint and realized that two of them had Roosevelt dimes missing San Francisco's S mintmark, which had been used on Proof coinage since 1968. Scott Schechter and Jeff Garrett write, "looking for a No S dime is something like searching for a needle in a haystack." This variety is ranked no. 1 in their popular book *100 Greatest U.S. Modern Coins*. To date, only two examples are verified, a PF-66 and a PF-68. The latter sold for $456,000 in September 2019!

	PF-63	PF-64	PF-65	PF-66	PF-67	PF-68
VARIETY	*See current pricing resources for the latest values.*					
NORMAL			$2.50	$4	$6	

1982, No P, Strong Strike

FS-10-1982-501a

Variety: Missing Mintmark, Strong Date

CONECA: MMO-001

PUP: Mintmark area near date

URS-12 · I-5 · L-4

Description: The P mintmark was omitted from this working die. All coins minted from the die exhibit a very strong strike (check the 82 of the date)—no exceptions!

Comments: The vast majority of this die variety was "dumped" in and around Toledo and Sandusky, Ohio, including the Cedar Point Amusement Park in Sandusky. Examples are found with and without Full Bands. Grades above MS-66 are very rare. In March 2020 an MS-67 coin with Full Bands sold for more than $10,000. Values shown here are for non–Full Bands coins.

	AU-50	MS-60	MS-63	MS-64	MS-65	MS-66
Variety	$75	$110	$135	$185	$265	$375
Normal					$7.50	$18

1982, No P, Weak Strike

FS-10-1982-501b

Variety: Missing Mintmark, Weak Date

CONECA: MMO-001

PUP: Mintmark area

URS-11 · I-4 · L-3

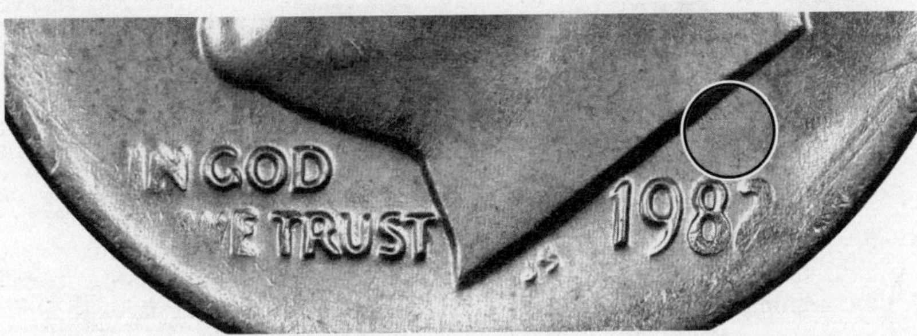

Description: The P mintmark was omitted from the working die. The numerals 82 in the date are weakly struck.

Comments: This variety is far scarcer than the strongly struck FS-10-1982-501, but because of lower demand, can be purchased for a lesser price. This is always seen with a weak 8 and almost nonexistent 2 in the date. No Full Bands coins have been verified. An MS-67 sold on eBay in November 2019 for $800. This issue was reportedly released in New Jersey.

	AU-50	MS-60	MS-63	MS-64	MS-65	MS-66
Variety	$60	$90	$105	$150	$210	$300
Normal					$7.50	$18

1983-D — FS-10-1983D-501

VARIETY: Repunched Mintmark **CONECA: RPM-001**
PUP: Mintmark
URS-3 · I-5 · L-5

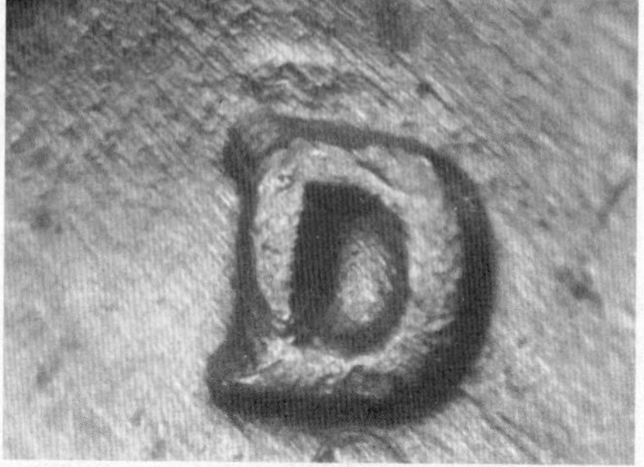

Description: A secondary D mintmark is visible protruding from the primary D. Only a small portion of the left upright bar of the underlying D is evident.

Comments: This is one of the latest-dated RPMs for the Roosevelt dime series. Apparently, this variety is very scarce, as there have been no verified sales and no slabbed pieces shown in the population reports. This is a good one to look for!

	EF-40	AU-50	MS-60	MS-63	MS-65	MS-66
VARIETY	n/a	n/a	n/a	n/a	n/a	n/a
NORMAL					$3.25	$8:50

1983-S, Proof, No S — FS-10-1983S-501

VARIETY: Missing Mintmark **CONECA: MMO-001**
PUP: Mintmark area near date
URS-8 · I-5 · L-5

Description: The S mintmark, normally located above the date, is missing.

Comments: Under normal circumstances, dies for San Francisco's 1983 Proof coinage were made from working hubs that had no mintmark, and all the working dies should have been punched with an S mintmark before going into production. That didn't happen for the die that created the 1983 No S dime. Since its discovery in mid-1983, only a few hundred examples of this variety have been found. They are almost always seen with notably deep or ultra cameo contrast. To avoid more such errors, starting in 1985 the Mint has made Proof dies from a production hub that includes the mintmark. This variety can still be cherrypicked!

	PF-63	PF-64	PF-65	PF-66	PF-67	PF-68
VARIETY	*See current pricing resources for the latest values.*					
NORMAL			$3	$4	$6	

1985-P, 1986-P, 1987-P — No FS#

Questionable Varieties

We have included the next three listings for several reasons. These varieties do catch the eye of many collectors, both novice and seasoned. Some variety enthusiasts believe them to be misplaced-mintmark varieties; however, while all three coins show an image that appears to be a misplaced mintmark, in our opinion there is simply not enough evidence to classify them conclusively. We do not intend to state categorically that they are *not* misplaced mintmarks; we just can't state for sure they are. We have not assigned Fivaz-Stanton numbers to them.

All the examples we have seen come from very late die states, as evidenced by the "orange peel" effect clearly visible on the coins' surfaces. We have not seen any of these in an earlier die state.

The inclusion of these die varieties in the *Cherrypickers' Guide* will provide a reference for understanding or describing them. Additionally, it will make it clear to the novice collector that there still are questions about their validity (and therefore their value).

1985-P — No FS#

Variety: Possible Misplaced Mintmark — **CONECA: N/L**

PUP: Area on neck and field

URS-7 · I-4 · L-3

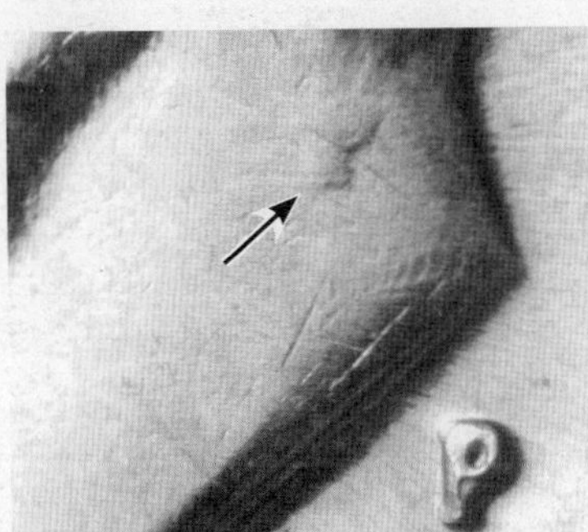

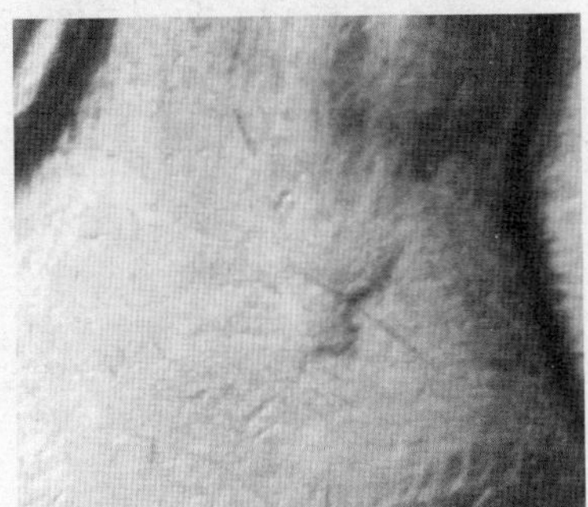

Description: A faint image is visible at the rear of the neck, just below President Roosevelt's hairline.

Comments: (See the introductory text preceding this entry.) Some enthusiasts believe this anomaly is a misplaced P mintmark. The coin, although questionable, is interesting and has a following within the variety market.

	AU-50	MS-60	MS-63	MS-65	MS-66
Variety	n/a	n/a	$50	n/a	n/a
Normal				$2.25	$5

1986-P

No FS#

VARIETY: Possible Misplaced Mintmark **CONECA: N/L**
PUP: Area on neck and field
URS-6 · I-4 · L-3

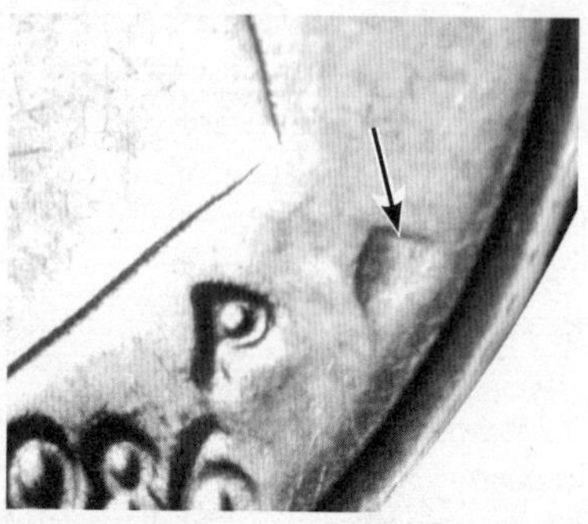
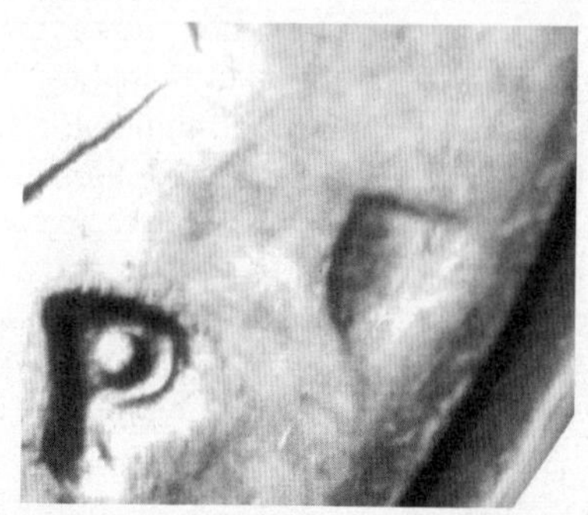

Description: A faint image is evident in the field near the rim, just to the right of the P mintmark.

Comments: (See the introductory text preceding this entry.) Some enthusiasts believe this anomaly is a misplaced P mintmark. Although its true nature is uncertain, the coin is interesting and it has a following within the hobby community.

	AU-50	MS-60	MS-63	MS-65	MS-66
VARIETY	n/a	n/a	$75	n/a	n/a
NORMAL				$2.50	$5

1987-P

No FS#

VARIETY: Possible Misplaced Mintmark **CONECA: N/L**
PUP: Area on neck and field
URS-8 · I-4 · L-3

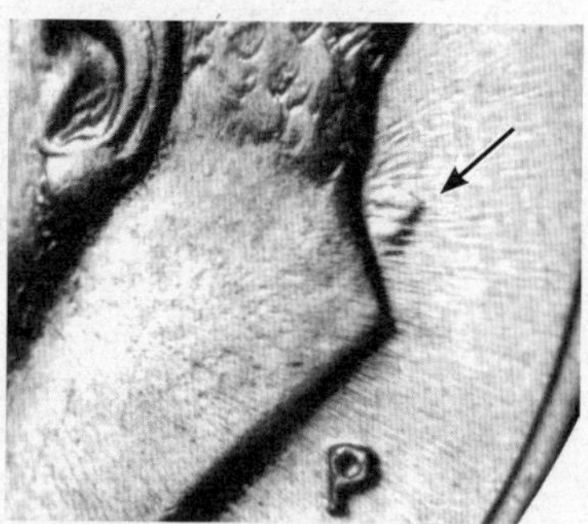
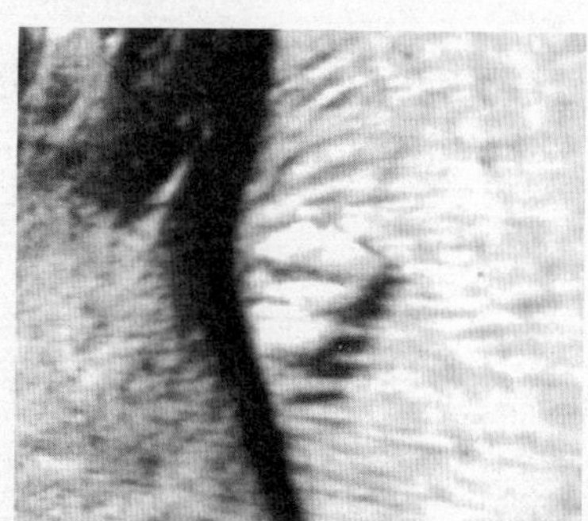

Description: A faint image can be seen in the field below President Roosevelt's neck hairline, on an even level with the bottom of his ear.

Comments: (See the introductory text preceding this entry.) Some collectors believe this anomaly is a misplaced P mintmark. The coin, although questionable as a misplaced mintmark, is interesting and has a following among variety enthusiasts.

	AU-50	MS-60	MS-63	MS-65	MS-66
VARIETY	n/a	n/a	$40	n/a	n/a
NORMAL				$2.25	$5

2004-D

FS-10-2004D-401

Variety: Curved Image

CONECA: N/L

PUP: Ear

URS-8 · I-5 · L-4

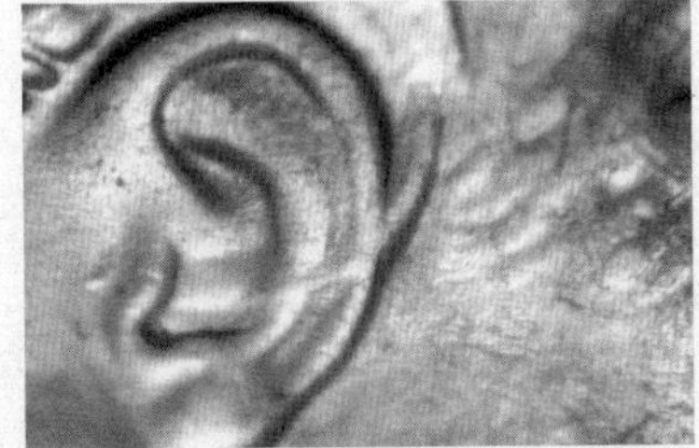

Description: A circular image overlaps the outer rim of the back of Roosevelt's ear.

Comments: An employee of the Denver Mint may have added the circular image to the die deliberately. Its size and shape are similar to those of images known on the reverse of the two 2004-D Wisconsin quarters (High Leaf and Low Leaf varieties), also featured in this volume. There is some unconfirmed evidence that this might be a doubled die. Since its discovery and inclusion in the *Cherrypickers' Guide*, this coin has proven to be fairly elusive. No Full Bands pieces have been verified.

	AU-50	MS-60	MS-63	MS-65	MS-66
Variety	$95	$125	$175	$275	$425
Normal				$2	$3

2015-P

FS-10-2015P-801

Variety: Doubled-Die Reverse

CONECA: DDR-003

PUP: Leaf overlapping torch

URS-6 · I-4 · L-3

Description: Nice doubling is visible on the reverse, with the leaf overlapping the torch.

Comments: A strong, localized doubling on the left leaf overlaps the torch to the east.

	EF-40	AU-50	MS-60	MS-63	MS-64	MS-65
Variety	n/a	n/a	n/a	*$100*	n/a	n/a
Normal						$2

Twenty-Cent Pieces, 1875–1878

This abbreviated denomination was produced for circulation only in 1875 and 1876, but Proof coinage was also struck in 1877 and 1878. Mintages were low for the circulation coinage, meaning very few production dies were used. As a result, the varieties that do exist are relatively common. In fact, misplaced dates for the 1875-S in this series are far more common than the date without the misplaced date.

For collectors seriously interested in these coins, we strongly recommend membership in the Liberty Seated Collectors Club, one of the best specialized clubs in numismatics. The LSCC attends more than twenty regional events each year, providing educational programs, exhibits at club tables, and meetings.

The award-winning *Gobrecht Journal*, the official publication of the club, is issued to members three times annually (in March, July, and November), in full color. This extensive publication is loaded with excellent educational articles. The *Gobrecht Journal* is research-orientated and contains articles on all Liberty Seated coinage denominations, from half dimes to trade dollars. You can preview sample articles online at https://nnp.wustl.edu/library/publisherdetail/2096

The Club also publishes *The E-Gobrecht*, a monthly email-based publication, distributed to club members and interested non-members at no cost. The *E-Gobrecht* contains information of a timely nature, such as recent auction sales, LSCC regional meeting or event announcements, and feature articles on new variety discoveries. You can download all back issues of *The E-Gobrecht* from the LSCC website's "E-Gobrecht Archives" page.

At the time of this publication, Liberty Seated Collectors Club membership dues are $30 per year—a bargain, considering the amount of resources available. If you join the LSCC, you will be connecting with the most serious and knowledgeable collectors and dealers in the hobby. For membership information, visit www.lsccweb.org, or write to

Liberty Seated Collectors Club
Leonard Augsburger, President
Email: leonard.augsburger@wustl.edu

New Twenty-Cent Pieces in the Sixth Edition, Volume II

Date, Variety	Fivaz-Stanton number	PUP
1876, Doubled Die Reverse	FS-20-1876-801	UNITED STATES OF AMERICA
1876-CC, Doubled-Die Obv., MPD	FS-20-1876CC-101	LIBERTY

1875-S FS-20-1875S-301

Variety: Misplaced Date, Repunched Mintmark **CONECA: RPM-001**
PUP: Denticles below 8 of date, mintmark
URS-12 · I-3 · L-2

Description: The top of a digit, likely an 8, is visible in the denticles below the primary 8. The S over S resembles a dollar sign.

Comments: The obverse comes with and without the repunched mintmark. This is a very common coin. With both the misplaced date and the repunched mintmark it brings a slight premium only because of the combination of errors. Coins without the misplaced date and repunched mintmark are very scarce.

	VG-8	F-12	VF-20	EF-40	AU-50	MS-60	MS-63
Variety	$120	$150	$175	$250	$350	$650	$1,000
Normal	$115	$140	$165	$240	$340	$645	$990

1875-S FS-20-1875S-302

Variety: Misplaced Date, Repunched Mintmark **CONECA: RPM-001**
PUP: Denticles below 7 of date, mintmark
URS-12 · I-3 · L-2

Description: The top of a digit, likely a 5, is visible in the denticles below the primary 7. The S mintmark is repunched with the secondary S evident and tilted.

Comments: Although common, this variety with the misplaced date and repunched mintmark brings a slight premium. Coins without the misplaced date and repunched mintmark are more scarce.

	VG-8	F-12	VF-20	EF-40	AU-50	MS-60	MS-63
Variety	$120	$150	$175	$250	$350	$650	$1,000
Normal	$115	$140	$165	$240	$340	$645	$990

1876

FS-20-1876-801

Variety: Doubled Die Reverse
PUP: UNITED STATES OF AMERICA
URS-8 · I-4 · L-3

Description: There is a light spread of doubling noticeable on UNITED STATES OF.

Comments: Although not major, the spread on the reverse makes the coin nice and highly collectible. This is a fairly rare coin that was unknown until recent years. This is the only collectible doubled die in the twenty-cent series.

	G-4	VG-8	F-12	VF-20	EF-40	AU-50
Variety	$245	$295	$400	$475	$550	$650
Normal	$235	$285	$390	$470	$545	$640

1876-CC

FS-20-1876CC-101

Variety: Doubled-Die Obverse, Misplaced Date
PUP: LIBERTY; 87 in dentils below date
URS-5 · I-5 · L-5

Description: LIBERTY on the shield shows major doubling. As a dual feature, digits 8 and 7 are visible in the denticles under the date.

Comments: This coin became a major rarity when Mint Director Henry Linderman ordered any/all silver coins held in U.S. banks to be melted for future silver coins. Today only 15 to 20 1876-CC twenty-cent pieces are known to exist. In the late 1970s, Art Kagin told Larry Briggs he once purchased three 1876-CC's from an elderly man. That man also showed Mr. Kagin an additional 10+ examples but refused to sell them. An interesting story, but never verified.

	VF-20	EF-40	AU-50	MS-60	MS-63
Variety					
Normal			$225,000	$325,000	$425,000

Capped Bust Quarters, 1815–1838

Capped Bust die varieties may be slightly different from what many of us are accustomed to encountering in late-nineteenth-century and more recent coinage. During the Bust era, the die-making process was somewhat different from that of later years. Often a matrix and punches were used to place many of the design elements, letters, and date numerals into the working die. (In later coinage, a hub would create master dies and working dies.) Because of this, it is not uncommon to see slight differences in positioning of these elements. In some cases, individual letter or number punches were used, which can account for one letter or number appearing over another.

Membership in a specialty club is always informative and well worth its relatively modest cost. The John Reich Collectors Society, which focuses on Capped Bust half dimes, dimes, quarters, and halves, is one of the most active and educational clubs in the United States.

The JRCS has a fabulous website, www.JRCS.org, with a membership application, club details, news, and educational material. The group also has a Meta (Facebook) page and holds quarterly gatherings online in addition to in-person meetings. Its print publication is the *John Reich Journal*. Contact the Society at

JRCS
Brad Karoleff, President
225 E. 6th Street, Suite 1
Cincinnati OH 45202

New Capped Bust Quarters in the Sixth Edition, Volume II

Date, Variety	Fivaz-Stanton number	PUP
1822, 25 Over 50	FS-25-1822-901	Denomination
1825, 5 Over 2	FS-25-1825-301	Date
1825, 5 Over 3	FS-25-1825-302	Date
1825, 5 Over 4	FS-25-1825-303	Date
1828, 25 Over 50	FS-25-1828-901	Denomination

1822, 25 Over 50 FS-25-1822-901

VARIETY: Overstruck Denomination **CONECA: N/L; BROWNING-2**
PUP: Denomination
URS-7 · I-5 · L-5

Description: The digits 25 are punched over the 50 in the denomination.

Comments: Three or more Proofs are known to exist. The reverse is actually from a botched 1818 leftover die. This variety is quite rare and seldom seen. Most are low grade (About Good to Fine) and have problems. They are always found with crisp denticles on the reverse and very weak to no denticles on the obverse—no exceptions!

	G-4	VG-8	F-12	VF-20	EF-40	AU-50
VARIETY	$5,000	$9,500	$16,000	$22,500	$32,000	$40,000
NORMAL	$400	$450	$850	$1,200	$1,650	$3,250

1825, 5 Over 2 FS-25-1825-301

VARIETY: Overdate **CONECA: N/L; BROWNING-1**
PUP: Star 13 and vertical upright of 5
URS-7 · I-5 · L-5

Description: The position of star 13 is high up on the curl compared to that on the 1825, 5 Over 3, and 1825, 5 Over 4, varieties. The obverse is from an 1815-1824 hub. On overlays, star 13 would fit between stars 12 and 13 on the 1825, 5 Over 3, and 1825, 5 Over 4. In addition, the vertical upright of the 5 is extra-thick, with a nodule protruding on the back of the curve.

Comments: This variety is very scarce to rare and is seldom seen. Fifty or more pieces were confirmed as of January 2021. It is easy to identify by star 13's position high up on the curl. It is usually found in low grades (About Good to Very Good.)

	G-4	VG-8	F-12	VF-20	EF-40	AU-50
VARIETY	$650	$1,250	$1,750	$3,750	$6,750	$9,250
NORMAL	$135	$250	$350	$750	$1,850	$2,500

1825, 5 Over 3 — FS-25-1825-302

Variety: Overdate — **CONECA:** N/L; **Browning-2**
PUP: Date
URS-12 · I-4 · L-4

Description: The variety is easily discerned by the curve of the 3 visible in the 5 of the date from the top right of the horizontal to the top curve.

Comments: This is by far the most common of the three varieties for this year. In comparison, probably 100 coins of the 5 Over 3 exist for every 5 Over 2; and 10 for every 5 Over 4. In late die state, the variety is found with a very nice and rare retained cud covering UNITED. It is sometimes found with an E or L counterstamp.

	G-4	VG-8	F-12	VF-20	EF-40	AU-50
Variety	$100	$145	$215	$400	$900	$1,600
Normal	$95	$140	$210	$395	$895	$1,590

1825, 5 Over 4 — FS-25-1825-303

Variety: Overdate — **CONECA:** N/L; **Browning-3**
PUP: Date
URS-10 · I-4 · L-4

Description: The variety is easily attributed by the right end of the crossbar on the 4 protruding at the lower left side of the vertical of the 5.

Comments: This is the second-scarcest of the three different varieties for this year. Much harder to find than the 5 Over 3, by a 10-to-1 margin! Although it is rare with the E or L counterstamps, it does exist. In later die states, it is found with a nicely retained cud over the arrowheads.

	G-4	VG-8	F-12	VF-20	EF-40	AU-50
Variety	$130	$175	$265	$500	$1,000	$1,900
Normal	$125	$170	$260	$490	$990	$1,890

1828, 25 Over 50 FS-25-1828-901

VARIETY: Overstruck Denomination **CONECA: N/L; BROWNING-3**
PUP: Denomination
URS-8 · I-5 · L-5

Description: A 25 is punched over the 50 in the denomination.

Comments: This one is rare in all grades, and progressively more so as grades escalate! It originated with a botched 1818 die that was first used in 1822, then was shelved and brought out again for use in 1828. By then, it had several areas of rust from humidity and improper storage of the die.

	G-4	VG-8	F-12	VF-20	EF-40	AU-50
VARIETY	$1,000	$1,500	$2,000	$2,750	$6,000	$9,000
NORMAL	$115	$250	$350	$650	$1,750	$2,400

1831, Large Letters FS-25-1831-301

VARIETY: Repunched Date **BROWNING-5, BROWNING-7**
PUP: Numeral 1's in date
B-5: URS-9 · I-3 · L-3
B-7: URS-6 · I-5 · L-4

Description: On this variety, a large-date logotype was used over a small-date logotype. The Large Letters reverse has large and small arrowheads. This obverse was mated with two reverses.

Comments: Browning-5 has large date numerals over small date numerals, a Large Letters reverse, and large arrowheads. It brings a small premium over the common type. Browning-7 has large date numerals over small date numerals, a Large Letters reverse, and small arrowheads. Browning-7 is rare.

	VF-20	EF-40	AU-50	MS-60	MS-63
BROWNING-5	$150	$350	$550	$2,000	$3,250
BROWNING-7	$350	$575	$875	$2,750	$4,500
NORMAL	$145	$345	$540	$1,990	$3,240

1833 FS-25-1833-901

VARIETY: Reverse Recut Legend **BROWNING-2**
PUP: Reverse legend
URS-10 · I-3 · L-3

Description: The entire reverse legend was recut, which is most evident on OF A. No period follows the C in the denomination (25 C.) The eagle has no tongue and the shield has only two vertical wide stripes.

Comments: Of the two similar varieties (of 1833 and 1834), this is the scarcer—but it is not rare. Two of every five 1833 quarters are Browning-2 (the other three are Browning-1.) There are only two varieties known (B-1 and B-2). Still, the variety brings a minimal premium.

	VF-20	EF-40	AU-50	MS-60	MS-63
VARIETY	$130	$345	$600	$1,900	$3,250
NORMAL	$125	$340	$590	$1,890	$3,240

1834 FS-25-1834-901

VARIETY: Reverse Recut Legend **BROWNING-1**
PUP: Reverse legend
URS-11 · I-3 · L-3

Description: The entire reverse legend on this variety was recut, most evidently on OF A. No period follows the C in the denomination (25 C.) The eagle has no tongue and the shield has only two vertical wide stripes.

Comments: This coin employs the same reverse die used on the 1833 B-2 variety. It was erroneously reported in previous *Cherrypickers' Guides* as very rare; in fact, it is the most common variety for the year. Although it brings no extra premium, it is popular because of the die-cutting error.

	VF-20	EF-40	AU-50	MS-60	MS-63
VARIETY	$110	$290	$500	$1,700	$3,000
NORMAL	$105	$285	$490	$1,690	$2,990

Liberty Seated Quarters, 1838–1891

Liberty Seated quarters are a paradise for die-variety enthusiasts. Significant varieties are known and can be found for nearly every date and mint. From minor repunched mintmarks to major doubled dies, and even major design changes, Liberty Seated die varieties are abundant.

Most of the varieties within the series are in high demand from the large number of Liberty Seated specialists. In general, their values have been rising even faster than for the normal coins. An eagle-eyed cherrypicker can easily earn a significant income by picking the varieties that go unnoticed by most coin dealers.

For collectors seriously interested in these coins, we strongly recommend membership in the Liberty Seated Collectors Club, one of the best specialized clubs in numismatics. The LSCC attends more than twenty regional events each year, providing educational programs, exhibits at club tables, and meetings.

The award-winning *Gobrecht Journal*, the official publication of the club, is issued to members three times annually (in March, July, and November), in full color. This extensive publication is loaded with excellent educational articles. The *Gobrecht Journal* is research-orientated and contains articles on all Liberty Seated coinage denominations, from half dimes to trade dollars. You can preview sample articles online at https://nnp.wustl.edu/library/publisherdetail/2096

The Club also publishes *The E-Gobrecht*, a monthly email-based publication, distributed to club members and interested non-members at no cost. The *E-Gobrecht* contains information of a timely nature, such as recent auction sales, LSCC regional meeting or event announcements, and feature articles on new variety discoveries. You can download all back issues of *The E-Gobrecht* from the LSCC website's "E-Gobrecht Archives" page.

At the time of this publication, Liberty Seated Collectors Club membership dues are $30 per year—a bargain, considering the amount of resources available. If you join the LSCC, you will be connecting with the most serious and knowledgeable collectors and dealers in the hobby. For membership information, visit www.lsccweb.org, or write to

Liberty Seated Collectors Club
Leonard Augsburger, President
Email: leonard.augsburger@wustl.edu

Liberty Seated Quarters Removed From the Fifth Edition, Volume II

Date, Variety	Fivaz-Stanton number	PUP
1843-O, Repunched Date	FS-25-1843o-301	Date
1876, Misplaced Date	FS-25-1876-301	Denticles

Note: Varieties removed are still considered *Cherrypickers' Guide* varieties (as opposed to being "delisted"); for example, they will continue to be cross-referenced and summarized in appendix H. (Exceptions include varieties debunked as counterfeits, or those which later research revealed to be erroneously classified. Those will be delisted completely).

New Liberty Seated Quarters in the Sixth Edition, Volume II

Date, Variety	Fivaz-Stanton number	PUP
1855, Doubled Die Obverse	FS-25-1855-101	Shield
1856, Mark in Shield	FS-25-1856-401	Shield
1857-O, Misplaced Date	FS-25-1857o-302	Date
1858, Multi-Denominational Clash	FS-25-1858-901	Lip
1861, Doubled-Die Obverse	FS-25-1861-101	Shield lines, LIBERTY
1861, Type 1 Reverse	FS-25-1861-901	Eye, Claws
1863, Repunched Date	FS-25-1863-301	Date
1872, Misplaced Date	FS-25-1872-302	Denticles
1872, Wavy Lines	FS-25-1872-401	Denticles
1876, Misplaced Date	FS-25-1876-306	Denticles
1876, Misplaced Date	FS-25-1876-307	Denticles
1876-CC, Doubled-Die Obverse	FS-25-1876CC-101	Shield

Don't get hung up on just the die varieties listed in this book. There are many nice, yet-to-be-discovered treasures out there waiting for you to cherrypick!

If you can't discern a variety with a 7x loupe, it probably isn't significant enough to earn the attention of other collectors.

Values provided in this book for die varieties are for raw (unslabbed) coins. Varieties correctly attributed, certified, and graded by a third-party grading service may *command higher premiums—but not necessarily. Ultimately, the marketplace of collectors determines a variety's value.*

1840-O, With Drapery

FS-25-1840o-501

VARIETY: Large O Mintmark
BRIGGS: REV. A
PUP: Mintmark
URS-7 · I-4 · L-4

Description: The O mintmark is 20 percent larger than that of its sister, the Small O, a difference visible to the naked eye.

Comments: Only one obverse and one reverse were paired for this variety, one of the rarest in its series. It was made when a No Drapery reverse die was held over at the New Orleans Mint and used until the Small O die arrived. In a later die state, the Large O die was reheated and recut, causing tiny spikes to protrude from each denticle. The reeding indicates four strikings of this die: doubled reeding is found in three different positions (with no reed slippage), and a fourth has no reed doubling. About 45 pieces exist, all in Fair-2 to VF-20, with most AG to VG. One scuffy Mint State piece is known, from the 1982 French Quarter–Meridian Hotel excavation.

	G-4	VG-8	F-12	VF-20	EF-40	AU-50
VARIETY	$1,500	$1,750	$2,250	$3,000	$4,250	$7,500
NORMAL	$45	$75	$115	$215	$450	$700

1841-O

FS-25-1841o-101

VARIETY: Doubled-Die Obverse
BRIGGS: OBV. 2
PUP: Shield, stars
URS-10 · I-4 · L-3

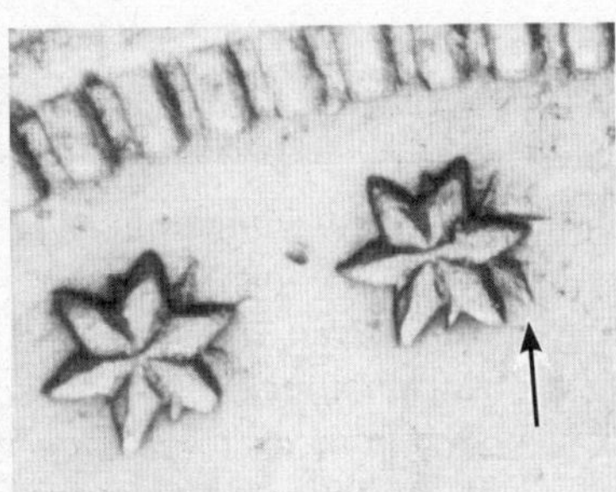

Description: Major doubling is evident on the shield, the first three stars on the left, the ribbon, the rock, and the gown.

Comments: Prior to 1982 this was a very rare coin. However, during the 1982 New Orleans–Meridian Hotel excavation, more than 500 pieces of this variety were among the hoard of coins discovered. Today it's readily available to collectors who want one! Choice, original, circulated pieces are still rare.

	VG-8	F-12	VF-20	EF-40	AU-50	MS-60	MS-63
VARIETY	$70	$100	$275	$425	$625	$1,000	$2,500
NORMAL	$65	$90	$165	$350	$425	$950	$2,000

1843-O — FS-25-1843o-501

Variety: Large O Mintmark **Briggs: Rev. F**
PUP: Mintmark
URS-8 · I-4 · L-3

Description: A larger-than-normal-sized O mintmark is virtually embedded in the juncture of the arrow and the stem.

Comments: A half dollar mintmark punch may have been used for this quarter dollar die. This very rare variety is usually found in grades AG to VG. Approximately 100 pieces are known, in all grades, with rarity escalating as the grade increases. Examples are peppered with rust lumps and pitting on the reverse, indicating this die sat around for quite a while before being used. The same reverse die was once again put into use on some 1844-O coins—they, too, are rare!

	G-4	VG-8	F-12	VF-20	EF-40	AU-50
Variety	$300	$475	$675	$1,250	$3,000	$6,000
Normal	$60	$85	$165	$400	$1,000	$1,750

1845 — FS-25-1845-301

Variety: Repunched Date **Briggs: Obv. 3**
PUP: Date
URS-9 · I-4 · L-3

Description: The primary 5 was punched over a smaller secondary 5, evident north.

Comments: A secondary 8 and 4 can be seen north on higher-grade specimens. These digits also appear smaller, supporting our theory that the initial date punch was likely intended for a half dime or dime. The Large 5 Over Small 5 is always visible, even on About Good coins.

	G-4	VG-8	F-12	VF-20	EF-40	AU-50
Variety	$45	$60	$85	$145	$210	$375
Normal	$40	$50	$75	$80	$165	$250

1847 FS-25-1847-301

VARIETY: Misplaced Date **BRIGGS: OBV. 3**

PUP: Rock area below shield tip and above 8

URS-8 · I-3 · L-3

Description: The lower portion of a numeral 8 is evident protruding from the rock above the primary 8.

Comments: This obverse is paired with three different reverses! All seemingly are scarce. The first twenty years of Liberty Seated coinage is a haven for misplaced dates, repunched dates, and overmintmarks; be on the lookout.

	G-4	VG-8	F-12	VF-20	EF-40	AU-50
VARIETY	$48	$65	$90	$165	$240	$400
NORMAL	$40	$60	$75	$95	$160	$275

1847 FS-25-1847-302 / 801

VARIETY: Doubled-Die Reverse, Repunched Date **BRIGGS: OBV. 2, REV. A**

PUP: Lettering

URS-8 · I-4 · L-3

Description: Nice doubling is visible on all of the lower half of the reverse design and lettering. The date shows repunching on the 47.

Comments: This reverse is paired with two different obverses: the Plain Date and this 7 Over 7, punched left. The variety shown here is far scarcer than its sister, the Plain Date / Doubled-Die Reverse. QUAR in QUARTER shows the strongest doubling.

	G-4	VG-8	F-12	VF-20	EF-40	AU-50	MS-60
VARIETY	$55	$75	$105	$195	$300	$475	$1,000
NORMAL	$50	$65	$75	$95	$160	$275	$750

1850 — FS-25-1850-301

Variety: Misplaced Digit — **Briggs: Obv. 1**
PUP: Denticles below date
URS-9 · I-4 · L-3

Description: The base of an extra 1 is punched on the rim below the 1 of the primary date.

Comments: The normal 1850 quarter is scarce; this variety is very scarce. The displaced 1 is barely visible on coins graded Fine and cannot be seen on lower grades. This variety shows up on approximately one out of every five 1850 quarters. Many coins of this date were melted, a factor that compounds the rarity.

	F-12	VF-20	EF-40	AU-50	MS-60
Variety	$165	$275	$425	$750	$1,875
Normal	$135	$225	$400	$650	$1,865

1853, No Arrows — FS-25-1853-301

Variety: Repunched Date — **Briggs: Obv. 1**
PUP: Date
URS-8 · I-5 · L-4

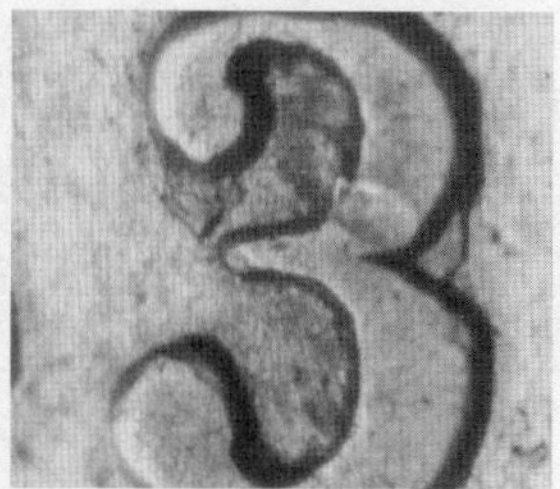

Description: The repunched date is visible at all grades, with light recutting on the 5 and major recutting on the 3.

Comments: The entire mintage of this coin features the repunched date. The coin was produced from one obverse and one reverse die. Old-time references refer to this variety as a 3 Over 2. Beware of any tooling on the last digit of the date, as many forgeries are tooled from 1858 coins. If the 3 doesn't show major recutting, especially at its top, the coin probably isn't genuine. Most of the original mintage was melted, as four pieces had a melt value of $1.10. The coin is very rare in all grades.

	G-4	VG-8	F-12	VF-20	EF-40	AU-50	MS-60
Variety	$1,250	$1,750	$2,750	$3,750	$4,750	$6,000	$7,500
Normal	$1,250	$1,750	$2,750	$3,750	$4,750	$6,000	$7,500

1853, Arrows and Rays

FS-25-1853-1301

VARIETY: Overdate **BRIGGS: OBV. 1**

PUP: Date and right arrow shaft

URS-9 · I-4 · L-3

RB

Description: In early die states, the year numerals 1853 are repunched over 854 and the right arrow is repunched.

Comments: This is a scarce variety in all grades, but it is not rare, and it still can be cherrypicked with diligence and some luck. In early die states, the overdate is quite clear, along with the repunching visible on the right arrow shaft. In later die states, the 85 over 85 fades, but the 3 over 4 and arrow shaft are still clear. The original discovery coin was About Uncirculated and brought $3,000 in 1980. The overdate can be seen in all grades, including About Good. (Note: This was erroneously listed as FS-25-1853-301 in the fifth edition.)

	G-4	VG-8	F-12	VF-20	EF-40	AU-50	MS-60
VARIETY	$50	$85	$150	$230	$425	$650	$1,500
NORMAL	$35	$40	$50	$60	$200	$350	$1,000

1853-O, Arrows and Rays

FS-25-1853o-501

VARIETY: Repunched Mintmark **BRIGGS: N/L**

PUP: Mintmark

URS-6 · I-4 · L-4

Description: When this coin's mintmark was repunched in the die, the O was struck over a horizontal O.

Comments: This is a very rare variety in all grades. It was discovered by Harry Smith and Larry Briggs in September 1993. Fewer than fifty pieces are known, none of them Uncirculated.

	G-4	VG-8	F-12	VF-20	EF-40	AU-50
VARIETY	$125	$175	$300	$525	$1,200	$3,000
NORMAL	$35	$40	$50	$60	$200	$350

1854-O, Arrows — FS-25-1854o-501

Variety: Huge O Mintmark — **Briggs: Rev. A**
PUP: Mintmark
URS-9 · I-4 · L-4

Description: The O mintmark is very thick and irregularly shaped. It was hand-carved and redone at the New Orleans Mint.

Comments: The mintmark is so large and irregular that this die, when striking the coin, "sucked" the metal away from UAR in QUARTER, the D of DOLLAR, and the tip of the stem above the mintmark. Stress is also evident in die cracks on top of QUAR and the denticles below these letters, especially along the rim. Two hoards are known to exist, one of about 145 pieces, the other of about 82. Only one true Uncirculated is known to exist; it was purchased as a type coin at the Indiana State Convention in 1974, then sold intact in a complete set to an Omaha collector and is now lost through decades of time. Most examples exist in AG to VG. EF coins are very rare, and AU coins are extremely rare.

	G-4	VG-8	F-12	VF-20	EF-40	AU-50
Variety	$750	$1,200	$1,700	$2,750	$4,500	$9,500
Normal	$50	$55	$65	$100	$125	$350

1855 — FS-25-1855-101

Variety: Doubled-Die Obverse — **Briggs: N/L; CONECA: N/L**
PUP: Shield
URS-6 · I-5 · L-4

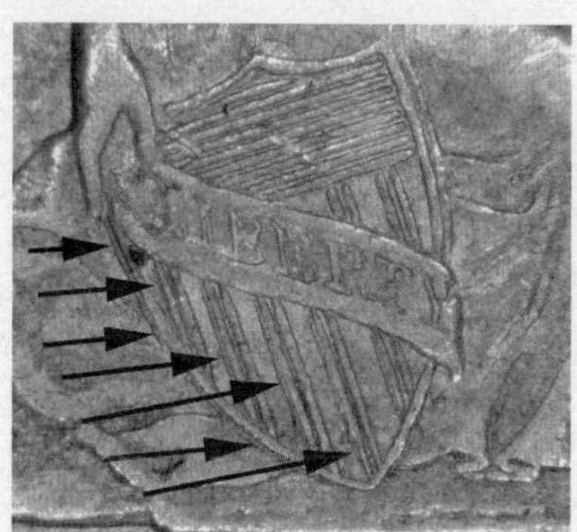

Description: There is very nice doubling on the obverse shield and LIBERTY.

Comments: This variety was discovered by Larry Briggs after his encyclopedia was published in 1996. It's a nice doubled die and a welcome addition for the Liberty Seated die-variety specialist. (An interesting side note: similar doubled dies exist on 1855 half dimes and 1855 dimes.)

	VG-8	F-12	VF-20	EF-40	AU-50	AU-55
Variety	$75	$125	$275	$425	$625	$975
Normal	$40	$45	$50	$125	$275	$300

1856 — FS-25-1856-301

VARIETY: Misplaced Digit — **BRIGGS: N/L**

PUP: Gown right of Y in LIBERTY

URS-7 · I-4 · L-3

Description: The top left and bottom of a numeral 1 is evident in the gown immediately right of the Y in LIBERTY. The top curve of a 6 is visible protruding from the rock below the foot.

Comments: This is a very scarce variety that, with perseverance, can be cherrypicked. There are few sales reported, but those validated are shown below in the "Variety" row.

	F-12	VF-20	EF-40	AU-50	MS-60	MS-63
VARIETY	n/a	$250	$350	$500	n/a	n/a
NORMAL	$45	$50	$85	$200	$350	$650

1856 — FS-25-1856-401

VARIETY: Mark in Shield — **BRIGGS: N/L; CONECA: N/L**

PUP: Shield

URS-5 · I-5 · L-4

Description: What appears as a possible top curvature on a 5 diagonally in the obverse shield.

Comments: Whether this anomaly is a serif or a curve of another digit, or just a die gouge—it's very interesting and very scarce. The variety was discovered in 2009 and it shows that new finds are still out there to be found.

	VG-8	F-12	VF-20	EF-40	AU-50	AU-55
VARIETY	n/a	n/a	$250	n/a	n/a	n/a
NORMAL	$40	$45	$50	$85	$200	$245

1856-S, S Over Small S — FS-25-1856S-501

VARIETY: Repunched Mintmark — **BRIGGS:** REV. E; **CONECA:** RPM-001
PUP: Mintmark
URS-8 · I-4 · L-4

Description: A larger S mintmark is punched over a much smaller S mintmark. The smaller S mintmark was probably intended for a dime.

Comments: This is by far the most desirable mintmark variety in the Liberty Seated quarter dollar series.

	VG-8	F-12	VF-20	EF-40	AU-50
VARIETY	$1,250	$1,750	$2,500	$6,000	$9,500
NORMAL	$575	$750	$850	$2,000	$3,750

1857 — FS-25-1857-401

VARIETY: Die Gouge — **BRIGGS:** N/L
PUP: Liberty's fingers and LIBERTY
URS-7 · I-3 · L-3

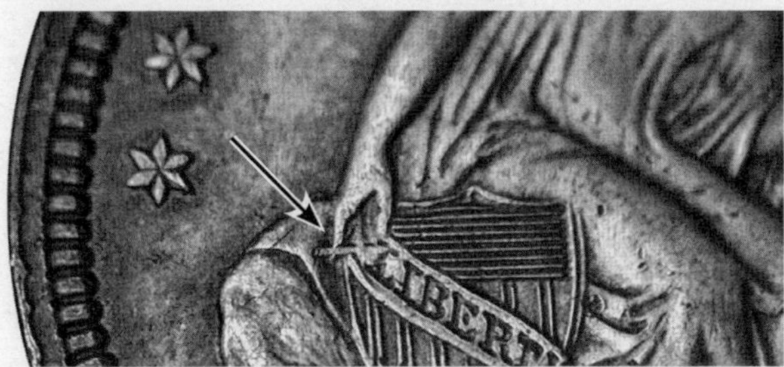

Description: A die gouge creates the appearance that Miss Liberty is holding a cigar or cigarette.

Comments: This variety is affectionately known among specialists as the "Smoking Liberty." It is very scarce but still can be cherrypicked with a little vim and vigor. Saverio Barbieri amassed a small hoard of 28 pieces over a period of eight years, starting in 2000. In 2009, he had Dominion Grading Service grade 26 of them, attribute them as "Smoking Liberty," and designate them as being from the "Barbieri Cache." "Variety" prices in the chart here are from verified sales.

	F-12	VF-20	EF-40	AU-50	MS-60	MS-63
VARIETY	n/a	$200	$325	$400	n/a	n/a
NORMAL	$45	$50	$85	$200	$375	$650

1857 — FS-25-1857-901

Variety: Multi-Denominational Clash — **Briggs: Rev. F**
PUP: Reverse at eagle's neck
URS-7 · I-5 · L-4

Description: The reverse of this 1857 Large Date quarter clashed with the reverse die of an 1857 Flying Eagle cent. Images of the cent reverse die are easily seen on either side of the eagle's neck, within the shield, and below the eagle's left (viewer's right) wing.

Comments: Refer also to the 1857 Flying Eagle cent with muled clashed dies, in the Cherrypickers' Guide, volume I. The 1857 is a common date, but this die variety is quite rare—more so than its sister, the 1857 Flying Eagle cent clashed with a Liberty Seated quarter reverse.

	VG-8	F-12	VF-20	EF-40	AU-50	MS-60	MS-63
Variety	$225	$325	$475	$850	$2,100	n/a	n/a
Normal	$40	$45	$50	$85	$200	$375	$650

1857-O — FS-25-1857o-301

Variety: Misplaced Digit — **Briggs: Obv. 7**
PUP: Denticles below date
URS-4 · I-4 · L-4

Description: The upper portion of a numeral 8 is evident protruding from the denticles below the right side of the primary 8.

Comments: In the fifth edition of the *Cherrypickers' Guide*, this variety was erroneously reported as not having been included in Larry Briggs's book on Liberty Seated quarters. After the 1990 publication of the discovery coin, only three specimens have come to light. After 30-plus years, only one verified sale has been recorded. It is listed below.

	F-12	VF-20	EF-40	AU-50	MS-60
Variety	n/a	n/a	$575	n/a	n/a
Normal	$100	$165	$300	$500	$1,300

1857-O

FS-25-1857o-302

VARIETY: Misplaced Date
PUP: Date
URS-1 · I-4 · L-3

CONECA: N/L
BRIGGS: 9-B

Description: The curve from the top of another 8 connects the bottom right loop of the 8 with the ball of the 5.

Comments: As of press time, this variety is unique! It was discovered in 2014, and to date no others are known. This listing will give variety collectors enlightenment and perhaps more will surface in the future.

	VG-8	F-12	VF-20	EF-40	AU-50	MS-60
VARIETY	n/a	n/a	n/a	n/a	n/a	n/a
NORMAL	$65	$100	$165	$300	$500	$1,300

1858

FS-25-1858-901

VARIETY: Reverse Die Clashed with Reverse of Flying Eagle Cent
PUP: Shield
URS-3 · I-5 · L-5

CONECA: N/L

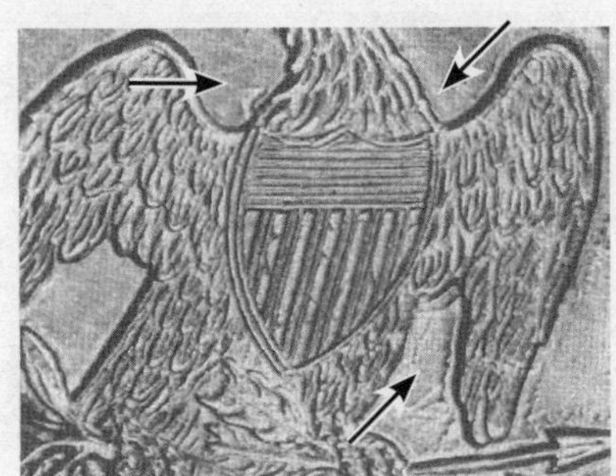

Description: This is a newly discovered clashed reverse die on an 1858 Liberty Seated quarter that is clashed with the reverse die of a Flying Eagle cent.

Comments: This variety appears to be very scarce or rare and few have turned up to date. Discovered in April of 2017 by Steve Feltner, no reported or verified sales have come to light. This exposure should allow more specimens to be found and it could be your lucky day. Clashing should be visible on virtually all grades VG and up.

	VG-8	F-12	VF-20	EF-40	AU-50
VARIETY	n/a	n/a	n/a	n/a	n/a
NORMAL	$40	$45	$50	$85	$200

1861 — FS-25-1861-101

VARIETY: Doubled-Die Obverse **BRIGGS: N/L; CONECA: N/L**
PUP: Obverse shield lines and LIBERTY
URS-5 · I-5 · L-5

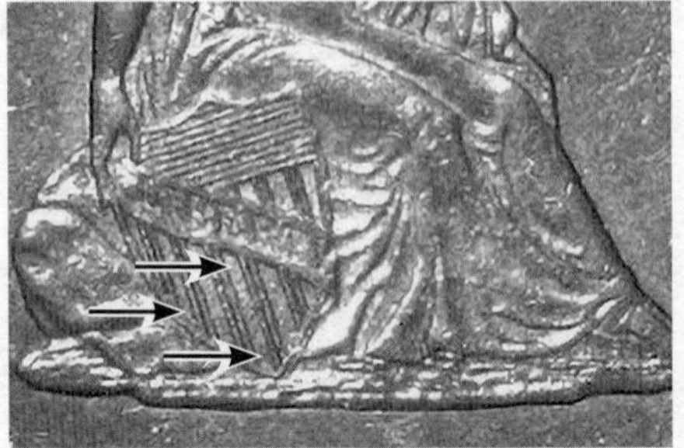

Description: There is a very nice doubling on the obverse shield's horizontal and vertical lines. There is also nice doubling on the shield outline, as well as LIBERTY.

Comments: This is a very rare variety that until now has had little publicity. One of only six verified doubled dies for the entire series, and one of the nicer examples, it was discovered by Larry Briggs in 1995. Ten pieces have been verified since that time. The normal 1861 quarter is a common date, making it affordable to cherrypick this rare variety.

	VG-8	F-12	VF-20	EF-40	AU-50	AU-55
VARIETY	n/a	n/a	$325	n/a	n/a	n/a
NORMAL	$45	$50	$65	$100	$200	$245

1861 — FS-25-1861-901

VARIETY: Type 1 Reverse **CONECA: N/L**
PUP: Eye, Claws
URS-7 · I-4 · L-3

Concave eye of Type 1 reverse.

Closed claw of Type 1 reverse.

Description: This coin has a Type 1 reverse with a concave eye and closed claws.

Comments: This variety has been very rare, in terms of locating, in any grade. It is easily discerned because of its concave eye and closed claws and must have had a short die run, creating its rarity. Two obverse dies were mated with one reverse die. It is rare in all grades and the finest-seen AU-50!

	G-4	VG-8	F-12	VF-20	EF-40	AU-50
VARIETY	$75	$125	$175	$250	$375	$525
NORMAL	$35	$45	$50	$65	$100	$200

1863 — FS-25-1863-301

VARIETY: Repunched Date — **CONECA: N/L**

PUP: Date

URS-4 · I-4 · L-4

Description: This is a nice repunching on the base of the 1 of the date. Although not major by some standards, it is actually impressive, as very few repunched dates exist on the Seated Civil War quarters.

Comments: This is a rare variety on an already scarce date Seated quarter. It was unknown at the time of printing for the *Comprehensive Encyclopedia of United States Liberty Seated Quarters* by Larry Briggs and Harry Smith, but was soon discovered by the former in 1992. Since the discovery of this variety, only three other specimens have come to light. Listed prices are for actual variety sales.

	VG-8	F-12	VF-20	EF-40	AU-50
VARIETY	n/a	n/a	$525	n/a	$875
NORMAL	$85	$115	$275	$500	$700

1872 — FS-25-1872-301

VARIETY: Repunched Date — **BRIGGS: N/L**

PUP: Date

URS-7 · I-3 · L-3

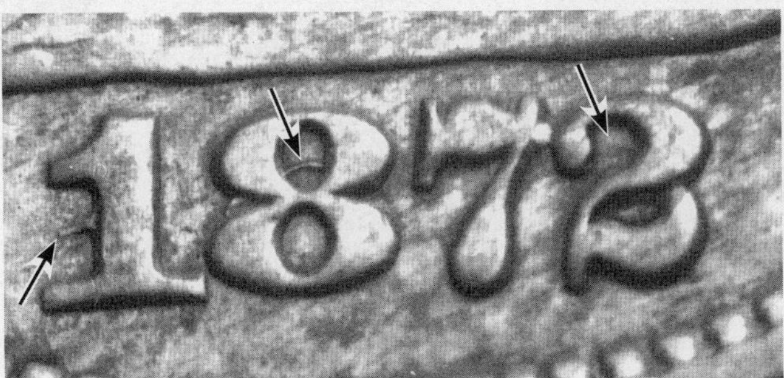

Description: The digits are repunched, with the secondary images south of the primary. Once the coin is examined, the secondary 7 is not noticeable, but the 1, 8, and 2 all are dramatic.

Comments: The variety was discovered after publication of Briggs's *Comprehensive Encyclopedia of United States Liberty Seated Quarters*. The normal coin is a scarce date to begin with, as many were melted in 1873 for their higher-than-face silver value. When found as a date, this affords a great opportunity to have an additional variety designation attached.

	F-12	VF-20	EF-40	AU-50	MS-60
VARIETY	$175	$275	$475	$625	$1,450
NORMAL	$170	$250	$400	$600	$1,250

1872 FS-25-1872-302

VARIETY: Misplaced Date **BRIGGS: 4-D; CONECA: N/A**
PUP: Denticles below date
URS-6 · I-5 · L-5

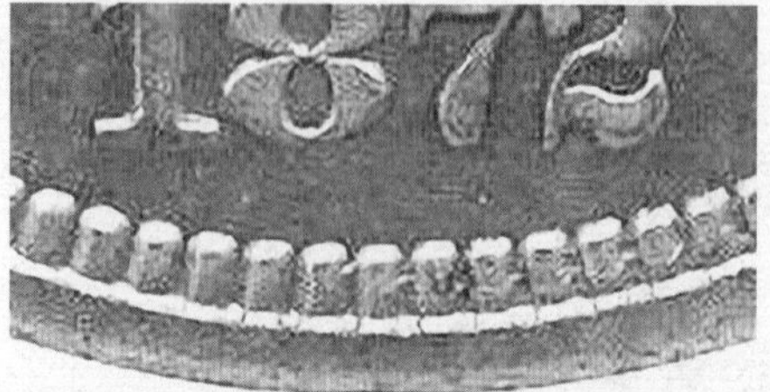

Description: This is a very nice misplaced date, visible in the denticles below the 87 of the date.

Comments: This coin is much rarer than the Liberty Seated quarter dollar census showed over the years. The reason is confusion with FS-25-1872-401 (see the next entry). As of 2023, 15 to 20 pieces have been truly confirmed for this variety. To make this and the following variety even scarcer, many of this date were melted in 1873 because they were worth more as silver than their face value.

	VG-8	F-12	VF-20	EF-40	AU-50
VARIETY	n/a	$250	$375	$525	n/a
NORMAL	$100	$170	$250	$400	$600

1872 FS-25-1872-401

VARIETY: Wavy Lines Through Denticles **BRIGGS: N/L; CONECA: N/L**
PUP: Denticles below date
URS-5 · I-5 · L-5

Description: A "squiggly line" appears in the denticles below the date.

Comments: This very scarce variety is shown here for comparison of the previous 1872 misplaced date variety. Every time the Liberty Seated Collectors Club has done a quarter dollar census, this variety has been declared a misplaced date—but it is not. No one has any idea what it truly is or what caused it. Prices shown below are derived from confirmed sales.

	VG-8	F-12	VF-20	EF-40	AU-50
VARIETY	n/a	$200	$300	n/a	$650
NORMAL	$100	$170	$250	$400	$600

1875 — FS-25-1875-301

Variety: Misplaced Date **Briggs: N/L**
PUP: Denticles below date
URS-7 · I-3 · L-3

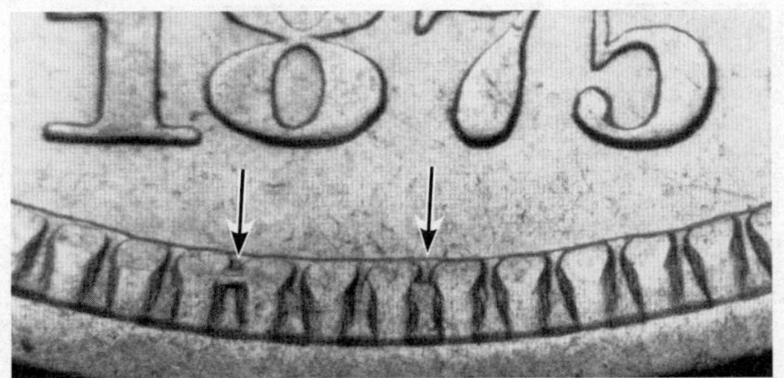

Description: The upper portion of numerals 8 and 7 can be seen within the denticles below the primary date.

Comments: This is another variety discovered after publication of the Briggs *Comprehensive Encyclopedia of United States Liberty Seated Quarters*—a very scarce variety that, with determination, can still be cherrypicked. This is a Type 2 reverse. (In Type 1, the letters TAT of STATES touch each other. In Type 2, they are separated.)

	F-12	VF-20	EF-40	AU-50	MS-60	MS-63
Variety	$65	$125	$175	$250	$375	n/a
Normal	$45	$50	$75	$160	$275	$550

1876 — FS-25-1876-302

Variety: Repunched/Misplaced Date **Briggs: N/L**
PUP: Date
URS-3 · I-4 · L-4

Description: The "flag" of a secondary numeral 1 is evident south and west of the primary 1, and a third 1 is south and west of the primary 8.

Comments: Although not known to be included in the Briggs encyclopedia, this variety was discovered by Larry Briggs in 1996. It appears to be quite rare, as only three pieces have been verified in addition to the original discovery coin. This is a Type 2 reverse. (In Type 1, the letters TAT of STATES touch each other. In Type 2, they are separated.)

	F-12	VF-20	EF-40	AU-50	MS-60	MS-63
Variety	n/a	$250	$350	$450	$650	n/a
Normal	$45	$50	$75	$160	$300	$550

1876 FS-25-1876-303

Variety: Misplaced Date **Briggs: N/L**
PUP: Rock above 87 in date
URS-6 · I-3 · L-3

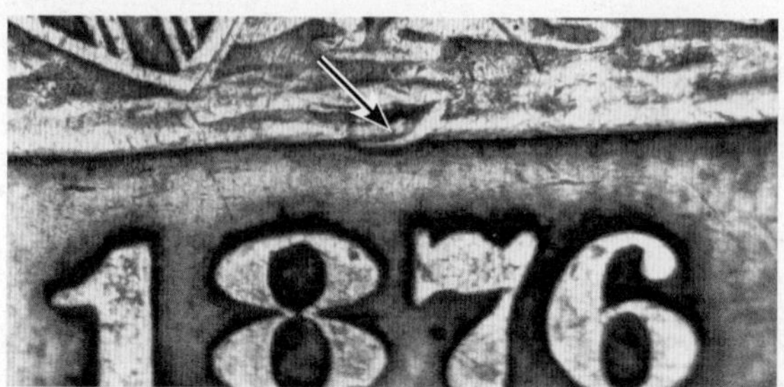

Description: The base of a numeral (likely a 6) is evident protruding from the rock above the date, between the 8 and the 7.

Comments: This is a very scarce variety, with just a few examples found since its discovery. With the abundance of varieties for 1876, specialists have concluded a novice was employed that year at the Mint, someone of little expertise—making for a cherrypicker's delight. Always check the rock and skirt on Liberty Seated coins. This is a Type 2 reverse. (In Type 1, the letters TAT of STATES touch each other. In Type 2, they are separated.)

	F-12	VF-20	EF-40	AU-50	MS-60	MS-63
Variety	$65	$95	$135	$375	$425	n/a
Normal	$45	$50	$75	$160	$300	$550

1876 FS-25-1876-304

Variety: Repunched Date **Briggs: Obv. 6**
PUP: Date
URS-8 · I-3 · L-3

Description: Repunching is evident as a triple-punched numeral 6, seen within the loop of the 6, and very slightly north on the base of the 1.

Comments: This is a very scarce variety that can still be cherrypicked if you're willing to look long and hard. You should always check all elements on the obverse and reverse of all Liberty Seated coins. This is a Type 2 reverse. (In Type 1, the letters TAT of STATES touch each other. In Type 2, they are separated.)

	F-12	VF-20	EF-40	AU-50	MS-60	MS-63
Variety	$65	$110	$165	$225	$375	n/a
Normal	$45	$50	$75	$160	$300	$550

1876 FS-25-1876-305

VARIETY: Misplaced Date **BRIGGS: OBV. 2**
PUP: Denticles Below Date
URS-7 · I-3 · L-3

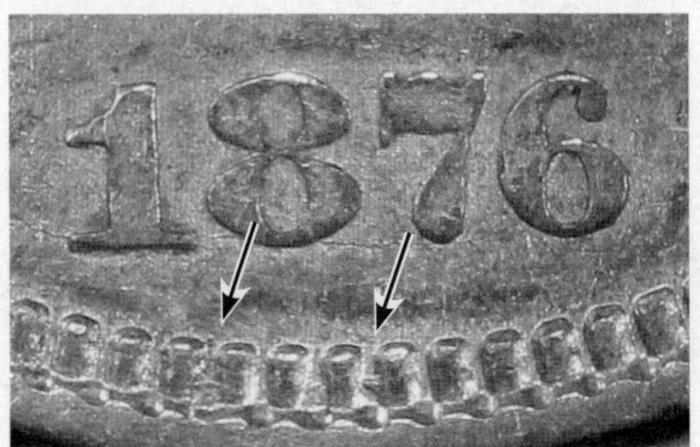

Description: The tops of a 1 and an 8 are evident in the denticles below the date.

Comments: This is another of several misplaced dates for this year. There is an amazing abundance of engraved errors for the 1876 Philadelphia, San Francisco, and Carson City quarters. No single year has more errors to offer in the entire series than 1876. This is a Type 2 reverse. (In Type 1, the letters TAT of STATES touch each other. In Type 2, they are separated.)

	F-12	VF-20	EF-40	AU-50	MS-60	MS-63
VARIETY	$75	$110	$150	$300	$475	n/a
NORMAL	$45	$50	$75	$160	$300	$550

1876 FS-25-1876-306

VARIETY: Misplaced Date **BRIGGS: N/L; CONECA: N/L**
PUP: Denticles below date
URS-6 · I-4 · L-4

Description: A digit is in the denticles below the 7 of the date.

Comments: For whatever reason, several very nice misplaced dates appear in this year. With the normal 1876 being a common-date coin, the collector or cherrypicker has an inexpensive opportunity to find this and other misplaced dates. This variety is a recent discovery, and its market pricing is still being established. This is a Type 2 reverse. (In Type 1, the letters TAT of STATES touch each other. In Type 2, they are separated.)

	VG-8	F-12	VF-20	EF-40	AU-50	AU-55
VARIETY	n/a	n/a	n/a	n/a	n/a	n/a
NORMAL	$40	$45	$50	$75	$160	$165

1876 — FS-25-1876-307

VARIETY: Misplaced Date — **BRIGGS:** N/L; **CONECA:** N/L
PUP: Dentils below date
URS-5 · I-4 · L-4

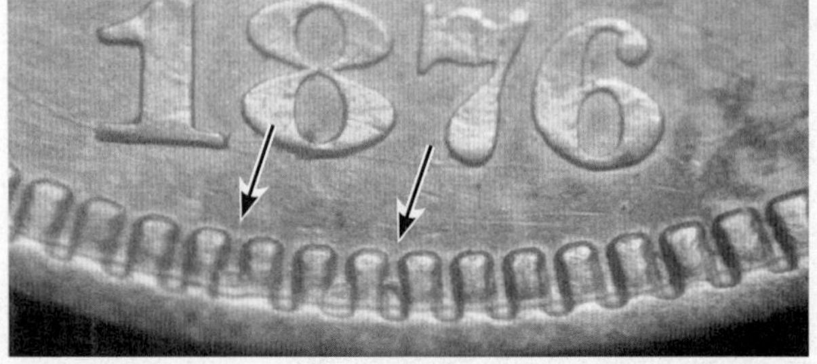

Description: There is a sharp misplaced date in the dentils below and between the 1 and the 8 of the date. Additionally, there is a possible second misplaced date under and below the right side of the 8 in the dentils.

Comments: This is a newly discovered and very sharp MPD in the dentils below the 1 and 8 of the date. A further digit appears also to the right of this sharp MPD. This is a very scarce variety on a very common date. With this exposure, surely more will be discovered.

	G-4	VG-8	F-12	VF-20	EF-40	AU-50
VARIETY	n/a	n/a	n/a	n/a	n/a	n/a
NORMAL	$35	$40	$45	$50	$75	$160

1876-S — FS-25-1876S-301

VARIETY: Misplaced Date — **BRIGGS:** N/L
PUP: Denticles below date
URS-7 · I-3 · L-3

Description: The tops of a 7 and a 6 can be seen in the denticles below the date.

Comments: While scarce, this variety can be cherrypicked with some effort. This is a Type 2 reverse. (In Type 1, the letters TAT of STATES touch each other. In Type 2, they are separated.)

	F-12	VF-20	EF-40	AU-50	MS-60	MS-63
VARIETY	$60	$75	$115	$225	$350	n/a
NORMAL	$45	$50	$75	$160	$275	$550

1876-S FS-25-1876S-302

Variety: Misplaced Date **Briggs: N/L**
PUP: Denticles below date
URS-7 · I-3 · L-3

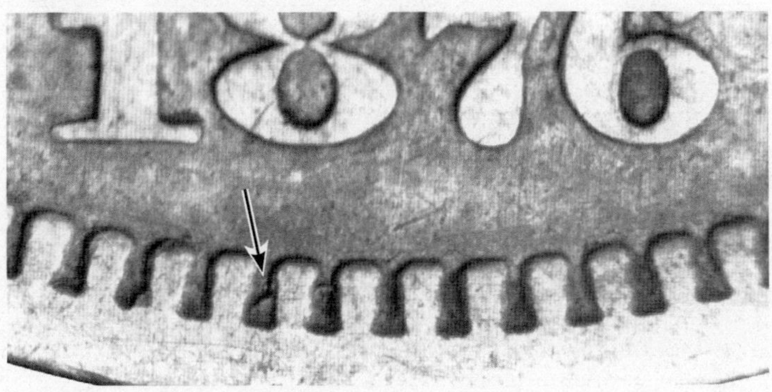

Description: The tops of two 8's are evident below the primary 8.

Comments: This variety is scarce, but it can be cherrypicked if you have time and patience. This is a Type 2 reverse. (In Type 1, the letters TAT of STATES touch each other. In Type 2, they are separated.)

	F-12	VF-20	EF-40	AU-50	MS-60	MS-63
Variety	$60	$75	$115	$225	$350	n/a
Normal	$45	$50	$75	$160	$275	$550

1876-CC FS-25-1876CC-101

Variety: Doubled-Die Obverse **Briggs: 13-L; CONECA: N/L**
PUP: Shield (LIBERTY)
URS-5 · I-5 · L-5

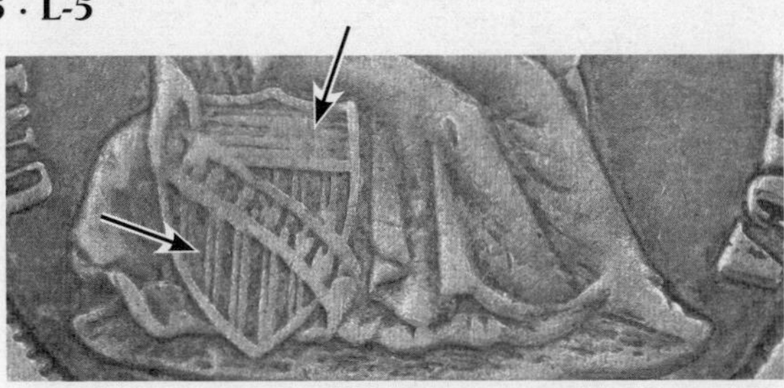

Description: There is a nice doubling on the obverse shield's vertical and horizontal lines, as well as LIBERTY. This variety has a large CC and a finely reeded edge.

Comments: This is one of the few doubled dies in the Liberty Seated quarter series—a very scarce variety on a fairly common coin, and one that can be cherrypicked with effort. Doubling can be seen even in low-grade pieces. Many times, an 1876-CC quarter will show most or all of LIBERTY and the obverse shield, while the reverse grades only AG, or worse. This is a Type 2 reverse. (In Type 1, the letters TAT of STATES touch each other. In Type 2, they are separated.) This obverse may be found with two reverses.

	VG-8	F-12	VF-20	EF-40	AU-50	AU-55
Variety	$225	n/a	$350	$500	n/a	n/a
Normal	$100	$125	$150	$225	$350	$425

1876-CC FS-25-1876CC-301

Variety: Repunched Date **Briggs: Obv. 1**
PUP: Date
URS-6 · I-3 · L-2

Description: Secondary digits for the 1, 8, and 7 are evident south of the primary digits. The secondary digits are very close to the primary.

Comments: In the fifth edition of the *Cherrypickers' Guide,* this variety was erroneously reported as unlisted in Briggs's encyclopedia (it is actually listed as Obverse 1). The reverse, a Type 1, was the exact die used on the rarest Liberty Seated quarter, the 1873-CC No Arrows. This is a very scarce variety, but it can be cherrypicked.

	F-12	VF-20	EF-40	AU-50	MS-60	MS-63
Variety	$135	$175	$275	$400	$600	$1,100
Normal	$125	$150	$225	$350	$590	$990

1877-CC FS-25-1877CC-301

Variety: Repunched Date **Briggs: Obv. 2**
PUP: Date
URS-8 · I-4 · L-3

Description: The two 7's of the date are strongly repunched south. The variety has a large CC mintmark.

Comments: This variety is very close to Briggs Obverse 1. The slight difference is in the date position. The 1 of the date shows slight recutting on the base, south. This is a Type 2 reverse. (In Type 1, the letters TAT of STATES touch each other. In Type 2, they are separated.)

	F-12	VF-20	EF-40	AU-50	MS-60	MS-63
Variety	$150	$200	$300	$435	$675	$1,150
Normal	$120	$150	$225	$325	$600	$1,140

1877-S, S Over Horizontal S — FS-25-1877S-501

Variety: Repunched Mintmark **Briggs: Reverse D; CONECA: RPM-001**
PUP: Mintmark
URS-8 · I-4 · L-4

Description: The initial S mintmark was punched into the die horizontally, then corrected with an upright S mintmark.

Comments: This is one of the most collectible mintmark varieties in the Liberty Seated quarter series, of longstanding fame—cherrypicked back to the 1950s. A small hoard of seven Mint State coins surfaced at the Indiana State Show in 1977; they were quickly dispersed among dealers at the show.

	F-12	VF-20	EF-40	AU-50	MS-60	MS-63
Variety	$95	$165	$250	$325	$475	$950
Normal	$45	$50	$75	$160	$275	$550

1891 — FS-25-1891-301

Variety: Misplaced Date
PUP: Denticles below date
URS-8 · I-4 · L-3

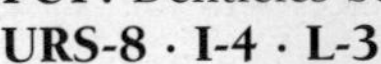

Description: The tops of an 8 and 9 are very evident protruding from the denticles below the primary date.

Comments: This is one of the more readily visible misplaced dates in the series—a very scarce and popular variety from the last year of the Liberty Seated quarter dollars.

	F-12	VF-20	EF-40	AU-50	MS-60	MS-63
Variety	$95	$150	$275	$375	$550	$925
Normal	$45	$50	$75	$160	$275	$550

Barber Quarters, 1892–1916

Some old-time collectors might still refer to the dimes, quarters, and half dollars that debuted in 1892 as *Liberty Head* types. But United States Mint chief engraver Charles E. Barber is so popularly connected to their designs that they're most widely known as "Barber coins."

For many years, the three coin series were neglected by collectors when it came to doubled dies, repunched mintmarks, overdates, and other die varieties. For many, the Barber quarter series was something of an afterthought in the search for nice varieties. This has changed in recent years, especially with the growth of the Barber Coin Collectors Society. Many new varieties are being discovered, reported, and cataloged, and are growing in popularity. We encourage close inspection of all Barber coins.

Only a small number of varieties were known in the Barber quarter series when the fourth edition of the *Cherrypickers' Guide* went to press. Collector interest was on the rise by the time the fifth edition was published in 2012. In this sixth edition, we have included more than a dozen Barber quarter entries. Some are already well established among collectors, and some are new and gaining interest. (The Barber dime section and, in volume III, the Barber half dollar section also have new listings.)

To obtain more knowledge on Barber coins in general, and Barber varieties in particular, we suggest seeking membership in the Barber Coin Collectors Society. Annual dues as of 2023 are only $20. Members receive four issues of the *Journal of the Barber Coin Collectors' Society*. The lively group attends more than twenty regional events every year, provides educational programs, exhibits at club tables, and encourages research, collecting, and networking. The BCCS website is at www.barbercoins.org, and President John Frost can be contacted by email at bccs@barbercoins.org.

Barber Quarters Removed From the Fifth Edition, Volume II

Date, Variety	Fivaz-Stanton number	PUP	Notes
1892, Repunched Date, Tripled-Die Obverse	FS-25-1892-301	Date, motto	Low collector interest
1892, Tripled-Die Reverse	FS-25-1892-801	Lettering	Low collector interest
1892-O, Doubled-Die Obverse	FS-25-1892o-101	Motto	Low collector interest

Note: Varieties removed are still considered *Cherrypickers' Guide* varieties (as opposed to being "delisted"); for example, they will continue to be cross-referenced and summarized in appendix H. (Exceptions include varieties debunked as counterfeits, or those which later research revealed to be erroneously classified. Those will be delisted completely.)

New Barber Quarters in the Sixth Edition, Volume II

Date, Variety	Fivaz-Stanton number	PUP
1909-S, Inverted Mintmark	FS-25-1909S-501	Mintmark

Reverse Types of 1892

Variety: Reverse Types

Description: There are two varieties of the 1892 Barber quarter reverse design, distinguished by the position of the eagle's wing tip relative to the E in UNITED. In Type 1, the wing covers only half of the E. In Type 2, the wing covers most of the E.

Description: 1892 quarters of Type 1 are somewhat scarcer than those of Type 2. However, the market has yet to make a significant distinction in their valuation. They may also be found on O-Mint coins.

1892 FS-25-1892-101

VARIETY: Doubled-Die Obverse **LAWRENCE-104**

PUP: Motto

URS-8 · I-2 · L-2

Description: Doubling is very evident on IN GOD WE TRUST.

Comments: The variety commands modest premiums. It is on the Type 2 reverse.

	VG-8	F-12	VF-20	EF-40	AU-50	MS-60	MS-63
VARIETY	$25	$35	$50	$95	$150	$265	$400
NORMAL	$15	$25	$45	$75	$135	$250	$375

1892-O FS-25-1892o-301

VARIETY: Repunched Date **LAWRENCE-102**

PUP: Date

URS-5 · I-4 · L-3

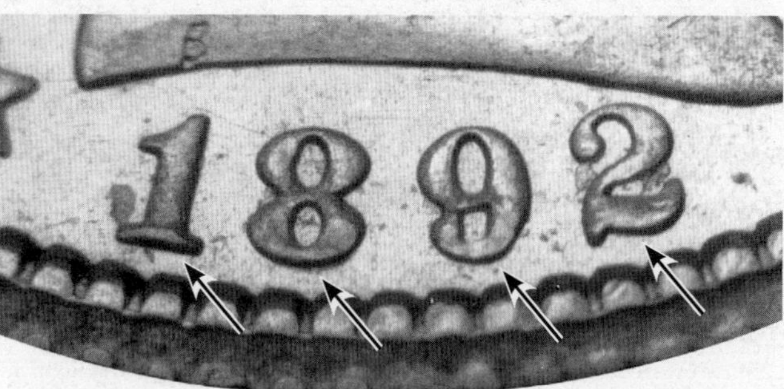

Description: Secondary digits are visible south on all numbers on the date, but most noticeable on the 2.

Comments: (*Note:* This variety was erroneously listed as FS-501 in the fourth edition.) This is a Type 2 reverse. Surprisingly, this coin has proven to be very elusive, to the point of being extremely rare. There are no verified sales and presently no specimens known for sale.

	VG-8	F-12	VF-20	EF-40	AU-50	MS-60	MS-63
VARIETY	n/a	n/a	n/a	n/a	n/a	n/a	n/a
NORMAL	$25	$50	$60	$100	$200	$350	$450

1892-O — FS-25-1892o-401 / 901

Variety: Clashed Dies, Covered E Reverse
PUP: Profile
URS-5 · I-4 · L-3

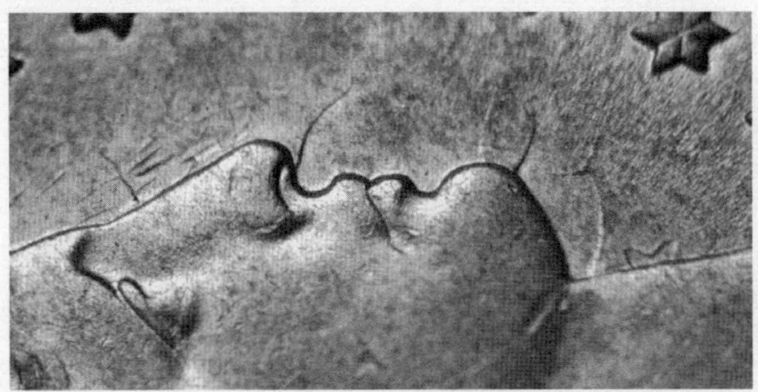

Description: This variety displays a strong clashed-die obverse and reverse (of Type 2). Stars transferred from the reverse die and jutting prominently from Miss Liberty's neck are the most visually dramatic aspect of this coin. Other obverse and reverse clash marks are evident.

Comments: First listed in the fifth edition, this variety has shown to be very elusive, despite the fact that its obverse clashing is so prominent. A leading factor confirming its rarity is the small number seen by the grading services. No verified sales could be confirmed.

	VG-8	F-12	VF-20	EF-40	AU-50	MS-60	MS-63
Variety	n/a	n/a	n/a	$200	n/a	n/a	n/a
Normal	$25	$50	$60	$100	$200	$350	$450

1892-S — FS-25-1892S-501

Variety: Repunched Mintmark — **Lawrence-101; CONECA: RPM-001**
PUP: Mintmark
URS-6 · I-4 · L-3

Description: A secondary S mintmark is evident northwest of the primary S.

Comments: Since its introduction to the *Cherrypickers' Guide*, this nice and very visible repunched mintmark has turned out to be more elusive than was first thought. Recent sales confirm its scarcity.

	VF-20	EF-40	AU-50	AU-58	MS-60	MS-63	MS-64
Variety	$225	$350	$575	$850	$1,000	$1,350	$2,200
Normal	$155	$250	$500	$525	$700	$1,150	$1,700

1899, Counterfeit

VARIETY: Doubled-Die Reverse **LAWRENCE: N/L; WEXLER: DDR-001**
PUP: DOLLAR
URS-4 · I-4 · L-4

Description: Very strong doubling is visible on the word DOLLAR, the arrows clutched in the eagle's claws, and the eagle's leg.

Comments: This entry was first listed in the *Cherrypickers' Guide* in the fifth edition. Recently it has been proven without a doubt to be a die-struck counterfeit. We are including it here to alert collectors of its changed status. Because it is a counterfeit, its former Fivaz-Stanton number (FS-25-1899-901) has been delisted.

	G-4	VG-8	F-12	VF-20	EF-40	AU-50
VARIETY	n/a	n/a	n/a	n/a	n/a	n/a
NORMAL	$12	$14	$28	$45	$75	$135

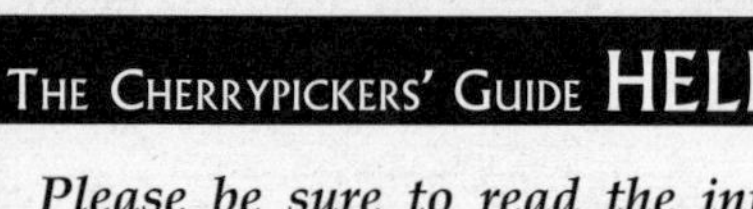

THE CHERRYPICKERS' GUIDE HELPFUL HINTS

Please be sure to read the information in the front of this book. It sets the tone for the material that follows and makes it easier to interpret the information for each listing.

The die varieties listed in this book are only the tip of the iceberg. Even more are yet to be discovered. Always examine closely any coin you obtain. You might discover a great variety that soon every collector wants! (Be sure to let us know when you do.)

Note: When you study auction results, especially for high-grade rarities, be aware of the "registry set effect." Two eager collectors who both want the #1-rated set can drive prices up and up—but their frenzy isn't necessarily a snapshot of the broader market.

1902-O — FS-25-1902o-301

Variety: Misplaced Date **Lawrence: N/L**
PUP: Denticles to right of and below 0 of date
URS-6 · I-3 · L-3

Description: The top of a digit (likely a 0) can be seen in the denticles below the 0 of the date.

Comments: This is one of the few listed misplaced dates for the Barber quarter series. So far, it has proven to be very scarce. No verified sales could be confirmed.

	VG-8	F-12	VF-20	EF-40	AU-50	MS-60	MS-63
Variety	n/a	n/a	n/a	n/a	n/a	n/a	n/a
Normal	$20	$55	$85	$150	$250	$550	$1,100

1907-D — FS-25-1907D-301

Variety: Repunched Date, Doubled-Die Obverse **Lawrence-102**
PUP: Date
URS-6 · I-4 · L-3

Description: Secondary digits are evident south on all four digits, most noticeably on the 9, 0, and 7. Minor doubling is evident on the first two stars on the left, and the ribbon ends.

Comments: Keep an eye out for this variety! Finding a high grade will be difficult but rewarding.

	VG-8	F-12	VF-20	EF-40	AU-50	MS-60	MS-63
Variety	n/a	$100	n/a	n/a	n/a	n/a	$2,250
Normal	$13	$27	$48	$70	$200	$375	$700

1907-S FS-25-1907S-501

VARIETY: Repunched Mintmark **LAWRENCE-104; CONECA: N/L**
PUP: Mintmark
URS-5 · I-5 · L-5

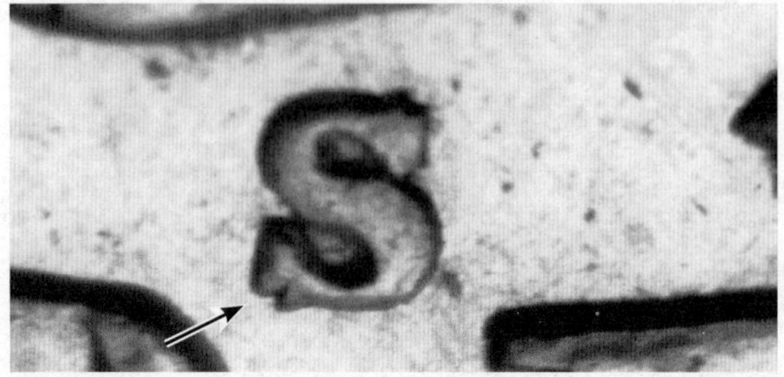

Description: This RPM is evident on the notched serifs of the S mintmark. The secondary S is rotated slightly.

Comments: This variety is rare to very rare. No auction records exist, and no confirmed sales. Fewer than ten specimens are known and of those verified, all are circulated. Finding this variety would make your day—perhaps even your year!

	VG-8	F-12	VF-20	VF-35	EF-40	AU-50
VARIETY	n/a	n/a	n/a	n/a	n/a	n/a
NORMAL	$22	$50	$80	$175	$190	$280

1908-D FS-25-1908D-301

VARIETY: Misplaced Date **LAWRENCE: N/L**
PUP: Denticles below 08
URS-4 · I-3 · L-3

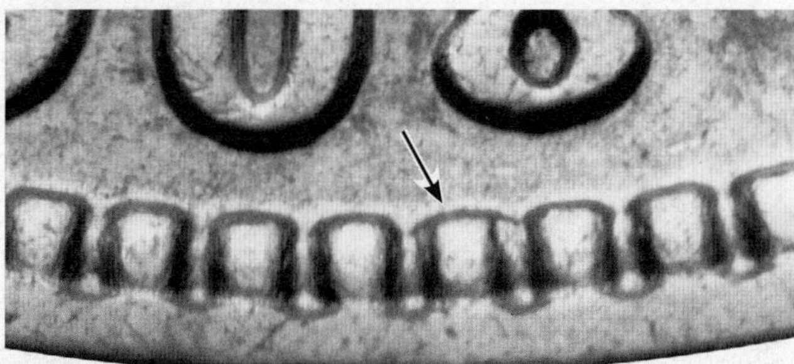

Description: The top of a digit (likely a 0) is visible in the denticles below the space between the 0 and the 8.

Comments: Very few misplaced dates are listed among Barber quarters. Although the misplaced digit is very clear in this variety, the Barber Coin Collectors Club die-variety survey indicates only one specimen (an AU coin) has come to light over the past decade. No others have been confirmed, and no sales are recorded.

	VG-8	F-12	VF-20	EF-40	AU-50	MS-60	MS-63
VARIETY	n/a	n/a	n/a	n/a	n/a	n/a	n/a
NORMAL	$13	$27	$45	$70	$135	$250	$375

1909-S FS-25-1909S-501

Variety: Inverted Mintmark **CONECA: N/L**
PUP: Mintmark
URS-6 · I-3 · L-3

Description: This is a recent discovery. The mintmark was inverted when it was punched into this die.

Comments: Check other San Francisco Barber coinage for other inverted mintmarks. Similar varieties among Barber half dollars are discussed in the sixth edition, volume III.

	VG-8	F-12	VF-20	EF-40	AU-50	MS-60
Variety	n/a	n/a	n/a	n/a	n/a	n/a
Normal	$20	$38	$55	$100	$225	$375

The Cherrypickers' Guide HELPFUL HINTS

A note of caution while you're studying auction results: Always be aware of the "Registry Set Effect." This happens when two strong bidders, competing to build the best registry set, push an auction price into the stratosphere. For some Roosevelt dime die varieties, for example, you might see very high prices for coins in ultra-high grades, especially those with Cameo designations (on Proofs) and those certified with Full Bands (PCGS) or Full Torch (NGC) details.

Keep in mind that an auction is a moment in time, and competition for the same coin variety might be completely different next time around.

This aggressive bidding, driven by registry set competition, is seen in other coin series, too, not just with Barber coinage.

1914-D FS-25-1914D-101

VARIETY: Doubled Die Obverse **LAWRENCE-102**
PUP: Motto
URS-6 · I-4 · L-3

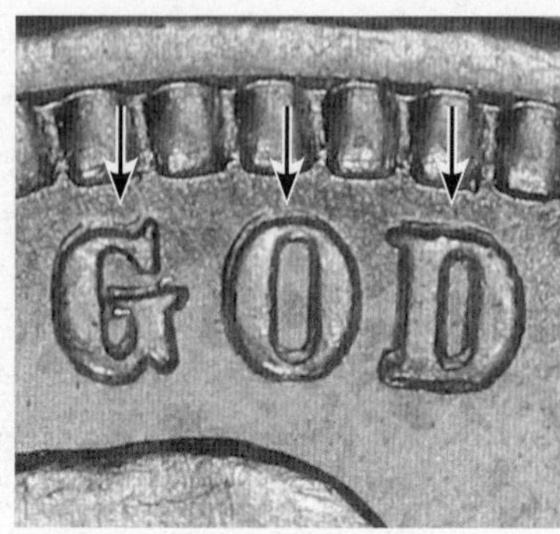

Description: Doubling is evident on all obverse lettering, the ribbon ends, and the stars.

Comments: This is a very nice doubled-die obverse that has proven to be very scarce. There have been no sales confirmed since 2000. Coins validated are few and far between, with grades ranging from Fine through MS-66.

	F-12	VF-20	EF-40	AU-50	MS-60	MS-63	MS-65	MS-66
VARIETY	n/a	n/a	n/a	n/a	n/a	n/a	n/a	n/a
NORMAL	$24	$45	$65	$135	$250	$375	$750	$875

1916-D FS-25-1916D-501

VARIETY: Repunched Mintmark **LAWRENCE-102; CONECA: RPM-002**
PUP: Mintmark
URS-9 · I-4 · L-3

Description: The secondary D mintmark is evident within the opening of the primary mintmark. We believe this is a large D over a small D. Other researchers feel it is just a D over D.

Comments: There are three repunched mintmarks for this date. The one illustrated is the most dramatic of the three and brings the highest price. The Barber Coin Collectors Club die-variety survey lists this as a large D over small D mintmark. On later die states, a die chip connects the upper-left serif of the D to a feather.

	VG-8	F-12	VF-20	EF-40	AU-50	MS-60	MS-63
VARIETY	$20	$35	$55	$95	$165	$275	$450
NORMAL	$13	$24	$45	$70	$120	$250	$375

Standing Liberty Quarters, 1916–1930

There are very few die varieties in the Standing Liberty quarter dollar series. Still, collector interest in the series is strong. This volume of the *Cherrypickers' Guide* adds several interesting new listings and introduces the concept of "incomplete shield" varieties.

Major varieties from the twentieth century seem to have occurred during wartime years, and the monster overdate of 1918-S, 8 Over 7, is a good example. One obvious reason for this is that the U.S. government did anything and everything possible to conserve strategic metals for use in ammunition and equipment. This would possibly explain the use of overdated dies for wartime coinage production.

Clashes involving an inverted E and L are known for almost every Standing Liberty date and mintmark. Several examples are included in this volume. The only dates for which they are not yet known are 1916, 1919-D, 1920-D, 1924-D, and 1929-D.

Also, due to heavy die polishing, several coins are known with incomplete shields; see FS-25-1930-401 for discussion. They include 1920-S, 1924-S, 1927, and 1930, with others possibly awaiting discovery.

More information about Standing Liberty quarter varieties is available at the website of CONECA, the national club devoted to the study of numismatic errors and varieties. This includes a complete list of all varieties in the CONECA register. Dr. James Wiles is the organization's primary attributor of twentieth-century die varieties. We strongly recommend membership in CONECA, which includes a subscription to the award-winning journal *Errorscope*, a free die-variety coin, access to the Members Only area of the website, and more benefits. Annual dues are $25 and up for individual adults and clubs, and $10 and up for Young Numismatists. Apply online at www.conecaonline.org.

STANDING LIBERTY QUARTERS REMOVED FROM THE FIFTH EDITION, VOLUME II

DATE, VARIETY	FIVAZ-STANTON NUMBER	PUP	NOTES
1930-S, Likely Repunched Mintmark	FS-25-1930S-501	Mintmark	Doubtful authenticity

Note: Varieties removed are still considered *Cherrypickers' Guide* varieties (as opposed to being "delisted"); for example, they will continue to be cross-referenced and summarized in appendix H. (Exceptions include varieties debunked as counterfeits, or those which later research revealed to be erroneously classified. Those will be delisted completely.)

NEW STANDING LIBERTY QUARTERS IN THE SIXTH EDITION, VOLUME II

DATE, VARIETY	FIVAZ-STANTON NUMBER	PUP	NOTES
1917-S, Obverse Doubled Die	FS-25-1917S-401	Last three bottom stars on left, bottom two-three stars on right	
1924-S, Repunched Mintmark	FS-25-1924S	Mintmark	Counterfeit.
1930, Incomplete Shield	FS-25-1930-401	Shield	

1917-D, Type 1 FS-25-1917D-801

VARIETY: Doubled-Die Reverse **WEXLER: WDDR-001; CONECA: DDR-001**
PUP: E PLURIBUS UNUM
URS-6 · I-4 · L-4

Description: A strong spread to the east shows on E PLURIBUS UNUM, MER of AMERICA, the lower left wing feathers, and some inner feather details on the right wing.

Comments: Very few doubled dies are known among Standing Liberty quarters, and this is a nice one! It's very scarce, with few specimens verified and few sales reported.

	VG-8	F-12	VF-20	EF-40	AU-50	MS-60	MS-63
VARIETY	$125	$175	$225	$350	n/a	n/a	n/a
NORMAL	$75	$100	$125	$200	$250	$325	$425

1917-S, Type 1 — FS-25-1917S-401

VARIETY: "Shish Kabab" **CONECA: N/L**
PUP: Last three bottom stars on left
URS-7 · I-4 · L-3

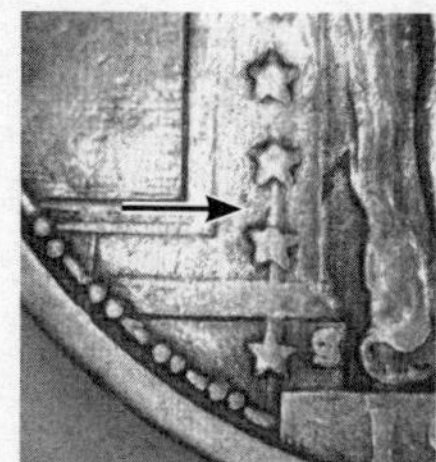

Description: The bottom three stars on the left have a large vertical gouge through them. Additionally, the obverse die was heavily polished before being retired, as evidenced by the letter B of LIBERTY almost polished off of the die. The top portion of Miss Liberty's "split" hair has also been scraped off completely, along with her shoulder under the letter B, showing very little definition.

Comments: Discovered by Rick DeSanctis, this is a very neat and scarce variety. It is a Type 1 variety. Prices shown are actual sales, and this variety will show up on coins even with no date visible!

	VG-8	F-12	VF-20	EF-40
VARIETY	$100	n/a	$175	n/a
NORMAL	$85	$115	$150	$200

1918-S, 8 Over 7 — FS-25-1918S-101

VARIETY: Overdate, Doubled-Die Obverse **CONECA: DDO-001**
PUP: Date
URS-11 · I-5 · L-4

Description: This clear overdate was caused by two different dated hubs being used when the die was made. The 7 is so bold this variety can be easily confirmed even in low grades.

Comments: This variety is extremely rare in high grades. We recommend professional third-party authentication because counterfeits and fraudulent alterations do exist. Genuine specimens have a small die chip above the pedestal, just to the left of the lowest star on the right. Full Head coins are very rare and bring substantial premiums.

	G-4	VG-8	F-12	VF-20	EF-40	AU-50
VARIETY	*Values range from $1,650 to $10,000+ (circulated), $20,000 to $30,000+ (Unc).*					
NORMAL	$20	$25	$35	$45	$85	$150

1920 FS-25-1920-401

VARIETY: Double-Clashed Obverse Die
PUP: Inverted doubled E in drapery
URS-7 · I-3 · L-2

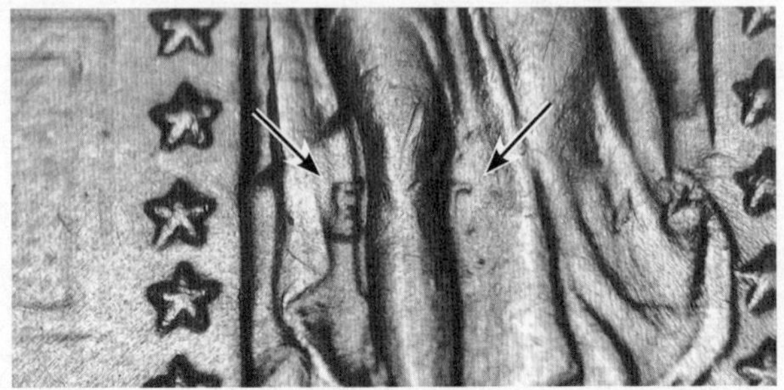

Description: The obverse shows typical elements of a strong clashed die. An inverted and doubled E of E PLURIBUS UNUM is evident protruding from the viewer's left of Liberty's right leg at the knee. An inverted L shows on the opposite side of her knee. A weak star is visible left of Liberty's head.

Comments: A single-clash is also known for this date (listed as Knauss: K-0077). Although known for some time, this variety has turned out to be fairly scarce. No Full Head coins are known.

	VG-8	F-12	VF-20	EF-40	AU-50	MS-60	MS-63	MS-65
VARIETY	n/a	n/a	n/a	n/a	$200	$400	n/a	n/a
NORMAL	$20	$25	$35	$50	$100	$200	$300	$1,500

1920-S FS-25-1920S-401

VARIETY: Clashed Obverse Die
PUP: Inverted doubled E in drapery
URS-6 · I-3 · L-2

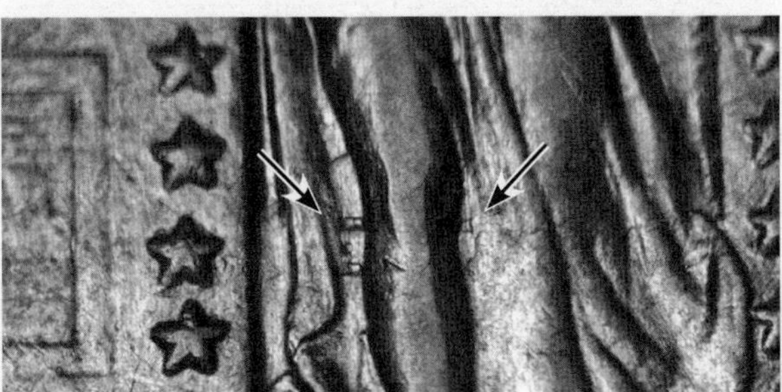

Description: The obverse shows typical elements of a strong clashed die. An inverted and doubled E of E PLURIBUS UNUM is evident protruding from the viewer's left of Liberty's right leg at the knee. An inverted L shows on the opposite side of her knee.

Comments: A single-clash is also known for this date (listed as Knauss: K-0078). At present, this variety is very scarce, with no Full Head coins known. Very few sales have been verified.

	VG-8	F-12	VF-20	EF-40	AU-50	MS-60	MS-63
VARIETY	$50	n/a	n/a	n/a	$250	$450	n/a
NORMAL	$25	$35	$50	$75	$200	$350	$1,000

1924-S (Counterfeit)

Variety: Repunched Mintmark, Counterfeit
PUP: Mintmark

Description: This "variety" is not a genuine mint product. It is a counterfeit coin that shows an S/S/S mintmark, the style of which is not that of the regular S.

Comments: This is a counterfeit coin and is included here for educational purposes only. The grading services will not encapsulate this piece.

	G-4	VG-8	F-12	VF-20	EF-40	AU-50
Variety	n/a	n/a	n/a	n/a	n/a	n/a
Normal	$25	$30	$50	$65	$150	$250

1928-S FS-25-1928S-501

Variety: Inverted Mintmark
PUP: Mintmark
URS-9 · I-4 · L-3

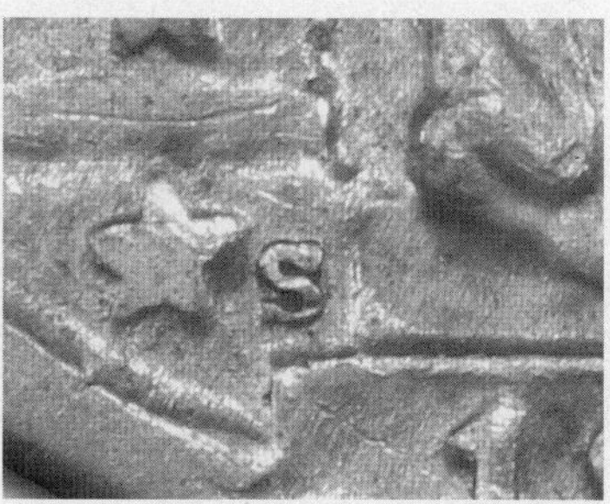

Description: An inverted S mintmark was clearly punched into the die.

Comments: This variety is very rare in Mint State and no Full Head coins are known. Inverted S-mintmark Standing Liberty quarters have been growing in popularity in recent years, as measured by sales and auction prices. On April 9, 2020, a VF-30 specimen of this variety sold on eBay for $853.

	VG-8	F-12	VF-20	EF-40	AU-50	MS-60	MS-63	MS-65
Variety	$100	$300	$450	$800	n/a	n/a	n/a	n/a
Normal	$10	$12	$22	$40	$75	$175	$250	$1,000

1928-S — FS-25-1928S-502

VARIETY: Repunched Mintmark — **CONECA: RPM-001**
PUP: Mintmark
URS-6 · I-4 · L-3

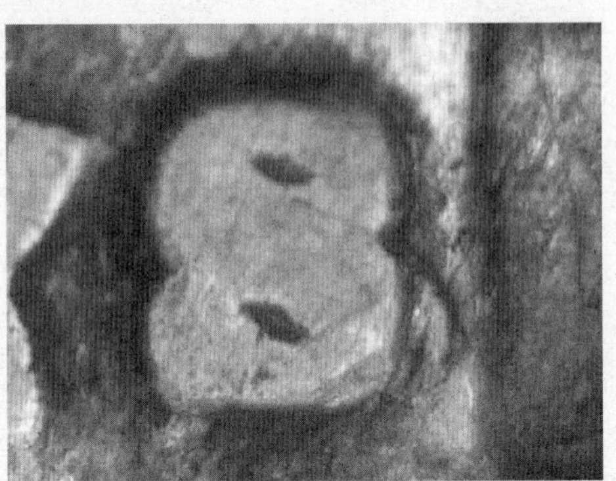

Description: The primary S mintmark is punched over a slightly east and tilted S.

Comments: Although scarce, this variety is known in virtually all circulated and Mint State grades. Also, it can be found with Full Head details.

	VG-8	F-12	VF-20	EF-40	AU-50	MS-60	MS-63	MS-65
VARIETY	$35	$60	$100	$200	$350	$400	$500	n/a
NORMAL	$10	$12	$22	$40	$75	$175	$250	$1,000

1929-S — FS-25-1929S-401

VARIETY: Clashed Obverse Die
PUP: Left of Liberty's right leg
URS-7 · I-4 · L-3

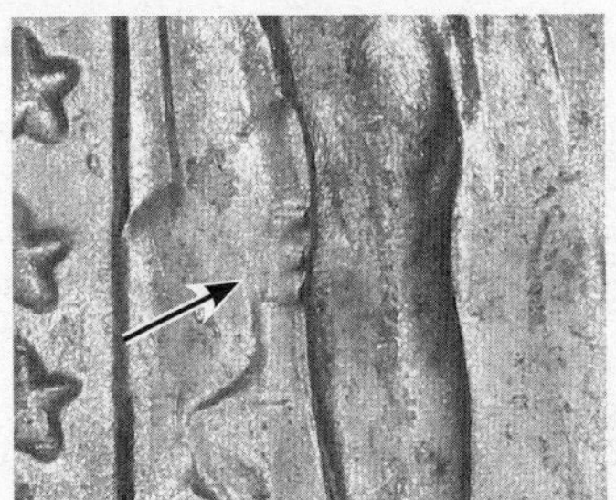

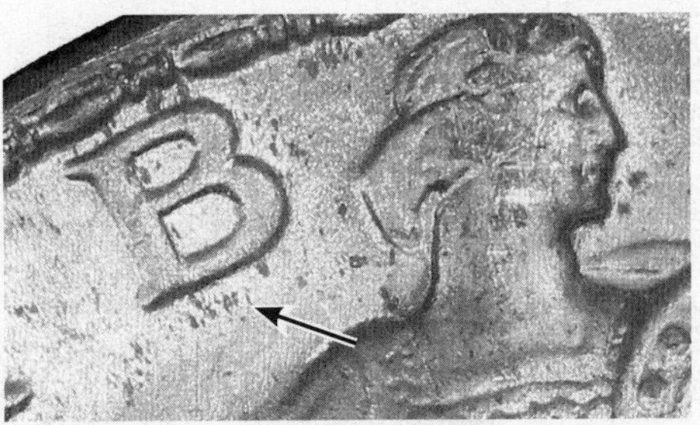

Description: This obverse die shows typical elements of a strong clashed die. An inverted E of E PLURIBUS is evident protruding from the viewer's left of Liberty's right leg. The letter I of AMERICA is evident below this B. Stars are visible left of Liberty's head.

Comments: This variety was growing in popularity when the fifth edition of the *Cherrypickers' Guide* was published, and interest has increased since. It has been found in virtually all circulated grades as well as Mint State, some with Full Head details.

	VG-8	F-12	VF-20	EF-40	AU-50	MS-60	MS-63	MS-65
VARIETY	$30	$40	$50	$75	$100	$175	$300	$475
NORMAL	$10	$12	$17	$40	$75	$165	$250	$470

1930 FS-25-1930-401

VARIETY: Incomplete Shield **CONECA: N/L**
PUP: Shield
URS-N/A · I-4 · L-3

Description: The upper portion of Miss Liberty's shield is missing.

Comments: Due to heavy die polishing, the upper portion of Liberty's shield is missing below the E in LIBERTY. To date, 1920-S, 1924-S, and 1927 have been found with incomplete shields as well, although the effect is not as dramatic. Possibly others await discovery.

	AU-50	AU-58	MS-60	MS-62	MS-63	MS-65
VARIETY	n/a	n/a	n/a	n/a	n/a	n/a
NORMAL	$75	$80	$175	$215	$250	$950

THE CHERRYPICKERS' GUIDE HELPFUL HINTS

For best cherrypicking results, make sure you read "How to Use This Book," in the front. It will help you interpret the information for each listing.

And remember, the die varieties in this book aren't the only ones in the series. Even more are waiting to be discovered. Always closely examine your coins, even the ones you get in pocket change. You might make an important discovery! (Be sure to let us know when you do.)

Be aware of the "registry set effect" when you study auction results, especially for high-grade rarities. If two collectors both aspire to the #1-rated set, and they both need a rare coin that's come up for bid, and they both have fat wallets, their bidding war might set a record. This momentary competition doesn't necessarily illustrate the rest of the market.

Washington Quarters, 1932 to Date

Collectors of Washington quarter die varieties are as avid as any group of numismatic specialists, and very serious in their quest for the most popular and rare specimens. They will actively compete for a hard-to-find coin.

When the first edition of the *Cherrypickers' Guide* went to press in 1989, this series was one of the "sleepers" for variety specialists. At that time, many of the better varieties were known only to a few collectors, so the pickings were relatively easy. However, since about 1990 the series has become increasingly more popular, making the search much more challenging—but still rewarding!

Interesting and rare varieties in the Washington quarter series include some spectacular doubled dies, significant repunched mintmarks, overmintmarks, and master die alterations. One of the few known totally separated repunched mintmarks, the 1940-D and D, is still considered one of the most elusive varieties. A couple of other very significant misplaced mintmarks have also been found in this series.

Very few reference books specializing in Washington quarters contain significant content on varieties. The most complete work is that of Dr. James Wiles, former president of the Combined Organizations of Numismatic Error Collectors of America (CONECA).

The varieties listed in this volume of the *Cherrypickers' Guide* are generally considered the best of the best. However, some of the lesser varieties are also included so that our Young Numismatists (YNs) and other novice enthusiasts can find some of the many nice varieties known in this series.

The fifth edition of the *Cherrypickers' Guide*, published in 2012, included many doubled dies from the popular State quarter series, including nine for the 2005 Minnesota quarter alone. Collector demand in recent years has focused on a few of the more interesting examples, which we've retained in this edition. We've also added more than a half dozen new varieties from the National Park quarters series.

If you're interested in learning as much as possible about Washington quarter errors and varieties, we highly recommend membership in CONECA, which gives you access to the complete list of varieties in the CONECA register. James Wiles is the organization's primary attributor of twentieth-century die varieties. Membership in CONECA also includes a subscription to the award-winning journal *Errorscope*, a free die-variety coin, access to the Members Only area of the website, and connection to hundreds of like-minded hobbyists. Annual dues are $25 and up for individual adults and clubs, and $10 and up for Young Numismatists. Apply online at www.conecaonline.org.

Washington Quarters Removed From the Fifth Edition, Volume II

Date, Variety	Fivaz-Stanton number	PUP	Notes
1934, Medium Motto	FS-25-1934-402	IN GOD WE TRUST	*
1934, Heavy Motto	FS-25-1934-403	IN GOD WE TRUST	*
1943-S, RPM	FS-25-1943S-504	Mintmark	Low collector interest
1945-S, TDO	FS-25-1945S-101	IN GOD WE TRUST	Low collector interest
1951-D, DDO	FS-25-1951D-101	LIBERTY	Low collector interest
1964, DDO	FS-25-1964-101	IN GOD WE TRUST	Low collector interest
1965, DDR	FS-25-1965-801	QUARTER DOLLAR	Low collector interest
1970-D, DDR	FS-25-1970D-801	QUARTER DOLLAR	Low collector interest
1970-D, DDR	FS-25-1970D-802	AMERICA, DOLLAR	Low collector interest
1979-S, Proof, Type II Mintmark	FS-25-1979S-501	Mintmark	Low collector interest
1981-S, Proof, Type II Mintmark	FS-25-1981S-501	Mintmark	Low collector interest
1982-S, Proof, DDO	FS-25-1982S-101	Date	Low collector interest
1996-P, Die Damage	FS-25-1996P-701		Not a die variety
2005-P, Minnesota, DDR	FS-25c-2005P-MN-801	Trees	Low collector interest
2005-P, Minnesota, DDR	FS-25c-2005P-MN-802	Trees	Low collector interest
2005-P, Minnesota, DDR	FS-25c-2005P-MN-804	Trees	Low collector interest
2005-P, Minnesota, DDR	FS-25c-2005P-MN-806	Trees	Low collector interest
2005-P, Minnesota, DDR	FS-25c-2005P-MN-807	Trees	Low collector interest
2005-D, Minnesota, DDR	FS-25c-2005D-MN-801	Trees	Low collector interest
2005-D, Minnesota, DDR	FS-25c-2005D-MN-802	Trees	Low collector interest
2005-P, Oregon, DDR	FS-25c-2005P-OR-801	Tall tree	Low collector interest
2005-P, Oregon, DDR	FS-25c-2005P-OR-802	Tall tree	Low collector interest
2007-P, Wyoming, DDR	FS-25c-2007P-WY-803	Saddle horn	Low collector interest

Note: Varieties removed are still considered *Cherrypickers' Guide* varieties (as opposed to being "delisted"); for example, they will continue to be cross-referenced and summarized in appendix H. (Exceptions include varieties debunked as counterfeits, or those which later research revealed to be erroneously classified. Those will be delisted completely.) * These listings were included in the fifth edition for informational purposes only. In this edition, photographs of the mottoes, for comparison, have been added to the listing for FS-25-1934-401.

NEW WASHINGTON QUARTERS IN THE SIXTH EDITION, VOLUME II

DATE, VARIETY	FIVAZ-STANTON NUMBER	PUP
1937-D, RPM	FS-25-1937D-501	Mintmark
1940-D, RPM	FS-25-1940D-502	Mintmark
1941-S, DDR	FS-25-1941S-801	Reverse lettering
1942-S, RPM	FS-25-1942S-501	Mintmark
1945-S, RPM	FS-25-1945S-501	Mintmark
1947, "Spitting Eagle"	FS-25-1947-901	Eagle's beak
1948-S, "Spitting Eagle"	FS-25-1948S-901	Eagle's beak
1951-S, RPM	FS-25-1951S-501	Mintmark
1959, Proof, DDO	FS-25-1959-102	IN GOD WE TRUST
1961-D, RPM	FS-25-1961D-503	Mintmark
1963, B Rev. Sub Var	FS-25-1963-901a	Arrow points
1964-D, RPM	FS-25-1964D-503	Mintmark
1968-S, Proof, Type E	FS-25-1968S-901	Leaves, Q in QUARTER
1968-S, Proof, Type F	FS-25-1968S-902	Leaves, Q in QUARTER
1970-S, Proof, DDR	FS-25-1970S-801	QUAR
1983, "Spitting Eagle"	FS-25-1983-901	Field below the eagle's beak
1989, No P	FS-25-1989-501	Mintmark area
1994, No P	FS-25-1994-501	Mintmark area

MAJOR DESIGN ALTERATIONS FOR WASHINGTON QUARTERS

Special thanks to José Cortez and José Miguel Gallego for their work on this section.

In 1932 the United States Mint began production of the George Washington quarter dollar. The popularity of the design, initially intended to commemorate the 200th anniversary of the president's birth, led the Mint to retain it for regular coinage. The motifs were in place from 1932 through 1998. From 1999 to 2021, John Flanagan's profile portrait of Washington was kept on the obverse, while the coin's reverse played host to dozens of designs celebrating various aspects of American history, geography, and culture. (In 2022, with the launch of the American Women quarters program, the obverse would change to a Washington portrait created by artist Laura Gardin Fraser in 1932.)

The Washington quarter has seen numerous obverse and reverse design alterations over the years.

OBVERSE DESIGN ALTERATIONS

From 1932 to 2022 there have been a total of 23 obverse design alterations, most of them relatively minor, but all significant in the minds of collectors. They could be categorized into seven major obverse designs minted at different years:

- 1932 through 1964 (11 alterations),
- 1965 through 1974 (3 alterations),
- 1776–1976 (1 design),
- 1977 through 1988 (3 alterations),
- 1989 through 1998 (2 alterations),
- State, DC, Territorial, National Park quarters from 1999 through 2021 (3 new designs)
- Those starting in 2022 with the American Women quarters with the Washington portrait by Fraser (1 new design)

Reverse Design Alterations and Designs

Similar to the obverse design alterations, the reverse design changes, with a total of 177 alternations and reverse new designs. They also can be categorized into seven major reverse designs minted at different years:

- 1932 through 1998 (14 alterations)
- 1776–1976 (1 design)
- State quarters from 1999 through 2008 (50 new designs)
- D.C. and Territories quarters in 2009 (6 new designs)
- America the Beautiful quarters from 2010 through 2021 (56 new designs)
- American Women quarters from 2022 through 2025 (20 new designs)

The alterations began in 1936 with the production of the first Proof coins of the series. The design alteration, or rather *enhancement,* produced a bolder view of the eagle's tail feathers, the leaves, and the arrows. This redesign is referred to as the Type B reverse. It was intended for use on Proof issues from 1936 to 1964.

The Type B reverse also exists on regular circulation-strike issues for Philadelphia from 1956 to 1964. All are considered scarce to very scarce. Mint sets of 1957, 1959, and 1960 are known with Type B reverse quarters.

Another reverse alteration began to be used with the introduction of the new copper-nickel clad coinage in 1965. This style became known as the Type C reverse. Close examination shows that it is a sharper version of the Type A reverse. It differs from Type A in that the leaves are sharper and more distinct. The leaf above the first L in DOLLAR is very distinct and almost touches the L. The leaf that faded in front of the bundle of arrow tips on the Type A reverse is very sharp in Type C and comes to a noticeable point at the tip of the top arrow. The tail feathers are sharper, showing lines in the center of the feathers that are now more distinct. The overall look of the Type C reverse is that it is flatter compared to the higher relief of Type A.

Although adopted for use on clad issues beginning with coins dated 1965, one Type C reverse die was mistakenly punched with a D mintmark and sent to the Denver Mint. This die was then used to produce silver quarters dated 1964. It is considered very scarce.

There has been speculation that there may be Denver-minted Washington quarters with the Type B reverse from 1956 to 1964; however, none have yet been confirmed.

The only year in which all three reverse types are known to have been used is 1964.

Reverse Hub Comparisons

Distinguishing among the reverse hubs is relatively easy after comparing their differences. In the following pages, we illustrate key areas of the three hubs, side by side.

TYPE A REVERSE (CONECA: RDV-001)

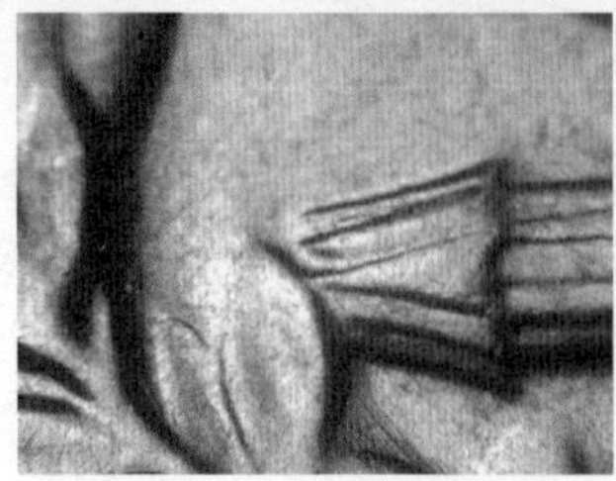

On the Type A reverse, the tip of the leaf is pointed and ends below the topmost arrow tips. The design overall is in lower relief and the leaves in the branches tend to fade into the field. The tip of the eagle's left wing (as viewed) is rounded.

The Type A reverse is known on all circulation strikes, from all mints, from 1932 through 1964, as well as on Proofs from 1936. All are common.

TYPE B REVERSE (CONECA: RDV-002)

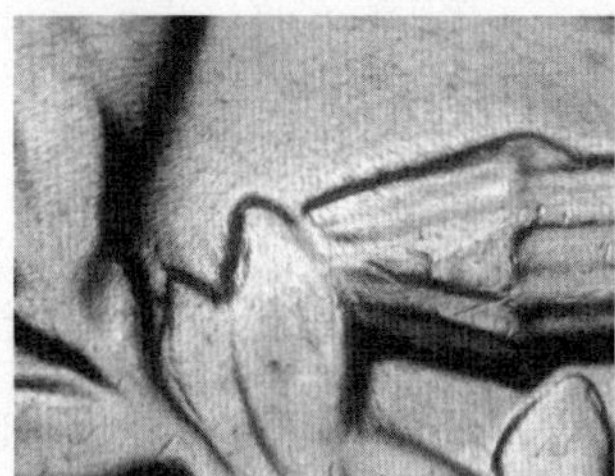

On the Type B reverse, the tip of the leaf is pointed, extending above the topmost arrow tip, and angles slightly to the left at the top. The overall design is in higher relief. The tip of the eagle's left wing (as viewed) is pointed.

The Type B reverse is known on some Philadelphia circulation strikes from 1956 through 1964, and on Proofs from 1937 through 1942 and from 1956 through 1964. The 1956 Type B reverse is the scarcest of the nine dates.

TYPE B REVERSE SUB-VARIETY (CONECA: RDV-002)

On the 1956 Type B Sub-Variety reverse, the tip of the leaf it is larger, ending pointed (like a nipple), angled strongly to the left, and extending above the topmost arrow tip. The tip of the eagle's left wing (as viewed) is pointed.

The Type B reverse is known on some Philadelphia circulation strikes from 1956 through 1964, and on Proofs from 1937 through 1942 and from 1956 through 1964. The 1956 Type B reverse is the scarcest of the nine dates, but the 1956 Type B Sub-Variety reverse is extremely rare.

TYPE C REVERSE (CONECA: RDV-003)

On the Type C reverse, the N in UNUM has a very slight serif at the top of the right-hand vertical bar and the tail feathers are stronger and sharper (with center lines in each) than they are on Type A and Type B.

The Type C reverse is known on the 1964-D, 1965, and 1967 strikes. The 1964-D and the 1967 are scarce to rare.

TYPE D REVERSE (CONECA: RDV-004)

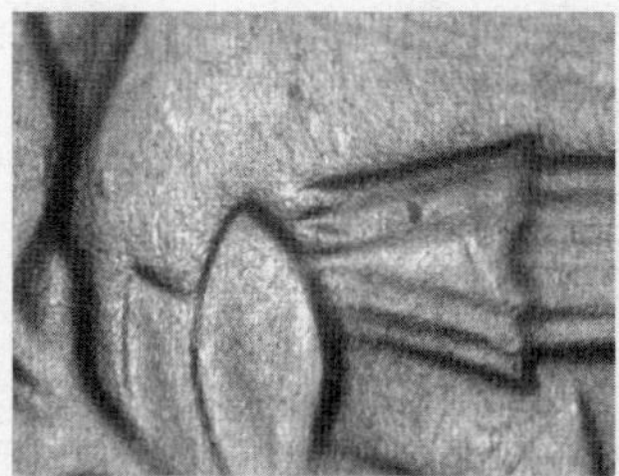

On the Type D reverse, the tip of the leaf is pointed and ends below the topmost arrow tip. The N in UNUM does not have a serif at the top of the right-hand vertical bar.

The Type D reverse is found on all of the following, and all are common: Philadelphia, 1965 through 1968; Denver, 1968 and 1969; and Special Mint Set coins of 1965 through 1967.

TYPE E REVERSE (CONECA: RDV-005)

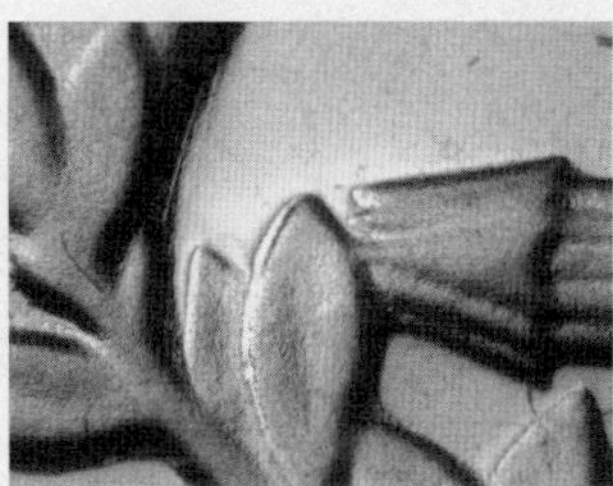

On the Type E reverse, the tip of the leaf is pointed and ends below the topmost arrow tip. The font on EPU is considerably thinner than any of the other reverse design types and it is easy to distinguish. There is no doubling on the Q in QUARTER. Another difference between Type D and Type E is that Type E has an incuse line on the inside edges of the vertical wing segments.

The Type E reverse is found on all of the following: Philadelphia, 1965 through 1968; Denver, 1968 and 1969; Special Mint Set coins of 1965 through 1967; and San Francisco, 1968. Of these, the 1968-S is extremely rare.

TYPE F REVERSE (CONECA: RDV-006)

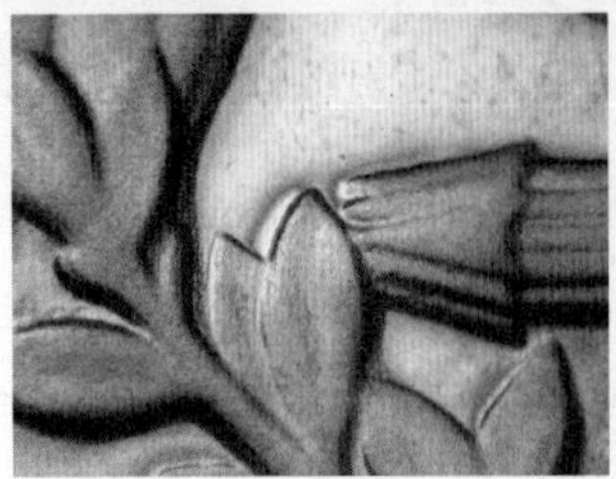

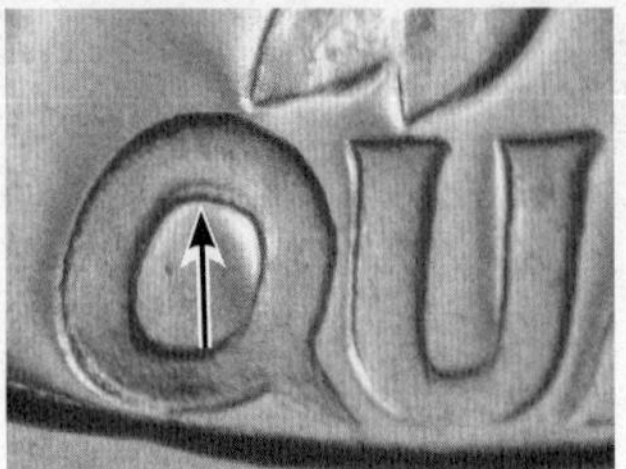

On the Type F reverse, the tip of the leaf is pointed and ends below the topmost arrow tip. The Q in QUARTER displays master-die doubling. The font on EPU is considerably thicker and easy to distinguish.

The Type F reverse is found on all of the following: Philadelphia, 1967 through 1972; Denver, 1968 through 1972; and San Francisco, 1968. The 1968-S is rare.

TYPE G REVERSE (CONECA: RDV-007)

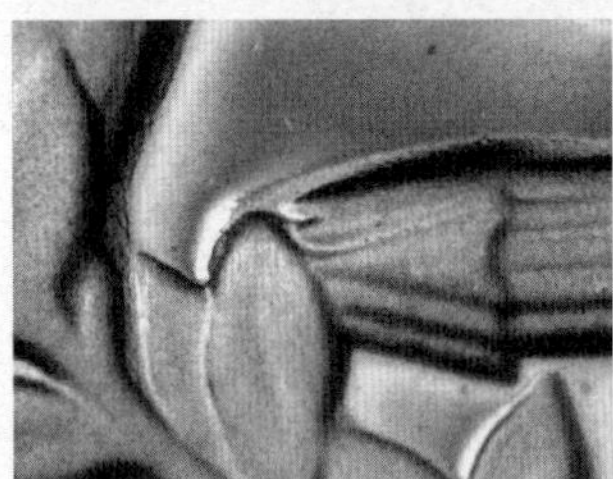

On the Type G reverse, the tip of the leaf is rounded and rests slightly below the topmost arrow tips. Doubling is evident on the Q in QUARTER. The N in UNUM has a very slight serif at the top of the right-hand vertical bar, similar to that on Type C but a bit more pronounced.

The Type G reverse is found on the 1968-S, 1969, and 1970-D, and all are common. The 1969-D is scarce and the 1970 is considered rare.

TYPE H REVERSE (CONECA: RDV-008)

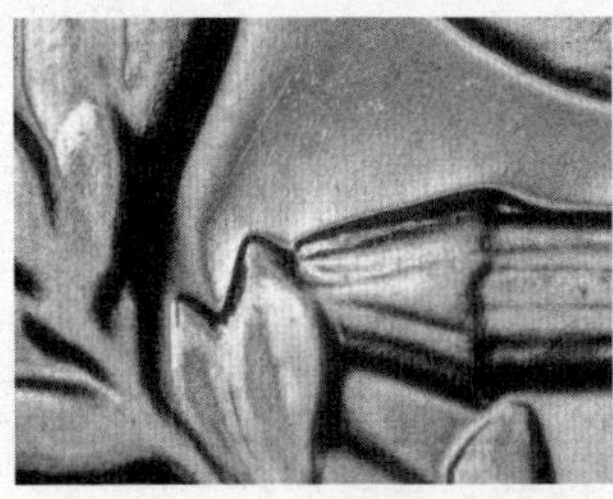

Very similar to the Type B reverse, the Type H reverse shows the leaf pointed and extending above the topmost arrow tips, and the overall design is in high relief. The font on E PLURIBUS UNUM is also considerably thinner and easy to distinguish. The tip of the eagle's left wing (as viewed) is pointed.

The Type H reverse is common in San Francisco coins from 1968 through 1972. Those produced from 1969 through 1972 in Denver are considered rare.

SEE THE CHARTS ON PAGES 172 AND 173 FOR ESTIMATED POPULATIONS OF THE SCARCE TO RARE VARIETIES.

Reverse Design Varieties (RDV) Quick Reference

The following is CONECA's nomenclature (e.g., RDV-001), followed by common naming (e.g., Type A), the die identification or Reverse Die Variety (e.g., IIa), and the years the particular Washington quarters were produced (e.g., 1937–1964). Next are the years and mintmarks to search, with Pick Up Points in order of priority.

To thoroughly verify any of the RDVs listed here, consult the presentation "Washington Quarters Reverse Design Varieties (RDV) From A to H, and Beyond," which has more detailed information about each of the reverse designs. Contact José Gallego at JMGallego@LosGallego.com or download it from http://www.heartlandcoinclub.com/links.html#link14.

RDV-001 (Type A) (I) (1932–1964)

All common. Weak strike. No serif on N of UNUM. No doubling on Q. Long-leg N.

RDV-002 (Type B) (IIa) (1937–1964)

1956–1964: Leaf above arrow tips. High relief. Pointed wingtip only on your left side. No serif on N of UNUM. No doubling on Q. Some of the leaves on the branches seem to fade into the field of the coin.

RDV-003 (Type C) (IIIo) (1964-D–1967)

1964-D, 1965 (circulation strike), 1967 (circulation strike): Serif on N of UNUM (best seen with the coin upside-down). No doubling on Q. Very sharp, raised tail feathers, and a centerline on each feather. Low profile, "flat" appearance. Sharp arrow tips. Arrows separated from the leaf. Left bud: slightly above the leaf.

RDV-004 (Type D) (IIIa1) (1965–1969-D)

1969D: No serif on N of UNUM. No doubling on Q. E PLURIBUS UNUM is in low relief, and wide. Widest left leaf. The inner edge of the eagle's left wing fades into the field. The far-left leaf looks tilted to the left compared with RDV-005. A very sharp-pointed leaf below arrow tips. Sharp arrow tips. Weak inner-right wing. Arrows separated from the leaf. Left bud: above the leaf.

RDV-005 (Type E) (IIIa2) (1965-1969D)

1968-S, Proof: No serif on N of UNUM. No doubling on Q. Thin and high-relief E PLURIBUS UNUM letters. The narrowest left leaf is pointed. The far-left leaf looks pointing up compared to RDV-004. An incuse outline next to the inner edge of the eagle's left wings. Weak left-inner wing. The top two arrow tips are quite far apart from the leaf. Left leaf with dip. Has an incuse line on the inside edges of the vertical wing segments. Left bud: above the leaf.

RDV-006 (Type F) (IIIb) (1967–1972-D)

1967(circulation strike), 1968-S, Proof, 1969-D: Serif on N of UNUM. Doubling on Q. Pointed leaf with doubling. Rounded arrow tips. The far-left leaf is shorter than others, leveled with bud. The left leaf shows a clear vertical and tighter pointed tip and with doubling.

RDV-007 (Type G/M) (IIIm) (1968-S–1970-D)

1969-D, 1970-P: Serif on N of UNUM. Doubling on Q. Rounded spoon-shape and doubled leaf. High relief secondary wings, sharp and well-defined. Sharp longer-pointed left leaf. Rounded arrow tips. Left bud: almost leveled.

RDV-008 (TYPE H) (IIB) (1968-S–1972-S)

1969-D, 1970-D, 1971-D, 1972-D: No serif on N of UNUM. No doubling on Q. Leaf above arrow tips. High relief. Both wingtips are pointed. The top two arrow tips are quite close to the leaf. Left bud: slightly above the leaf. Bottom barbwire missing. Centerlines added to tail feathers.

(ESTIMATED POPULATIONS)
SILVER WASHINGTON QUARTERS, 1932–1964

DATE(S)	RDV-001	RDV-002	RDV-002	RDV-003
	TYPE A	TYPE B	TYPE B SUB-VARIETY	TYPE C
	I	IIA	IIA	IIIO
1932–1964	Common			
1936, Proof	Common			
1937–1964, Proofs		Common		
1956	Common	Scarce		
1957	Common	Uncommon		
1958	Common	Uncommon		
1959	Common	Uncommon		
1960	Common	Uncommon		
1961	Common	Uncommon		
1962	Common	Uncommon		
1963	Common	Uncommon	Extremely Rare	
1964	Common	Uncommon		
1964-D	Common			Very Scarce

(ESTIMATED POPULATIONS)
CLAD WASHINGTON QUARTERS, 1965–1972

DATE(S)	RDV-003	RDV-004	RDV-005	RDV-006	RDV-007	RDV-008
	TYPE C	TYPE D	TYPE E	TYPE F	TYPE M (G)	TYPE H
	IIIO	IIIA1	IIIA2	IIIB	IIIM	IIB
1965	Very Scarce	Common	Common			
1965, SMS	Uncommon	Common	Common			
1966	Unconfirmed	Common	Common			
1966, SMS	Unconfirmed	Common	Common			
1967	Unconfirmed	Common	Common	Rare		
1967, SMS	Scarce	Common	Common	Unconfirmed		
1968		Common	Common	Common		
1968-D		Common	Common	Common		
1968-S, Proof			Very Scarce	Very Scarce	Common	Common
1969				Common	Common	

Date(s)	RDV-003	RDV-004	RDV-005	RDV-006	RDV-007	RDV-008
	Type C	Type D	Type E	Type F	Type M (G)	Type H
	IIIo	IIIa1	IIIa2	IIIb	IIIm	IIb
1969-D		Scarce		Uncommon	Scarce	Scarce
1969-S, Proof						Common
1970				Common	Very Scarce	
1970-D				Common		Very Scarce
1970-S, Proof						Common
1971				Common		
1971-D				Common		Rare
1971-S, Proof						Common
1972				Common		
1972-D				Common		Rare
1972-S, Proof						Common

Build a Set of Reference Washington Quarter RDVs By Collecting Common Varieties

Use the table below to build your own set of the nine common reverse varieties. Use them as reference to confirm your finds of the 'uncommon' to 'rare' RDVs listed in the two charts on the previous pages. For example, a 1959 Type B can be confirmed by comparing it with a 1964 Proof (common).

RDV	Type	Class	Common Issues*	Recommended Sample for Set
RDV-001	Type A	I	1932-1964, 1932D-1964D CS and 1936 Proof	1964
RDV-002	Type B	IIa	1937-1942 Proofs, 1956-1964 Proofs	1964 Proof
RDV-003	Type C	IIIo	Not Common (1965, 1967, 1964-D CS)	Not Common (1965 Type C)
RDV-004	Type D	IIIa1	1965-1968, 1968D-1969D CS, and 1965-1967 SMS	1965 (Look for wide letters EPU)
RDV-005	Type E	IIIa2	1965-1968, 1968D-1969D CS, 1965-1967 SMS, and 1968S Proof	1967 SMS
RDV-006	Type F	IIIb	1967-1970, 1972, 1968D-1970-D, 1972-D, CS 1968S Proof	1968D CS (or a 1968S Proof)
RDV-007	Type M (or G)	IIIm	1970-1971, 1969D-1971-D CS, 1968S Proof	1970D CS
RDV-008	Type H	IIb	1969D-1972D CS, 1968S-1972S Proof	1970S Proof
RDV-009		IIIc	1973-1974, 1973D-1974D CS, 1973S-1974S Proof	1973D CS

* CS = circulation strike

1932 FS-25-1932-101

VARIETY: Doubled-Die Obverse **CONECA: DDO-001**
PUP: Earlobe, nostril
URS-7 · I-4 · L-3

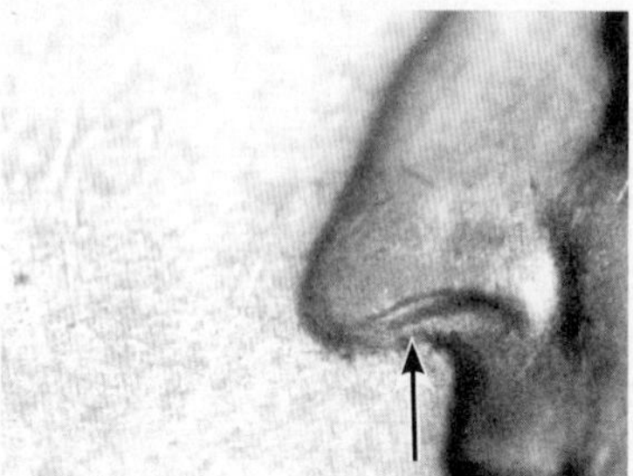
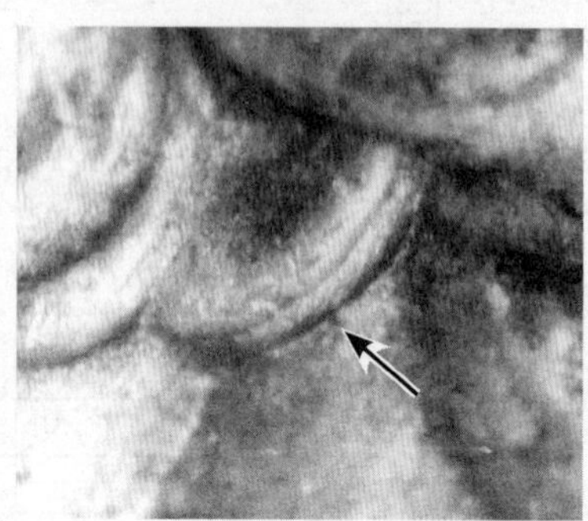

Description: Doubling is evident as a doubled earlobe, with additional doubling visible on the nostril and the back of George Washington's queue.

Comments: This doubled die is one of many in the series that continues to grow in popularity. Although it is very scarce, supply has been able to fill demand.

	VF-20	EF-40	AU-50	MS-60	MS-63	MS-65
VARIETY	$30	$45	$95	$210	$400	$1,350
NORMAL	$13	$15	$16	$25	$60	$275

1934 FS-25-1934-101

VARIETY: Doubled-Die Obverse **CONECA: DDO-001**
PUP: IN GOD WE TRUST
URS-10 · I-4 · L-4

Description: Very strong doubling is evident on IN GOD WE TRUST, on LIBERTY, and on the date. This is a Medium Motto obverse.

Comments: This obverse, one of the strongest and most popular of all Washington quarter varieties, can also be found matched with a significant Class VI reverse doubled die (CONECA DDR-001) that is overshadowed by the DDO and largely ignored by mainstream buyers. Growing interest in Washington quarters has slowly but steadily increased pricing for this variety. Several years ago, an MS-66+ specimen brough $6,500 in a major auction, and an MS-67+ garnered $8,519.

	VG-8	F-12	VF-20	EF-40	AU-50	MS-60	MS-63	MS-65
VARIETY	$65	$100	$125	$250	$475	$800	$1,500	$2,750
NORMAL	$8	$8.50	$9	$10	$24	$45	$70	$180

1934 — FS-25-1934-401

VARIETY: Light Motto — **CONECA: ODV-001**
PUP: IN GOD WE TRUST
URS-13 · I-3 · L-3

Light Motto.

Medium Motto.

Heavy Motto.

Description: Notice the considerable weakness in the letters of IN GOD WE TRUST. In addition, the center tip of the W is pointed.

Comments: See the photos above for comparison between the Light, Medium, and Heavy Motto styles. In 2014 an MS-67+ Light Motto coin brought more than $8,500, most likely sold to an avid registry-set collector. (Although the Medium and Heavy Motto coins are common, in higher grades of MS-66+ to MS-67+ they command strong prices.)

	VF-20	EF-40	AU-50	MS-60	MS-63	MS-65	MS-66
VARIETY	$10	$15	$25	$50	$75	$185	$375
NORMAL	$9	$10	$24	$45	$70	$180	$365

1934-D — FS-25-1934D-501

VARIETY: Small Mintmark of 1932 — **CONECA: MMS-001**
PUP: Mintmark
URS-9 · I-3 · L-2

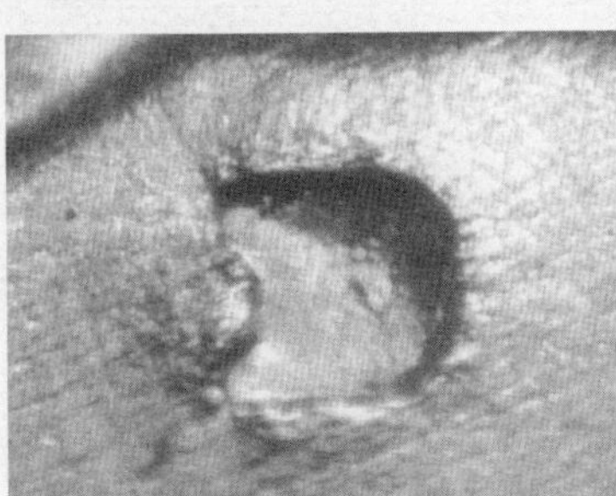

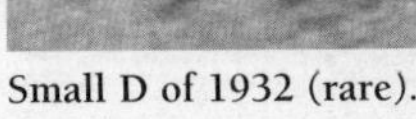

Small D of 1932 (rare).

Normal D of 1934 (common).

Description: The D mintmark is smaller than the common D of 1934.

Comments: This is the D mintmark of 1932, likely the result of a single die left over from that earlier year. This is a scarce variety in circulated grades, and Mint State coins are very scarce. It is paired with both Medium and Heavy Motto obverse dies.

	VF-20	EF-40	AU-50	AU-55	MS-60	MS-63	MS-65
VARIETY	$50	$75	$95	$120	$200	$360	$500
NORMAL	$12	$25	$85	100	$175	$225	$425

1935 FS-25-1935-101

Variety: Doubled-Die Obverse **CONECA: DDO-1**
PUP: IN GOD WE TRUST
URS-7 · I-3 · L-2

Description: Doubling is visible on IN GOD WE TRUST and on the L of LIBERTY.

Comments: To date, very few specimens have come to light and no transactions have been verified. Although minor, compared to some doubled-die obverses this variety is still very collectible.

	VF-20	EF-40	AU-50	AU-55	MS-60	MS-63	MS-65
Variety	$13	$17	$20	$30	$55	$75	$125
Normal	$9	$11	$14	$18	$22	$35	$70

1936 FS-25-1936-101

Variety: Doubled-Die Obverse **CONECA: DDO-001**
PUP: IN GOD WE TRUST
URS-8 · I-5 · L-4

YN

Description: Very strong doubling is evident on IN GOD WE TRUST, on LIBERTY, and on the date.

Comments: This very rare variety is always in demand. Grades range from AG through MS. It is extremely rare in Mint State.

	G-4	VG-8	F-12	VF-20	EF-40	AU-50	AU-55	MS-60	MS-63
Variety	$35	$50	$100	$200	$300	$400	$575	$800	$1,500
Normal	$5	$5.50	$5.75	$7	$8	$10	$15	$25	$35

1937 — FS-25-1937-101

Variety: Doubled-Die Obverse — **CONECA: DDO-001**
PUP: IN GOD WE TRUST
URS-8 · I-5 · L-5

Description: Very strong doubling is evident on IN GOD WE TRUST, on LIBERTY, on the date, and on the end of the hair ribbons.

Comments: This variety is considered one of the most important in the Washington quarter series. It is a very rare coin, and brings strong prices when available. The first MS-65 coin sold privately for $15,000 in 2004.

	G-4	VG-8	F-12	VF-20	EF-40	AU-50	AU-55	MS-60	MS-63	MS-65
Variety	$125	$175	$225	$350	$750	$1,250	$1,750	$2,350	$4,250	$8,500
Normal	$5	$5.50	$6	$8	$9	$12	$25	$30	$45	$100

1937-D — FS-25-1937D-501

Variety: Repunched Mintmark — **CONECA: RPM-003**
PUP: Mintmark
URS-6 · I-4 · L-4

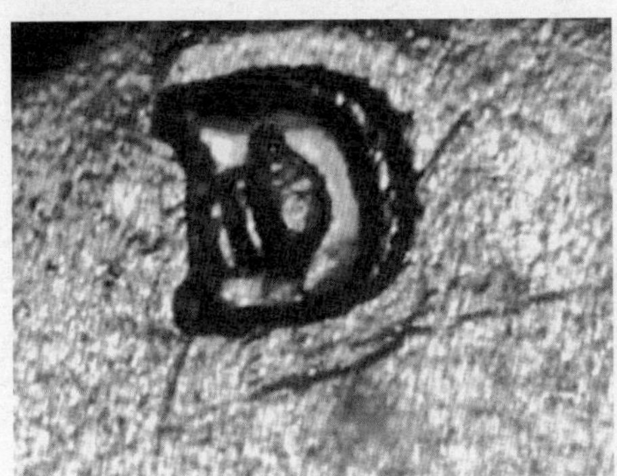

Description: The D mintmark is doubled nicely to the southeast.

Comments: This is a very scarce coin that has been known for some time but has had very few sales. Interest in repunched mintmarks has been increasing, and the keen-eyed attention of cherrypickers could bring to light more examples of the 1937-D.

	EF-40	AU-50	MS-60	MS-63	MS-65	MS-66
Variety	n/a	n/a	n/a	n/a	n/a	n/a
Normal	$24	$35	$75	$90	$135	$275

1939-D, D Over S — FS-25-1939D-501

VARIETY: Overmintmark **CONECA: N/L**
PUP: Mintmark
URS-7 · I-4 · L-3

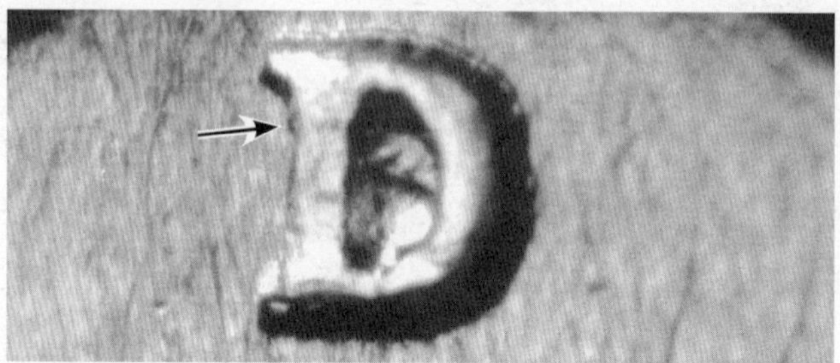

Description: This particular reverse die illustrates a D mintmark punched over an S mintmark. The center curve of the S is clearly evident within the opening of the D, and the left-most upper curve of the S is evident immediately left of the upright of the D.

Comments: There is a coin listed as FS-12.3 in *Over Mintmarks and Hot Repunched Mintmarks*. That coin is shown as being a refuted over mintmark, but is not the same die as listed here. More study is needed.

	EF-40	AU-50	AU-55	MS-60	MS-63	MS-65
VARIETY	$40	$55	$70	$90	$125	$200
NORMAL	$13	$20	$24	$45	$50	$95

1939-S — FS-25-1939S-101

VARIETY: Doubled-Die Obverse **CONECA: DDO-001**
PUP: IN GOD WE TRUST
URS-8 · I-3 · L-2

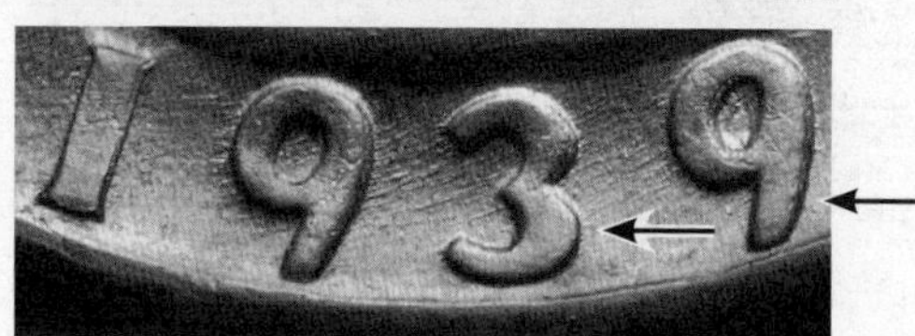

Description: Doubling is evident on the motto, LIBERTY, and the date.

Comments: This variety has proven scarce. Collectors of doubled dies as well as registry set collectors have kept this variety—although minor—in demand. Prices have held steady.

	VF-20	EF-40	AU-50	AU-55	MS-60	MS-63	MS-65
VARIETY	$17	$50	$65	$75	$105	$150	$350
NORMAL	$9	$29	$60	$65	$100	$135	$265

1940-D — FS-25-1940D-101

Variety: Doubled-Die Obverse **CONECA: DDO-001**
PUP: IN GOD WE TRUST
URS-5 · I-5 · L-5

Description: Strong doubling is evident on the motto, and lesser doubling is visible on LIBERTY and the date.

Comments: This is a very attractive doubled die! This variety has shown to be quite elusive. A very rare variety of an already scarce date.

	VF-20	EF-40	AU-50	AU-55	MS-63	MS-65	MS-66
Variety	n/a	n/a	n/a	n/a	$500	$1,000	$3,500
Normal	$10	$38	$65	$70	$165	$255	$375

1940-D — FS-25-1940D-501

Variety: Repunched Mintmark **CONECA: RPM-002**
PUP: Mintmark
URS-6 · I-5 · L-5

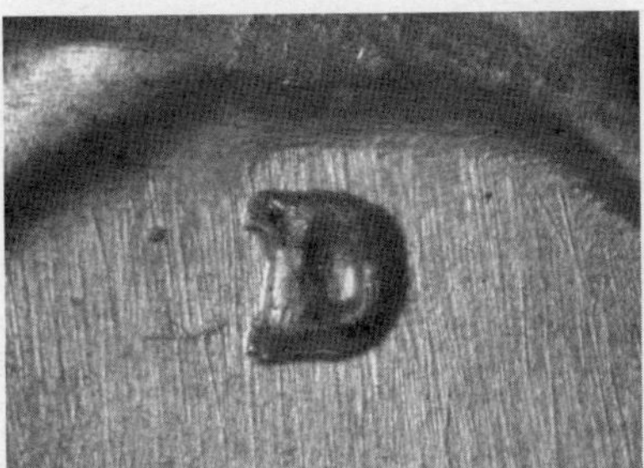

Description: This highly unusual repunched mintmark shows a secondary D totally separated and west of the primary D.

Comments: This is one of about 10 known repunched mintmarks that are totally separated. Discovered by Lee Hiemke, this is a very rare variety and is in very high demand. The reverse is actually a doubled die repunched mintmark with serifs plus an entirely separate D west of the other two D over Ds. It is a very nice rare coin.

	AU-50	AU-60	AU-63	MS-64	MS-65	MS-66
Variety	$75	$150	$300	$400	$600	$1,500
Normal	$65	$75	$100	$200	$255	$375

1940-D

FS-25-1940D-502

Variety: Repunched Mintmark — **CONECA: N/L**

PUP: Mintmark

URS-3 · I-5 · L-4

Description: The repunched D mintmark appears very clearly, south of the secondary mintmark.

Comments: The normal coin this variety appears on (the 1940-D Washington quarter) is moderately scarce. The repunched mintmark is a recent discovery; this demonstrates that new varieties are still out there waiting to be found.

	AU-50	MS-60	MS-63	MS-64	MS-65	MS-66
Variety	$100	$175	$350	$450	$650	$1,700
Normal	$65	$140	$165	$200	$255	$375

1941

FS-25-1941-101

Variety: Doubled-Die Obverse — **CONECA: DDO-003**

PUP: IN GOD WE TRUST

URS-6 · I-4 · L-4

Description: The doubling is most evident on GOD WE and the UST of TRUST.

Comments: The doubling is very obvious. This is a very scarce coin with nice doubling on "GOD WE -UST." With interest level growing on doubled dies, this, as well as others in this series, have grown in popularity as well as price in recent years!

	EF-40	AU-50	AU-55	MS-60	MS-63	MS-65
Variety	$20	$25	$30	$50	$150	$225
Normal	$8	$9	$10	$12	$15	$40

1941 FS-25-1941-102

VARIETY: Doubled-Die Obverse **CONECA: DDO-006**
PUP: IN GOD WE TRUST, LIB, date
URS-7 · I-4 · L-4

Description: There is very nice doubling on the motto, IN GOD WE TRUST, as well as the 94 of the date! Doubling is slightly visible on LIBERTY as well.

Comments: There are several 1941 doubled die obverse quarters but the three listed here are in the highest demand. This is a nice doubled die obverse and has proven to be quite scarce.

	EF-40	AU-50	AU-55	MS-60	MS-63	MS-65
VARIETY	$20	$25	$30	$45	$125	$200
NORMAL	$8	$9	$10	$12	$15	$40

1941 FS-25-1941-103

VARIETY: Doubled-Die Obverse **CONECA: DDO-004**
PUP: IN GOD WE TRUST, 19 of date **WEXLER: WDDO-002**
URS-5 · I-4 · L-3

Description: A strong Class II spread toward the center shows on IN GOD WE TRUST, the date, LIBERTY, and Washington's queue.

Comments: Of the many 1941 doubled-die obverses for this date, this is one of the better ones. This variety, although a relatively new listing to the *Cherrypickers' Guide*, has been known for some time in the variety community. It has proven to be a very scarce variety.

	EF-40	AU-50	AU-55	MS-60	MS-63	MS-65	MS-66
VARIETY	$35	$50	$75	$125	$175	$250	$700
NORMAL	$8	$9	$10	$12	$15	$40	$65

1941 — FS-25-1941-801

VARIETY: Doubled-Die Reverse — **CONECA: DDR-004**
PUP: Eagle's beak
URS-6 · I-4 · L-3

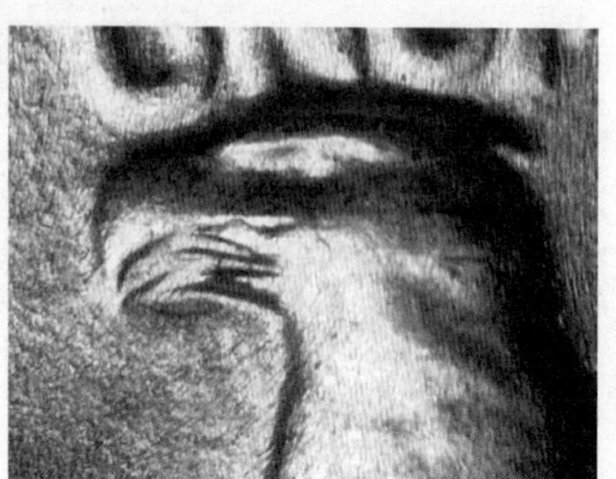

Description: Doubling is evident on the eagle's beak, doubled south. Other doubling is also visible on portions of QUARTER DOLLAR.

Comments: CONECA lists at least 20 other reverse doubled dies for 1941-(P) that are somewhat similar to this variety. All command a nice premium. It is suggested to have any similar variety accurately attributed.

	EF-40	AU-50	AU-55	MS-60	MS-63	MS-65
VARIETY	$40	$75	$100	$125	$200	$475
NORMAL	$8	$9	$10	$12	$15	$40

1941-D — FS-25-1941D-101

VARIETY: Doubled-Die Obverse — **CONECA: DDO-001**
PUP: IN GOD WE TRUST, nose, eye
URS-6 · I-4 · L-3

Description: Doubling is evident on portions of IN GOD WE TRUST and, lightly, in the 41 of the date, nostril, and eye.

Comments: Known for many years, this variety has always been popular with specialists. It has enjoyed even greater interest since its inclusion in the *Cherrypickers' Guide*.

	EF-40	AU-50	AU-55	MS-60	MS-63	MS-65	MS-66
VARIETY	$20	$30	$75	$150	$225	$575	$2,250
NORMAL	$8	$14	$15	$50	$55	$70	$120

1941-D FS-25-1941D-801

Variety: Doubled-Die Reverse **CONECA: DDR-001**
PUP: Reverse Lettering
URS-7 · I-4 · L-4

Description: The doubling is most evident on STATES OF AMERICA, with a light spread on the D of UNITED and the AR of DOLLAR.

Comments: This reverse doubled die is considered rare and in demand by Washington variety enthusiasts.

	EF-40	AU-50	AU-55	MS-60	MS-63	MS-65	MS-66
Variety	$50	$75	$100	$130	$175	$250	$450
Normal	$8	$14	$15	$50	$55	$70	$120

1941-S FS-25-1941S-501

Variety: Large S Mintmark **CONECA: MMS-002**
PUP: Mintmark
URS-8 · I-5 · L-5

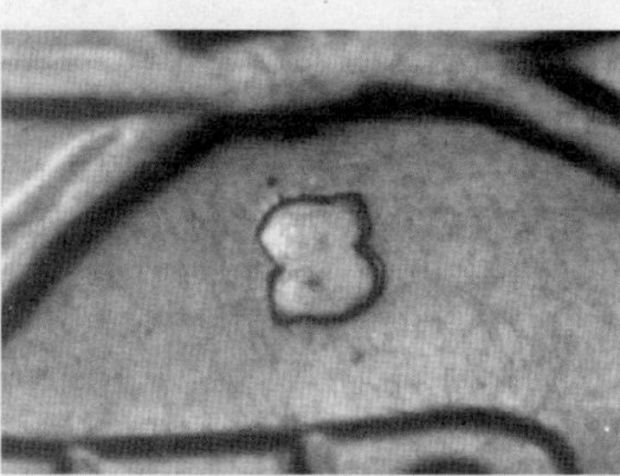

Normal, Small S

Scarce Large S

Description: The S mintmark on a very few 1941-S coins exhibits the Large S, or "Trumpet-Tail" style mintmark. Compare to the normal or small S mintmark. Some of the Large S varieties have a filled upper loop.

Comments: There are 10 known reverse dies with this Large S mintmark. One Large S die has the same style S as on the Large S nickels with a triangular lower serif. As the grade increases, so does rarity. High-end Mint State coins are quite rare.

	EF-40	AU-50	AU-55	MS-60	MS-63	MS-65
Variety	$25	$45	$65	$120	$200	$325
Normal	$8	$12	$15	$45	$50	$70

1941-S — FS-25-1941S-503

VARIETY: Large S Mintmark — **CONECA: MMS-002**
PUP: Mintmark
URS-8 · I-5 · L-5

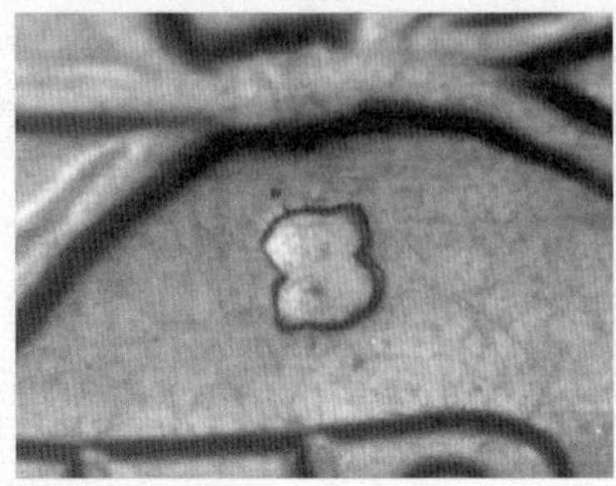
Normal, Small S

Large Triangular Serif S

Description: This Large S mintmark, with triangular lower serif, is the same Large S as found on scarce 1941-S Large S nickels.

Comments: Only one reverse die is known as of this writing. This is a very difficult variety to find.

	EF-40	AU-50	AU-55	MS-60	MS-63	MS-65
VARIETY	$27	$50	$75	$145	$225	$375
NORMAL	$8	$12	$15	$45	$50	$70

1941-S — FS-25-1941S-801

VARIETY: Doubled-Die Reverse — **CONECA: N/L**
PUP: Reverse lettering
URS-4 · I-4 · L-4

Description: Strong doubling is evident on the reverse lettering.

Comments: The distinct doubling of letters and leaves on the reverse is especially visible on DOLLAR and AMERICA. Market values for this newly listed variety will emerge and mature over time.

	EF-40	AU-50	AU-55	MS-60	MS-63	MS-65	MS-67
VARIETY	n/a	n/a	n/a	n/a	n/a	n/a	n/a
NORMAL	$8	$12	$15	$45	$50	$70	$425

1942 — FS-25-1942-101

Variety: Doubled-Die Obverse — **CONECA: DDO-003**
PUP: IN GOD WE TRUST
URS-7 · I-4 · L-4

Description: Doubling is evident on the lower portions of the motto. Secondary images are especially evident on GOD and TRUST.

Comments: Other obverse doubled dies are known for this date, but all are less evident.

	EF-40	AU-50	MS-60	MS-63	MS-65
Variety	$30	$50	$75	$125	$225
Normal	$8	$9	$10	$12	$30

1942 — FS-25-1942-801 (014)

Variety: Doubled-Die Reverse — **CONECA: DDR-002**
PUP: Reverse Lettering
URS-7 · I-5 · L-5

Description: Clockwise doubling is extremely strong on United States of America, with lesser doubling, although evident, on QUARTER DOLLAR.

Comments: Although known for some time, very few specimens have surfaced over the years! The reverse has the widest doubling of the year. Be careful not to confuse this variety with the next one.

	EF-40	AU-50	MS-60	MS-63	MS-65
Variety	$125	$200	$325	$450	$750
Normal	$8	$9	$10	$12	$30

1942 — FS-25-1942-802 (014.3)

VARIETY: Doubled-Die Reverse — **CONECA: DDR-005**
PUP: Reverse lettering, major on QUARTER DOLLAR
URS-6 · I-5 · L-5

Description: This is one of the strongest reverse doubled dies known for the Washington series. The doubling is evident on all reverse lettering, with a clockwise spread.

Comments: This variety has turned out to be rare in all grades!

	EF-40	AU-50	MS-60	MS-63	MS-64	MS-65
VARIETY	$200	$325	$500	$1,000	$1,500	n/a
NORMAL	$8	$9	$10	$12	$20	$30

1942 — FS-25-1942-803

VARIETY: Doubled-Die Reverse — **CONECA: DDR-006**
PUP: Eagle's beak, neck
URS-6 · I-3 · L-4

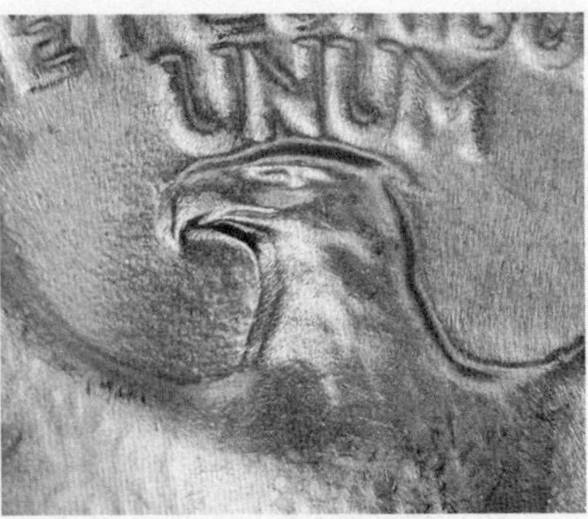

Description: The doubling on this variety can be seen on the eagle's right side (viewer's left), and is most evident as a strongly doubled lower beak and neck, as well as the left thigh and left wreath.

Comments: This is a very attractive and elusive variety. However, it lacks the appeal of the previous 1942 listed doubled die reverses. The variety is still eagerly sought after.

	EF-40	AU-50	MS-60	MS-63	MS-65	MS-65
VARIETY	$100	$150	$225	$350	$500	n/a
NORMAL	$8	$9	$10	$12	$30	$30

1942-D — FS-25-1942D-101 (015)

Variety: Doubled-Die Obverse **CONECA: DDO-001**
PUP: IN GOD WE TRUST, LIBERTY
URS-8 · I-5 · L-5

Description: Doubling is evident, with a very strong spread, on LIBERTY, the date, and the motto. This is one of the most popular Washington quarter varieties.

Comments: Many low grade examples exist from G to F! However, any coin VF or above is a treasure and very few pieces exist in MS grades. If you can locate a high-grade example, you will have no trouble selling it.

	VG-8	F-12	VF-20	EF-40	AU-50	MS-60	MS-63	MS-64	MS-65
Variety	$95	$125	$200	$375	$1,000	$1,500	$2,500	$5,000	n/a
Normal	$7	$7.25	$7.50	$8	$9	$20	$22	$30	$35

1942-D — FS-25-1942D-801 (016)

Variety: Doubled-Die Reverse **CONECA: DDR-001**
PUP: Eagle's beak, branch, lower left section
URS-7 · I-5 · L-5

Description: The doubling on this variety is most prominent on the eagle's beak, the arrows, and the branch above the mintmark.

Comments: This variety is very scarce in all grades, with very few circulated coins known, as well as very few pieces known above MS-65! The finest graded to date is MS-66+. Be sure to carefully examine this variety; note that DDR-002 is very similar, and DDR-002 commands a slightly lower premium.

	EF-40	AU-50	MS-60	MS-63	MS-65
Variety	$250	$425	$750	$1,300	$2,250
Normal	$8	$9	$20	$22	$35

1942-S — FS-25-1942S-501

Variety: Repunched Mintmark — **CONECA: RPM-004**
PUP: Mintmark — **WRPM-002**
URS-5 · I-4 · L-3

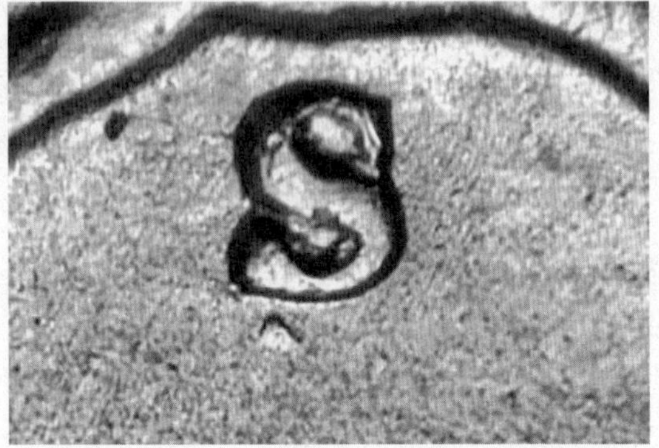

Description: The mintmark on this variety is strongly repunched south.

Comments: The doubled (first) S mintmark is seen well below the strong S. This is a very nice repunched mintmark and well worth looking for.

	AU-58	MS-60	MS-63	MS-64	MS-65	MS-66	MS-67
Variety	n/a	n/a	n/a	n/a	n/a	n/a	n/a
Normal	$45	$75	$115	$120	$135	$155	$550

1943 — FS-25-1943-101 (16.5)

Variety: Doubled-Die Obverse — **CONECA: DDO-005**
PUP: IN GOD WE TRUST
URS-7 · I-5 · L-5

Description: The doubling is very strong northwest on the motto, and to a lesser degree on LIBERTY.

Comments: This variety was discovered by Glenn Jeong. It has proven to be very rare, and is highly in demand!

	EF-40	AU-50	AU-55	MS-60	MS-63	MS-64	MS-65
Variety	$100	$150	$175	$350	$1,000	$1,500	$3,000
Normal	$6.50	$7.50	$8	$10	$11	$20	$40

1943 — FS-25-1943-102

Variety: Doubled-Die Obverse — **CONECA: DDO-017**
PUP: LIBERTY
URS-7 · I-5 · L-5

Description: Doubling is very strong on LIBERTY, with lesser doubling on the date and the motto.

Comments: This variety is very popular among Washington specialists. The popularity of Washington quarter varieties has led to a very strong demand of all varieties over the past few years. In fact, all high-end varieties continually set new records with every auction.

	EF-40	AU-50	AU-55	MS-60	MS-63	MS-65	MS-66
Variety	$75	$125	$150	$200	$275	$400	$600
Normal	$6.50	$7.50	$8	$10	$11	$40	$85

1943 — FS-25-1943-103 (016.7)

Variety: Doubled-Die Obverse — **CONECA: DDO-011**
PUP: IN GOD WE TRUST
URS-7 · I-5 · L-5

Description: This very strong doubled die was discovered about 1993 or 1994 by Eric Striegel. The doubling is very strong on the motto, LIBERTY, and the date, and appears very similar to the popular and well-known 1943-S.

Comments: This coin's addition to the *Red Book* makes it imperative for verification. Easily confused with FS-101, it has a far greater spread on IN GOD WE TRUST. For value reasons, confirmation is a must. Before most people realized its rarity and popularity, early sales brought very little, although, on March 20, 2011, an AU-53 (PCGS) brought $3,900 in a public auction. More recently in December 2019, a PCGS AU-55 brought $2,655. This coin may not exist in high grades of MS-65 or better. It is rare in any grade and an easy seller.

	VG-8	F-12	VF-20	EF-40	AU-50	MS-60	MS-63	MS-64	MS-65
Variety	$350	$875	$1,500	$2,500	$3,500	$5,000	$7,500	$10,000	$12,500
Normal	$5.75	$6	$6.25	$6.50	$7.50	$10	$11	$20	$40

1943-D — FS-25-1943D-101

VARIETY: Doubled-Die Obverse — **CONECA: DDO-004**
PUP: Ear, chin, lips
URS-7 · I-4 · L-4

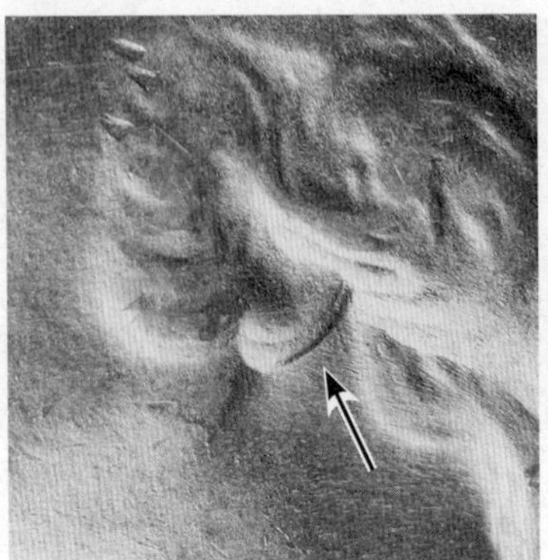

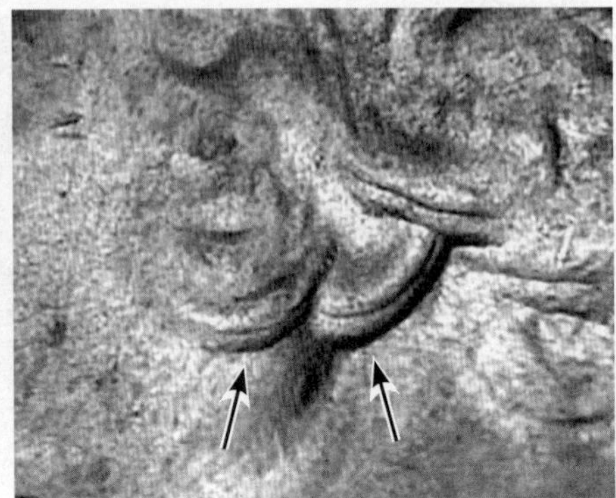

Description: The doubling is evident on the chin, ear, hair curls, and queue.

Comments: This is a most interesting variety. This coin has turned out to be far scarcer than originally thought. A very nice doubled-die obverse of an intriguing variety.

	EF-40	AU-50	MS-60	MS-63	MS-65
VARIETY	$40	$60	$100	$175	$350
NORMAL	$9	$11	$30	$40	$60

1943-S — FS-25-1943S-101 (17)

VARIETY: Doubled-Die Obverse — **CONECA: DDO-001**
PUP: IN GOD WE TRUST, date, LIBERTY
URS-9 · I-5 · L-4

Description: Very strong doubling is evident on the motto, LIBERTY, the designer's initials, and the date.

Comments: This dramatic doubled die has long been known to collectors. Values for this variety are generally firm, but do change with market conditions and demand fluctuations. Because of market fluctuations, be sure to check current price guides and the most recent sales for accurate pricing.

	G-4	VG-8	F-12	VF-20	EF-40	AU-50	MS-60	MS-63	MS-64	MS-65
VARIETY	$30	$50	$75	$115	$160	$225	$450	$650	$800	$1,350
NORMAL	$6	$7	$8	$9	$10	$15	$40	$45	$50	$60

1943-S — FS-25-1943S-401

Variety: "Goiter" **CONECA: N/L**
PUP: Washington's throat
URS-8 · I-4 · L-4

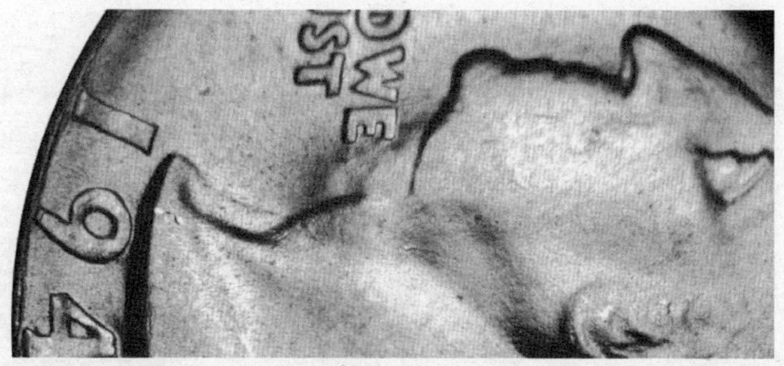

Description: Severe deterioration of the obverse die occurred due to unknown causes. Washington's mouth and chin are flat and lack definition; the area below his jaw is sunken while the area of field in front of his Adam's apple is buckled upward.

Comments: This variety has been known for decades, but it is apparently rare, as few have surfaced. It is affectionately referred to as the "Goiter" variety by old-time collectors. Most coins seen are in low circulated grades, with MS coins very scarce to rare.

	EF-40	AU-50	MS-60	MS-63	MS-64	MS-65
Variety	$250	$325	$475	$700	$900	$1,500
Normal	$10	$15	$40	$45	$50	$60

1943-S — FS-25-1943S-501

Variety: Trumpet-Tail S **CONECA: MMS-002**
PUP: Mintmark
URS-6 · I-4 · L-3

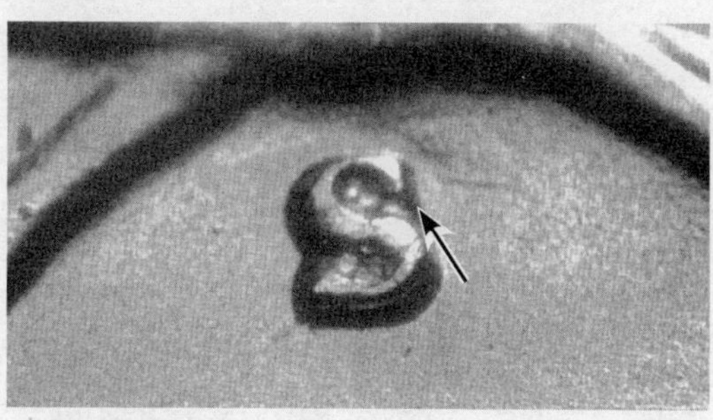

Trumpet Tail

Description: The upper serif is pointed downward, not up and down as on the Large S varieties common to this date.

Comments: This variety is infinitely rarer than the 1941-S Trumpet Tail. A handful of specimens in AU or higher are known. Some experts feel that the difference between this S mintmark and he normal one is more a matter of punch strength than actual size.

	EF-40	AU-50	AU-55	MS-60	MS-63	MS-65
Variety	$50	$65	$100	$175	$250	$400
Normal	$10	$15	$20	$40	$45	$60

1943-S — FS-25-1943S-502

Variety: Medium S Mintmark — **CONECA: N/L**
PUP: Mintmark
URS-6 · I-5 · L-4

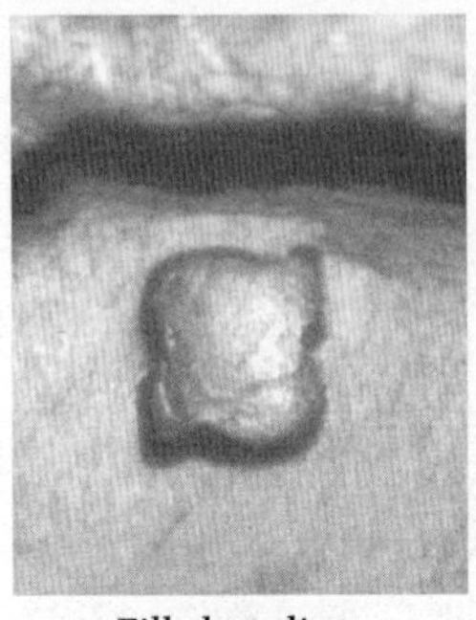

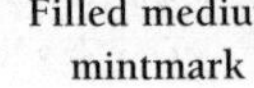

Filled medium mintmark

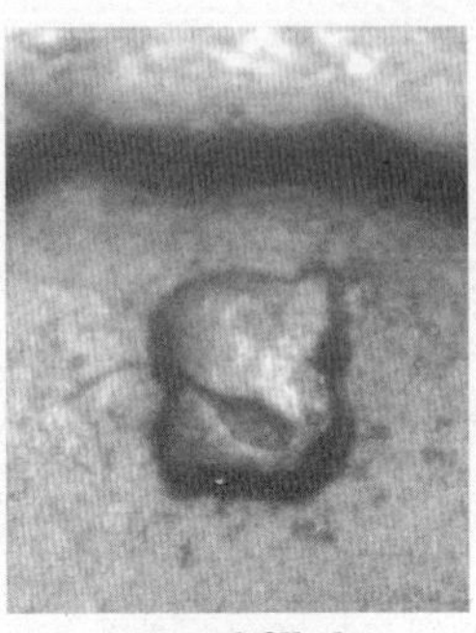

Partial filled medium mintmark

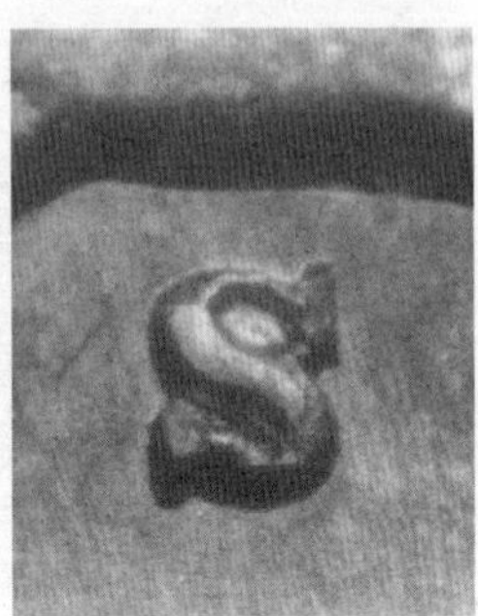

Large S (common) medium mintmark

Description: This variety exhibits a slightly smaller medium S mintmark. Shown for comparison is the Large S (common).

Comments: This variety was unknown for this date until recently.

	EF-40	AU-50	AU-55	MS-60	MS-63	MS-65
Variety	$35	$50	$60	$75	$110	$300
Normal	$10	$15	$20	$40	$45	$60

1943-S — FS-25-1943S-503

Variety: Repunched Mintmark — **CONECA: RPM-002**
PUP: Mintmark
URS-7 · I-4 · L-4

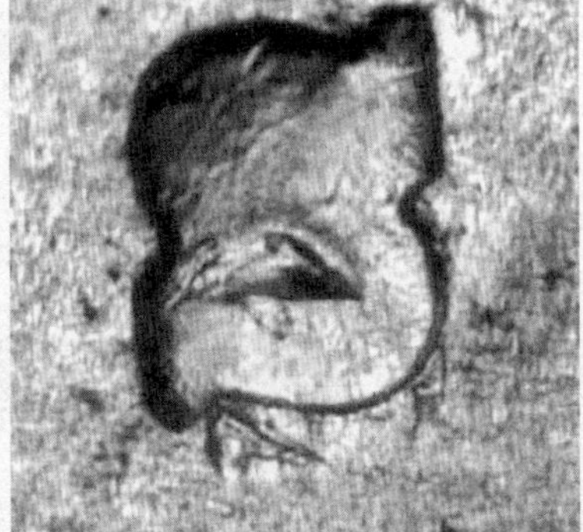

Description: The secondary S mintmark is evident south of the primary S on the medium S variety.

Comments: This filled medium S over S variety has proven to be rare. Very few specimens have surfaced over the years!

	EF-40	AU-50	AU-55	MS-60	MS-63	MS-65
Variety	$35	$50	$65	$110	$175	$325
Normal	$10	$15	$20	$40	$45	$60

1944 FS-25-1944-101

Variety: Doubled-Die Obverse **CONECA: DDO-006**
PUP: IN GOD WE TRUST
URS-9 · I-4 · L-3

Description: Doubling is evident south on the motto IN GOD WE TRUST, with a medium spread, and somewhat evident on LIBERTY and the date.

Comments: All 1944 quarters are from a doubled master die (nose, earlobe). There are several similar doubled dies for this date. Keep searching! Although not a major spread on IN GOD WE TRUST, this variety has proven to be elusive and thus has grown in popularity and demand.

	EF-40	AU-50	AU-55	MS-60	MS-63	MS-65
Variety	$20	$25	$30	$45	$60	$150
Normal	$7	$8	$9	$10	$12	$30

1944-D FS-25-1944D-101

Variety: Doubled-Die Obverse **CONECA: DDO-002**
PUP: LIBERTY
URS-8 · I-4 · L-3

Description: Strong spread on ERTY with light spread on LIB, date, queue, and the designer's initials.

Comments: This is another of the many doubled dies known for this series. This variety has proven to be very scarce and has grown in popularity and demand the last few years.

	EF-40	AU-50	AU-55	MS-60	MS-63	MS-65
Variety	$30	$40	$50	$70	$95	$150
Normal	$7	$10	$12	$15	$20	$40

1944-S — FS-25-1944S-101 (017.5)

Variety: Doubled-Die Obverse — **CONECA: DDO-001**
PUP: IN GOD WE TRUST
URS-9 · I-4 · L-3

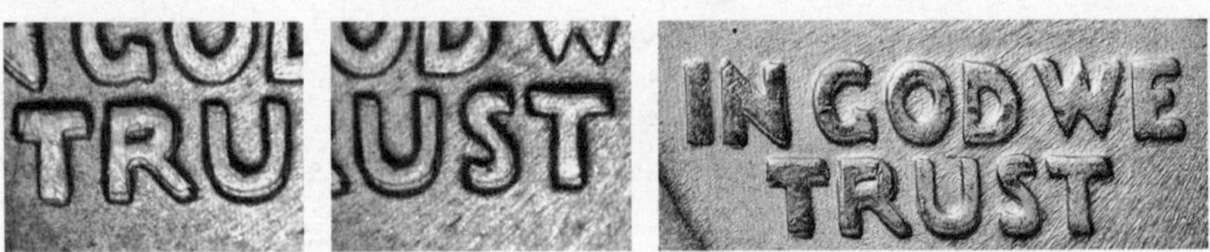

Description: Doubling is evident south on the motto, and slightly on LIBERTY, the date, and the designer's initials.

Comments: This variety, although very evident, is relatively easy to find with enough looking. It is a very nice doubled-die obverse quarter that, while not rare, is still scarce and has grown in popularity and value over the past few years.

	EF-40	AU-50	AU-55	MS-60	MS-63	MS-65
Variety	$15	$20	$30	$40	$55	$95
Normal	$7	$10	$12	$15	$20	$35

1945 — FS-25-1945-101 (018)

Variety: Doubled-Die Obverse — **CONECA: DDO-001**
PUP: IN GOD WE TRUST
URS-7 · I-4 · L-3

Description: Doubling is most evident slightly northwest on the motto, on LIBERTY, and on the date.

Comments: This variety has proven to be very tough to locate in any grade and is rare in high MS grades.

	EF-40	AU-50	AU-55	MS-60	MS-63	MS-65
Variety	$45	$75	$100	$175	$275	$500
Normal	$7	$8	$9	$10	$12	$35

1945-S FS-25-1945S-102

Variety: Doubled-Die Obverse **CONECA: DDO-004**
PUP: IN GOD WE TRUST
URS-7 · I-4 · L-3

Description: Extreme extra thickness is evident on the motto, with doubling also evident on LIBERTY.

Comments: This is another very tough variety to locate. Since its inception in the *Cherrypickers' Guide*, this coin has grown in interest and price over the years, with few recent auction records indicating its rarity!

	EF-40	AU-50	MS-60	MS-63	MS-64	MS-65
Variety	$120	$200	$290	$400	$675	$1,250
Normal	$7	$8	$10	$13	$20	$35

1945-S FS-25-1945S-501

Variety: Repunched Mintmark **CONECA: N/L**
PUP: Mintmark
URS-7 · I-4 · L-3

Description: The S mintmark is very clearly repunched.

Comments: This is a very nice, unmistakable example of a repunched mintmark. Its discovery is recent, and it's presently very scarce to rare—though more specimens will surely come to light with its publication in the *Cherrypickers' Guide*.

	AU-50	MS-60	MS-63	MS-64	MS-65	MS-66
Variety	$10	$15	$20	$30	$50	$100
Normal	$8	$10	$13	$20	$35	$80

1946 FS-25-1946-101

VARIETY: Doubled-Die Obverse **CONECA: DDO-002, DDR-001**
PUP: Date
URS-7 · I-5 · L-4

Description: Nice separation is visible on the 4 of the date. This portion of the obverse is class II. IN GOD WE TRUST, LIBERTY, and the rest of the date are class IV.

Comments: This is a rare and elusive variety. Very nice doubling is visible on the date.

	EF-40	AU-50	MS-60	MS-63	MS-64	MS-65
VARIETY	$35	$50	$75	$125	$175	$225
NORMAL	$7	$8	$10	$12	$20	$40

1946 FS-25-1946-102/802 (018.2)

VARIETY: Doubled-Die Obverse, Doubled-Die Reverse **CONECA: DDO-008, DDR-002**
PUP: IN GOD WE TRUST, STATES OF, E PLURIBUS UNUM **WEXLER: WDDR-003**
URS-5 · I-4 · L-5

Description: The doubling is most evident on E PLURIBUS UNUM, STATES OF, and IN GOD WE TRUST; it is slightly visible on AMERICA. There is a very minor DDO paired with this reverse die, listed as CONECA DDO-008.

Comments: This is yet another variety that may be very difficult to locate in high grade and has proven to be quite rare in any grade! Note the correction to the Fivaz-Stanton number of the previous entry to FS 101/801, which also affected the change to the FS number of this variety.

	EF-40	AU-58	MS-60	MS-63	MS-65
VARIETY	n/a	$750	n/a	n/a	$1,000
NORMAL	$7	n/a	$10	$12	$40

1946-D

FS-25-1946D-501

Variety: Repunched Mintmark **CONECA: N/L**
PUP: Mintmark
URS-6 · I-4 · L-4

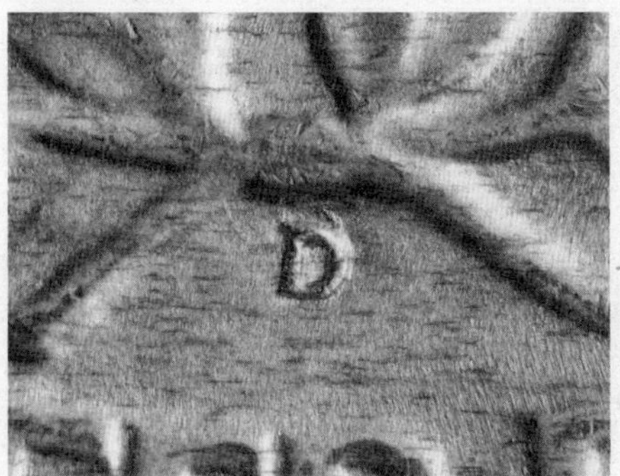

Description: The secondary D is weak but evident north of the primary D, and touching the branch above.

Comments: This RPM is not currently listed by CONECA. Since its inception in the *Cherrypickers' Guide*, very few pieces have been found! In fact, this variety has turned out to be rare!

	EF-40	AU-50	MS-60	MS-63	MS-64	MS-65
Variety	n/a	n/a	$215	$375	$525	n/a
Normal	$7	$8	$10	$12	$20	$30

1946-S

FS-25-1946S-501

Variety: Repunched Mintmark **CONECA: RPM-002**
PUP: Mintmark
URS-10 · I-4 · L-3

Description: A secondary S is evident north of and within the primary mintmark.

Comments: This RPM is in fairly high demand.

	EF-40	AU-50	MS-60	MS-63	MS-65	MS-66
Variety	$15	$20	$30	$50	$75	$100
Normal	$7	$8	$10	$12	$35	$60

1947 FS-25-1947-101

VARIETY: Doubled-Die Obverse **CONECA: DDO-001**
PUP: LIBERTY
URS-6 · I-5 · L-4

Description: Doubling is evident mainly on LIBERTY, with an extremely weak spread on the date, the designer's initials, and the motto IN GOD WE TRUST.

Comments: This variety has shown to be very scarce with very few pieces trading hands the past few years. Prices have been all over the board, but seem to have climbed up the past three years.

	EF-40	AU-50	AU-55	MS-60	MS-63	MS-64	MS-65
VARIETY	n/a	n/a	$100	$150	$225	$400	$500
NORMAL	$7	$8	$9	$11	$19	$25	$35

1947 FS-25-1947-901

VARIETY: "Spitting Eagle" **CONECA: N/L**
PUP: Eagle's beak
URS-5 · I-4 · L-4

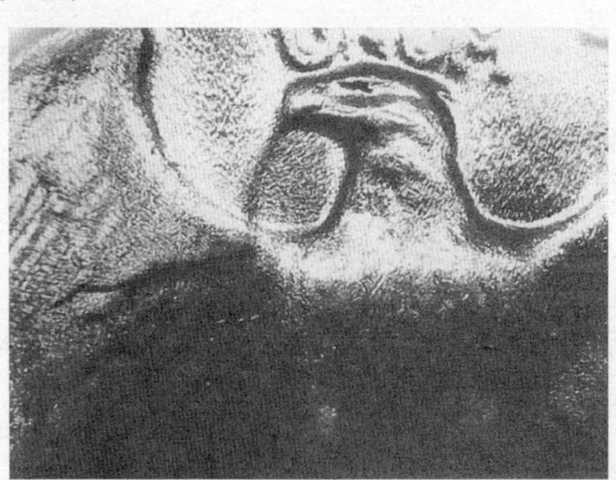

Description: A clashed die is visible in the area of the eagle's beak.

Comments: The clash mark from the obverse gives the eagle the appearance of spitting.

	EF-40	AU-50	AU-58	MS-60	MS-63	MS-64	MS-65	MS-66
VARIETY	$40	$60	$75	$100	$175	$425	$575	n/a
NORMAL	$7	$8	$9	$11	$19	$25	$35	$65

1947-S FS-25-1947S-501 / 101

VARIETY: Repunched Mintmark, Doubled-Die Obverse **CONECA: RPM-001, DDO-001**
PUP: Mintmark / IN GOD WE TRUST
URS-7 · I-4 · L-3

Description: The weaker S is evident west of the primary S. The most prominent portion of the underlying S is the upper left loop, protruding left of the primary. Light doubling is seen mainly on IN GOD WE TRUST.

Comments: This is a highly collectible RPM. The RPM comes mated with DDO-001 in DDO-001 Stage C, D, and E! In other words, it's the nice RPM-001 and DDO-001 in Stage C, D, or E of DDO-001's life. This combo adds a bonus to the avid collector. The FS number was changed from 501 to 501/101.

	EF-40	AU-50	AU-55	MS-60	MS-63	MS-65
VARIETY	$15	$20	n/a	$25	$40	$70
NORMAL	$7	$8	$9	$10	$15	$25

1947-S FS-25-1947S-502

VARIETY: Repunched Mintmark **CONECA: RPM-002**
PUP: Mintmark
URS-6 · I-5 · L-5

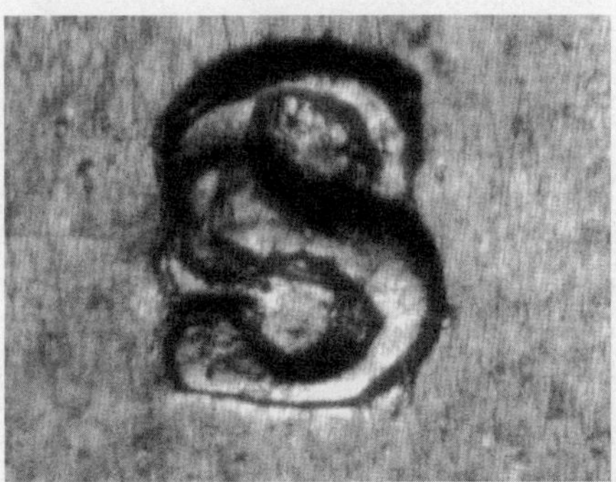

Description: The secondary S is evident south of the primary S. There is also a third S mintmark protruding from the upper left loop of the primary S mintmark.

Comments: This is an outstanding RPM in earlier die states (as shown here). Later die states show less doubling. This is actually an S/S/S/S!

	EF-40	AU-50	MS-60	MS-63	MS-64	MS-65	MS-66
VARIETY	n/a	n/a	n/a	$60	$75	$100	$200
NORMAL	$7	$8	$10	$15	$20	$25	$45

1948-S — FS-25-1948S-501

VARIETY: Repunched Mintmark **CONECA: RPM-002**
PUP: Mintmark
URS-4 · I-5 · L-5

Description: The tops of two different S mintmarks are visible north of the primary, and a total of at least three are evident within the lower loop of the primary. It seems there are four different mintmark punches on this die.

Comments: This is one of the most dramatic repunched mintmarks in the entire series. This variety has proven to be quite rare!

	EF-40	AU-50	MS-60	MS-63	MS-64	MS-65
VARIETY	n/a	$250	n/a	n/a	$1,500	n/a
NORMAL	$7	$8	$10	$12	$20	$40

1948-S — FS-25-1948S-901

VARIETY: "Spitting Eagle" **CONECA: N/L**
PUP: Eagle's beak
URS-5 · I-4 · L-4

Description: There is a clashed die at the eagle's beak.

Comments: The clash mark from the obverse gives the illusion that the eagle is spitting.

	EF-40	AU-50	AU-58	MS-60	MS-63	MS-64	MS-65	MS-66
VARIETY	n/a	n/a	n/a	n/a	n/a	n/a	n/a	n/a
NORMAL	$7	$8	$9	$10	$12	$20	$40	$75

1949-D FS-25-1949D-501

Variety: Repunched Mintmark **CONECA: N/L**
PUP: Mintmark
URS-5 · I-5 · L-4

Description: This very interesting RPM shows what appears to be a secondary D northeast of the primary, and another west of the primary. The image west may be the remains of either an inverted D or a horizontal D. Further study may prove the image west as one way or the other.

Comments: This variety may actually be a die gouge; it needs more study.

	EF-40	AU-50	MS-60	MS-63	MS-64	MS-65
Variety	$100	$150	$200	$250	$300	$500
Normal	$10	$12	$18	$38	$45	$55

The Cherrypickers' Guide HELPFUL HINTS

Please be sure to read the information in the front of this book. It sets the tone for the material that follows and makes it easier to interpret the information for each listing.

The die varieties listed in this book are only the tip of the iceberg. Even more are yet to be discovered. Always examine closely any coin you obtain. You might discover a great variety that soon every collector wants! (Be sure to let us know when you do.)

Note: When you study auction results, especially for high-grade rarities, be aware of the "registry set effect." Two eager collectors who both want the #1-rated set can drive prices up and up—but their frenzy isn't necessarily a snapshot of the broader market.

1949-D, So-Called D Over S — FS-25-1949D-601 (018.8)

VARIETY: Over Mintmark — **CONECA: RPM-003**
PUP: Mintmark
URS-8 · I-5 · L-4

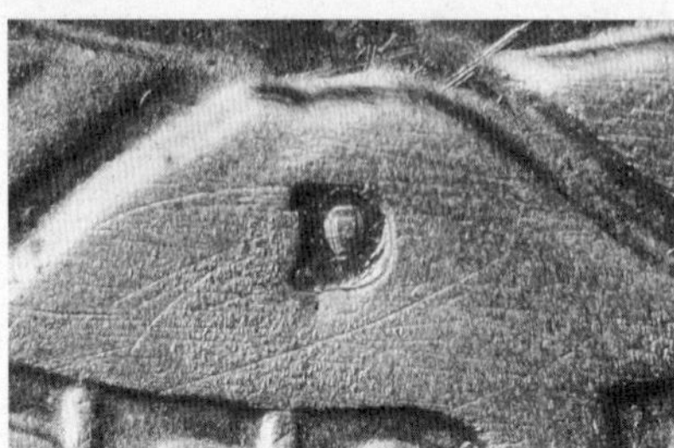

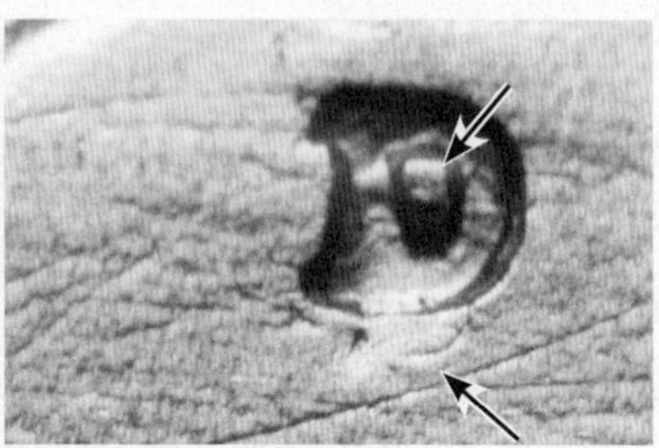

Description: The remnants of a secondary mintmark are evident south of the primary D. Some specialists believe this to be a D/D and not a D/S. However, it is still the opinion of the authors that the underlying mintmark is an S, as evidenced by the curvature of the lower bar on the underlying image. Additionally, the overall width of the underlying image appears too narrow to be that of a D.

Comments: The coin illustrated above is obviously a later die state. Questions about the underlying mintmark may be answered definitively if an earlier die state is discovered.

	AU-55	AU-58	MS-60	MS-63	MS-64	MS-65	MS-66
VARIETY	$45	$60	$75	$175	$325	$500	$750
NORMAL	$15	$16	$18	$38	$45	$55	$100

1950 — FS-25-1950-801 (019)

VARIETY: Doubled-Die Reverse — **CONECA: DDR-001**
PUP: Eagle's beak, entire left reverse
URS-9 · I-4 · L-3

Description: Doubling is most evident on the eagle's beak, the lower-left wing edges, and the leaves and stems on the left side.

Comments: An early-die-state specimen will command higher values.

	EF-40	AU-50	MS-60	MS-63	MS-65
VARIETY	$10	$25	$45	$85	$225
NORMAL	$7	$8	$10	$12	$35

1950-D FS-25-1950D-501

Variety: Repunched Mintmark **CONECA: RPM-002**
PUP: Mintmark
URS-8 · I-4 · L-3

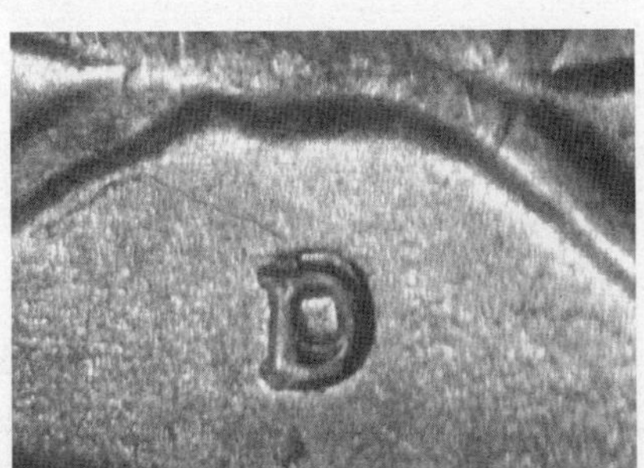

Description: The secondary mintmark is evident north of the primary D.

Comments: This variety is one of the more attractive RPMs for the date, and the series. This variety was erroneously listed in previous editions as FS-502.

	EF-40	AU-50	MS-60	MS-63	MS-65
Variety	$35	$40	$50	$80	$225
Normal	$7	$8	$10	$12	$40

1950-D FS-25-1950D-801 (020)

Variety: Doubled-Die Reverse **CONECA: DDR-001**
PUP: Eagle's talons, lower left body of the eagle, wing
URS-8 · I-4 · L-3

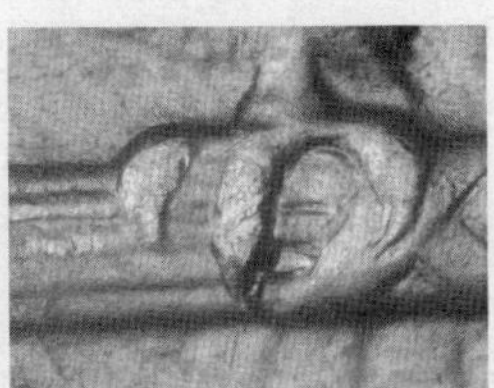
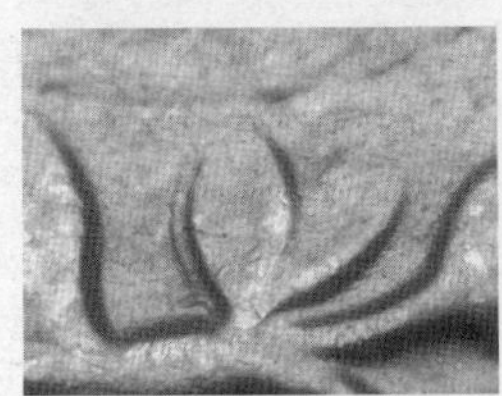
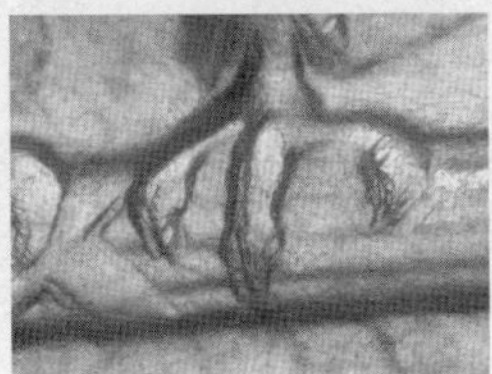

Description: Doubling is evident on the eagle's talons, the arrow points, and the feathers on the legs.

Comments: Discovered by Del Romines, this variety can be found with some searching.

	EF-40	AU-50	MS-60	MS-63	MS-65
Variety	$20	$30	$75	$175	$350
Normal	$7	$8	$10	$12	$40

1950-D FS-25-1950D-802

VARIETY: Doubled-Die Reverse **CONECA: DDR-002**
PUP: Reverse lettering
URS-7 · I-4· L-3

Description: As with all Class VI doubled dies, this variety exhibits the typical extra thickness on all reverse lettering. This extra thickness is especially strong on UNITED and QUARTER DOLLAR, where some separation in the letters may be evident.

Comments: For a Class VI, most of which aren't much to get excited about, this is a strong variety and worth hunting for.

	EF-40	AU-50	MS-60	MS-63	MS-65
VARIETY	$25	$50	$75	$175	$325
NORMAL	$7	$8	$10	$12	$40

1950-D, D Over S FS-25-1950D-601 (021)

VARIETY: Over Mintmark **CONECA: OMM-001**
PUP: Mintmark
URS-11 · I-5 · L-5

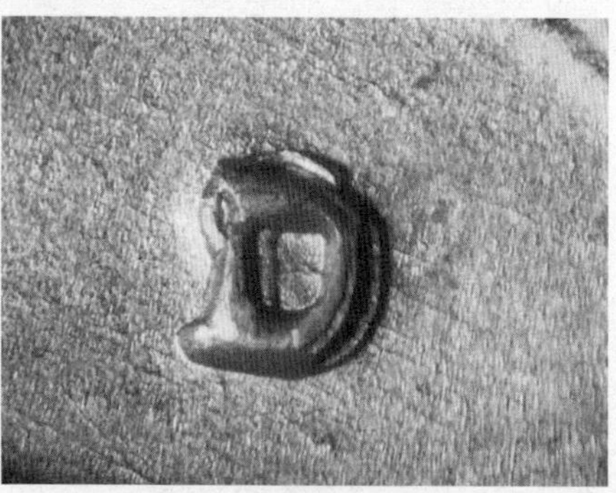

Description: The upper left curve of the underlying S is evident west and north of the D.

Comments: Most specimens exhibit strike doubling on the D, and have brilliant surfaces. The mintmark, besides heavy strike doubling, is also a D/D as well! Many low-grade VG-VF specimens exist.

	EF-40	AU-50	MS-60	MS-63	MS-65	MS-66
VARIETY	$150	$190	$325	$950	$3,600	$7,500
NORMAL	$7	$8	$10	$12	$40	$70

1950-S FS-25-1950S-801

Variety: Doubled-Die Reverse **CONECA: DDR-003**
PUP: Large leaf at arrow points
URS-8 · I-5 · L-4

Description: Doubling is visible on the lower arrows and on some of the lower leaves.

Comments: The large leaf at the arrow tips appears to indicate a Type B over Type A reverse, as the tip points distinctly to the left. This variety may be DDR-001, 003, or 004. Although a relatively minor doubled die, it is featured as an example of some of the varieties that still wait to be found!

	EF-40	AU-50	MS-60	MS-63	MS-65	MS-66
Variety	$40	$50	$75	$125	$300	$750
Normal	$7	$8	$10	$16	$35	$60

1950-S FS-25-1950S-501

Variety: Repunched Mintmark **CONECA: RPM-001**
PUP: Mintmark
URS-9 · I-5 · L-4

Description: The weaker S mintmark is evident wide north of the primary S.

Comments: This is considered a very wide repunching on a mintmark. This is one of the more desirable RPMs.

	EF-40	AU-50	MS-60	MS-63	MS-65	MS-66
Variety	$25	$35	$55	$100	$275	$600
Normal	$7	$8	$10	$16	$35	$60

1950-S, S Over D — FS-25-1950S-601 (022)

VARIETY: Over Mintmark — **CONECA: OMM-001**
PUP: Mintmark
URS-10 · I-5 · L-5

Description: The underlying D mintmark is clearly visible beneath the primary S.

Comments: This is certainly one of the most popular Washington varieties. Most Uncirculated specimens have a frosty luster, compared to the brilliant surfaces on most Uncirculated 1950-D, D/S quarters. Many low-grade specimens exist in VG-VF grades. In terms of graded coins, the S/D has fewer than the D/S!

	EF-40	AU-50	MS-60	MS-63	MS-65	MS-66
VARIETY	$175	$275	$475	$775	$1,250	$2,000
NORMAL	$7	$8	$10	$16	$35	$60

1951-D — FS-25-1951D-501

VARIETY: Repunched Mintmark — **CONECA: RPM-004**
PUP: Mintmark
URS-6 · I-4 · L-4

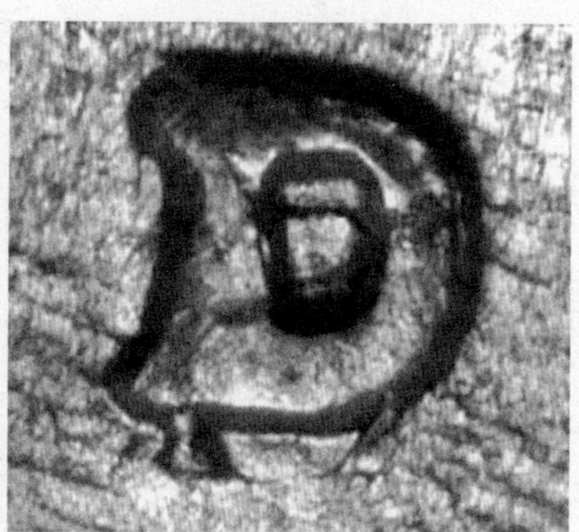

Description: A relatively strong secondary mintmark can be seen to the south of the primary D.

Comments: While thought by some to be a D/S, this coin has been determined to be a D/D RPM-004.

	EF-40	AU-50	MS-60	MS-63	MS-65	MS-66
VARIETY	$60	$80	$150	$400	$750	$1,000
NORMAL	$7	$8	$9	$10	$35	$65

1951-S — FS-25-1951S-501

VARIETY: Repunched Mintmark — **CONECA: N/L**
PUP: Mintmark
URS-4 · I-5 · L-4

Description: The mintmark is strongly repunched south.

Comments: This is one of the strongest repunched mintmarks in the Washington quarter series. Collector interest in the variety is strong. Valuations will be reported in the next edition.

	AU-58	MS-60	MS-63	MS-64	MS-65	MS-66	MS-67
VARIETY	n/a	n/a	n/a	n/a	n/a	n/a	n/a
NORMAL	$10	$11	$15	$20	$35	$75	$155

1952, Proof — FS-25-1952-901

VARIETY: Engraving Error, "Superbird" — **CONECA: N/L**
PUP: Eagle's breast
URS-13 · I-4 · L-3

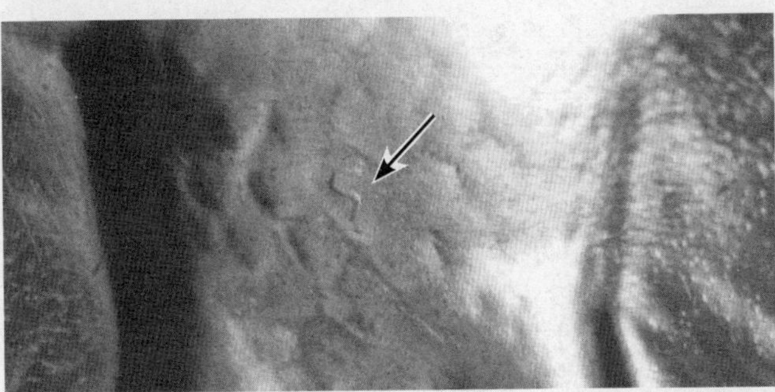

Description: There is an unusual S-shaped mark on the breast of the eagle. The cause of this mark is unknown.

Comments: The nickname for this well-known variety is, suitably, "Superbird!" This variety is featured in *Mega Red*. With due diligence and luck, this variety can still be cherrypicked. The values are for non-cameo coins.

	PF-63	PF-64	PF-65	PR-66	PR-67
VARIETY	$50	$100	$150	$250	$425
NORMAL	$35	$40	$45	$55	$100

1952, Proof — FS-25-1952-902 / 101

VARIETY: Hand-Engraved Tail Feathers, "Superbird" **CONECA: DDO-004**
PUP: Tail feathers, eagle's breast **RED-001**
URS-9 · I-5 · L-5

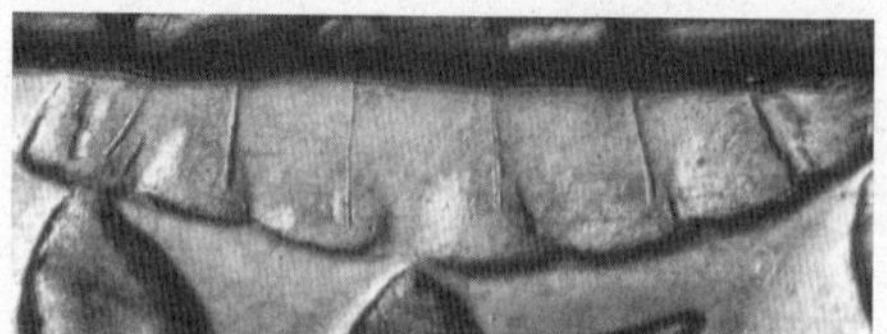

Description: This is a later die state of the so-called "Superbird" variety. At this stage, part of the lower loop of the S is worn or polished away, and the tail-feather details have been strengthened by hand engraving.

Comments: This coin is popular among hobbyists for the "Superbird" feature. Few specialists actually realize that the late die state displays enhanced wing feathers, which in itself is probably more interesting than the S on the eagle's breast. The obverse of this coin is a minor doubled die. Two other Washington quarter dates, 1953 and 1957-D, are known with hand-engraved feathers. Compared to the regular "Superbird," this "Superbird" with re-engraved feathers is rare! Cameo coins for this variety are very rare. 101 has been added to the FS number, which previously was just 902.

	PF-63	PF-64	PF-65	PF-66	PF-67
VARIETY	$100	$175	$225	$450	$675
NORMAL	$35	$40	$45	$55	$100

1952-D — FS-25-1952D-101

VARIETY: Doubled-Die Obverse **CONECA: DDO-001**
PUP: LIBERTY, IN GOD WE TRUST
URS-7 · I-5 · L-4

Description: Moderate doubling is evident on the date, the motto, and LIBERTY.

Comments: This variety can still be located with a little searching, yet has proven to be very scarce!

	EF-40	AU-50	MS-60	MS-63	MS-64	MS-65
VARIETY	$100	$200	$350	$575	$850	n/a
NORMAL	$7	$8	$9	$10	$20	$30

1952-D

FS-25-1952D-501

Variety: Huge Mintmark
PUP: Mintmark
URS-9 · I-5 · L-4

CONECA: MMS-004

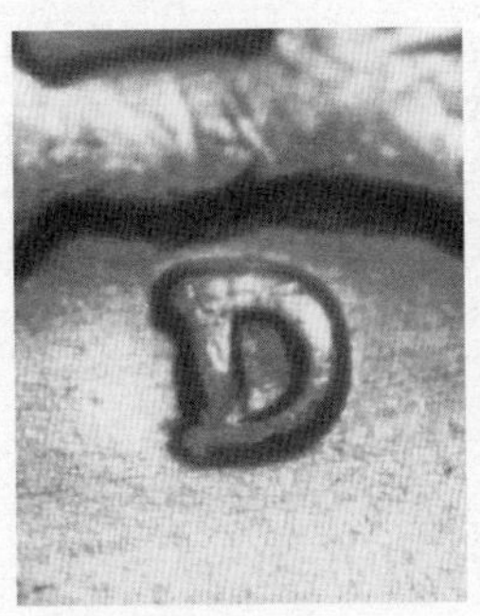
Huge D

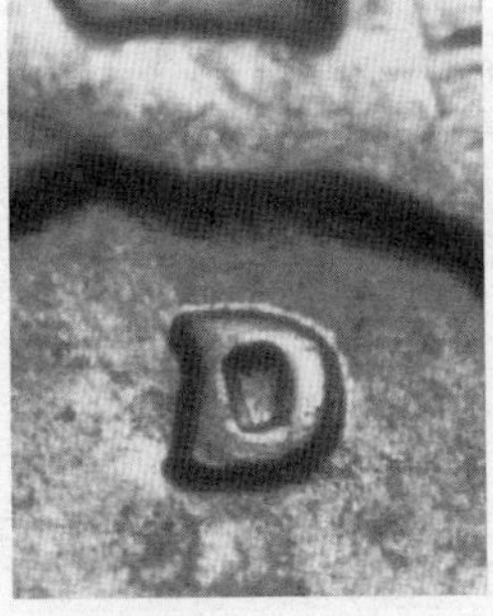
Medium D

Small D

Description: A medium and small D are shown for comparison.

Comments: The huge D is considered very rare in all grades (including circulated) with very few specimens known in Uncirculated. Cherrypicking one of these in Brilliant Uncirculated would surely make your day!

	EF-20	EF-40	AU-50	MS-60	MS-63	MS-64	MS-65
Variety	$40	$75	$125	$250	$500	$750	$1,250
Normal	$6	$7	$8	$9	$10	$20	$30

1952-S

FS-25-1952S-501

Variety: Repunched Mintmark
PUP: Mintmark
URS-9 · I-5 · L-5

CONECA: RPM-001

Description: This is a triple-punched mintmark, with a secondary S evident north of the primary, and another overlapping the primary.

Comments: RPMs in the Washington quarter series are becoming highly collectible. This is one of the nicer RPMs of the series, and, as such, is very popular.

	EF-40	AU-50	MS-60	MS-63	MS-65	MS-66
Variety	$18	$25	$45	$65	$100	$150
Normal	$7	$8	$13	$20	$40	$60

1952-S — FS-25-1952S-502

VARIETY: Repunched Mintmark — **CONECA: RPM-002**
PUP: Mintmark
URS-7 · I-4 · L-3

Description: The secondary mintmark is evident north of the primary.

Comments: New RPMs in the Washington quarter series are being reported every year! RPM-002 gives the collector or cherrypicker an added bonus for this year. It is a very scarce coin with few sales.

	EF-40	AU-50	MS-60	MS-63	MS-65	MS-66
VARIETY	$25	$50	$100	$150	$350	$550
NORMAL	$7	$8	$13	$20	$40	$60

1953, Proof — FS-25-1953-101 (022.1)

VARIETY: Doubled-Die Obverse — **CONECA: DDO-001**
PUP: IN GOD WE TRUST, date
URS-9 · I-4 · L-3

Description: Doubling is evident on all obverse lettering, very strongly so on the motto, date, and designer's initials.

Comments: This is a fairly well known variety, but it can still be cherrypicked! This variety comes in non-cameo and cameo. The prices below are for regular-struck Proof coins.

	PF-63	PF-65	PF-66
VARIETY	$50	$100	$150
NORMAL	$26	$40	$45

1953, Proof, Re-engraved Tail

FS-25-1953-901

Variety: Re-Engraved Tail Feathers

CONECA: RED-001

PUP: Tail feathers

URS-8 · I-5 · L-5

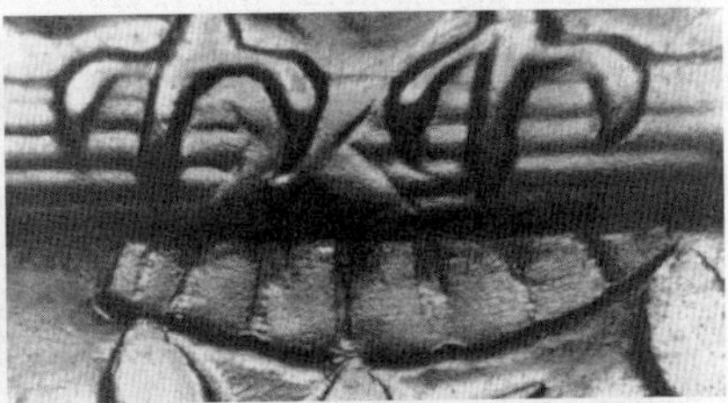

Description: Many of the tail-feather details were polished away, resulting in the removal of the incuse separation lines between the feathers. The design was then strengthened by the cutting in of crude tail-feather outlines that are raised. The lower edges of the feathers were also strengthened in the same manner.

Comments: This variety appears to be rare, as very few have surfaced. Two other Washington quarter dates, 1932 (Proof) and 1957-D, are known with hand-engraved tail-feather outlines.

	PF-63	PF-65	PF-66
Variety	$175	$300	$500
Normal	$26	$40	$45

1953-D

FS-25-1953D-801 (022.2)

Variety: Doubled-Die Reverse

CONECA: DDR-001

PUP: UNITED STATES OF AMERICA, QUARTER DOLLAR

URS-9 · I-4 · L-3

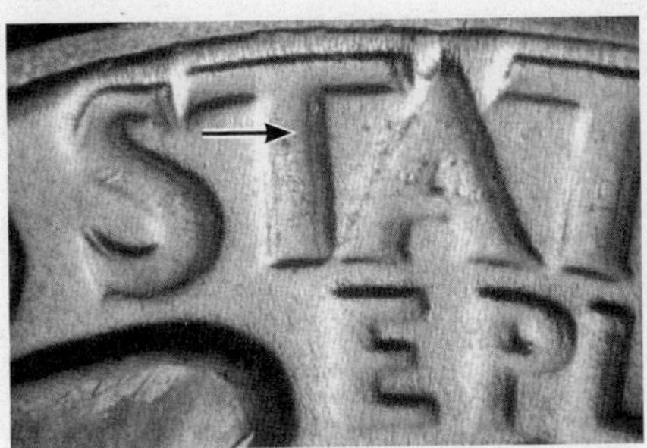

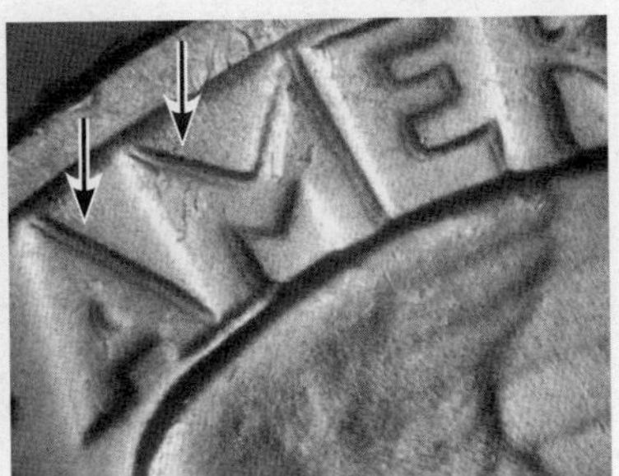

Description: Doubling is evident on all reverse lettering, strongest on UNITED STATES OF AMERICA, and weaker on QUARTER DOLLAR.

Comments: This variety is one of the strongest reverse doubled dies in the series. (Note: This variety was wrongly listed as FS-25-1953D-101 in the fourth edition, volume II.) In this case, the higher the grade, the rarer the coin.

	EF-40	AU-50	MS-60	MS-63	MS-65
Variety	n/a	n/a	$35	$75	$200
Normal	$7	$8	$9	$10	$35

1953-D

FS-25-1953D-501

Variety: Repunched Mintmark
CONECA: RPM-001
PUP: Mintmark
URS-5 · I-5 · L-5

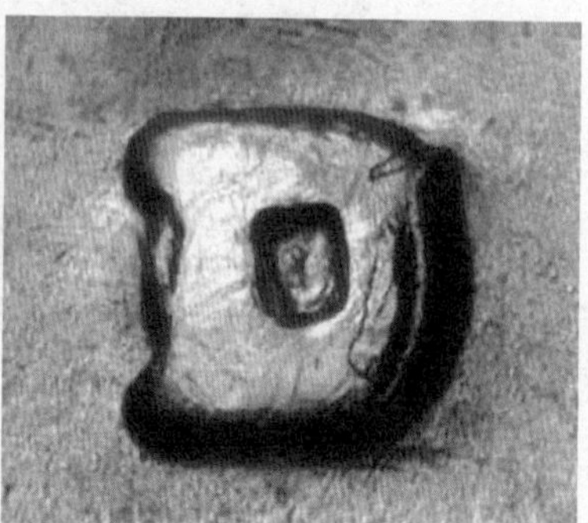

Description: The primary D mintmark is punched over what is believed to be an inverted mintmark. Further study may determine the underlying D to be horizontal, but the current photos lean more toward the inverted orientation.

Comments: This is an extremely popular variety and has proved to be very scarce.

	EF-40	AU-50	MS-60	MS-63	MS-64	MS-65
Variety	$100	$150	$275	$400	$600	$1,000
Normal	$7	$8	$9	$10	$20	$35

1953-D, D Over S

FS-25-1953D-601 (022.3)

Variety: Over Mintmark
CONECA: OMM-001
PUP: Mintmark
URS-9 · I-4 · L-4

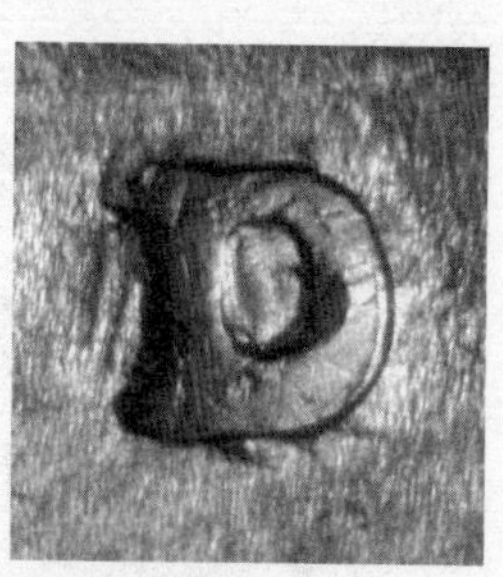

Early die state

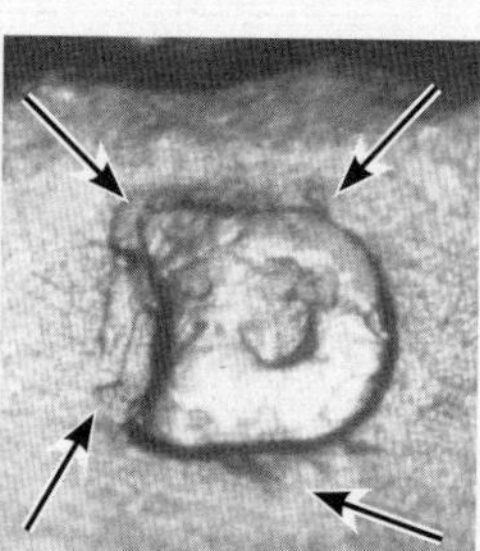

Middle die state

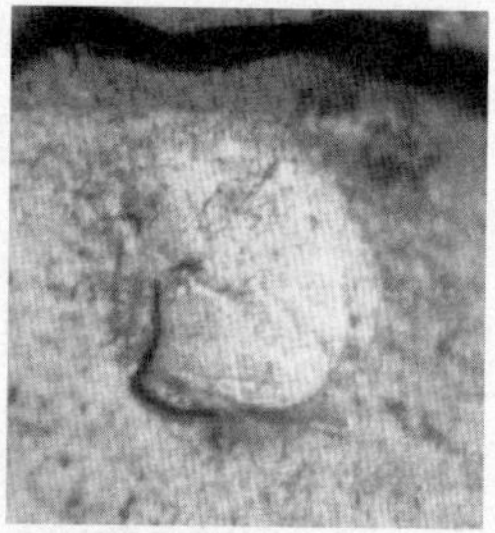

Late die state

Description: Multiple mintmark punches produced this fascinating variety, creating a D/D/D/S/S over mintmark. Some specialists consider only one underlying S, but these photos clearly show at least two S mintmark punches.

Comments: This variety is not very well known, but can be found with some searching. The values shown are for the early die state. The late die stage (illustrated above) is often overlooked as not saleable.

	EF-40	AU-50	MS-60	MS-63	MS-65
Variety	n/a	$45	$75	$145	$375
Normal	$7	$8	$9	$10	$35

1956, Proof — FS-25-1956-101

VARIETY: Doubled-Die Obverse
PUP: IN GOD WE TRUST
URS-7 · I-4 · L-4

Description: Nice doubling is visible on the motto IN GOD WE TRUST.

Comments: Very thick letters are seen in IN GOD WE TRUST, with nice separation of doubling, especially on TRUST. This is a great one to look for! Cameo Proofs bring extra premiums.

	PF-60	PF-63	PF-64	PF-65	PF-66	PF-67
VARIETY	n/a	n/a	n/a	n/a	n/a	n/a
NORMAL	$11	$12	$14	$20	$35	$50

1956, Proof — FS-25-1956-701

CONECA: N/L

VARIETY: Reverse Die Gouge
PUP: Area under talons
URS-9 · I-5 · L-5

Description: A very unusual die gauge is evident on the arrows below the eagle's right talons. Another die scratch is evident under the eagle's left talons.

Comments: The causes of these gouges are unknown, but they are extremely interesting. The first example was found by Larry Briggs in 1996. Since then, very few more have surfaced—even though interest is high and cherrypickers are on the hunt.

	PF-63	PF-65	PF-66	PF-67
VARIETY	$100	$200	$300	$425
NORMAL	$12	$20	$35	$50

1956–1964, Type B Reverses

VARIETY: Type B Reverse **CONECA: N/L**
PUP: Eagle's tail feathers, STATES
URS-4 · I-3 · L-4

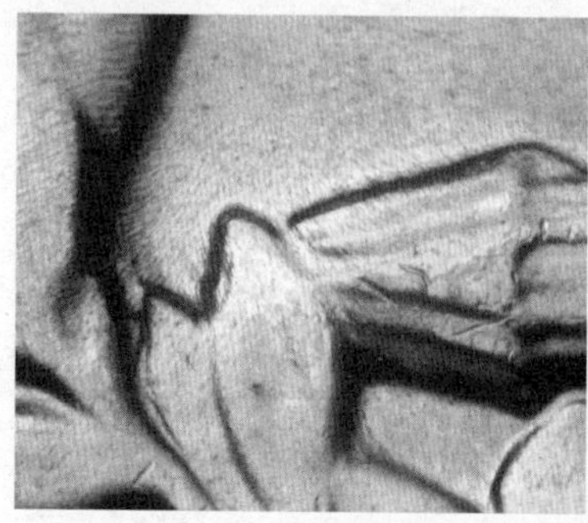

As discussed on page 167, Washington quarters are known with at least eight different reverse varieties. The Type B reverses and their valuations are listed here. The Type B reverse is characterized by a pointed tip to the leaf nearest the arrow points; by the fact that this leaf tip extends above the topmost arrow tips; and by the fact that the design overall is in higher relief. This reverse style is known on all Philadelphia circulation strikes from 1956 through 1964 (which are listed here), as well as on Proofs from 1937 through 1942 and from 1950 through 1964. The 1956 Type B reverse is scarce.

1956, FS-25-1956-901, CONECA: RDV-002

	AU-50	MS-60	MS-63	MS-65
VARIETY	$25	$35	$75	$200
NORMAL	$8	$9	$10	$20

1957, FS-25-1957-901, CONECA: RDV-002

	AU-50	MS-60	MS-63	MS-65
VARIETY	$25	$35	$45	$75
NORMAL	$8	$9	$10	$20

1958, FS-25-1958-901, CONECA: RDV-002

	AU-50	MS-60	MS-63	MS-65
VARIETY	$25	$33	$65	$125
NORMAL	$8	$9	$10	$20

1959, FS-25-1959-901, CONECA: RDV-002

	AU-50	MS-60	MS-63	MS-65
VARIETY	$35	$60	$125	$225
NORMAL	$8	$9	$10	$20

1960, FS-25-1960-901, CONECA: RDV-002

	AU-50	MS-60	MS-63	MS-65
VARIETY	$30	$55	$115	$225
NORMAL	$8	$9	$10	$20

1961, FS-25-1961-901, CONECA: RDV-002

	MS-60	MS-63	MS-65
VARIETY	$50	$75	$160
NORMAL	$9	$10	$25

1962, FS-25-1962-901, CONECA: RDV-002

	MS-60	MS-63	MS-65
VARIETY	$20	$25	$95
NORMAL	$9	$10	$25

1963, FS-25-1963-901, CONECA: RDV-002

	MS-60	MS-63	MS-65
VARIETY	$75	$150	$250
NORMAL	$9	$10	$25

1964, FS-25-1964-901, CONECA: RDV-002

	AU-55	MS-60	MS-63	MS-65	MS-66
VARIETY	$25	$30	$45	$80	$150
NORMAL	$8	$9	$10	$25	$55

1956-D — FS-25-1956D-501 (022.4)

VARIETY: Inverted Repunched Mintmark — **CONECA: RPM-001**
PUP: Mintmark
URS-9 · I-4 · L-4

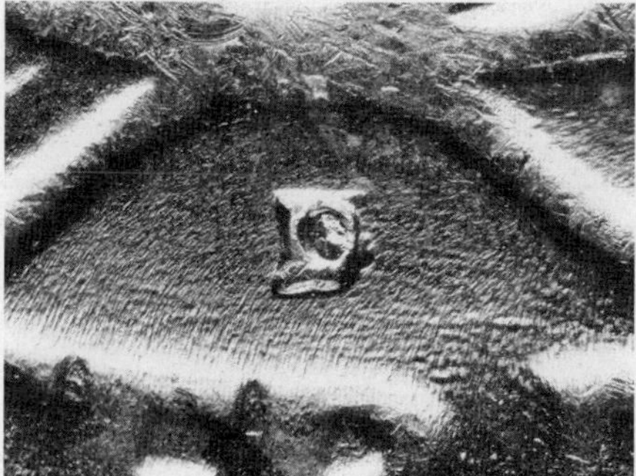

Description: The initial mintmark was punched into the die inverted, and then the second (primary) mintmark was punched correctly, creating this variety.

Comments: This is a very interesting and popular variety. Although not rare, it is scarce. With a lot of hard work and some luck, it can still be cherrypicked. This coin is a conditional rarity.

	AU-50	MS-60	MS-63	MS-65
VARIETY	$20	$50	$90	$325
NORMAL	$8	$9	$10	$25

1957-D FS-25-1957D-901

VARIETY: Re-Engraved Tail Feathers **CONECA: RED-001**
PUP: Tail feathers
URS-5 · I-5 · L-5

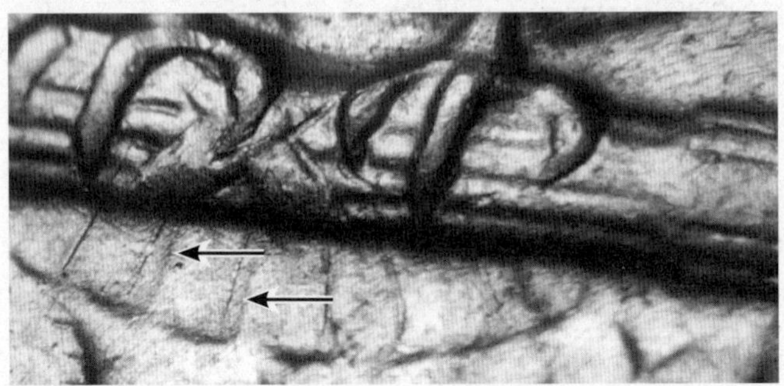

Description: Many of the tail-feather details were polished or abraded away; the design was then strengthened by the cutting in of crude tail-feather outlines.

Comments: Two other Washington quarter dates, 1952 and 1953 (both Proofs), are known with hand-engraved tail-feather outlines. At present, it has shown to be very elusive and rare. There are only three verified sales. This coin would make your day.

	AU-50	MS-60	MS-63	MS-64	MS-65
VARIETY	$300	$750	$1,500	$2,250	n/a
NORMAL	$8	$9	$10	$16	$25

1957-D FS-25-1957D-902

VARIETY: Separated Mintmark **CONECA: N/L**
PUP: Mintmark
URS-11 · I-4 · L-4

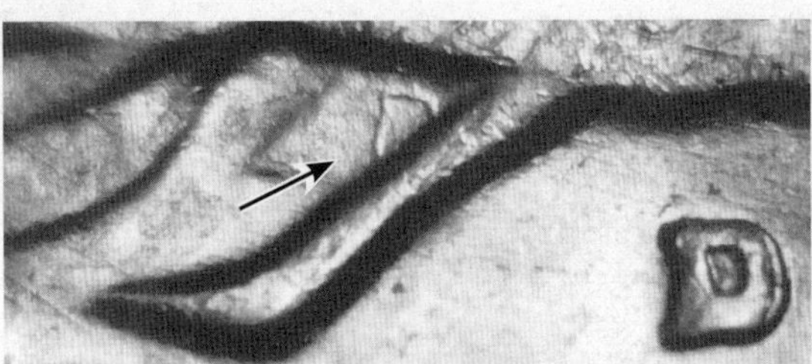

Description: An apparent D mintmark shows above the left olive branch.

Comments: This variety was previously listed with Fivaz-Stanton number FS-501. This particular mark is known on several reverse dies, suggesting the original might have been intended to be a working die, blundered, set aside, and then mistakenly used as a master die (which in turn was used to make a working hub with which several working dies were created). Most specialists accept as a "Master Die RPM" while others believe it to be a form of hub damage. Some specialists attempt to own one from each die. Note that the doubling on the primary D below the wreath is strike doubling—not an RPM.

	AU-55	MS-60	MS-63	MS-64	MS-65
VARIETY	$30	$45	$75	$100	$150
NORMAL	$7	$9	$10	$15	$25

1959, Proof — FS-25-1959-101

Variety: Doubled-Die Obverse — **CONECA: DDO-004**
PUP: IN GOD WE TRUST
URS-9 · I-3 · L-3

Description: Doubling is dramatic to the north on all obverse lettering, especially on IN GOD WE TRUST.

Comments: There are at least five different obverse doubled dies for the 1959 Proofs. This is by far the nicest. Prices shown here are for non–Cameo coins.

	PF-63	PF-65	PF-66
Variety	$40	$75	$140
Normal	$7	$14	$24

1959, Proof — FS-25-1959-102

Variety: Doubled-Die Obverse — **CONECA: DDO-002**
PUP: IN GOD WE TRUST
URS-5 · I-3 · L-3

Description: Strong doubling is visible on the motto IN GOD WE TRUST.

Comments: On this Proof 1959 issue, nice doubling is present to the south—in contrast to the doubling to the *north* on FS-25-1959-101. Market values will solidify over time. Cameos will undoubtedly command extra premiums.

	PF-60	PF-63	PF-64	PF-65	PF-66	PF-67
Variety	n/a	n/a	n/a	n/a	n/a	n/a
Normal	$6	$7	$13	$14	$24	$35

1959-D

FS-25-1959D-501

VARIETY: Repunched Mintmark
CONECA: RPM-001
PUP: Mintmark
URS-7 · I-4 · L-3

Description: Secondary D mintmarks are evident north and southeast of the primary D.

Comments: While relatively new, this coin has proven to be very scarce. A very nice RPM that has had few pieces enter the slab field!

	AU-50	MS-60	MS-63	MS-64	MS-65
VARIETY	$30	$50	$100	$175	$350
NORMAL	$8	$9	$10	$15	$20

1960, Proof

FS-25-1960-801

VARIETY: Doubled-Die Reverse
CONECA: DDR-002
PUP: QUARTER DOLLAR
URS-10 · I-3 · L-3

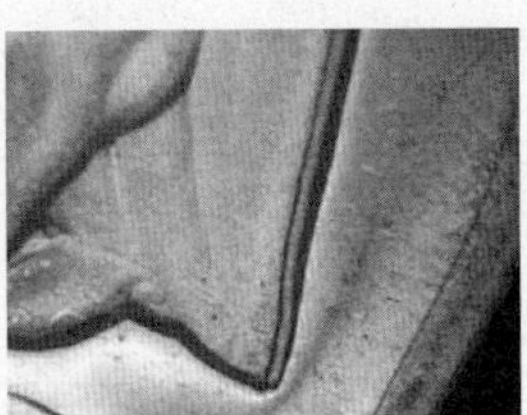

Description: The doubling on this variety is evident on all reverse lettering, and many of the other design elements. A strong spread is evident on the eagle's wings, the leaf stems, and especially QUARTER DOLLAR.

Comments: This is one of the strongest Proof reverse doubled dies in the Washington series. Prices are for non cameo or deep cameo coins.

	PF-63	PF-65	PF-66
VARIETY	$35	$75	$125
NORMAL	$10	$13	$25

1961, Proof FS-25-1961-101

Variety: Doubled-Die Obverse **CONECA: DDO-001**
PUP: IN GOD WE TRUST
URS-8 · I-3 · L-2

Description: Moderate doubling is evident on the date, the designer's initials, and the motto.

Comments: There are several other obverse doubled dies for the 1961 Proof.

	PF-63	PF-65	PF-66
Variety	$25	$65	$125
Normal	$10	$13	$25

1961-D FS-25-1961D-501

Variety: Repunched Mintmark **CONECA: RPM-005**
PUP: Mintmark
URS-5 · I-5 · L-5

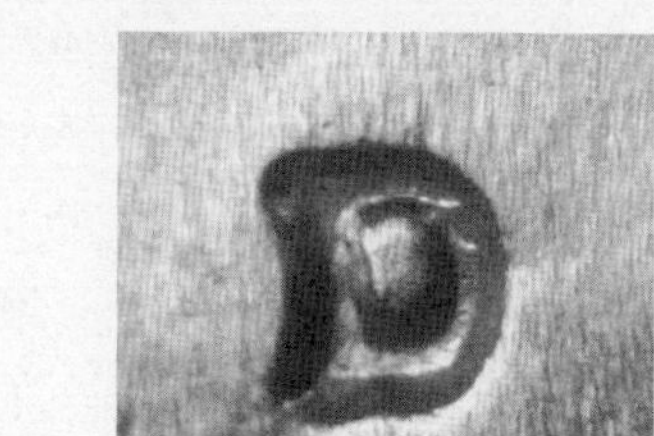

Description: The secondary D is evident north of the primary D.

Comments: This is a fairly strong RPM for the Washington quarter series. It has proven to be quite elusive, but when available brings a substantial premium!

	AU-50	MS-60	MS-63	MS-64	MS-65
Variety	$50	$100	$300	$500	$750
Normal	$8	$9	$10	$16	$25

1961-D — FS-25-1961D-502

Variety: Repunched Mintmark **CONECA: RPM-004**
PUP: Mintmark
URS-6 · I-4 · L-4

Description: The secondary D is evident north of the primary D.

Comments: This listing is clearly different from the previous one and has also proven to be rare!

	AU-50	MS-60	MS-63	MS-64	MS-65
Variety	$50	$100	$200	$350	n/a
Normal	$8	$9	$10	$16	$25

1961-D — FS-25-1961D-503

Variety: Repunched Mintmark **CONECA: RPM-001**
PUP: Mintmark
URS-5 · I-4 · L-4

Description: The D mintmark is repunched to the west.

Comments: This is a very strong repunched mintmark—more dramatic than FS-25-1961D-501 and -502.

	AU-50	MS-60	MS-63	MS-64	MS-65
Variety	n/a	n/a	n/a	n/a	n/a
Normal	$8	$9	$10	$16	$25

1962 — FS-25-1962-101

Variety: Doubled-Die Obverse — **CONECA: DDO-004**
PUP: IN GOD WE TRUST
URS-8 · I-5 · L-5

Description: The extra thickness on all lettering is typical of the Class VI doubled die. However, close examination will show four separate hubbings, especially on the R of TRUST and the end of the ribbon. This is a circulation-strike coin.

Comments: This is an extremely strong Class VI variety. It has proven to be very scarce and sales have been supportive of such. Finding this little cherry will definitely make your day.

	EF-40	AU-50	MS-60	MS-63	MS-64	MS-65	MS-66
Variety	n/a	n/a	$100	$250	$375	$500	$750
Normal	$7	$8	$9	$10	$16	$25	$55

1962-D — FS-25-1962D-501

Variety: Repunched Mintmark — **CONECA: RPM-003**
PUP: Mintmark
URS-7 · I-4 · L-4

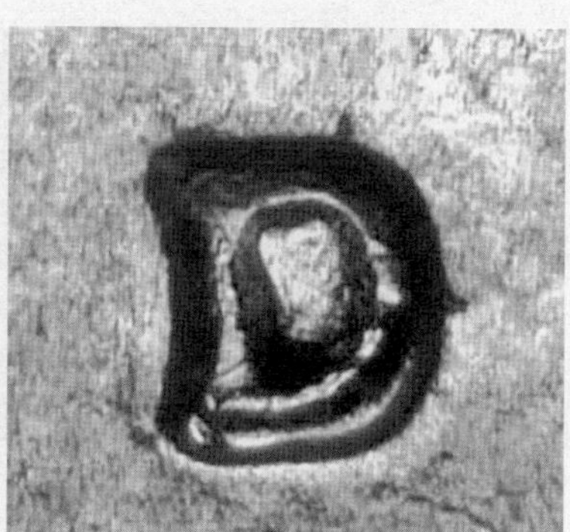

Description: Remnants of a secondary D mintmark are evident northeast of the primary D. The vertical of the secondary D is protruding from the upper right portion of the primary D.

Comments: An earlier die state of this RPM would be a great find! This is a scarce coin with much interest but has not yet reached its potential value.

	MS-60	MS-63	MS-65
Variety	$40	$105	$175
Normal	$9	$10	$25

1963 FS-25-1963-101 (023)

VARIETY: Doubled-Die Obverse **CONECA: DDO-001**
PUP: IN GOD WE TRUST
URS-12 · I-5 · L-4

Description: Doubling is evident on all obverse lettering and the date.

Comments: This variety can be found in Mint sets. This has been a known packaged variety for several years. Although not rare, because of the nice doubling, this coin is popular and quite sellable.

	MS-60	MS-63	MS-64	MS-65	MS-66
VARIETY	$20	$40	$55	$75	$175
NORMAL	$9	$10	$15	$25	$55

1963 FS-25-1963-102 / 803

VARIETY: Doubled-Die Obverse, Doubled-Die Reverse **CONECA: DDO-007, DDR-001**
PUP: IN GOD WE TRUST, AMERICA
URS-9 · I-5 · L-4

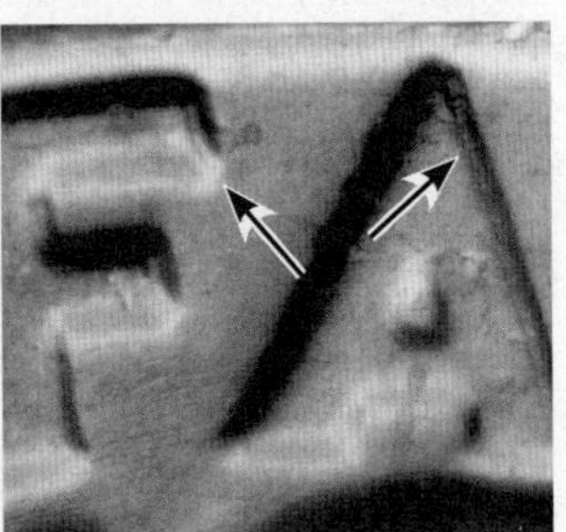

Description: The reverse is doubled on all lettering around the rim. This variety is in a different direction and is not the same as FS-101. We are correcting this mistake at this time.

Comments: This variety can also be found in Mint sets.

	MS-60	MS-63	MS-65	MS-66
VARIETY	$35	$75	$225	$400
NORMAL	$9	$10	$25	$55

1963 FS-25-1963-103

Variety: Doubled-Die Obverse **CONECA: DDO-005**
PUP: Date
URS-7 · I-5 · L-4

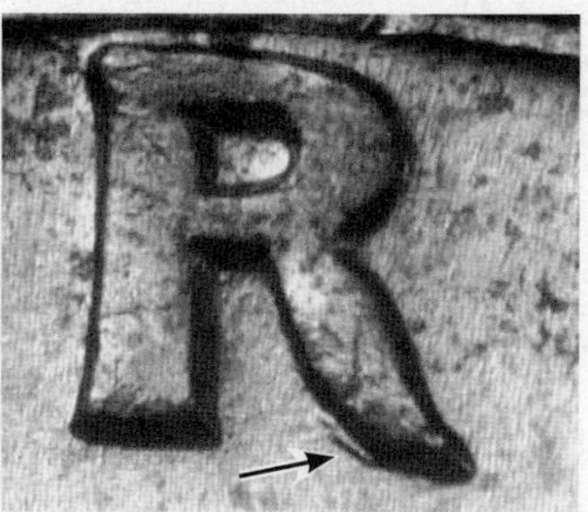

Description: The doubling is most evident on the 6 and 3 of the date. The secondary 6 is clear to the right of the loop of the primary 6.

Comments: This is one of the most interesting doubled dies for this date. It has turned out to be quite scarce.

	MS-60	MS-63	MS-65	MS-66
Variety	$100	$175	$300	$450
Normal	$9	$10	$25	$55

1963 FS-25-1963-801

Variety: Doubled-Die Reverse **CONECA: DDR-004**
PUP: AMERICA
URS-7 · I-4 · L-3

Description: Doubling is evident only left of the left upright on M of AMERICA, inside the upper loop on C of AMERICA, and to the left of the first T of STATES.

Comments: This is a very unusual variety. This variety has proven to be quite scarce.

	MS-60	MS-63	MS-65	MS-66
Variety	$100	$175	$300	$450
Normal	$9	$10	$25	$55

1963 — FS-25-1963-901a

VARIETY: Space Between Arrow Point and Leaf **CONECA: N/L**
PUP: Arrow points
URS-4 · I-5 · L-5

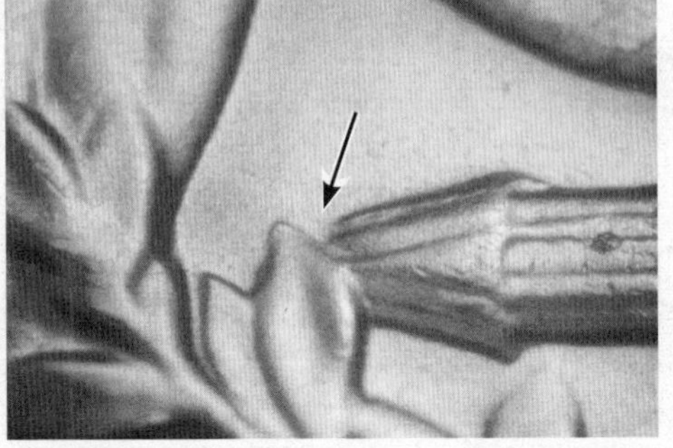

Description: The top arrowhead on this Type B reverse is much farther away from the leaf.

Comments: This variety is quite rare and apparently overlooked all these years! It was discovered by Robert Lawson in 2015. Presently only six or seven examples are known, with one verified sale of $500 for MS-64. More surely exist; publication in the *Cherrypickers' Guide* should bring additional coins to light.

	AU-50	MS-60	MS-63	MS-64	MS-65	MS-66
VARIETY	n/a	n/a	n/a	n/a	n/a	n/a
NORMAL	$8	$9	$10	$14	$25	$55

1963, Proof — FS-25-1963-802

VARIETY: Doubled-Die Reverse **CONECA: DDR-006**
PUP: AMERICA
URS-7 · I-4 · L-3

Description: Doubling is evident on all reverse lettering, but strongest on AMERICA and DOLLAR.

Comments: This is one of six or more DDR 1963 Proof quarters.

	PF-63	PF-65	PF-66
VARIETY	$75	$175	$275
NORMAL	n/a	$13	n/a

1963-D FS-25-1963D-101

Variety: Doubled-Die Obverse **CONECA: DDO-004**
PUP: LIBERTY
URS-6 · I-4 · L-3

Description: Doubling is evident on all obverse lettering, strongest on LIBERTY, lesser on IN GOD WE TRUST and the date.

Comments: This is a rare coin in all grades and the interest level is very high. Pricing, however, is very moderate for its rarity.

	EF-40	AU-50	MS-60	MS-63	MS-64	MS-65
Variety	n/a	n/a	$65	$100	$150	n/a
Normal	$7	$8	$9	$10	$18	$25

1964 FS-25-1964-801

Variety: Doubled-Die Reverse **CONECA: DDR-001**
PUP: QUARTER DOLLAR
URS-8 · I-5 · L-5

Description: Doubling is evident on all reverse lettering with a very strong spread, strongest on QUARTER DOLLAR.

Comments: This variety is in extremely high demand by specialists. It has turned out to be one of the nicest late-date DDR coins in the series. Also, it has turned out to be very scarce and brings a nice premium. To date, one MS-65 is the top population. The majority are circulated.

	AU-50	AU-55	MS-60	MS-63	MS-64	MS-65	MS-66
Variety	$100	$150	$200	$300	$500	n/a	n/a
Normal	$8	$8.50	$9	$10	$18	$25	$55

1964 FS-25-1964-802

Variety: Doubled-Die Reverse **CONECA: DDR-002**
PUP: QUARTER DOLLAR
URS-6 · I-5 · L-5

Description: Doubling is evident with a nice spread on QUARTER DOLLAR.

Comments: This is one of at least 11 reverse doubled dies for this date. This variety has proven to be quite elusive. When available for sale, it brings a strong premium. Few coins have come to light and fewer sales have been confirmed.

	EF-45	AU-55	MS-60	MS-63	MS-64
Variety	n/a	$100	$200	$350	$500
Normal	$7.50	$8.50	$9	$10	$18

1964 FS-25-1964-803

Variety: Doubled-Die Reverse **CONECA: DDR-003**
PUP: AMERICA
URS-6 · I-5 · L-5

Description: Doubling is moderate on UNITED STATES OF AMERICA, being strongest on STATES and AMERICA.

Comments: This variety is very scarce in all grades, and with very few confirmed sales.

	AU-55	MS-60	MS-63	MS-64	MS-65	MS-66
Variety	$50	$100	$200	$300	n/a	n/a
Normal	$8.50	$9	$10	$18	$25	$55

1964 — FS-25-1964-804

Variety: Doubled-Die Reverse — **CONECA: DDR-004**
PUP: QUARTER DOLLAR
URS-7 · I-4 · L-5

Description: The doubling is very strong on QUARTER DOLLAR, weaker on UNITED, and very light on STATES.

Comments: This is a rare variety, and always in demand. Very, very few sales have been reported! At present, only two have been certified above MS-64.

	AU-55	MS-60	MS-63	MS-64	MS-65	MS-66
Variety	$100	$200	$400	$550	n/a	n/a
Normal	$8.50	$9	$10	$18	$25	$55

1964-D — FS-25-1964D-101

Variety: Doubled-Die Obverse — **CONECA: DDO-001**
PUP: IN GOD WE TRUST
URS-9 · I-4 · L-3

Description: The doubling is most evident on the motto IN GOD WE TRUST.

Comments: This is very similar to FS-25-1963-101. As doubled dies have grown in popularity, varieties such as this have increased in value.

	AU-55	MS-60	MS-63	MS-65	MS-66
Variety	$55	$75	$160	$450	n/a
Normal	$8.50	$9	$10	$25	$75

1964-D — FS-25-1964D-501

Variety: Repunched Mintmark **CONECA: RPM-003**
PUP: Mintmark
URS-5 · I-4 · L-4

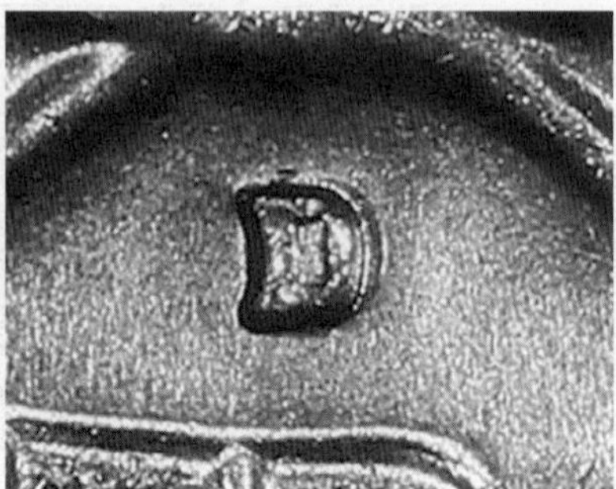

Description: The secondary D mintmark is evident east of the primary D.

Comments: This is one of the nicer repunched mintmarks for this date. It appears to be very rare, and few sales have been recorded. Note: The FS-502 variety in earlier editions was erroneously listed as a repunched mintmark. It has been changed to a misplaced mintmark (see FS-902 below). That is why there is no FS-502 in this volume.

	AU-55	MS-60	MS-63	MS-65	MS-66
Variety	$100	$250	$450	n/a	n/a
Normal	$8.50	$9	$10	$25	$75

1964-D — FS-25-1964D-503

Variety: Repunched Mintmark **CONECA: RPM-001**
PUP: Mintmark
URS-6 · I-4 · L-3

Description: There is a very widely spread repunching of the mintmark north and inside the final D mintmark.

Comments: This is a very nicely spread repunched mintmark. It may be scarcer than traditionally thought, with so many modern silver coins melted for their bullion value over the years.

	AU-50	MS-60	MS-63	MS-64	MS-65	MS-66
Variety	n/a	n/a	n/a	n/a	n/a	n/a
Normal	$8	$9	$10	$15	$25	$75

1964-D — FS-25-1964D-801 (025)

Variety: Doubled-Die Reverse — **CONECA: DDR-001**
PUP: AMERICA
URS-9 · I-4 · L-4

Description: Doubling is very strong on OF AMERICA and DOLLAR, with a medium spread on STATES, QUARTER, and E PLURIBUS UNUM.

Comments: This is a very dramatic doubled-die reverse. It has proven popular and scarce, as confirmed by each sale when available.

	AU-55	MS-60	MS-63	MS-65	MS-66
Variety	$40	$75	$125	$225	n/a
Normal	$8.50	$9	$10	$25	$75

The Cherrypickers' Guide HELPFUL HINTS

For best cherrypicking results, make sure you read "How to Use This Book," in the front. It will help you interpret the information for each listing.

And remember, the die varieties in this book aren't the only ones in the series. Even more are waiting to be discovered. Always closely examine your coins, even the ones you get in pocket change. You might make an important discovery! (Be sure to let us know when you do.)

Be aware of the "registry set effect" when you study auction results, especially for high-grade rarities. If two collectors both aspire to the #1-rated set, and they both need a rare coin that's come up for bid, and they both have fat wallets, their bidding war might set a record. This momentary competition doesn't necessarily illustrate the rest of the market.

1964-D FS-25-1964D-901

VARIETY: Type C Reverse **CONECA: RDV-003**
PUP: Eagle's tail feathers, leaf at arrow tips
URS-11 · I-5 · L-5

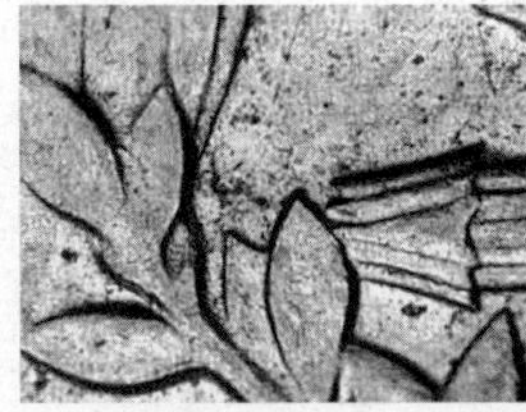

Description: A very small quantity of 1964-D coins is known to have the Type C reverse intended for use starting in 1965. Type C coins show the leaves above the AR in DOLLAR sharp and almost touching the letters, where the Type A is weak and the Type B is bold, but with the one leaf touching the A of DOLLAR. The tail feathers on Type C have a very distinct centerline. Additionally, the leaves below the tail feathers are sharp and barely touch those tail feathers. The leaf in front of the arrow tips comes to a distinct point in front of the arrow tips. On Type B, this leaf rises above the top arrow point, and the leaf end tips left. On Type A it is very weak.

Comments: This coin is very scarce in all grades. Most known coins are circulated. Mint State examples are rare, especially MS-63 and finer. Finding any Brilliant Uncirculated specimen will definitely help make your day.

	EF-40	AU-50	AU-55	MS-60	MS-63	MS-64	MS-65
VARIETY	$30	$45	$125	$225	$375	$525	$775
NORMAL	$7	$8	$8.50	$9	$10	$15	$25

1964-D — FS-25-1964D-902

Variety: Misplaced Mintmark — **CONECA: N/L**
PUP: Branch above mintmark
URS-4+ · I-4 · L-4

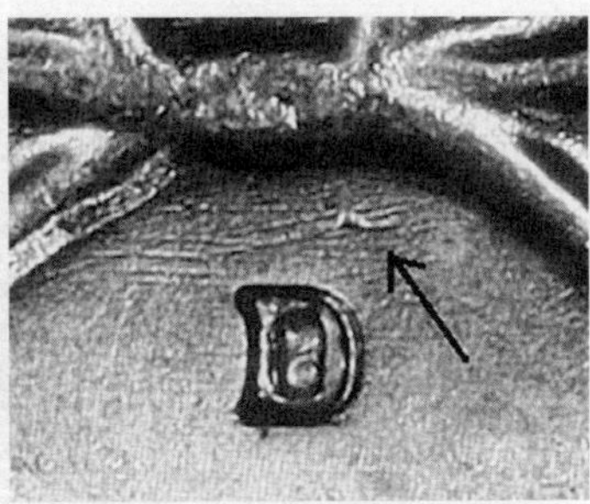

Description: On this very visually dramatic variety, a secondary D mintmark is evident protruding from the branch above the normal mintmark area.

Comments: This is one of very few completely separated mintmark varieties. Only a small number of specimens have surfaced since its discovery. Note: This variety in earlier editions was erroneously listed as a repunched mintmark (FS-502). It has been changed to a misplaced mintmark (FS-902).

	AU-55	MS-60	MS-63	MS-64	MS-65	MS-66
Variety	$65	$100	$250	$400	n/a	n/a
Normal	$8.50	$9	$10	$15	$25	$50

1965 — FS-25-1965-101

Variety: Doubled-Die Obverse — **CONECA: DDO-001**
PUP: IN GOD WE TRUST, LIBERTY
URS-6 · I-5 · L-5

Description: This doubling is very strong on all obverse lettering, the eye, and the date.

Comments: This variety is extremely rare and sells very quickly at auction. There are no recent verified sales. Only one sale has been shown, from 2007.

	EF-40	AU-50	AU-55	MS-60	MS-63	MS-65	MS-66
Variety	n/a	n/a	n/a	n/a	n/a	n/a	n/a
Normal					$2	$9	$20

1965 — FS-25-1965-102

Variety: Doubled-Die Obverse — **CONECA: DDO-002**
PUP: LIBERTY
URS-5 · I-4 · L-4

Description: Doubling is very strong on LIBERTY.

Comments: This variety is typical of a Class V doubled die, with doubling evident on one area only. It has proven to be very scarce, with few confirmed sales—another rare and underrated doubled die!

	EF-40	AU-50	AU-55	MS-60	MS-63	MS-65	MS-66
Variety	n/a	$75	$150	$250	$500	$750	n/a
Normal					$2	$9	$20

1966 — FS-25-1966-801

Variety: Doubled-Die Reverse — **CONECA: DDR-001**
PUP: UNITED STATES OF AMERICA, QUARTER DOLLAR
URS-5 · I-5 · L-5

Description: Very strong doubling is evident on all reverse lettering, including E PLURIBUS UNUM.

Comments: Discovered by Roger Gray, this variety has proven to be very rare. There are no recent verified sales, thus no reliable values for input. Only one MS coin has been verified—all others are EF–AU. *Note:* This is *not* the Special Mint Set issue!

	AU-55	MS-60	MS-63	MS-65	MS-66
Variety	n/a	n/a	n/a	n/a	n/a
Normal			$2	$7	$20

1967, Special Mint Set — FS-25-1967-101

Variety: Doubled-Die Obverse — **CONECA: DDO-002**
PUP: IN GOD WE TRUST
URS-10 · I-4 · L-3

Description: Strong doubling is evident on IN GOD WE TRUST and LIBERTY, with moderate doubling on the date.

Comments: Most examples of this variety are known with strike doubling. Those without strike doubling command far more than the values shown here. Several have come to light over the past few years, satisfying most of the demand and lowering values, but it is still a desirable variety.

	MS-65	MS-66	MS-67
Variety	$125	$225	$375
Normal	$10	$20	$35

1967, Special Mint Set — FS-25-1967-801

Variety: Doubled-Die Reverse — **CONECA: DDR-002**
PUP: QUARTER DOLLAR
URS-7 · I-5 · L-4

Description: Moderate doubling is evident on the stems and QUARTER DOLLAR.

Comments: More specimens of this variety are sure to be uncovered. This is a very scarce coin with a lot of collector interest, but it brings modest prices when sold.

	MS-60	MS-63	MS-65	MS-66	MS-67
Variety	n/a	n/a	$75	$110	$175
Normal			$10	$20	$35

1968-D FS-25-1968D-801

VARIETY: Doubled-Die Reverse **CONECA: DDR-001**
PUP: UNITED STATES OF AMERICA, QUARTER DOLLAR
URS-5 · I-5 · L-5

Description: Very strong doubling is evident on all reverse lettering, the leaves, the branches, and the eagle's wing tips.

Comments: Keep an eye open for this very strong doubled die. It's extremely rare in all grades—finding this coin would make your year, and help pay a few bills!

	AU-55	MS-60	MS-63	MS-65	MS-66
VARIETY	$800	$1,000	$1,500	$2,000	n/a
NORMAL			$2	$6	$15

1968-S, Proof FS-25-1968S-101

VARIETY: Doubled-Die Obverse **CONECA: DDO-001**
PUP: Date, LIBERTY, IN GOD WE TRUST
URS-7 · I-4 · L-4

Description: Doubling is evident on the motto IN GOD WE TRUST, LIBERTY, and the date.

Comments: This is an extremely rare variety! It has proven to be quite elusive, and just one more reason to check every coin in a 1968-S Proof set.

	PF-63	PF-65	PF-66
VARIETY	$100	$175	$275
NORMAL	$2	$6	$10

1968-S, Proof

FS-25-1968S-501

VARIETY: Repunched Mintmark

CONECA: RPM-004

PUP: Mintmark

URS-7 · I-4 · L-4

Description: The secondary S mintmark is evident north of the primary S.

Comments: Prior editions had this variety listed as RPM-003 in error (it is actually RPM-004, as corrected here). This is a nice, scarce, collectible variety.

	PF-63	PF-65	PF-66	PF-67
VARIETY	$40	$75	$100	$175
NORMAL	$2	$6	$10	$15

1968-S, Proof

FS-25-1968S-801

VARIETY: Doubled-Die Reverse

CONECA: DDR-001

PUP: QUARTER DOLLAR

URS-9 · I-4 · L-3

Description: The doubling is on all lettering around the rim and the leaf tips.

Comments: Several specimens have surfaces in recent years, filling the previous supply void and helping to lower prices in response to collector demand.

	PF-63	PF-65	PF-66	PF-67
VARIETY	$40	$100	$125	$150
NORMAL	$2	$6	$10	$15

1968-S, Proof — FS-25-1968S-901

VARIETY: Type E Reverse — **CONECA: N/L**
PUP: Leaves, Q in QUARTER
URS-7 · I-3 · L-3

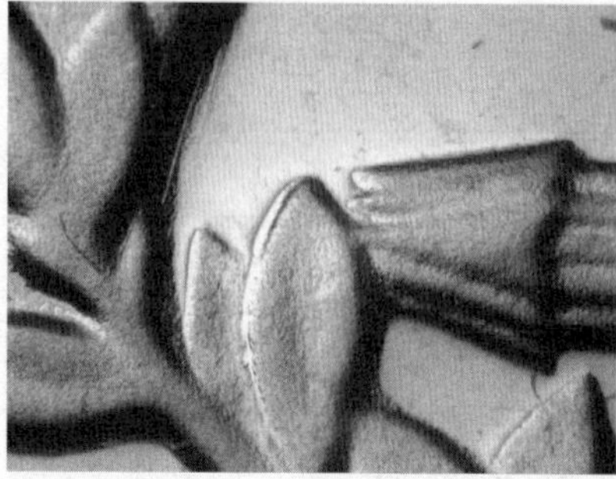

Description: This is the Type E reverse, with pointed leaves and no doubling inside the upper part of the Q in QUARTER.

Comments: The leaf tips are pointed near the arrow tips. The serif of the last S in STATES is higher than the E serif. The key diagnostic is there *is* no doubling at the upper inner part of the Q in QUARTER.

	PF-63	PF-65	PF-66	PF-67
VARIETY	n/a	n/a	n/a	n/a
NORMAL	$2	$6	$10	$15

1968-S, Proof — FS-25-1968S-902

VARIETY: Type F Reverse — **CONECA: N/L**
PUP: Leaves, Q in QUARTER
URS-5 · I-4 · L-4

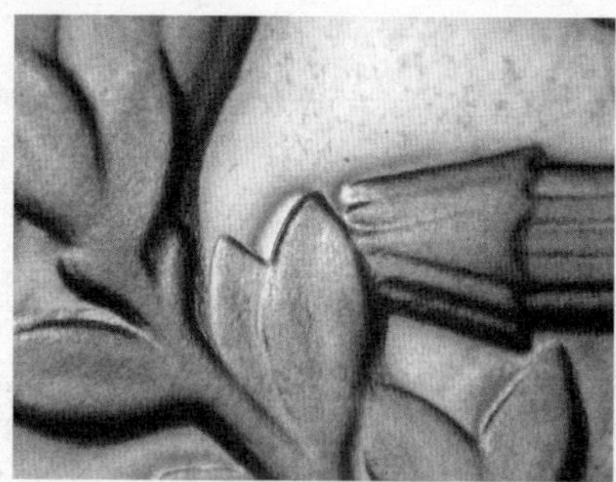

Description: This is a Type F reverse (with pointed leaf and doubling on the Q in QUARTER).

Comments: The leaf tips are pointed near the arrow tips, and the serif on the last S in STATES is higher than the serif on the E. The key diagnostic on this variety is that the Q in QUARTER is doubled at the upper inside.

	PF-63	PF-65	PF-66	PF-67
VARIETY	n/a	n/a	n/a	n/a
NORMAL	$2	$6	$10	$15

1969-D — FS-25-1969D-501

Variety: Repunched Mintmark — **CONECA: RPM-001**
PUP: Mintmark
URS-9 · I-3 · L-3

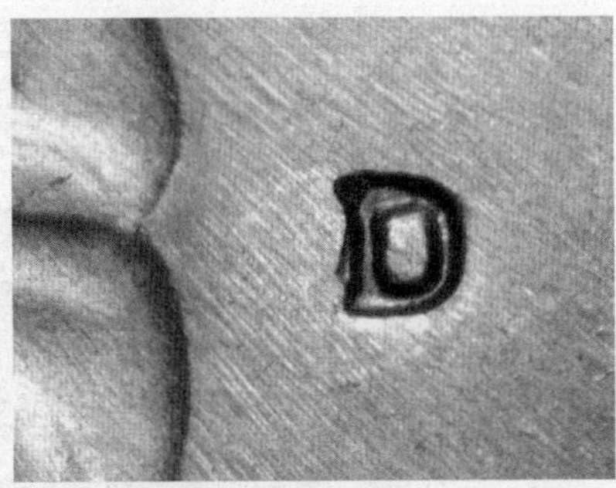

Description: The secondary D mintmark is slanted slightly west of the primary D.

Comments: This variety can be found in Mint sets.

	MS-63	MS-64	MS-65	MS-66
Variety	$30	$45	$100	$135
Normal	$2.50	$5	$10	$25

1969-D — FS-25-1969D-502

Variety: Repunched Mintmark — **CONECA: RPM-003**
PUP: Mintmark
URS-5 · I-4 · L-5

Description: The secondary D mintmark is slightly west of the primary D.

Comments: This variety is reported to have been found in Mint sets. While known for years, it has proven to be very rare, with no sales confirmed.

	MS-62	MS-64	MS-65
Variety	n/a	n/a	n/a
Normal	$2	$5	$10

1969-S, Proof — FS-25-1969S-101

VARIETY: Doubled-Die Obverse — **CONECA: DDO-001**
PUP: Date, LIBERTY
URS-6 · I-4 · L-4

Description: The doubling is extremely strong on all obverse lettering and on the date.

Comments: This is a rare variety and it provides a solid reason to check all 1969-S Proof sets.

	PF-63	PF-65	PF-66
VARIETY	$125	$225	$350
NORMAL	$4	$5	$10

1969-S, Proof — FS-25-1969S-501 / 102

VARIETY: Repunched Mintmark and Doubled-Die Obverse — **CONECA: RPM-001, DDO-002**
PUP: Mintmark, date, IN GOD WE TRUST
URS-6 · I-4 · L-4

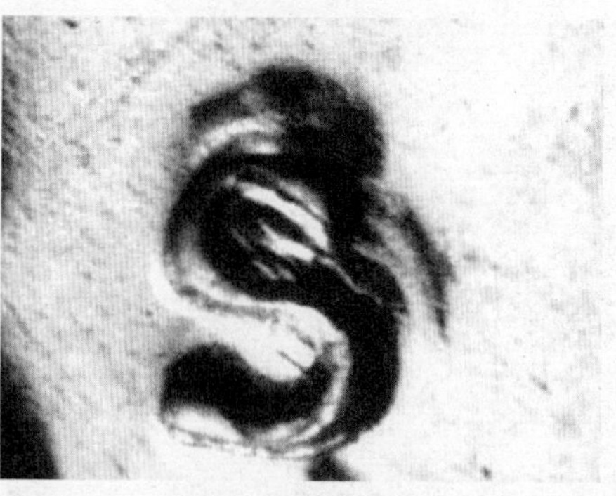

Description: This RPM exhibits an S/S/S, with both secondary punches slightly north of the primary S mintmark.

Comments: Previously reported as RPM-002, this variety in fact is RPM-001. Note also that the obverse is a doubled die, DDO-002.

	PF-63	PF-65	PF-66	PF-67
VARIETY	n/a	$225	$350	n/a
NORMAL	$4	$5	$10	$15

1970-D FS-25-1970D-101

Variety: Doubled-Die Obverse **CONECA: DDO-001**
PUP: IN GOD WE TRUST
URS-6 · I-5 · L-4

Description: This is a very strong doubled die, with doubling evident on the date, IN GOD WE TRUST, and ERTY of LIBERTY.

Comments: This variety, long considered to be extremely rare, has proven to be very elusive!

	EF-40	AU-50	AU-55	MS-60	MS-63	MS-65
Variety	$300	$750	$1,250	$1,500	$2,000	$2,500
Normal					$2	$6

1970-D FS-25-1970D-102

Variety: Doubled-Die Obverse **CONECA: DDO-002**
PUP: LIBERTY
URS-4 · I-5 · L-5

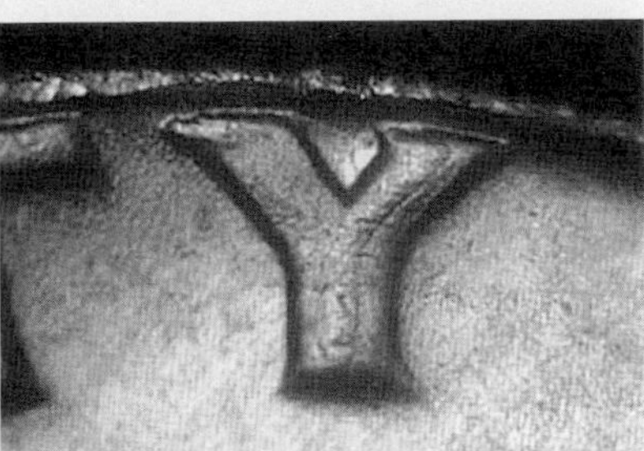

Description: The doubling on this extremely rare variety is evident on the date, IN GOD WE TRUST, and LIBERTY. Both hubbings were of equal depth, causing the differences in the two to be faint. However, the wide separation, evidenced by the split serifs, is very dramatic.

Comments: This variety is extremely rare—far rarer than DDO-001—with only three examples reported to date, and only two public sales confirmed. The coins certified were graded AU-58, MS-62, and MS-65 (the latter sold in 2012 for $2,875).

	EF-40	AU-50	MS-60	MS-62	MS-63	MS-65
Variety	n/a	$750	n/a	$1,500	n/a	$3,000
Normal					$2.25	$6

1970-S, Proof FS-25-1970S-801

Variety: Doubled-Die Reverse **CONECA: N/A**
PUP: QUAR DOL
URS-3 · I-4 · L-4

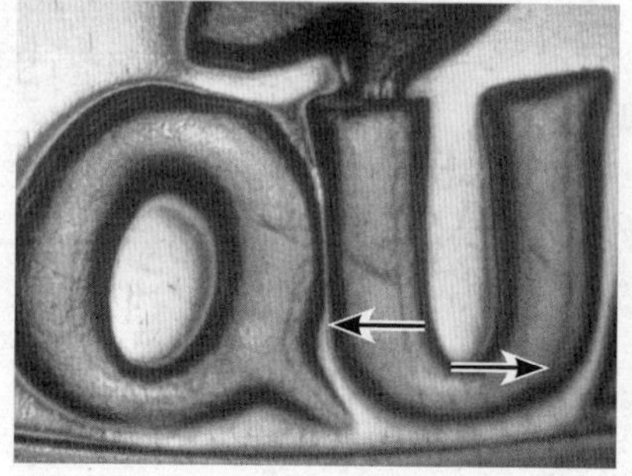

Description: This is a very nice doubled-die reverse with very noticeable separation on QUAR and DOL.

Comments: At present, this is a very rare variety. To date, only three pieces have been confirmed. Inclusion in the *Cherrypickers' Guide* should change that in the future. The inclusion of this new variety gives cherrypickers another nice coin to look for.

	PF-60	PF-63	PF-64	PF-65	PF-66	PF-67
Variety	n/a	n/a	n/a	n/a	n/a	n/a
Normal				$5	$10	$15

1971-D FS-25-1971D-801

Variety: Doubled-Die Reverse **CONECA: DDR-001**
PUP: UNITED STATES OF AMERICA
URS-5 · I-4 · L-4

Description: Strong doubling is evident on UNITED STATES OF AMERICA.

Comments: At present, this is a very rare coin with very few specimens verified. The finest verified to date is an MS-62. *Note:* This variety value is higher than the following 1976-D DDO because of low supply and high demand from registry-set collectors.

	EF-40	AU-50	AU-55	MS-60	MS-62
Variety	$300	$600	n/a	n/a	$1,500
Normal	$0.30	$0.35	$0.40	$0.50	$0.75

1976-D FS-25-1976D-101

Variety: Doubled-Die Obverse **CONECA: DDO-001**
PUP: LIBERTY
URS-8 · I-5 · L-5

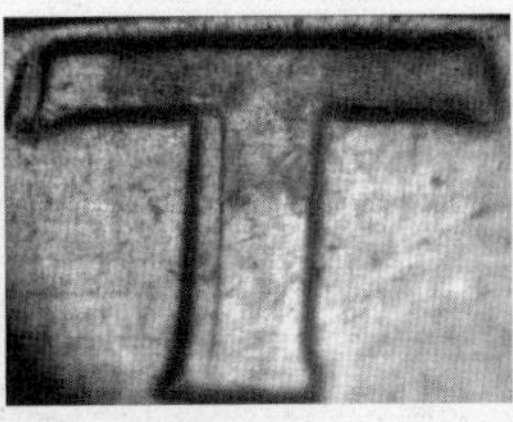
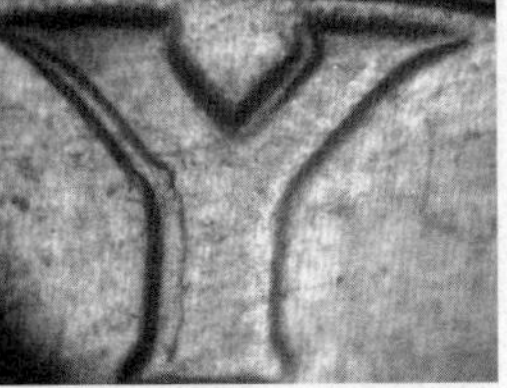

Description: Very strong doubling is evident on LIBERTY, and very slight doubling on the motto IN GOD WE TRUST and the date.

Comments: Generally, only early die state specimens will show doubling on the motto. This is a rare coin with substantial demand; sale prices are high when it's available.

	AU-50	AU-55	AU-58	MS-60	MS-63	MS-65
Variety	$600	$750	$1,000	$1,250	$1,500	$3,500
Normal	$0.50	$0.60	$0.70	$0.85	$1	$6

1976-D FS-25-1976D-102

Variety: Doubled-Die Obverse **CONECA: DDO-002**
PUP: LIBERTY
URS-9 · I-3 · L-3

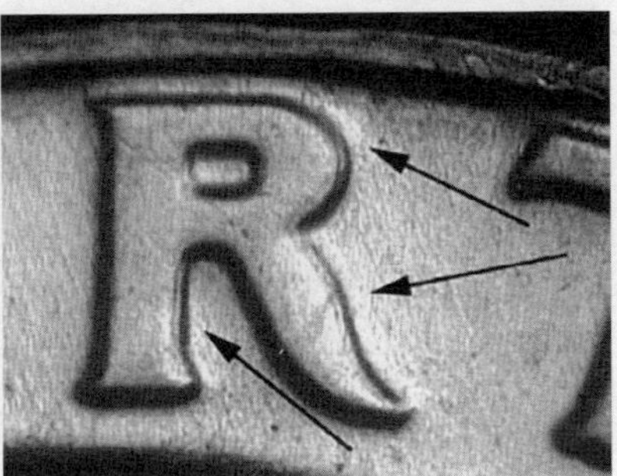

Description: Moderate doubling is evident only on LIBERTY.

Comments: This coin has proven scarce, but not rare. An interesting anomaly: 99.9 percent have been graded choice to gem Brilliant Uncirculated.

	AU-55	MS-60	MS-63	MS-65	MS-66
Variety	n/a	$75	$125	$225	$350
Normal	$0.60	$0.70	$1	$6	$15

1983-P — FS-25-1983-901

VARIETY: "Spitting Eagle" **CONECA: N/L**
PUP: Field below the eagle's beak
URS-6 · I-5 · L-5

Description: A clash mark from Washington's throat on the obverse is visible from the eagle's beak to the top of its wing.

Comments: Visually, this clash mark makes the eagle look like it's spitting. Heavy die polishing surrounds the clash in the field. Presently this variety is very scarce or even rare.

	AU-50	MS-60	MS-63	MS-64	MS-65	MS-66
VARIETY	n/a	n/a	n/a	n/a	n/a	n/a
NORMAL	$8	$12	$30	$45	$65	$200

1989-P — FS-25-1989-501

VARIETY: No P **CONECA: N/L**
PUP: Mintmark area
URS-8 · I-5 · L-4

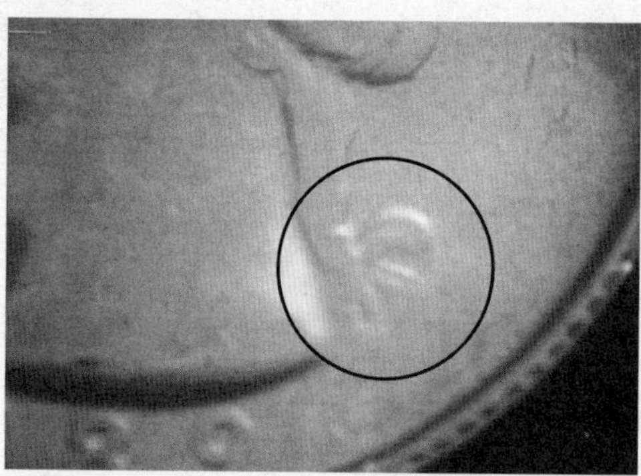

Description: The mintmark—most likely a P, for Philadelphia—is missing from the lower-right field of the obverse.

Comments: The missing mintmark was likely caused by grease clogging the obverse die in the normal mintmark area. The result is visually interesting, and collectible.

	AU-50	MS-60	MS-63	MS-64	MS-65	MS-66
VARIETY	$25	$45	$95	$175	n/a	n/a
NORMAL	$0.50	$0.75	$1	$5	$12	$30

1989-D

FS-25-1989D-501

CONECA: RPM-001

Variety: Repunched Mintmark
PUP: Mintmark
URS-2 · I-5 · L-5

Description: The secondary D mintmark is evident west of the primary D.

Comments: Presently, two examples of this variety are known. Neither has been professionally graded and there are no verified sales.

	MS-60	MS-63	MS-65	MS-66
Variety	n/a	n/a	n/a	n/a
Normal	$0.50	$1	$7	$25

1990-S, Proof

FS-25-1990S-101

CONECA: DDO-001

Variety: Doubled-Die Obverse
PUP: Date, Mintmark
URS-7 · I-5 · L-4

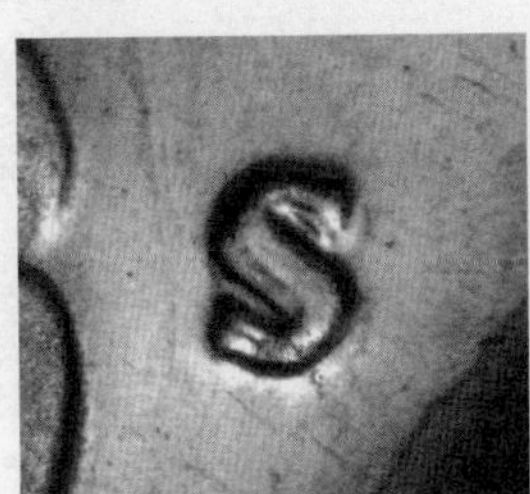

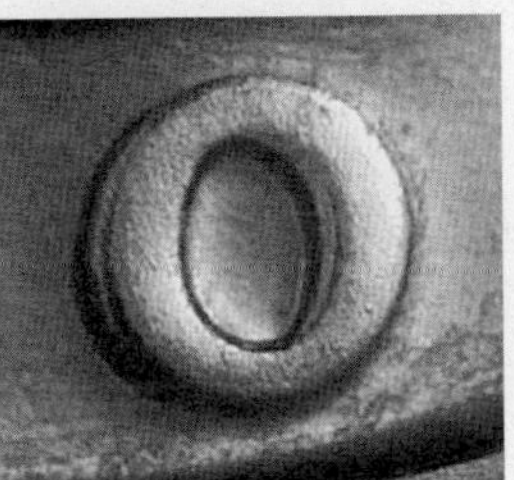

Description: Very strong doubling is evident on the date and the mintmark, and slightly on IN GOD WE TRUST.

Comments: This is a nice doubled die that seems to only come in deep cameo!

	PF-65	PF-66	PF-67	PF-68	PF-69
Variety	$100	$200	$400	$600	$800
Normal	$4	$6	$8	$12	$25

1994-P — FS-25-1994-501

VARIETY: No P — **CONECA: N/L**
PUP: Mintmark area
URS-5 · I-5 · L-5

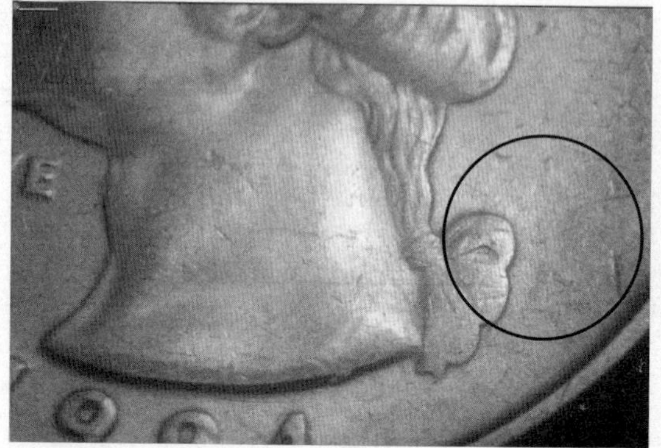

Description: The mintmark is missing from its normal position in the lower-right field of the obverse.

Comments: This is similar to the 1989 No P quarter—the result of a grease-filled die. At present we classify it as rare. Be on the lookout and you might cherrypick one!

	EF-40	AU-50	AU-58	MS-60	MS-63	MS-64	MS-65
VARIETY	$45	$75	$100	$150	$225	$325	n/a
NORMAL					$1	$4	$10

1995-S, Proof, Clad — FS-25-1995S-101

VARIETY: Doubled-Die Obverse — **CONECA: DDO-001**
PUP: Date, ribbon end, mintmark
URS-6 · I-4 · L-3

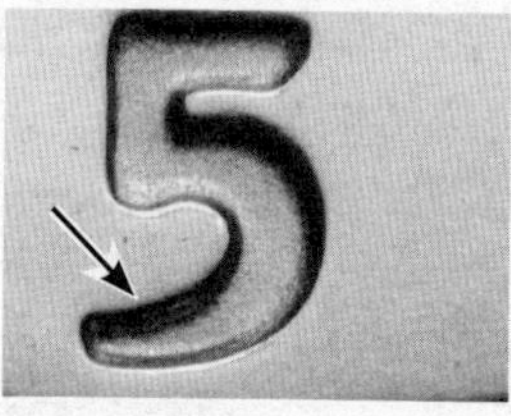
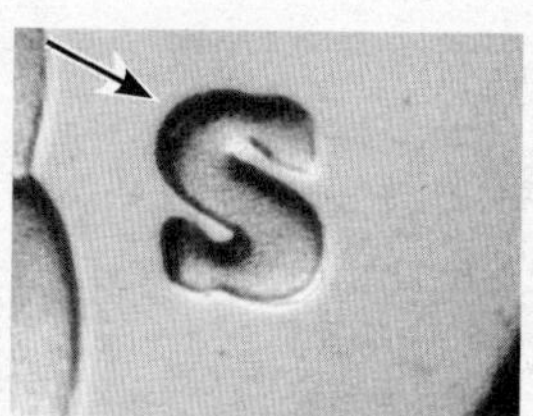
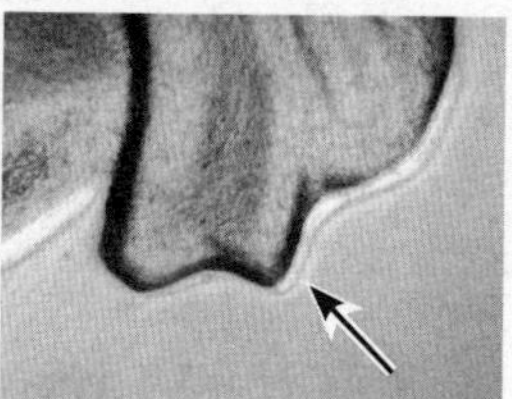

Description: Very close doubling is visible on the date, the mintmark, the ribbon, and Washington's hair.

Comments: This may be difficult to pick up, as doubling is often hard to see on Proof coins with heavy frosting. The lowest graded coins for all services are PF-67 Deep Cameo. All pieces to date have been graded Deep Cameo. A combination of rarity plus strong demand from registry-set collectors has kept prices high.

	PF-67	PF-68	PF-69
VARIETY	$500	$650	$800
NORMAL	$10	$20	

2004-D, Wisconsin (Extra Leaf High) FS-25-2004D-901

Variety: Design Manipulation **CONECA: N/L**
PUP: Reverse—left corn leaf
URS-15 · I-5 · L-5

Description: An image was added to the working die, creating an upward line to the left cornhusk.

Comments: Many collectors and dealers refer to this as the "Extra Leaf High" variety. It is our belief that the additional lines on this and the next variety of Wisconsin quarter were deliberately added to the reverse dies. Apparently, a tool with a rounded edge was impressed into the working dies to create images that were not a part of the intended design. Initial discovery coins sold for very high prices. However, more than 8,500 pieces have since been slabbed, keeping prices reasonable.

	AU-55	MS-60	MS-63	MS-65	MS-66	MS-67
Variety	$40	$75	$100	$200	$300	$600
Normal	$0.40	$0.75	$1	$10	$15	$30

2004-D, Wisconsin (Extra Leaf Low) FS-25-2004D-902

Variety: Design Manipulation **CONECA: N/L**
PUP: Reverse—left corn leaf
URS-15 · I-5 · L-5

Description: Images were added to the working die, creating two downward lines to the left cornhusk.

Comments: This is commonly known as the "Extra Leaf Low" variety. We believe that additional lines on this and the preceding variety were deliberately added to their reverse dies. It appears a tool with a rounded edge was impressed into the working dies to create images not intended for the original design. Initial discovery pieces brought high prices. To date, however, almost 12,000 pieces have been graded. Even with high demand, that supply keeps prices affordable.

	AU-55	MS-60	MS-63	MS-65	MS-66	MS-67
Variety	$35	$60	$75	$150	$225	$600
Normal	$0.40	$0.75	$1	$10	$15	$30

2005-P, Minnesota — FS-25-2005P-MN-803

VARIETY: Doubled-Die Reverse **CONECA: DDR-004; WEXLER: WDDR-004**
PUP: Portion of "extra tree" right of fourth tree
URS-7 · I-4 · L-3

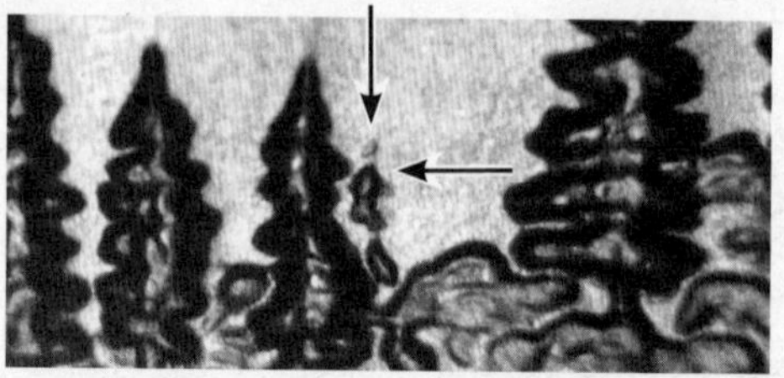

Description: Doubling is seen as a free-floating portion of the fourth evergreen tree east of the state outline.

Comments: This coin is found in Mint sets and has a satin finish. On the Minnesota quarters, more than 100 known doubled dies affect the centermost tree (and other centralized areas of the design). They are found on coins from all mints and include the San Francisco Proofs, both clad and silver. The vast majority are minor but collectible nonetheless. This, FS-803, is one of few doubled-die Minnesota quarters that PCGS designates as an "Extra Tree." Confusion among the many varieties abounds within the hobby community. The market is unsettled as to pricing.

	AU-55	MS-60	MS-63	MS-65	MS-66	MS-67
VARIETY	n/a	n/a	n/a	*$50*	*$100*	n/a
NORMAL	$0.50	$0.60	$1	$5	$10	$30

2005-P, Minnesota — FS-25-2005P-MN-805

VARIETY: Doubled-Die Reverse **CONECA: DDR-007; WEXLER: WDDR-007**
PUP: Portion of "extra tree" right of the fourth tree
URS-9 · I-4 · L-3

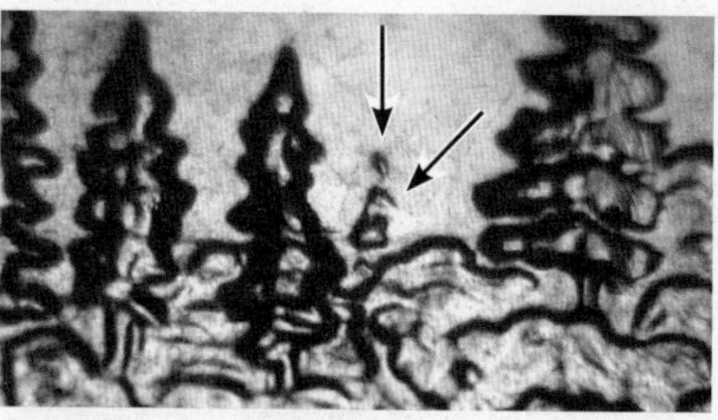

Description: Similar to FS-803 (see preceding), this variety involves a portion of the fourth tree to the right of the state outline, with doubling fully displaced from its point of origin.

Comments: More than 100 doubled dies affect the centermost tree (and other centralized areas of the design) of the Minnesota quarter. These anomalies are found on coins from all mints and include the San Francisco Proofs, both clad and silver. The vast majority are minor but still collectible. FS-805 is one of few doubled-die Minnesota quarters that PCGS designates as an "Extra Tree."

	AU-55	MS-60	MS-63	MS-65	MS-66	MS-67
VARIETY	n/a	n/a	n/a	$50	$100	n/a
NORMAL	$0.50	$0.60	$1	$5	$10	$30

2005-S, Kansas, Proof, Silver — FS-25-2005S-KS-901

Variety: Large Die Dent Reverse — **Potter: VCR-001**
PUP: Hoof-shaped die dent on bison's hindquarter
URS-6 · I-5 · L-4

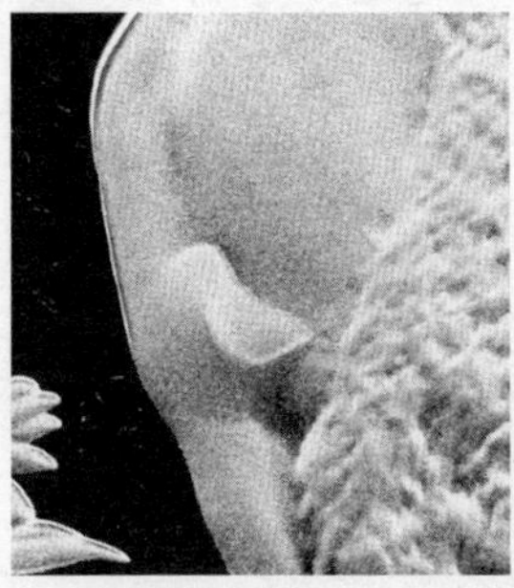

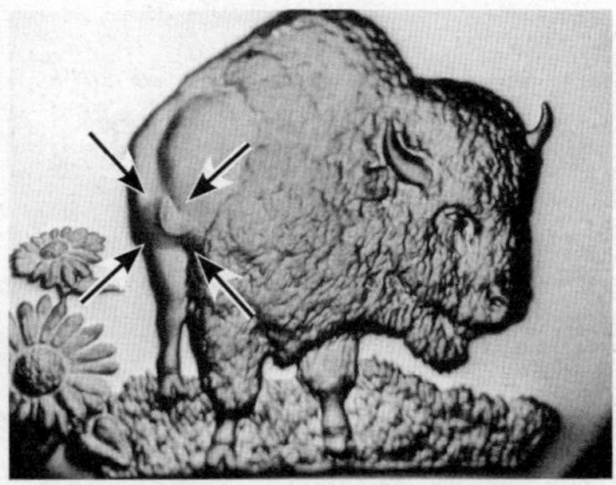

Description: A large, hoof-shaped die dent can be seen just above the bison's right rear leg. It appears to be a deliberate addition to the die, but the cause and origin are unknown.

Comments: This die aberration is significantly larger in area than those found on the two well-known 2004-D "Extra Leaf" Wisconsin quarters, to which this Kansas variety is sometimes compared due to the flaw's curved shape. Although known for several years now, this coin still has few verified specimens and has proven to be rare. All coins are Deep Cameo!

	PF-67	PF-68	PF-69
Variety	$200	$300	$400
Normal	$25	$40	$60

2007-P, Wyoming — FS-25-2007P-WY-801

Variety: Doubled-Die Reverse — **CONECA: DDR-018; Wexler: WDDR-005**
PUP: Saddle horn
URS-6 · I-4 · L-3

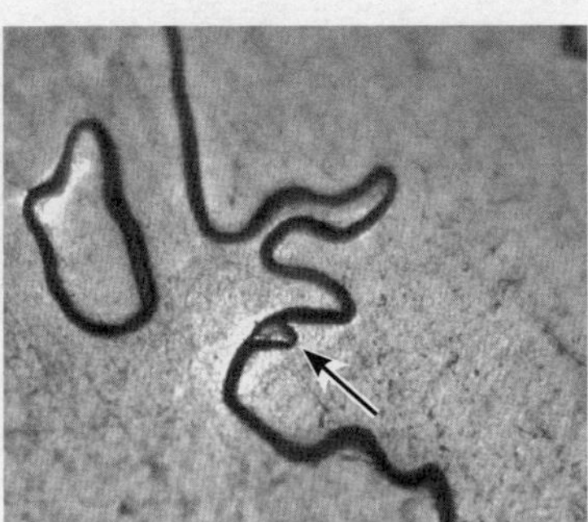

Description: This variety displays very strong doubling of the saddle horn. It's one of the strongest of several Wyoming varieties in which this area of the design is affected.

Comments: Many other doubled dies exist for this date and type, but most of them are less significant. At present, there are only two reliable auction sales (both MS-64, at $104 and $105).

	AU-55	MS-60	MS-63	MS-65	MS-66
Variety	n/a	n/a	$75	$150	n/a
Normal	$0.40	$0.50	$0.75	$4	$10

2007-P, Wyoming — FS-25-2007P-WY-802

Variety: Doubled-Die Reverse — **CONECA: DDR-008; Wexler: WDDR-014**
PUP: Saddle horn
URS-6 · I-3 · L-3

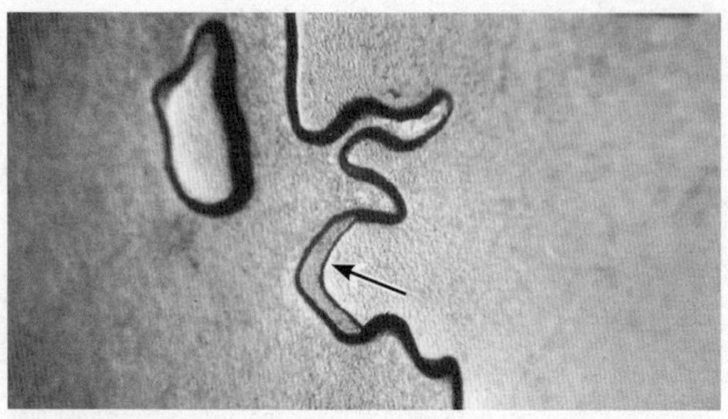

Description: Very strong doubling of the saddle appears just below the saddle horn. This is the strongest of several varieties in which this area of the design is affected.

Comments: Many other doubled dies exist for this date and type, but most of them are less significant. These can be found in Mint sets. Coins graded by the grading services are listed as specimens.

	AU-55	MS-60	MS-63	MS-65	MS-66
Variety	n/a	n/a	n/a	$150	$200
Normal	$0.40	$0.50	$0.75	$4	$10

2009-P, District of Columbia — FS-25-2009P-DC-801

Variety: Doubled-Die Reverse — **CONECA: DDR-012**
PUP: Piano keys, E of ELLINGTON
URS-6 · I-5 · L-5

Description: A strong secondary black key appears centered between the two normal black keys next to Duke Ellington's left arm, in addition to a bit of doubling to the lower left of the E in ELLINGTON.

Comments: This is one of more than a dozen doubled-die reverses known of this date and type for Philadelphia; the others are relatively minor. Although very scarce, the Philadelphia DDR coins do not enjoy the demand of the D.C. Denver coin, FS-25-2009D-DC-801.

	AU-55	MS-60	MS-63	MS-65	MS-66
Variety	n/a	$100	$175	$350	n/a
Normal	$0.40	$0.50	$1	$2	$10

2009-P, District of Columbia — FS-25-2009P-DC-802

Variety: Doubled-Die Reverse — **CONECA: DDR-004**
PUP: Piano key below the E of ELLINGTON
URS-6 · I-5 · L-5

Description: A strong secondary black key is centered between the two normal black keys next to Ellington's left arm.

Comments: This is one of more than a dozen doubled-die reverses known of this date and type for Philadelphia; the others, however, are relatively minor. This variety is as nice as or nicer than FS-801. This die, FS-802, is scarcer than FS-801 of the D.C. "P" DDR coins, but it lacks the demand of its previous counterpart.

	AU-55	MS-60	MS-63	MS-65	MS-66
Variety	n/a	n/a	$100	$175	$300
Normal	$0.40	$0.50	$1	$2	$10

2009-D, District of Columbia — FS-25-2009D-DC-801

Variety: Doubled-Die Reverse — **CONECA: DDR-001**
PUP: ELL of ELLINGTON
URS-6 · I-5 · L-5

Description: This variety boasts extremely strong doubling of the ELL in ELLINGTON, as well as some doubling of the two most westerly piano keys, the lower edge of the piano keys, the upper lip of the panel below them, and Duke Ellington's thumb, due to tilt and counterclockwise shift.

Comments: This is the very strongest of the State/Territorial quarter doubled dies, and has proven to be very rare and in demand. The Mint must have caught this one early. It is also the only doubled-die reverse known from the Denver Mint for this issue.

	AU-55	MS-60	MS-63	MS-65	MS-66
Variety	$400	$750	$1,000	$1,500	$2,250
Normal	$0.40	$0.50	$1	$2	$10

America the Beautiful Quarter Varieties

There are many America the Beautiful quarters that are more interesting than they are valuable. Some of the more noteworthy varieties of these coins are included in this volume, all of which are new to the *Cherrypickers' Guide*.

The quarters range from 2013 to 2016, and hail from the Philadelphia and Denver Mints, with the first being the 2013-P, Perry's Victory and International Peace Memorial (Ohio) "Chip on His Shoulder" variety—featuring a large die chip on Master Commandant Oliver Hazard Perry's shoulder.

Three varieties are found with the 2015-P, Homestead National Monument (Nebraska) quarter, one being a doubled die reverse with very strong doubling on the window of the house.

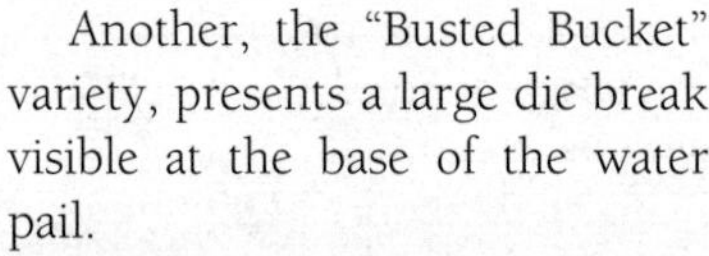

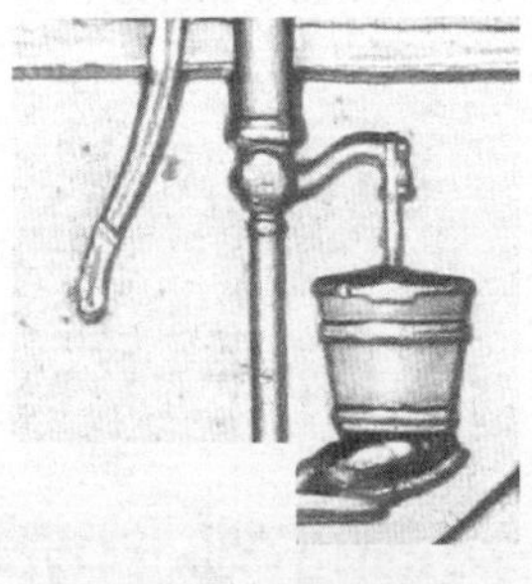

Another, the "Busted Bucket" variety, presents a large die break visible at the base of the water pail.

The third variety, "Snow on the Roof," displays large die breaks, which are visible on both sides of the roof of the pioneer house, giving the illusion of accumulated snow.

Moving onto the 2015-D, Kisatchie National Forest (Louisiana) quarter, there are die chips visible below the wild turkey's tail feathers and under the talons. This is known as the "Extra Tail Feathers and Talons" variety.

Next is the "Extra Rock" variety of the 2016-P, Shawnee National Forest (Illinois) quarter, wherein a small extra rock is visible on top of the large rock on the left.

Last but not least is the "Pigtail" variety of the 2016-P, Cumberland Gap National Historical Park (Kentucky) quarter. Large die breaks are visible on the Kentucky frontiersman's neck and shoulder, while "Button" die breaks are seen on top of his hat. Collector demand is modest for these varieties, but they do attract curious cherrypickers and inject some more fun into the modern quarter dollar series. Values may increase and solidify if interest (and therefore demand) goes up.

Appendix A
Doubled Dies vs. Other Forms of Doubling

The difference between die doubling (doubled dies, repunched dates, and repunched mintmarks, among others) and the more confusing forms of doubling can be very challenging to explain, and even more difficult for a novice to comprehend. Additionally, there are times when determining the difference can be frustrating even for a very experienced collector. This section will help you learn the differences. But reading alone will not do it all; you must examine numerous coins before you can expect to have a solid grasp of the differences between die doubling and other forms of doubling.

Die Doubling: Those Abnormalities We Love to Collect!

Die doubling is the type of doubling that exhibits a doubled image on the die itself, even before the coin is struck. Die doubling includes doubled dies, repunched dates, repunched mintmarks, overdates, over mintmarks, and repunched letters. It almost always exhibits splits in the serifs of the letters and/or numerals, with rounded, secondary images.

On this Jefferson nickel, the distinctive splits in the serifs are evident, and the secondary images are "rounded" and can easily be detected.

The photograph shown here of a true 1969-S doubled-die Lincoln cent exhibits the typical rounded secondary images. Notice also the "crease" between the images.

Many nineteenth-century coins have letters and numerals that are flat on their top surfaces as compared to the rounded appearance of most twentieth-century letters and numerals. Therefore, the key to identifying true die doubling on nineteenth-century coins is the distinctive splits in the serifs.

There is one class of doubled die that would not exhibit the normal characteristics mentioned for die doubling. Known as Class VI doubled dies, these exhibit extra thickness on

The splits in the serifs on this 1887 Indian Head cent doubled-die obverse are typical of what one would expect for most nineteenth-century coins with true die doubling.

some letters and numbers. Most widely known on Lincoln cents, the doubling sometimes exhibits letters that are slightly misshapen, such as the lower bar of an E being curved. This curved shape often is convex. Although some specialists may disagree, Class VI doubled dies *generally* command very small premiums—except in rare cases.

Notice the extra thickness of the letters in LIBERTY. This is typical of a Class VI doubled die, shown here on a Lincoln cent.

STRIKE DOUBLING

Strike doubling is the type of doubling most often confused with, and very often misidentified as, a doubled die or repunched mintmark. Not only do novices confuse this type of doubling with doubled dies, but specialists disagree as to what the correct terminology should be.

This LIBERTY on a Lincoln cent exhibits typical strike doubling. Notice the flat, shelf-like appearance of the secondary image.

Strike doubling (the term we prefer) is generally accepted to be caused by die bounce due to looseness in the tooling-to-die assembly, the die holder, or the die(s) within that holder. This causes excessive vibration during press operation, much as excessive vibration may set up in a running automobile with a broken motor mount. In effect, the vibration causes a coin to bounce or slide against the die within the split second after it is struck, just before or during ejection. In its most common form, strike doubling is characterized by a flat, shelf-like area of doubling bordering a design; this represents metal from the original raised image that has been smashed by the die down into the field of the coin. According to Mint technicians, strike doubling is usually eliminated when loose bolts, etc., are tightened.

Some might argue that the striking of the coin ends when the hammer die reaches the very end of its stroke. By this argument, this should not be called *strike doubling,* but rather *mechanical* or *machine doubling.* In our opinion, this is like trying to split a hair. Additionally, we feel that *machine* or *mechanical* doubling can be even more confusing, as neither term indicates in which part of the minting process this happens. Either of those terms could refer to the coin counters at the end of the process! We feel *strike doubling* is best suited to indicate the point of the minting process in which this doubling occurs.

Furthermore, numismatists agree there are three basic areas of the minting process: planchet, die, and striking. This doubling occurs during the striking process, and not in the die-making or planchet-making process. (We don't refer to incomplete planchets as a machine problem, although a machine causes them.)

Whether you refer to this as *strike doubling, machine doubling, mechanical doubling,* or *ejection doubling,* your primary focus should be to understand the differences and educate others.

Typically, strike doubling exhibits a flat, shelf-like secondary image, not like the rounded secondary images of true die doubling. Usually this secondary image is low to the field. There are no splits in the serifs. On most Uncirculated and Proof coins, strike doubling gives the appearance that the metal has been "moved," much like that on hobo nickels or love tokens, and has a very shiny appearance. (Other less common forms of strike doubling exist that are not covered here.)

On this 1937 Buffalo nickel, the secondary images exhibit the flat, shelf-like doubling typical of strike doubling. The secondary image is low, close to the field.

Strike doubling can affect all lettering on one or both sides, or could be detected on only one letter or a small portion of a device. Proof coins often exhibit strike doubling due to the excessive force employed in their manufacture. Strike doubling can also be evident on a coin with a true doubled die or true repunched mintmark.

There are several dates (and runs of dates) in several series that are well known for strike doubling. Examples include Mercury dimes from 1936 through 1942 and Lincoln cents from 1968 through 1972.

Compare this 1969-S Lincoln cent doubled die with the strike-doubling specimen to the right.

In this 1969-S cent, strike doubling is evident on the date and mintmark. Whenever the date and mintmark both are doubled, odds are that the doubling is strike doubling.

Although it can be difficult for a novice to understand, strike doubling might affect only the mintmark on a coin, creating what some may interpret as a repunched mintmark. In fact, this is fairly common, especially on Franklin halves and Washington quarters. This is often because strike doubling first affects the deepest part of the die (the highest part of the coin), which in many cases is the deeply punched mintmark.

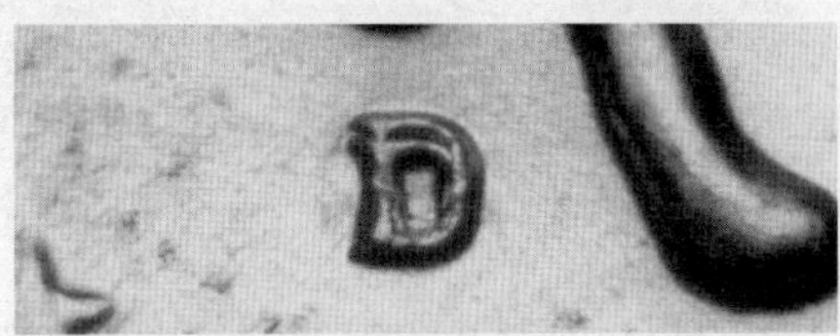

This is a genuine repunched mintmark on a Kennedy half dollar. Compare the doubling here with the next, which was caused by strike doubling.

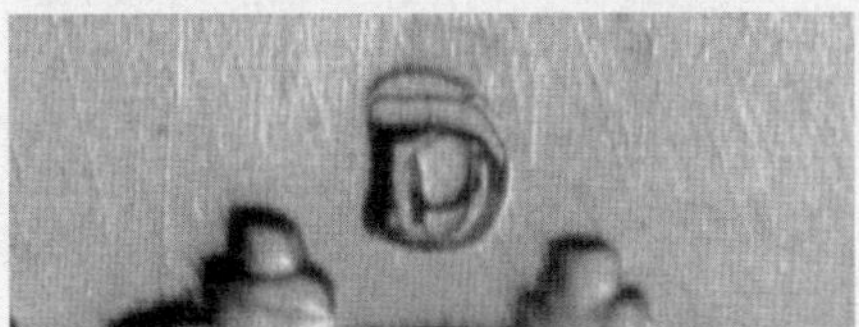

This mintmark on a Franklin half dollar is the result of strike doubling. Notice the flat, shelf-like doubling, which is the primary characteristic of strike doubling.

Other Forms of Doubling

In addition to strike doubling, there are other forms of doubling that are often mistaken for die doubling. Among these are doubling caused by die deterioration, and doubling that is typical on coins designed by James B. Longacre, possibly intentionally.

Die Deterioration

Die deterioration doubling is very often confused with doubled dies, repunched mintmarks, and other collectible forms of die doubling. In general, as a die deteriorates, its letters and numerals (among other design elements) will develop doubling, twisting, mushrooming, and similar effects. The exact result often depends on the type of die steel used, composition of planchets struck, geometry of die design, and length of time the die(s) remain in service. These effects normally begin on elements closest to the rim and move inward to a point of leaving random die-deterioration patches that may appear to be misplaced mintmarks in strange places (e.g., on Roosevelt's cheek). This is due to stress in the metal of the die. This doubling will often, but not always, occur in combination with an "orange-peel" effect on the fields of the coin, created by the stress in the metal on the dies.

Die deterioration is very evident and extreme in this Jefferson nickel. Notice the secondary images on both sides of the letters, and the "orange-peel" effect on the field.

Here is another example of die deterioration. Notice the edges of the I and T appearing to merge into the field. Also, the letters have less definition than one would expect.

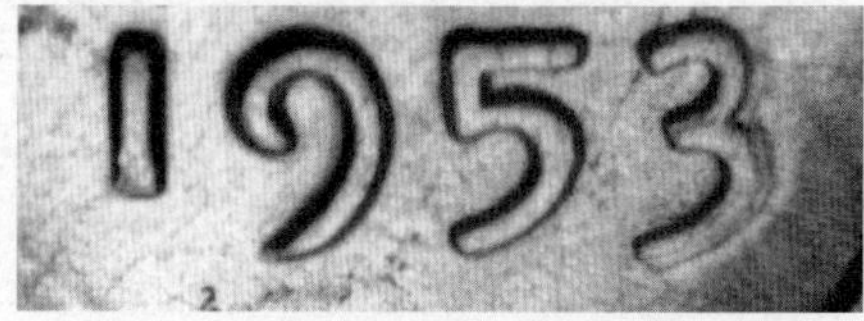

Die deterioration doubling is found on many Lincoln cents, in particular those of the 1950s and earlier. One such deteriorated 1955 cent was often promoted by dealers as "the poor man's doubled die."

Die deterioration is very common on Washington quarters from the 1980s and 1990s, Jefferson nickels from 1955 to date, and Roosevelt dimes from 1965 to date. Die deterioration is a prime example of what can happen when the Mint tries to get maximum production out of every single die.

"Longacre" Doubling

In this Indian Head cent, the doubling that is typical on many of Longacre's designs is evident. Notice that the secondary image is visible on both sides of the letters.

This term was coined by J.T. Stanton as an easy way to describe the doubling that is typical on many coins designed by James Barton Longacre. These include Indian Head cents, nickel three-cent pieces, Shield nickels, and many gold issues. We're certain many readers have seen this doubling before; almost all of the letters are doubled, with the secondary image appearing on both sides of the letters. Some specialists believe this is from the shoulder of the punch penetrating the die, causing the secondary step. Others feel it was an intentional design on Longacre's part, to help the metal flow into the tight crevices of the die. Although this doubling is evident on many of the coins that Longacre designed, it is not seen on all of his coins. This would likely remove the theory that the secondary or "stepped" image was planned to help with metal flow.

Longacre doubling does not add premium to a coin's value.

Summary

We hope this long, but educational, article will help our readers learn the difference between die doubling and other forms of doubling. However, the best learning tool is experience. In that light, we suggest that you look—and look carefully—at as many coins as possible, especially in the date ranges mentioned. Look especially carefully at Proof quarters from 1968 and 1969 for strike doubling, Indian Head cents from the 1860s, 1870s, and 1880s for "Longacre" doubling, nickels from the 1980s for die deterioration, and Franklin half dollars for strike doubling on the mintmark. Don't pass up the opportunity to buy a good example of one of these for your reference, if it's not too expensive.

Die-Doubling I.Q. Test

The 10 photographs here exhibit some examples of die doubling, strike doubling, and even some other forms of doubling. Take a few minutes to see for yourself whether you can accurately identify the various forms of doubling.

Note: Most variety collectors feel coins exhibiting other forms of doubling should not command a premium. However, some collectors believe they are collectible and actively seek them. We feel there is absolutely nothing wrong with this and encourage those who decide to take this course. The question is and should be, "Are you having *fun* in your collecting pursuits?"

Test photo 1

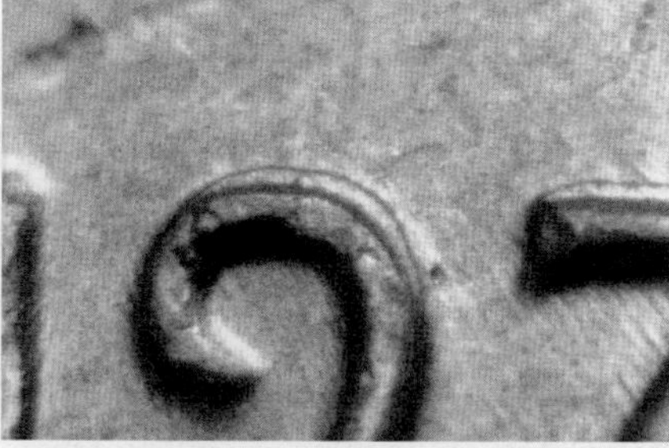

Test photo 2

Test photo 3

Test photo 4

Test photo 5

Test photo 6

Test photo 7

Test photo 8

Test photo 9

Test photo 10

Answers to the test photographs:

1. strike doubling; 2. strike doubling; 3. doubled die; 4. strike doubling; 5. doubled die; 6. die deterioration; 7. strike doubling; 8. repunched mintmark; 9. doubled die; 10. strike doubling.

In test photo 10, notice that the date and the mintmark both exhibit similar doubling. This should be a red flag. There are very few examples on which a doubled die and a repunched mintmark both are evident on the same side of the same coin. Keep in mind that until very recently, the mintmark was punched into the die after the die was made. Therefore, if the die is doubled, the mintmark is not necessarily doubled.

Appendix B

The Minting Process

WHY STUDY THE MINTING PROCESS?

In the study of Mint errors and varieties—and the study of the "regular" segment of numismatics, as well—a basic knowledge of the minting process is vital. If you do not understand how an error or variety occurred, you will not be able to determine whether it is genuine. The description that follows is an abbreviated one, but the basics remain the same.

There are three basic processes that take place at the U.S. Mint, and in each process errors and varieties can occur. First is the die-making process, in which the coin is designed, a model is engraved, and the design is transferred to a "die steel" to strike the coin. The second process is the making of planchets—coin blanks that are created and specially prepared for striking. The last process is the striking of these planchets to make them into coins.

These three processes—die making, planchet production, and striking—are where errors and varieties occur. Some have described this trio of areas as "P-D-S" (planchets, dies, and striking); the resemblance of these initials to the P, D, and S mintmarks of the three primary minting facilities (Philadelphia, Denver, and San Francisco) makes it easy to remember these areas of production.

Error vs. Variety

Occasionally there is disagreement as to whether a certain aberrant coin is an error or a variety. Generally speaking, most specialists consider an error a one-time occurrence that is not repeated in exactly the same way, and a variety an occurrence that *is* repeated in exactly the same way. An off-center strike, therefore, would be considered an error. True, some off-center strikes look quite similar, but generally speaking, each one will be different. However, a doubled die will repeat exactly with each strike, and is thus considered a variety.

THE DIE-MAKING PROCESS

Artists are employed by the Mint to design coins and medals and to sculpt and engrave other designs into workable subjects for coining. Highly trained medallic sculptors take a design from a drawing, painting, or other two-dimensional rendering and transform it onto a plaster model, approximately 15 inches in diameter, that will ultimately be transferred to a coin or medal. The design on the model is always raised above the surrounding area (i.e., it is "positive" or "in relief"), just as it will appear on the finished coin. This plaster sculpture, after slight changes and improvements, is coated with epoxy resins that act as a preservative and a hardener. The epoxy-coated plaster sculpture is called a *galvano* and is forwarded to the die-making area of the Mint.

Technology has developed tremendously in the last few years. As a result many modern coin designs are developed with the use of CAD (Computer Aided Design) programs. In fact some short-run coins have the designs cut directly into the steel dies by laser.

Since the galvano is usually many times larger than the intended coin, its design must be reduced. Traditionally, the galvano would be placed onto a Janvier transfer-reducing machine. This machine traces the design on the galvano and, using the principle of the fulcrum, transfers the design onto the end of a piece of steel bar the actual size of the coin to be produced. This is called the *reducing* stage of die production, and this finished piece of steel is called the *master hub.* When the master hub has been produced, it is heated to extreme temperature, then quenched (cooled) quickly in a vat of oil. This heating-and-cooling process, called *tempering,* hardens the steel even further.

The large galvano is reduced on a Janvier transfer-reducing machine to create a master hub (a "positive") at the actual size of the coin.

The master hub has the design in the same relief design as on the galvano and as it will appear on the finished coin. It is placed into a hydraulic hubbing press, opposite a piece of die steel that is about four inches long. When each is seated into the press, hydraulic force brings the two together, transferring the image from the master hub onto the end of the die steel. When complete, this is called the *master die,* with the design pressed (incused) into its surface.

This operation, known as *hubbing,* used to take several impressions to bring the design to the depth specifications. After each hubbing, the die would be annealed to make the steel soft for the next hubbing. If the die were to receive the image deep enough in the first hubbing, stress on the die steel would result and very likely create cracks, or at least would weaken the die. Strength and durability are stringent requirements. This process is now done by the "single-squeeze method," using one high-pressure compression.

Initially, it was thought that this would ring the death knell to doubled dies. Cherrypickers, however, have found this to be false. The single-squeeze–hubbing method still produces doubled dies, but they are generally located in the center of the coin with limited spreads. Hundreds of doubled dies have been cataloged on coins produced by this new hubbing method.

After the master die is produced, it is placed into the hubbing press to create the working hub in the same manner. Several working hubs are produced. These working hubs then produce working dies in the manner described before. The working dies are then placed into the coining presses to strike coins and medals.

Traditionally, all dies were made in the Philadelphia Mint. Until 1985 the dies were produced without mintmarks, which were added by hand with punches before the dies were shipped to the branch-mint facilities for completion. However, beginning in 1985 the mintmark was added to the master die for Proof coinage, and in 1989–90 it was added to the master dies for circulation coinage. In the late 1990s the mintmark was made part of the original plaster sculpture and a reduction was made for each mint. Subsequently, the mintmark is transferred to the master hub and on down the die-production chain. Beginning in 1996, the Denver Mint started producing dies for its own use and for the San Francisco Mint's production facilities.

Remember that the plaster sculpture, the galvano, the master hub, and the working hub all have the image of the coin in relief, or positive, just as the finished coin will appear. Master dies and working dies have the image coin incuse, or negative—a mirror image of the finished coin.

Planchet Making

Cent and nickel planchets are primarily made outside the Mint, as is the sheet metal for the other denominations. However, the process is much the same as when the Mint produced its own planchets and metal. Raw metal, after being melted, is rolled into long sheets until it is the proper thickness for the intended coin. These long sheets are then coiled for storage, shipping, and eventual use. The sheets are uncoiled and fed into a blanking press—which is nothing more than a series of punches that cut blanks out of the metal coils—either at the outside facility or at the Mint. Notice the word "blank" instead of "planchet": Technically speaking, a *blank* is a disc of metal that has not yet been prepared for striking, whereas a *planchet* is a blank that has been further prepared for striking, as described below.

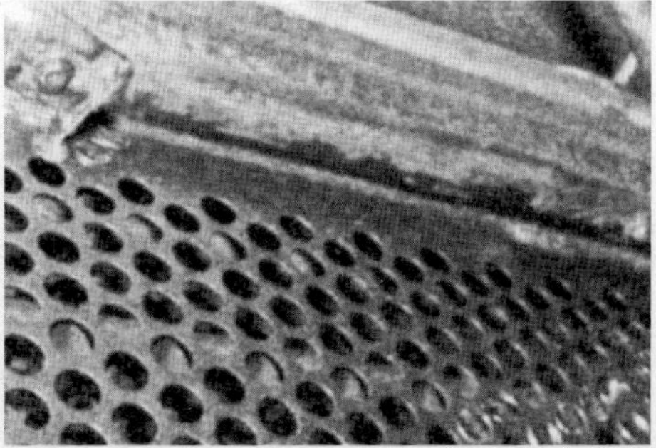

Once the blanks are produced, they pass through what is known as a riddler, which removes imperfectly-sized blanks.

Once the blanks are produced, they pass through what is known as a *riddler*, which passes the blanks over a three-tiered, vibrating screen, with holes in the first tier slightly larger than the intended blanks. The blanks that are of proper diameter drop through, and blanks that are too large are retained on the upper tier and carried to a scrap bin. The second-tier screen has holes slightly smaller than a proper-sized blank. Blanks that are too small pass through these holes to the third tier, from which they are carried away to the scrap bin. The blanks that remain on the second tier are presumed to be of accurate size, and are forwarded to the next process.

At this point, the blanks must be annealed and cleaned. The annealing process softens the blanks to improve striking and reduce wear on the dies. The blanks are fed into a furnace. This furnace is much like a long dryer with the blanks being fed in one end and tumbled as they travel through the furnace. When the blanks exit the furnace, they are washed in a chemical bath and slowly tumbled dry.

The blanks are then ready for the *upset mill*. This is a machine with two primary components: (1) a stationary die with V-shaped grooves, and (2) a rotating die in the center, also with V-shaped grooves. Blanks are fed into one end of the upset mill, fitting into the grooves. As the center die rotates, the blanks pass between the outer, stationary die and the inner, rotating die. As the blanks go through the mill, the spacing between the two dies is gradually reduced, forcing the metal on the edge of the blank to be raised above the flat surfaces. When the disc of metal exits the upset mill, generally with raised metal all around the edge, it is considered a planchet.

The reason for putting raised edges on planchets before striking is that it greatly helps in coin production: it helps force the metal, during striking, toward the center of the coin and then into the crevices of the die; it also helps the coins stack neatly for use in commerce.

A blank remains a blank until it has been through the upsetting mill and received a raised edge, at which time it becomes a planchet. Blanks are frequently (and erroneously) referred to as "Type 1 planchets," but because they do not have raised edges, they should not be called planchets of any kind. There are no Type 1 or Type 2 planchets; the disc of metal is either a blank or a planchet, period.

STRIKING

In the Mint's older presses, the striking process begins with the planchets being brought to the coining presses via overhead conveyors with small bins. These conveyors deposit the planchets into a hopper above the coining presses. From that point the planchets are fed by gravity through feeder tubes and down into the *coining chamber* (the area of the coining press where striking takes place).

The planchets drop from the feeder tubes into *feeder fingers,* each of which has a slot in the end to push out the struck coin and a hole a couple of inches back that holds the next planchet to be deposited into the chamber. These fingers slide back and forth over a smooth steel surface.

The coining chamber consists primarily of the anvil (lower) die, hammer (upper) die, collar, and feeder fingers. The *anvil die,* which usually strikes the reverse of the coin, moves only when coins are being ejected and planchets received. The *hammer die,* which usually strikes the obverse, comes down and strikes the planchet. The *collar* is a metal ring that retains the planchet during the strike, preventing the metal from expanding outside the desired diameter. The collar also serves as a third die, creating the reeding or lettering on coins intended to have reeded or lettered edges.

When the planchet is deposited on the anvil die and within the collar by the feeder finger, the finger retracts and the hammer die comes down and strikes the planchet. As the hammer die retracts, the anvil die (riding on a cam) rises; the feeder finger pushes the struck coin out of the chamber, continues forward, and deposits another planchet onto the anvil die. The feeder finger retracts and the striking process begins again. The finished coins pass through an additional riddler to catch errors; this has greatly reduced the number of error coins escaping the Mint.

The Mint's newer presses strike coins with dies that move horizontally rather than up and down. The rest of the process is generally as described above.

COUNTING AND BAGGING

Once the coins are ejected from the coining press, they fall down a chute and accumulate in large bulk bags that hold thousands of pounds of coinage. These are stored temporarily on-site. The bagged coins are then shipped to the various Federal Reserve banks.

Appendix C

What Are the Best Magnifiers?

"What level of magnification should I use when searching for varieties?" "Which magnifier is the best to use?" "Do I need a microscope?" These are three of the more common questions ever broached concerning this subject. All too often a collector will believe *more* magnification is better—when in fact less is usually best. With coin collecting in general and variety collecting in particular, the strength of the magnification is not as important as the *quality*.

Virtually every variety of any significance can be detected with a 7x glass, if it's of good quality. (A good 7x magnifier is also the recommended loupe for the most accurate coin grading.) A lesser-quality magnifier will only distort the image, making proper identification even more difficult. On the other hand, a good-quality glass with too much magnification is almost always overkill, as it can cause you to overlook key identification points.

An H.E. Harris magnifier (or *loupe,* pronounced "loop") is a common sight at coin shows. You will see dealers and collectors slip them out of their pocket to examine interesting coins. (Some wear them on a chain or string around their neck, for constant easy access.) These magnifiers fold into their chrome cases to protect the lens, which is usually 4x to 8x or greater strength.

Most serious collectors and almost all dealers use a Hastings triplet magnifier; usually a 7x or 10x power is preferred. "Hastings" is not a brand but a method of manufacture. The Hastings triplet has a three-glass (or plastic) optic, which ensures clarity throughout the entire lens and produces virtually no distortion.

Some manufacturers use 10x or 17x designations. However, without good-quality optics, the 10x or 17x means nothing. We've seen some magnifiers marked as 17x, compared to which a 10x Hastings triplet provides more detail, better clarity, and a wider field of view. And remember, if you can't see a variety with a 7x glass, it's likely not worth searching for.

A good 7x Bausch & Lomb Hastings triplet will normally run about $45. However, with some searching on the Internet, you can find a good 7x Hastings triplet for less than $25.

Stereoscopes (microscopes) are handy, fun, and very educational, but these are not absolutely necessary for the study of varieties. Should you have the desire to add one to your array of collecting tools, a good stereoscope can be obtained for as little as $200 (though most will run around $500 or more). Be sure to get a stereoscope—one that has two eyepieces. This will allow the very best in clarity and use. A stereoscope is great for taking photographs, and for studying the minute differences evident on every coin.

Check with your local supplier or favorite online dealers. See what they recommend. We strongly advise spending a little more for a good-quality product. You'll reap the rewards soon afterward.

Appendix D

Popular Varieties From Proof and Mint Sets

This is a general guide to Proof sets and Mint sets that contain significant varieties. Proof listings in **bold** type are considered the most desirable.

Mint Sets

1948	1¢	S/S–repunched mintmark
1949	5¢	D/S–over mintmark (although known, most have already been removed)
1954	5¢	doubled-die reverse
1959	1¢	D/D–repunched mintmark
1960	1¢	D/D–repunched mintmark (RPM-001, RPM-023)
1961	50¢	D/D–repunched mintmark
1963	1¢	D/D–repunched mintmark (RPM-012, RPM-016)
1963	5¢	D-doubled-die reverse
1963	10¢	(P)–doubled-die obverse
1963	25¢	(P)–doubled-die obverse (DDO-001, DDO-008)
1963	25¢	(P)–doubled-die obverse and doubled-die reverse (DDO-007 and DDR-001)
1963	25¢	D-doubled-die obverse (DDO-001, DDO-002)
1963	50¢	(P)–doubled-die obverse
1963	50¢	(P)–doubled-die reverse (DDR-001, DDR-004)
1966 SMS	50¢	doubled-die obverse
1966 SMS	50¢	no engraver's initials
1967 SMS	25¢	doubled-die obverse
1967 SMS	25¢	doubled-die reverse
1967 SMS	50¢	doubled-die obverse
1968	10¢	(P)–doubled-die obverse
1968	25¢	D–doubled-die reverse
1969	10¢	D/D–repunched mintmark
1969	25¢	D/D–repunched mintmark
1969	50¢	D–doubled-die reverse (DDR-001, DDR-004)
1970	1¢	D/D–repunched mintmark
1970	1¢	S/S–repunched mintmark
1970	10¢	D–doubled-die reverse (DDR-001, DDR-003, DDR-004, DDR-005)
1970	25¢	D–doubled-die reverse (DDR-001, DDR-002, DDR-004)
1970	50¢	D–doubled-die reverse (DDR-001, DDR-002, DDR-003, DDR-004, DDR-005, DDR-006, DDR-007, DDR-008, DDR-009)
1971	5¢	D/D–repunched mintmark (RPM-001, RPM-004)
1971	10¢	D/D–repunched mintmark
1971	10¢	D–doubled-die reverse
1971	50¢	D–doubled-die obverse (DDO-004, DDO-006, DDO-007)
1972	5¢	D–doubled-die reverse
1972	50¢	D–doubled-die reverse
1973	50¢	(P)–doubled-die reverse
1973	50¢	D–doubled-die obverse
1974	50¢	D–doubled-die obverse

Mint Sets

1974	50¢	D–doubled-die reverse
1976	25¢	D–doubled-die obverse
1976	50¢	D–doubled-die obverse
1981	5¢	D–doubled-die reverse
1981	25¢	P–doubled-die obverse
1984	50¢	D/D–repunched mintmark
1987	10¢	D/D–repunched mintmark
1989	5¢	D–doubled-die reverse
1989	10¢	P–doubled-die reverse
1989	25¢	P–doubled-die obverse
1989	50¢	D/D–repunched mintmark
1991	5¢	D–doubled-die reverse (DDR-001, DDR-002, DDR-003, DDR-004)
2005	5¢ Bison	P–doubled-die obverse (DDO-001, DDO-002, DDO-003, DDO-004)
2005	5¢ Ocean in View	P–doubled-die reverse (many)
2005	25¢ Minnesota	P–doubled-die reverse (many)
2005	25¢ Oregon	P–doubled-die reverse (many)
2005	25¢ Oregon	D–doubled-die reverse (many)
2007	25¢ Wyoming	P–doubled-die reverse (many)
2008	25¢ New Mexico	D–doubled-die reverse (many)
2009	1¢ Formative Years	D–doubled-die reverse (many)
2009	25¢ Washington, D.C.	P–doubled-die reverse
2015	25¢ Nebraska	doubled-die reverse

Proof Sets

1950	10¢	doubled-die reverse
1950	50¢	doubled-die obverse
1951	1¢	doubled-die obverse
1951	**5¢**	**doubled-die obverse**
1952	**25¢**	**“Superbird”**
1953	1¢	doubled-die obverse
1953	**5¢**	**doubled-die obverse**
1953	25¢	doubled-die obverse
1953	25¢	recut tail feathers
1954	5¢	doubled-die obverse
1954	10¢	doubled-die obverse
1954	50¢	doubled-die obverse
1955	1¢	doubled-die obverse
1955	1¢	doubled-die reverse
1955	**5¢**	**tripled-die reverse**
1956	1¢	doubled-die obverse
1956	1¢	doubled-die reverse
1956	5¢	doubled-die obverse
1956	10¢	doubled-die obverse
1956	25¢	reverse die gouge
1956	50¢	doubled-die obverse
1956	50¢	doubled-die reverse
1956	50¢	Variety 1 reverse
1957	**5¢**	**quadrupled-die obverse**
1957	50¢	doubled-die reverse
1959	25¢	doubled-die obverse
1960, Small Date	**1¢**	**doubled-die obverse (Large/Small)**

Proof Sets

1960, Small Date	**1¢**	**doubled-die obverse (Small/Large)**
1960	1¢	doubled-die reverse
1960	5¢	doubled-die reverse
1960	10¢	doubled-die obverse
1960	**10¢**	**doubled-die reverse**
1960	**25¢**	**doubled-die reverse**
1960	50¢	doubled-die obverse
1961	5¢	doubled-die reverse
1961	25¢	doubled-die obverse
1961	**50¢**	**doubled-die reverse**
1962	1¢	doubled-die reverse
1962	50¢	doubled-die obverse
1962	**50¢**	**poss. misplaced mintmark**
1963	**1¢**	**doubled-die reverse**
1963	**10¢**	**doubled-die reverse**
1963	25¢	doubled-die reverse
1964	5¢	tripled-die reverse
1964	10¢	doubled-die obverse
1964	1¢	doubled-die reverse
1964	50¢	doubled-die obverse
1964	50¢	Accented Hair
1968-S	1¢	doubled-die obverse
1968-S	5¢	repunched mintmark
1968-S	10¢	doubled-die obverse
1968-S	**10¢**	**doubled-die reverse**
1968-S	**10¢**	**doubled-die obverse**
1968-S	**10¢**	**No S**
1968-S	**25¢**	**doubled-die reverse**
1968-S	**50¢**	**doubled-die obverse**
1969-S	5¢	repunched mintmark
1969-S	25¢	doubled-die obverse
1969-S	**25¢**	**repunched mintmark**

1970-S	**10¢**	**No S**
1970-S	50¢	doubled-die obverse
1971-S	1¢	doubled-die obverse
1971-S	**5¢**	**No S**
1971-S	50¢	doubled-die obverse
1975-S	**10¢**	**No S**
1976-S, clad	50¢	doubled-die reverse
1979-S	1¢	Type II mintmark
1979-S	5¢	Type II mintmark
1979-S	10¢	Type II mintmark
1979-S	25¢	Type II mintmark
1979-S	50¢	Type II mintmark
1979-S	$1	Type II mintmark
1981-S	1¢	Type II mintmark
1981-S	5¢	Type II mintmark
1981-S	10¢	Type II mintmark
1981-S	25¢	Type II mintmark
1981-S	50¢	Type II mintmark
1981-S	$1	Type II mintmark
1983-S	**10¢**	**No S**
1988-S	**50¢**	**doubled-die obverse**
1990-S	**1¢**	**No S**
1990-S	5¢	doubled-die obverse
1990-S	25¢	doubled-die obverse
1992-S	50¢	doubled-die obverse
1992-S	50¢	doubled-die obverse
1995-S	25¢	doubled-die obverse
1999-S	25¢ PA, clad	doubled-die obverse
2004-S	25¢ MI, clad	doubled-die obverse
2005-S	25¢ MN, clad, silver	many doubled-die reverses
2005-S	25¢ OR, clad, silver	many doubled-die reverses
2007-S	25¢ WY, clad, silver	many doubled-die reverses

Appendix E

When Cherrypickin', Use Courtesy and Respect!

Many years ago, a dealer friend of ours indicated he would never let anyone, other than a few people, cherrypick his stock (fortunately, we were among that select group). He had legitimate complaints regarding most of those who try to cherrypick varieties. His experiences are not unlike those of many dealers. Too often, collectors who are most interested in cherrypickin' varieties disregard the dealer's other (and potentially more profitable) customers. Many cherrypickers will take up space and time, and then walk away without a single purchase. Is that right? Is that fair to the dealer?

Before we get directly into the *courtesy* aspect of this article, we would like to remind you that there is nothing wrong with cherrypickin'. We use our knowledge just as another dealer or collector would use their knowledge to buy the best deal. A dealer trying to buy an 1892-S Barber quarter in Fine condition for a client will usually cherrypick to get the best possible value. Dealers with excellent grading skills can cherrypick undergraded coins, making a nice profit in a later sale. That has been occurring for decades in our hobby.

When the term *cherrypick* is used today, most hobbyists automatically think of those who search for varieties among a stock of normal coins. Those of us involved with varieties have studied long and hard for our knowledge. However, to make the most of this knowledge, we must use some common sense, and we must *always* respect a dealer's main objective—to earn a living. Dealers are at shows and in the coin business to make money to support their families. This is their livelihood, and we must always respect their time and space. If you don't feel you can afford them this courtesy, don't consider cherrypickin' for varieties. Those of us who do respect a dealer's time and space do not want a few inconsiderate people to ruin the pickings for the rest of us.

There are a few "courtesy" pointers that we'd like you to keep in mind. Remember that you are very likely a small customer for the typical dealer. They can almost certainly make more money from another customer in a tenth of the time they might spend with you. Remember that *you need the dealers* for cherrypickin'—they could make their living without cherrypickers!

If you're at a show and you've spotted a dealer whose stock you would like to search, and that dealer is busy, simply go to another dealer for a while. If you are seated at a dealer's table looking over their stock, and they start to get busy, let them know in a respectful way that you realize you're taking up their space and time, and that you will come back when they aren't as busy. We promise the dealer will remember your courtesy and respect, and you're more likely to be welcomed back when time permits.

We've often had dealers ask what we're looking for. We generally tell them that we're looking for various varieties, and that will usually suffice. Don't lie. Never lie! But you don't have to tell everything. If the dealer persists, you might tell them about a few of the more scarce varieties, and explain that there is a market for those varieties. Remember most dealers couldn't care less about the popular varieties that aren't listed in the *Red Book* or *Mega Red*. They will usually say "fine," and you can continue looking.

However, the best-case scenario is that you can teach this dealer something about varieties. As you become better acquainted, the dealer might start to look for some of the varieties, and save them for you. Sure, you'll likely pay a little more for them than the price of the normal coin, but far less than the actual value of the variety. In short, you'll have added a pair of eyes to *your* cherrypickin'. You'll get a new supply for varieties and at prices that will enable you to realize a very nice profit. We've even had dealers tell us to name the price, and we've had dealers ask for only the value of the normal coin.

Here's a tip that we think is extremely important. If you're at a dealer's table, and if for some reason you need to reach into your pocket or lap, plainly open your hands above the table, turn them over and rub them together, then do what you need to do. You don't need to say anything, and don't make a big deal of it, but make sure it's obvious. Why? The dealer will know for sure that you are not "palming" a coin. Do this with dealers you know well, and with dealers you don't know. Make it a habit. The main point here is to *never* give any dealer any opportunity to even think you are doing something wrong. We've seen people who hold a want list or magnifier in their lap, then take the coin below the table's surface, out of view of the dealer. That is very wrong, whether cherrypickin' or not, and will often discourage a dealer from welcoming you back. Always think of how you would want a customer to act if you were the dealer, and *always be respectful*—even if the dealer may seem rude.

Here are some other important points: Never let a dealer feel cheated when you buy a coin, or you'll never be welcomed back. Never brag about what you've purchased from a dealer if there is any way possible it could get back to the dealer. Always be polite and courteous—and being friendly doesn't hurt, either. Try to put yourself in their shoes once in a while. Usually, a dealer's main objective is to sell for a profit coins they have and know best. Many dealers specialize in certain areas, and leave other coins to others. We cherrypickers are the ones who know varieties best, and so they will usually leave this area for us.

One last tip: Suppose you find a super variety for the price of a regular coin, and for some reason you don't want the dealer to key in on that one coin. You might buy a few other coins at the same time to draw less attention to the coin you really want. Who cares about the added expense? You'll make a bundle on that nice cherry! And if the extra coins are ones with firm markets, such as an MS-63 Morgan dollar or a Proof set, you'll be able to turn around and sell them quickly.

Above all, *always use courtesy and respect* in all your dealings, be honest, and always act in a professional manner. You'll make some friends along the way, and we guarantee you'll come out ahead in the long run!

Appendix F

1979-S and 1981-S Proof-Mintmark Varieties

The Type 1 and Type 2 mintmark varieties for the 1979-S and 1981-S Proof sets are very well known, yet many people become confused when trying to differentiate them. This appendix Hllustrates the four mintmark styles for each denomination.

Compare these descriptions to the photos, and you'll be able to identify the correct types:

- The *1979-S Type 1* mintmark has a squared, filled S, very indistinct.
- The *1979-S Type 2* mintmark is clear and well formed.
- The *1981-S Type 1* is a worn version of the 1979-S Type 2.
- The *1981-S Type 2,* although somewhat similar to the Type 1, is distinguishable by the flattened top surface of the S. Some specialists argue that the S must be clear in both loops. Most agree that the S can show some slight filling, but the mintmark punch must show that flattened top surface. This is usually the most difficult type to comprehend. But the key is really very simple—that flatness on the top surface.

Dimes

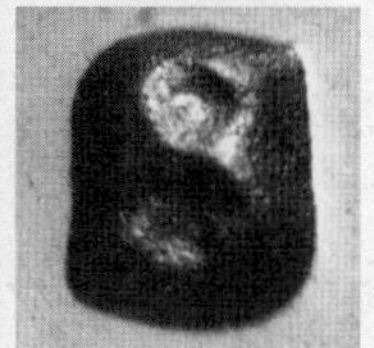
1979-S Type 1

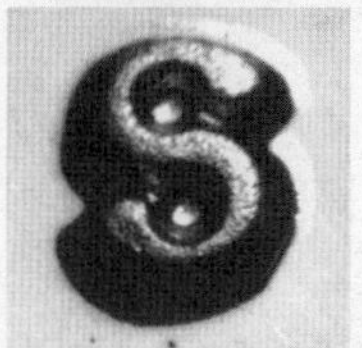
1979-S Type 2

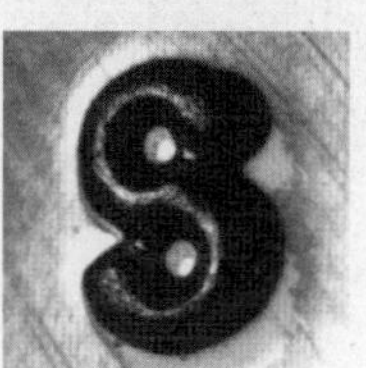
1981-S Type 1

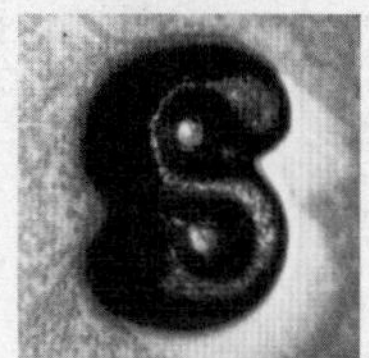
1981-S Type 2

Quarter Dollars

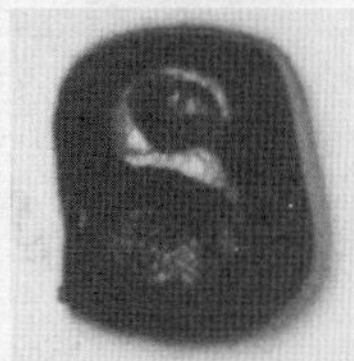
1979-S Type 1

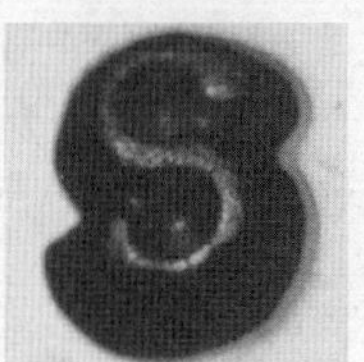
1979-S Type 2

1981-S Type 1

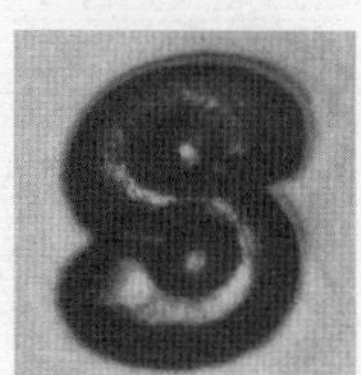
1981-S Type 2

Appendix G
Recommended Reading

The axiom "Buy the book before the coin" applies even more strongly to error/variety collectors than to the regular segment of the hobby. This list of recommended readings is by no means complete—new books become available regularly—but it gives you an excellent foundation for building your knowledge. Most of these books are available online, or through any coin dealer. Some are out of print, but can be found in the secondary market.

One book that should begin any numismatic library is *A Guide Book of United States Coins,* by R.S. Yeoman (senior editor Jeff Garrett, research editor Q. David Bowers, editor emeritus Kenneth Bressett). Popularly known as the "Red Book," it covers not only regular coins, but the more popular errors and varieties, as well.

The following books highlight specific coin series or subjects covered in the sixth edition, volume II, of the *Cherrypickers' Guide*. Each is a tremendous asset for anyone seriously interested in the particular topic. Also take note, all references by James Wiles are cataloging the CONECA variety files.

The periodicals listed are magazines that regularly feature die varieties and errors.

Half Dimes

Blythe, Al. *The Complete Guide to Liberty Seated Half Dimes.*
Bowers, Q. David. *A Guide Book of Liberty Seated Silver Coins.*
Logan, Russell, and John McCloskey. *Federal Half Dimes 1792–1837.*
Newlin, H.P. *The Early Half-Dimes of the United States.*
Valentine, D.W. *The United States Half Dimes.*

Dimes

Ahwash, Kamal M. *Encyclopedia of United States Liberty Seated Dimes 1837–1891.*
Bateson, Richard. *Richard's Roosevelt Dime Review: The Silver Years, 1946–1965.*
Bowers, Q. David. *A Guide Book of Barber Silver Coins.*
Bowers, Q. David. *A Guide Book of Liberty Seated Silver Coins.*
Bowers, Q. David. *A Guide Book of Mercury Dimes, Standing Liberty Quarters, and Liberty Walking Half Dollars.*
Davis, David, Russell Logan, Allen Lovejoy, John McCloskey, and William Subjack. *Early United States Dimes 1796–1837.*
Fortin, Gerry. *Liberty Seated Dimes Web-Book.* www.seateddimevarieties.com.
Greer, Brian. *The Complete Guide to Liberty Seated Dimes.*
Lange, David W. *The Complete Guide to Mercury Dimes,* second ed.
Lawrence, David. *The Complete Guide to Barber Dimes.*
Wexler, John, et al. *The Authoritative Reference on Roosevelt Dimes.*

Twenty-Cent Pieces

Brunner, Lane J., and John M. Frost. *Double Dime: The United States Twenty-Cent Piece.*

Quarter Dollars

Bowers, Q. David. *A Guide Book of Barber Silver Coins.*
Bowers, Q. David. *A Guide Book of Liberty Seated Silver Coins.*
Bowers, Q. David. *A Guide Book of Mercury Dimes, Standing Liberty Quarters, and Liberty Walking Half Dollars.*
Bowers, Q. David. *A Guide Book of Washington Quarters.*
Briggs, Larry. *The Comprehensive Encyclopedia of United States Seated Quarters.*
Browning, A.W. *The Early Quarter Dollars of the United States, 1796–1838.*
Cline, J.H. *Standing Liberty Quarters,* third ed.
Knauss, Robert H. *Standing Liberty Quarters: Varieties & Errors.*
Lawrence, David. *The Complete Guide to Barber Quarters.*
Rea, Rory, Glenn Peterson, Bradley Karoleff, and John Kovach. *Early Quarter Dollars of the U.S. Mint, 1796–1838.*
Tompkins, Steve M. *Early United States Quarters, 1796–1838.*
Wexler, John, et al. *The Best of the Washington Quarter Doubled Dies.*
Wiles, James. *The Washington Quarter Dollar Book,* vols. 1–3.

General Error and Die-Variety Books

Brown, Nicholas P., David J. Camire, and Fred Weinberg. *100 Greatest U.S. Error Coins.*
Margolis, Arnold. *Error Coins From A to Z.*
Margolis, Arnold. *The Error Coin Encyclopedia.*
Wexler, John A., and Robert Wilharm. *Error-Variety News Classics,* books I and II.
Herbert, Alan. *Official Price Guide to Mint Errors,* seventh ed.
Byers, Mike. *World's Greatest Mint Errors.*
Thurman, Sam, and Arnold Margolis. *The Cud Book.*
Wexler, John. *The Encyclopedia of Doubled Dies,* vols. 1 and 2.
Wexler, John, et al. *Over Mintmarks and Hot Repunched Mintmarks.*
Wexler, John, and Tom Miller. *The RPM Book.*
Potter, Ken, and Brian Allen. *Strike It Rich With Pocket Change: Error Coins Bring Big Money,* third ed.
Wiles, James. *Ultra Modern Doubled Dies (1996–2012).* (ebook)
Wiles, James. *What Are Die Varieties?* (ebook).

Periodicals

ErrorScope. The bi-monthly magazine of CONECA (Combined Organizations of Numismatic Error Collectors of America), the national error/variety club. Membership information is available online at www.conecaonline.org.

Error Trends Coin Magazine. This highly educational monthly magazine was devoted to the error/variety hobby, weighted toward errors.

The Hub. This was the bi-monthly magazine of the National Collectors Association of Die Doubling.

Appendix H
Fivaz-Stanton Numbers Cross-Reference Chart

The Fivaz-Stanton numbering system changed in the fourth edition of the *Cherrypickers' Guide*. The earlier numbering system was very confined, limiting the number of new listings that could be added. The newer system is rational and infinite. For details, consult the "How to Use This Book" section.

This chart cross-references the current FS numbers assigned to all previous listings. It covers denominations covered in this volume of the *Cherrypickers' Guide*. The first column indicates the *new* FS number, with other columns showing the old FS number (if there was a listing), the date and mint of the coin, and a brief description. Due to space limitations, the description is very short and should not be used in an attempt to identify a variety.

These numbers can easily be used in an abbreviated format, by using only the final three or four digits in the full number. A variety is always described with the denomination and date, so duplicating that number in a description is not really necessary. The final digits will describe the variety's FS number when the denomination and date are identified.

FS#	Old FS#	Issue	Brief Description
CAPPED BUST HALF DIMES			
H10-1829-301	000.1	1829	Overdate (9 Over 8)
H10-1834-301	000.3	1834	RPD (3 Over Inverted 3)
H10-1836-301		1836	RPD
LIBERTY SEATED HALF DIMES			
H10-1838-901		1838	Rusted Die Rev
H10-1839o-501		1839-O	Rev of '38 (Large O Mintmark)
H10-1840o-501		1840-O	No Drapery, Huge O
H10-1840o-901	000.5	1840-O	Transitional Rev (Large Letters reverse; open buds)
H10-1842o-301		1842-O	RPD (8 and 2)
H10-1843-301	000.6	1843	RPD (1, 8, and 4 south)
H10-1844-301	000.63	1844	RPD (1 and 8 north and south; 4 south)
H10-1845-301	000.65	1845	MPD (84 protruding south from base of rock)
H10-1845-302	000.66	1845	RPD (all digits northwest)
H10-1848-301	001	1848	Large Date
H10-1848-302	001.3	1848	Possible Overdate (8 Over 7 Over 6)
H10-1849-301	001.5	1849	Overdate (9 Over 6)
H10-1849-302	001.55	1849	Overdate (possibly 9 Over 6)
H10-1849-303		1849	Overdate (9 Over So-Called 8)
H10-1853-301	001.8	1853	MPD (protruding from rock)

FS#	Old FS#	Issue	Brief Description
H10-1853-401		1853	Arrows; Dot Below 5 of Date
H10-1855-101		1855	DDO, Clashed Dies (lower edge of skirt)
H10-1856-301	001.9	1856	MPD (8 in rock above primary 8)
H10-1858-301	002	1858	RPD; V-10
H10-1858-302	003	1858	RPD (Date Over Inverted Date)
H10-1861-301	003.6	1861	Possible Overdate (1 Over 0)
H10-1863S-301		1863-S	Misplaced Date
H10-1865S-301	003.8	1865-S	RPD (circulation strike of V-1 and -4)
H10-1871-301	003.9	1871	MPD (portion of a digit in rock)
H10-1872-101	004	1872	DDO (V-6)
H10-1872S-301	005	1872-S	MPD and RPD (1 in skirt)
H10-1872S-302		1872-S	MPD (left of and below pendant; also Mintmark Below Bow)
BUST DIMES			
10-1814-901		1814	Close STATESOFAMERICA
10-1820-901		1820	Close STATESOFAMERICA
10-1829-301	001	1829	Curl-Base 2
10-1829-901	002	1829	Small Over Large 10 C.
10-1829-902		1829	Extra Large 10 C.
10-1830-301	003	1830	Overdate (30 Over 29)

APPENDIX H: FIVAZ-STANTON NUMBERS CROSS-REFERENCE CHART

FS#	Old FS#	Issue	Brief Description
LIBERTY SEATED DIMES–SMALL STARS OBVERSE, NO DRAPERY, CLOSED BUD REVERSE–1838–1840			
10-1838-801	003.27	1838	DDR (all of this type are the DDR)
LIBERTY SEATED DIMES–LARGE STARS OBVERSE, NO DRAPERY, CLOSED BUD REVERSE–1838–1840			
10-1838-802	003.27	1838	DDR (same reverse die as FS-801)
LIBERTY SEATED DIMES–LARGE STARS OBVERSE, PARTIAL DRAPERY, CLOSED BUD REVERSE–1838–1839			
10-1839o-501	003.28	1839-O	RPM (O Over O); Large O
10-1839o-502		1839-O	Huge O Mintmark
LIBERTY SEATED DIMES–LARGE STARS OBVERSE, WITH DRAPERY, OPEN BUD REVERSE–1840–1853, 1856–1860-S			
10-1841o-901	003.3	1841-O	Transitional Rev (closed bud; Small O Mintmark)
10-1841o-902		1841-O	Transitional Rev (closed bud; Large O Mintmark)
10-1843-301		1843	RPD
LIBERTY SEATED DIMES–ARROWS ADDED			
10-1853-301		1853	RPD
10-1855-101		1855	DDO
10-1856-101		1856 SD	DDO; Small Date
10-1856o-301		1856-O	RPD, Large O
10-1872-301	003.45	1872	RPD
10-1872-302		1872	MPD (outer curve of 2 above 7)
10-1872-801		1872	DDR (reverse rotated about 170 degrees)
LIBERTY SEATED DIMES–NO ARROWS, CLOSE 3			
10-1873-301		1873	RPD
LIBERTY SEATED DIMES–WITH ARROWS			
10-1873-101	003.5	1873	DDO
10-1875-301		1875	MPD (1 in denticles)
10-1876CC-101	004	1876-CC	DDO (Level CC Mintmark)
10-1876CC-102	004	1876-CC	DDO (Right C High)
10-1876CC-103	004	1876-CC	DDO (Right C Low)
10-1876CC-301	003.7	1876-CC	MPD (digits in skirt by shield)
10-1876CC-801		1876-CC	DDR
10-1876CC-901	005	1876-CC	Type II Reverse
10-1876S-301		1876-S	RPD (18 of date)
10-1877CC-301		1877-CC	Overdate (7 Over 6)
10-1887S-501		1887-S	RPM (S Over S)
10-1888S-501		1888-S	RPM (S Over S); Greer-101
10-1889-801	005.3	1889	DDR (also RPD)
10-1890-301	005.5	1890	MPD (9 in gown)
10-1890-302	005.6	1890	MPD (digits in drapery)

FS#	Old FS#	Issue	Brief Description
10-1890S-501		1890-S	RPM; Greer-102
10-1890S-502		1890-S	RPM
10-1891-301		1891	MPD (denticles between 8 and 9)
10-1891o-501	008	1891-O	RPM (O Over Horizontal O)
10-1891S-501	007	1891-S	RPM; Greer-101
BARBER DIMES			
10-1892-301	008.3	1892	RPD
10-1892-302	008.4	1892	RPD
10-18920-301	008.5	1892-O	RPD
10-1893-301		1893	So-Called 3 Over 2
10-1893S-501	009	1893-S	RPM
10-1895S-301	009.2	1895-S	RPD (9 and 5)
10-1896-301	009.3	1896	RPD (8, 9, and 6)
10-1897-301		1897	RPD
10-1897-302		1897	RPD
10-1897-303		1897	RPD
10-1899o-301		1899-O	RPD
10-18990-501		1899-O	RPM
10-1901o-501	010	1901-O	RPM (O Over Horizontal O)
10-1903-301		1903	RPD
10-1903o-301		1903-O	RPD
10-1905o-501		1905-O	Micro O
10-1906-301		1906	RPD
10-1906-302		1906	RPD
10-1906D-501		1906-D	OMM (D Over O)
10-1906D-302		1906-D	RPD, RPM
10-1906D-303		1906-D	RPD, MPD
10-1906o-301		1906-O	RPD, MPD
10-1906S-301/501		1906-S	RPD, RPM
10-1907-301		1907	RPD
10-1907D-301		1907-D	RPD
10-19070-501		1907-O	RPM
10-1908-301		1908	RPD
10-1908-302		1908	Possible Overdate (08 Over 07)
10-1908-303		1908	RPD (multiple punches)
10-1908D-301	010.220	1908-D	RPD (possible overdate)
10-1908D-302	010.210	1908-D	RPD
10-1908D-303	010.200	1908-D	Overdate
10-1908D-304	010.225	1908-D	RPD
10-1908D-305	010.230	1908-D	RPD
10-1908D-306	010.235	1908-D	RPD
10-1908D-307	010.240	1908-D	RPD
10-19080-301	010.250	1908-O	RPD
10-19080-302	010.260	1908-O	RPD
10-1912D-501		1912-D	RPM
10-1912S-101		1912-S	DDO (UNITED and all letters)
10-1912S-401		1912-S	Die Chips (lip and jaw)
MERCURY DIMES			
10-1919-101		1919	DDO
10-1926-101		1926	DDO
10-1928S-501		1928-S	Large S Mintmark

FS#	Old FS#	Issue	Brief Description
10-1929S-101	010.3	1929-S	DDO
10-1931D-101		1931-D	DDO
10-1931S-101		1931-S	TDO (date, motto)
10-1934D-501		1934-D	RPM
10-1935-101		1935	DDO (date)
10-1935S-501		1935-S	RPM (also strike doubling on mintmark)
10-1936-101	010.5	1936	DDO
10-1936D-501		1936-D	RPM
10-1936S-110		1936-S	Possible Overdate
10-1937-101		1937	DDO
10-1937S-101		1937-S	DDO
10-1939-101		1939	DDO
10-1939D-501		1939-D	RPM (D Over D)
10-1940S-501		1940-S	RPM (S Over S Over S Over S)
10-1940S-101/801		1940-S	DDO; DDR
10-1941-101		1941	DDO
10-1941D-101/801	010.58	1941-D	DDO; DDR
10-1941S-501	010.6	1941-S	RPM
10-1941S-502		1941-S	RPM
10-1941S-511	010.65	1941-S	Large S Mintmark
10-1941S-801		1941-S	DDR
10-1942-101	010.7	1942/1	DDO
10-1942D-101	010.8	1942/1-D	DDO (also RPM)
10-1942D-501		1942-D	RPM
10-1942S-501		1942-S	IMM
10-1942S-502		1942-S	RPM
10-1943D-501		1943-D	RPM
10-1943S-501		1943-S	RPM (S Over S)
10-1943S-511		1943-S	Large, Trumpet Tail S Mintmark
10-1944D-501		1944-D	RPM
10-1945D-101/501		1945-D	RPM (D Over D)
10-1945D-502		1945-D	RPM
10-1945D-503		1945-D	RPM
10-1945S-503	011	1945-S	RPM (S Over Horizontal S)
10-1945S-504		1945-S	Inverted S
10-1945S-511		1945-S	RPM (possible S Over D)
10-1945S-512		1945-S	Micro S Mintmark
ROOSEVELT DIMES			
10-1946-101/803	011.4	1946	DDO-004, DDR-003
10-1946-102/804		1946	DDO (same obv die as above, but no DDR)
10-1946-103/805	011.5	1946	DDO
10-1946-104		1946	DDO
10-1946-801		1946	DDR
10-1946-802		1946	DDR
10-1946D-501		1946-D	RPM (D Over D)
10-1946D-502		1946-D	RPM (D Over D)
10-1946D-503		1946-D	RPM (D Over D)

FS#	Old FS#	Issue	Brief Description
10-1946S-501/801	011.7	1946-S	RPM (also DDR-001)
10-1946S-502/802	011.6	1946-S	RPM (also DDR-002)
10-1946S-503		1946-S	RPM (S Over S Over S, possibly RPM-013)
10-1946S-504		1946-S	Sans Serif S Mintmark
10-1946S-505		1946-S	RPM
10-1947-101	011.9	1947	DDO
10-1947D-101		1947-D	DDO-003
10-1947D-102		1947-D	DDO-001 (LIBERTY, IN GOD WE TRUST)
10-1947S-501	013	1947-S	OMM (S Over D)
10-1947S-502	012	1947-S	OMM (S Over D)
10-1947S-503		1947-S	RPM (S Over S)
10-1947S-504		1947-S	RPM (S Over Horizontal S)
10-1947S-801	013.5	1947-S	DDR
10-1948-801		1948	DDR
10-1948S-501		1948-S	RPM-001
10-1949S-401		1949-S	"Bugs Bunny"
10-1950-801		1950 PF	DDR
10-1950D-501		1950-D	OMM (D Over S)
10-1950D-502		1950-D	RPM
10-1950D-801	014	1950-D	DDR
10-1950S-501	014.5	1950-S	RPM (S Over Inverted S)
10-1951D-501		1951-D	RPM-001
10-1952S-501		1952-S	RPM-001
10-1953D-501		1953-D	RPM (D Over Horizontal D)
10-1953S-401		1953-S	"Bugs Bunny"
10-1953S-501		1953-S	RPM-002
10-1953S-901		1953-S	Acorn Variety
10-1954-101		1954 PF	DDO
10-1954-801		1954	DDR (base of torch and oak stem)
10-1954S-501		1954-S	RPM
10-1954S-401		1954-S	Missing Designer's Initials
10-1955S-401		1955-S	"Bugs Bunny"
10-1956-101		1956 PF	DDO
10-1957-101		1957	DDO
10-1959D-501	014.8	1959-D	RPM (D Over Inverted D)
10-1959D-502		1959-D	RPM (D Over D)
10-1959D-503		1959-D	RPM (D Over D)
10-1959D-504		1959-D	RPM-001
10-1960-101		1960 PF	DDO
10-1960-102a	015	1960 PF	DDO (early die state)
10-1960-102b	015	1960 PF	DDO (late die state)
10-1960-103		1960 PF	DDO-004 (designer's initials, TRUST)
10-1960-104		1960 PF	DDO-007 (like FS-101 but stronger on N)
10-1960-105		1960 PF	DDO-008 (TRUST)
10-1960-801	015.5	1960 PF	DDR
10-1960D-501		1960-D	RPM (D Over D Over D)
10-1961D-801	015.8	1961-D	DDR
10-1962D-501		1962-D	RPM (D Over Horizontal D)

FS#	Old FS#	Issue	Brief Description
10-1963-101	016	1963	DDO
10-1963-801	017	1963 PF	DDR
10-1963-802	017.5	1963 PF	DDR
10-1963-803	018	1963 PF	DDR
10-1963-804		1963 PF	DDR
10-1963-805		1963	DDR
10-1963D-801	018.2	1963-D	DDR
10-1964-101	018.4	1964 PF	DDO
10-1964-801		1964	DDR
10-1964-802	018.3	1964	DDR
10-1964D-501		1964-D	RPM (D Over D northeast)
10-1964D-502	018.7	1964-D	Misplaced Mintmark (D protruding from torch)
10-1964D-503		1964-D	RPM (D Over D south)
10-1964D-504		1964-D	RPM (D Over D south)
10-1964D-505		1964-D	RPM (D Over D south)
10-1964D-506		1964-D	RPM (D Over D south)
10-1964D-801	018.5	1964-D	DDR
10-1964D-802		1964-D	DDR
10-1966-401		1966	"5" on Cheek
10-1967-101	019	1967	DDO
10-1968-101	019.5	1968	DDO
10-1968S-101	020	1968-S PF	DDO
10-1968S-102	020.2	1968-S PF	DDO
10-1968S-501		1968-S PF	Missing Mintmark
10-1968S-502		1968-S PF	RPM (also minor DDO)
10-1968S-801	020.3	1968-S PF	DDR
10-1968S-802		1968-S PF	DDR
10-1969-901		1969	Rev of '68 (deeper lines in flame); RDV-002
10-1969D-501	020.4	1969-D	RPM (D Over D northeast)
10-1970-801	020.6	1970	DDR
10 -1970-901		1970	Rev of '68 (deeper lines in flame); RDV-002
10-1970D-801		1970-D	DDR
10-1970D-802		1970-D	DDR
10-1970D-901		1970-D	Rev of '68 (deeper lines in flame); RDV-002
10-1970S-501		1970-S	No S
10-1971D-501		1971-D	RPM
10-1975S-501		1975-S PF	RPM (S Over S)
10-1975S-502		1975-S	No S
10-1982-501a	021	1982	Missing Mintmark
10-1982-501b		1982	Missing Mintmark
10-1983D-501		1983-D	RPM (D Over D)
10-1983S-501		1983-S	No S
10-1985P-501		1985-P	Possible Misplaced Mintmark ("ghost" in nec; similar to a P)
10-1986P-501		1986-P	Possible Misplaced Mintmark ("ghost" in nec; similar to a P)
10-1987P-501		1987-P	Possible Misplaced Mintmark ("ghost" in nec; similar to a P)
10-2004D-401		2004-D	DDO (ear, rotated die)
10-2015P-801		2015-P	DDR

FS#	Old FS#	Issue	Brief Description
TWENTY-CENT PIECES			
20-1875S-301		1875-S	MPD (8 in denticles; also RPM)
20-1875S-302		1875-S	Possible MPD (denticles below 7; also RPM)
20-1876-801		1876	DDR
20-1876CC-101		1876-CC	DDO, MPD
BUST QUARTERS			
25-1822-901		1822	25 Over 50
25-1825-301		1825	5 Over 2
25-1825-302		1825	5 Over 3
25-1825-303		1825	5 Over 4
25-1828-901		1828	25 Over 50
25-1831-301		1831	RPD (1 and 8 south)
25-1833-901		1833	DDR
25-1834-901		1834	Recut "OF A" in UNITED STATES OF AMERICA
LIBERTY SEATED QUARTERS			
25-18400-501		1840-O	Large O Mintmark
25-18410-101	001	1841-O	DDO-001
25-18430-301		1843-O	RPD (1 and 8 north)
25-18430-501	001.5	1843-O	Large O Mintmark
25-1845-301		1845	RPD (Large 5 Over Small 5)
25-1847-301	002.3	1847	MPD (8 protruding from base of rock)
25-1847-302/801	002	1847	DDR-001 (also RPD)
25-1850-301		1850	RPD (1 in denticles)
25-1853-301		1853	RPD (5 and 3 below the primary digits, slanted)
LIBERTY SEATED QUARTERS–ARROWS AND RAYS			
25-1853-1301	003	1853	Overdate (3 Over 4)
25-18530-501		1853-O	RPD (O Over Horizontal O)
25-18540-501	004	1854-O	Huge O Mintmark
25-1855-101		1855	DDO
25-1856-301		1856	MPD (1 and 6 punched in gown)
25-1856-401		1856	Mark in Shield
25-1856S-501	005	1856-S	Large S / Small S Mintmark
25-1857-401		1857	Die Gouge (Liberty's fingers; resembles a cigar)
25-1857-901	006	1857	Rev Die Clash (with reverse of Flying Eagle cent)
25-18570-301	006.2	1857-O	MPD (1 and 8 in denticles)
25-1857o-302		1857-O	MPD
25-1858-901		1858	Multi-Denominational Clash
25-1861-101		1861	DDO
25-1861-901		1861	Type 1 Reverse
25-1863-301		1863	RPD
25-1872-301		1872	RPD (1 and 8 repunched south)
25-1872-302		1872	MPD
25-1872-401		1872	Wavy Lines

FS#	Old FS#	Issue	Brief Description
25-1875-301	006.75	1875	MPD (1 and 7 in denticles)
25-1876-301		1876	MPD (top of a 6 in denticles below 6)
25-1876-302	006.8	1876	MPD (1 southwest of primary 1)
LIBERTY SEATED QUARTERS			
25-1876-303	06.85	1876	MPD (6 in rock)
25-1876-304		1876	RPD (triple 6)
25-1876-305		1876	MPD (top of 1 and 8 in denticles)
25-1876-306		1876	MPD
25-1876-307		1876	MPD
25-1876CC-101		1876-CC	DDO
25-1876CC-301		1876-CC	RPD (1, 8, and 7 close south)
25-1876S-301	006.88	1876-S	MPD (7 and 6 in denticles)
25-1876S-302		1876-S	MPD (digit in denticles under 8)
25-1877CC-301		1877-CC	RPD (1, 8, and 7 close south)
25-1877S-501	007	1877-S	RPM (S Over Horizontal S)
25-1891-301	007.5	1891	MPD
BARBER QUARTERS			
25-1892-101	007.7	1892	DDO (IN GOD WE TRUST)
25-1892-301		1892	RPD (also minor TDO)
25-1892-801		1892	TDR
25-18920-101	007.8	1892-O	DDO (IN GOD WE TRUST)
25-18920-301	007.9	1892-O	RPD
25-1892o-401/901		1892-O, Covered E Reverse	Obv Die Clash (Liberty's profile)
25-1892S-501		1892-S	RPM
25-1897S-501		1897-S	Mintmark Position
25-19020-301		1902-O	MPD (denticles)
25-1907D-301		1907-D	RPD (also DDO)
25-1907S-501		1907-S	RPM
25-1908D-301		1908-D	MPD (denticles)
25-1909S-501		1909-S	Inverted Mintmark
25-1914D-101	007.99	1914-D	DDO
25-1916D-501	008	1916-D	RPM
STANDING LIBERTY QUARTERS			
25-1917D-801		1917-D, Type 1	DDR-001 (motto)
25-1917S-401		1917-S	"Shish Kabab"
25-1918S-101	008.5	1918-S	DDO-001 (also Overdate, 8 Over 7)
25-1920-401		1920	Obv Die Clash (drapery)
25-1920S-401		1920-S	Obv Die Clash (drapery)
25-1928S-501		1928-S	IMM
25-1928S-502		1928-S	RPM
25-1929S-401		1929-S	Obv Die Clash
25-1930-401		1930	Incomplete Shield

FS#	Old FS#	Issue	Brief Description
WASHINGTON QUARTERS			
25-1932-101		1932	DDO (earlobe)
25-1934-101	009	1934	DDO-001
25-1934-401		1934	Light Motto
25-1934-402		1934	Medium Motto
25-1934-403		1934	Large Motto
25-1934D-501	009.5	1934-D	Small D (D of 1932)
25-1935-101	010	1935	DDO-001
25-1936-101	011	1936	DDO-001
25-1937-101	012	1937	DDO-001
25-1937D-501		1937-D	RPM
25-1939D-501	012.3	1939-D	OMM (D Over S)
25-1939S-101		1939-S	DDO
25-1940D-101	012.5	1940-D	DDO-001
25-1940D-501	012.4	1940-D	RPM (D Over D to left)
25-1940D-502		1940-D	RPM
25-1941-101	012.7	1941	DDO
25-1941-102	012.9	1941	DDO
25-1941-103		1941	DDO-004 (date and IN GOD WE TRUST)
25-1941-801	013	1941	DDR-004 (tripled)
25-1941D-101		1941-D	DDO-001 (date and IN GOD WE TRUST); Breen 4309
25-1941D-801		1941-D	DDR-001 (OF AMERICA, QUARTER DOLLAR)
25-1941S-501		1941-S	Large Mintmark (Trumpet Tail style)
25-1941S-503		1941-S	Large Mintmark (triangular lower serif)
25-1941S-801		1941-S	DDR
25-1942-101		1942	DDO
25-1942-801	014	1942	DDR
25-1942-802	014.3	1942	DDR
25-1942-803		1942	DDR
25-1942D-101	015	1942-D	DDO
25-1942D-801	016	1942-D	DDR
25-1942S-501		1942-S	RPM
25-1943-101	016.5	1943	DDO (motto, LIB, and date)
25-1943-102		1943	DDO (LIBERTY, motto, and date)
25-1943-103	016.7	1943	DDO (motto, LIB, and date)
25-1943D-101		1943-D	DDO (eye, hair curls, initials, lip, chin)
25-1943S-101	017	1943-S	DDO
25-1943S-401		1943-S	Die Deformation (Washington's throat; "Goiter" variety)
25-1943S-501	017.3	1943-S	Mintmark Style (Trumpet Tail S)
25-1943S-502		1943-S	Slightly smaller and slightly different S (Large S is common)
25-1943S-503		1943-S	RPM (south; filled upper loop of primary mintmark)
25-1943S-504		1943-S	RPM (knob south of primary mintmark)

APPENDIX H: FIVAZ-STANTON NUMBERS CROSS-REFERENCE CHART

FS#	Old FS#	Issue	Brief Description
25-1944-101		1944	DDO (IN GOD WE TRUST, date, and LIB)
25-1944D-101		1944-D	DDO (LIBERTY)
25-1944S-101	017.5	1944-S	DDO
25-1945-101	018	1945	DDO
25-1945S-101		1945-S	DDO (IN GOD WE TRUST, date, and TY of LIBERTY)
25-1945S-102		1945-S	DDO (IN GOD WE TRUST, LIBERTY)
25-1945S-501		1945-S	RPM
25-1946-101/801		1946	DDO (IN GOD WE TRUST, date, and LIBERTY); DDR (OF and AM)
25-1946-102/802		1946	DDR (lettering; also DDO)
25-1946D-501		1946-D	RPM (north of primary)
25-1946S-501		1946-S	RPM (S Over S)
25-1947-101		1947	DDO (LIBERTY)
25-1947-901		1947	"Spitting Eagle"
25-1947S-501/101		1947-S	RPM (S Over S); DDO
25-1947S-502		1947-S	RPM (S Over S)
25-1948S-501	018.4	1948-S	RPM (S Over S Over S Over S)
25-1948S-901		1948-S	"Spitting Eagle"
25-1949D-501		1949-D	RPM (D Over D Over D)
25-1949D-601		1949-D	Possible OMM (D Over S)
25-1950-801	019	1950	DDR (eagle's beak, wings)
25-1950D-801	020	1950-D	DDR (talons, feathers, and arrow tips)
25-1950D-802		1950-D	DDR (lettering, esp. QUARTER DOLLAR)
25-1950D-501		1950-D	RPM (D Over D)
25-1950D-601	021	1950-D	OMM (D Over S)
25-1950S-501		1950-S	RPM (S Over S north)
25-1950S-601	022	1950-S	OMM (S Over D)
25-1950S-801		1950-S	DDR
25-1951D-101		1951-D	DDO (LIBERTY, IN GOD WE TRUST, date)
25-1951D-501		1951-D	RPM-004
25-1951S-501		1951-S	RPM
25-1952-901		1952 PF	"Superbird" (unusual S evident on breast of eagle)
25-1952-902/101		1952 PF	"Superbird" plus Recut Tail Feathers and DDO
25-1952D-101		1952-D	DDO
25-1952D-501		1952-D	Huge D Mintmark
25-1952S-501		1952-S	RPM (S Over S Over S)
25-1952S-502		1952-S	RPM (S Over S)
25-1953-101		1953 PF	DDO
25-1953-901		1953 PF	Recut Tail Feathers
25-1953D-801	022.2	1953-D	DDR (UNITED STATES OF AMERICA, E PLURIBUS UNUM)
25-1953D-501		1953-D	RPM (Inverted D Over D)
25-1953D-601		1953-D	OMM (D Over D Over D Over S Over S)
25-1956-101		1956 PF	Rev Die Gouges
25-1956-701		1956 PF	Rev Die Gouge
25-1956-901		1956	Type B Rev on Circ Strike (intended for Proofs)
25-1956D-501		1956-D	RPM (D Over Inverted D)
25-1957-901		1957	Type B Rev on Circ Strike (intended for Proofs)
25-1957D-501		1957-D	RPM (master die; separate D above olive branch)
25-1957D-901		1957-D	Recut Tail Feathers
25-1958-901		1958	Type B Rev on Circ Strike (intended for Proofs)
25-1959-101	022.45	1959 PF	DDO (IN GOD WE TRUST)
25-1959-102		1959 PF	DDO
25-1959-901		1959	Type B Rev on Circ Strike (intended for Proofs)
25-1959D-501		1959-D	RPM (D Over D)
25-1960-801	022.5	1960 PF	DDR
25-1960-901		1960	Type B Rev on Circ Strike (intended for Proofs)
25-1961-101		1961 PF	DDO (IN GOD WE TRUST)
25-1961-901		1961	Type B Rev on Circ Strike (intended for Proofs)
25-1961D-501		1961-D	RPM (D Over D northeast)
25-1961D-502		1961-D	RPM (D Over D)
25-1961D-503		1961-D	RPM
25-1962-101		1962 PF	DDO (lettering)
25-1962-901		1962	Type B Rev on Circ Strike (intended for Proofs)
25-1962D-501		1962-D	RPM (D Over D)
25-1963-101	023	1963	DDO (date, motto, and LIBERTY)
25-1963-102/803		1963	DDO; DDR
25-1963-103		1963	DDO (63 of date)
25-1963-801		1963	DDR (C and M of AMERICA, first T of STATES)
25-1963-802		1963 PF	DDR (AMERICA)
25-1963-901		1963	Type B Rev on Circ Strike (intended for Proofs)
25-1963-901a		1963	B Rev. Sub Var
25-1963D-101		1963-D	DDO-004 (lettering and date)
25-1964-101		1964	DDO (IN GOD WE TRUST)
25-1964-801		1964	DDR (lettering)
25-1964-802	024.5	1964	DDR (QUARTER DOLLAR)
25-1964-803		1964	DDR (STATES OF AMERICA)
25-1964-804		1964	DDR (UNITED)
25-1964-901		1964	Type B Rev on Circ Strike (intended for Proofs)
25-1964-902		1964	Type C Rev (intended for production beginning in 1965)
25-1964D-101		1964-D	DDO (IN GOD WE TRUST)
25-1964D-501		1964-D	RPM (D Over D)
25-1964D-502		1964-D	RPM (D Over D)
25-1964D-503		1964-D	RPM
25-1964D-801	025	1964-D	DDR (STATES OF AMERICA, QUARTER DOLLAR)

FS#	Old FS#	Issue	Brief Description
25-1964D-901		1964-D	Type B Rev on Circ Strike (intended for Proofs)
25-1964D-902		1964-D	Type C Rev (intended for production beginning in 1965)
25-1965-101	026	1965	DDO (lettering)
25-1965-102		1965	DDO (LIBERTY)
25-1965-801		1965	DDR (QUARTER DOLLAR)
25-1966-801	026.3	1966	DDR (lettering)
25-1967-101	026.5	1967 SMS	DDO (lettering)
25-1967-801		1967 SMS	DDR (lower branches, leaves, QUARTER DOLLAR)
25-1968D-801		1968-D	DDR (lettering)
25-1968S-101		1968-S PF	DDO (lettering)
25-1968S-501		1968-S PF	RPM (S Over S north)
25-1968S-801	027	1968-S PF	DDR (lettering)
25-1968S-901		1968-S PF	Type E
25-1968S-902		1968-S PF	Type F
25-1969D-501	027.06	1969-D	RPM (D Over D)
25-1969D-502		1969-D	RPM (D Over D)
25-1969S-101	027.08	1969-S PF	DDO (lettering and date)
25-1969S-501/102	027.1	1969-S PF	RPM (S Over S Over S); DDO
25-1970D-101	027.3	1970-D	DDO (lettering)
25-1970D-102		1970-D	DDO (LIBERTY)
25-1970D-801		1970-D	DDR (lettering)
25-1970D-802		1970-D	DDR (lettering)
25-1970S-801		1970-S	DDR
25-1971-801	027.7	1971	DDR (lettering)
25-1971D-801	027.8	1971-D	DDR (UNITED STATES OF AMERICA)
25-1976D-101	028	1976-D	DDO (LIBERTY)
25-1976D-102		1976-D	DDO-002 (LIBERTY)
25-1979S-501		1979-S PF	Type II Mintmark
25-1981S-501		1981-S PF	Type II Mintmark
25-1982S-101		1982-S PF	DDO (IN GOD WE TRUST, date)
25-1983-901		1983	"Spitting Eagle"
25-1989-501		1989	No P
25-1989D-501		1989-D	RPM (D Over D)
25-1990S-101		1990-S PF	DDO (date and mintmark)
25-1994-501		1994	No P
25-1995S-101		1995-S PF	DDO (date, mintmark, ribbon, hair, west on LIBERTY and IN GOD WE TRUST)
25-2004D-901		2004-D, WI	Extra Leaf High (lines pointing up)
25-2004D-902		2004-D, WI	Extra Leaf Low (lines pointing down)
25-2005P-MN-801		2005-P, MN	DDR-001 (right of 4th tree)
25-2005P-MN-802		2005-P, MN	DDR-002 (right of 4th tree)
25-2005P-MN-803		2005-P, MN	DDR-004 (right of 4th tree)
25-2005P-MN-804		2005-P, MN	DDR-006 (left of 4th tree)
25-2005P-MN-805		2005-P, MN	DDR-007 (right of 4th tree)
25-2005P-MN-806		2005-P, MN	DDR-008 (right of 4th tree)
25-2005P-MN-807		2005-P, MN	DDR-012 (right of 4th tree)
25-2005D-MN-801		2005-D, MN	DDR-001 (left of 4th tree)
25-2005D-MN-802		2005-D, MN	DDR-003 (left of 4th tree)
S25-2005S-KS-901		2005-S, KS, PF, 90% Silver	Large Die Dent Rev (bison's hindquarter)
25-2005P-OR-801		2005-P, OR	DDR-001 (tallest tree, right side of coin)
25-2005P-OR-802		2005-P, OR	DDR-002 (two trees on right side of coin)
25-2007P-WY-801		2007-P, WY	DDR-018 (saddle horn)
25-2007P-WY-802		2007-P, WY	DDR (saddle horn)
25-2007P-WY-803		2007-P, WY	DDR (saddle horn)
25-2009D-DC-801		2009-D, DC	DDR-001 (ELL of ELLINGTON)
25-2009P-DC-801		2009-P, DC	DDR-012 (piano keys)
25-2009P-DC-802		2009-P, DC	DDR-004 (piano key below ELL)

ABOUT THE AUTHORS AND EDITOR

Bill Fivaz

Bill Fivaz, a coin collector since 1950, has earned recognition as one of the most respected authorities on numismatic errors and die varieties. His awards include the highest recognition of the American Numismatic Association, which presented him its top honor, the Farran Zerbe Memorial Award, in 1995. He was elected to the ANA Hall of Fame in 2002.

Bill is widely known as an engaging teacher and a speaker on numismatic topics. He has written hundreds of articles on a wide array of numismatic topics, and has been a consultant to several coin-authentication services. His contributions are noted in many of today's most popular and respected hobby books, including the *Guide Book of United States Coins* (the "Red Book").

Bill has served on the board of governors of the ANA and on the board of directors of CONECA (the Combined Organizations of Numismatic Error Collectors).

To honor his reputation as a teacher and writer, since 2010 Whitman Publishing and the ANA have endowed and managed the Bill Fivaz Young Numismatist Literary Award, for young numismatists aged 8 to 12.

J.T. Stanton

J.T. Stanton started collecting coins in 1959 and began specializing in errors and varieties in 1982. Well known as a teacher and lecturer in the die-variety field, he instructed American Numismatic Association Summer Seminar courses for 11 years and started the ANA's annual "Errors and Varieties and Modern Minting Process" class.

The ANA recognized J.T.'s contributions to the hobby with awards including the Medal of Merit, the Glenn Smedley Memorial Award, the Outstanding Adult Supervisor Award, and two Presidential Awards.

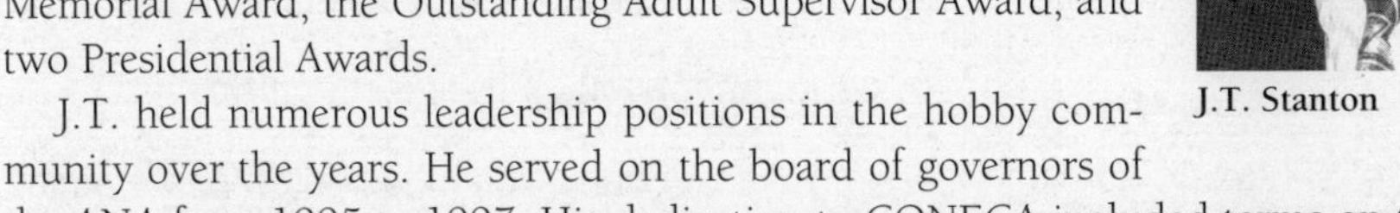

J.T. held numerous leadership positions in the hobby community over the years. He served on the board of governors of the ANA from 1995 to 1997. His dedication to CONECA included terms on the board of directors and as the group's president. He was elected to CONECA's Hall of Fame.

Larry Briggs

Larry Briggs is a professional numismatist, authenticator, author, and researcher. He has supported the American Numismatic Association in numerous roles, including as president of its Authentication Committee. Larry served in the United States Air Force and worked for Ford Motor Company before launching his business, Larry Briggs Rare Coins, in 1978. He is an official contributor to the *Guide Book of United States Coins*, specializing in Liberty Seated coinage and early American coppers, and is well known to cherrypickers as an active dealer and an authority in the field. While Larry is a longtime contributor to the *Cherrypickers' Guide*, the sixth edition, volume II, is his first effort as a volume editor. In this position he coordinated resources including a network of specialists from around the country, and contributed his own original research and photography.

IMAGE CREDITS

In this volume of the *Cherrypickers' Guide*, obverse and reverse designs illustrated in the introduction of each coin type are from Whitman Publishing's archives. Within each denomination, die-variety images are credited below by Fivaz-Stanton number. For varieties illustrated by more than one image, credit is given in left-to-right / top-to-bottom order.

Abbreviation key: **Briggs** = Larry Briggs Rare Coins. **Fivaz** = Bill Fivaz. **Fortin** = Gerry Fortin Rare Coins. **Frost** = John Frost. **Gallego** = José Gallego. **HA** = Heritage Auctions. **Lawson** = Robert Lawson. **NGC** = Numismatic Guaranty Company. **PCGS** = Professional Coin Grading Service. **SBG** = Stack's Bowers Galleries. **VV** = Variety Vista. **Wexler** = John Wexler. **Whitman** = Whitman Publishing Archives. **Wiles** = Dr. James Wiles.

Half Dimes

FS-H10-1834-301 .... NGC
FS-H10-1836-301 .... NGC
FS-H10-1838-901 . PCGS; PCGS; PCGS
FS-H10-1839o-501 . Whitman; Whitman
FS-H10-1840o-501 ...... Fivaz; Whitman
FS-H10-1840o-901 .... PCGS; HA
FS-H10-1843-301 .... NGC
FS-H10-1844-301 .... NGC
FS-H10-1845-301 .... Fivaz
FS-H10-1845-302 .... NGC
FS-H10-1848-301 .... PCGS
FS-H10-1848-302 .... NGC
FS-H10-1849-301 .... NGC
FS-H10-1849-302 .... NGC; NGC
FS-H10-1849-303 .... PCGS, PCGS
FS-H10-1853-301 .... NGC
FS-H10-1856-301 .... SBG
FS-H10-1858-301 .... NGC
FS-H10-1858-302 .... NGC
FS-H10-1861-301 .... PCGS
FS-H10-1863S-301 .... Whitman
FS-H10-1865S-301 .... PCGS
FS-H10-1872-101 .... NGC; NGC
FS-H10-1872S-301 .... NGC; NGC
FS-H10-1872S-302. Whitman; Whitman

Dimes

FS-10-1814-901 .... NGC; SBG
FS-10-1820-901 .... NGC; SBG
FS-10-1829-301 .... NGC; SBG
FS-10-1829-901 .... NGC
FS-10-1829-902 .... SBG; SBG
FS-10-1830-301 .... NGC
FS-10-1838-801 ... PCGS; PCGS; PCGS
FS-10-1838-802 .... PCGS; PCGS
FS-10-1839o-501 .... NGC
FS-10-1839o-502 .... Whitman
FS-10-1841o-901 .... NGC; SBG
FS-10-1841o-902 ...... NGC; NGC; NGC
FS-10-1843-301 .... NGC
FS-10-1853-301 .... NGC
FS-10-1855-101 .... PCGS
FS-10-1856-101 .... Whitman; Whitman; NGC
FS-10-1856o-301 .... NGC; Whitman; Whitman
FS-10-1872-302 ..... Whitman; Whitman
FS-10-1872-801 ...... Fivaz; Fivaz; Fivaz; Fivaz; Fivaz
FS-10-1873-301 .... NGC
FS-10-1873-101 .... NGC; NGC
FS-10-1875-301 .... NGC
FS-10-1876CC-101, 102, 103.... Fivaz; Fivaz; Fivaz; Fivaz; Fivaz
FS-10-1876CC-301 .... Whitman
FS-10-1876CC-801 .... Fivaz
FS-10-1876CC-901 .... Fivaz; Fivaz
FS-10-1876S-301 .... Whitman
FS-10-1877CC-301 . Whitman; Whitman
FS-10-1887S-501 .... Whitman
FS-10-1888S-501 .... NGC
FS-10-1889-801 ..... Whitman; Whitman
FS-10-1890-301 .... PCGS
FS-10-1890-302 .... PCGS
FS-10-1890S-501 .... PCGS
FS-10-1891-301 .... PCGS
FS-10-1891o-501 .... NGC
FS-10-1891S-501 .... PCGS
FS-10-1893-301 .... PCGS
FS-10-1893S-501 .... NGC
FS-10-1901o-501 .... NGC
FS-10-1905o-501 .... NGC; NGC
FS-10-1906-302 .... Frost
FS-10-1906D-501 .... Frost
FS-10-1906o-301 .... PCGS
FS-10-1906S-301/501 .... PCGS; PCGS
FS-10-1907-301 .... Whitman
FS-10-1907o-501 .... Whitman
FS-10-1908D-303 .... Whitman
FS-10-1912D-501 .... Tanner Scott
FS-10-1912S-101 .... Fivaz; Fivaz
FS-10-1912S-401 .... Whitman
FS-10-1919-101 .... Whitman
FS-10-1926-101 .... Whitman
FS-10-1928S-501 ... Whitman; Whitman
FS-10-1929S-101 .... NGC; NGC
FS-10-1931D-101 .... NGC
FS-10-1931S-101 .... NGC
FS-10c-1934D-501 .... Wiles
FS-10-1935-101 .... Whitman
FS-10-1935S-501 .... NGC
FS-10-1936-101 .... PCGS; PCGS
FS-10-1936D-501 ... Whitman; Whitman
FS-10-1936S-110 .... Fivaz
FS-10-1937S-101 .... NGC; NGC
FS-10-1939D-501 .... NGC
FS-10-1940S-501 .... Whitman
FS-10-1940S-101/801 ...... All Whitman
FS-10-1941-101 .... NGC
FS-10-1941D-101/801 .... Whitman; Whitman
FS-10-1941S-501 .... NGC
FS-10-1941S-502 .... NGC
FS-10-1941S-511 .... Fivaz; SBG
FS-10-1942-101 .... NGC; PCGS
FS-10-1942D-101 .... NGC; Wiles
FS-10-1942D-501 .... NGC
FS-10-1942S-501 .... Whitman
FS-10-1942S-502 .... Whitman
FS-10-1943D-501 .... Whitman
FS-10-1943S-501 .... NGC
FS-10-1943S-511 .... NGC
FS-10-1944D-501 .... NGC
FS-10-1945D-101/501 .. Whitman; NGC
FS-10-1945D-502 .... PCGS
FS-10-1945D-503 ... Whitman; Whitman
FS-10-1945S-503 .... Wiles
FS 10-1945S-504 .... VV; VV
FS-10-1945S-512 .... Whitman; Wiles
FS-10-1946-101/803 ... Wexler; Wexler

FS-10-1946-102/804... Wexler; Wexler
FS-10-1946-103/805.........Wexler; VV
FS-10-1946-104.......................PCGS
FS-10-1946-801.....................VV; VV
FS-10-1946-802.....Whitman; Whitman
FS-10-1946D-501...............PCGS; VV
FS-10-1946D-502..............PCGS; VV
FS-10-1946D-503................ Whitman
FS-10-1946S-501/801...........VV; VV
FS-10-1946S-502/802...........VV; VV
FS-10-1946S-503.........................VV
FS-10-1946S-504.......................NGC
FS-10-1946S-505..........Whitman; VV
FS-10-1947-101........ VV; VV; VV; VV
FS-10-1947D-101..........Whitman; VV
FS-10-1947S-501.......................NGC
FS-10-1947S-502.........................VV
FS-10-1947S-503.......................NGC
FS-10-1947S-504.........................VV
FS-10-1947S-801 ....VV; VV
FS-10-1948S-501.........................VV
FS-10-1949S-401................Jon Potts
FS-10-1950D-501.............Fivaz; Fivaz
FS-10-1950D-502..................VV; VV
FS-10-1950D-801 ....VV; VV; VV
FS-10-1950S-501.........................VV
FS-10-1951D-501................ Whitman
FS-10-1952S-501.......................NGC
FS-10-1953D-501..................VV; VV
FS-10-1953S-401................ Whitman
FS-10-1953S-501.........................VV
FS-10-1953S-901.. Whitman; Whitman; Whitman
FS-10-1954-101.............PCGS; PCGS
FS-10-1954-801....................... PCGS
FS-10-1954S-501................ Whitman
FS-10-1954S-401................ Whitman
FS-10-1955S-401................ Whitman
FS-10-1956-101....................... PCGS
FS-10-1957-101.....................VV; VV
FS-10-1959D-501.........................VV
FS-10-1959D-502.................... PCGS
FS-10-1959D-504.......................NGC
FS-10-1960-101.....Whitman; Whitman
FS-10-1960-102a............VV; VV; VV
FS-10-1960-102b..............PCGS; VV
FS-10-1960-103.....Whitman; Whitman
FS-10-1960-801.....Whitman; Whitman
FS-10-1960D-501.........................VV
FS-10-1961D-801............VV; VV; VV
FS-10-1962D-501......................... VV
FS-10-1963-101..........................VV
FS-10-1963-801 .... PCGS
FS-10-1963-802 ....VV; VV
FS-10-1963-803 ....VV; VV
FS-10-1963-804..........................VV
FS-10-1963-805...................VV; VV
FS-10-1963D-801..................VV; VV
FS-10-1964-101 .... VV; VV; VV; VV
FS-10-1964-801............... NGC; NGC
FS-10-1964-802 ....VV; VV; VV
FS-10-1964D-501........................ VV
FS-10-1964D-502 VV
FS-10-1964D-801..................VV; VV
FS-10-1964D-802..................VV; VV
FS-10-1966-401.................. Whitman
FS-10-1967-101 ....VV; VV
FS-10-1968-101.... Whitman; NGC; VV
FS-10-1968S-101 VV
FS-10-1968S-102 ....VV; VV
FS-10-1968S-501................ Whitman
FS-10-1968S-502........................ VV
FS-10-1968S-801 .. Whitman; Whitman
FS-10-1969D-501 VV
FS-10-1969-901.....Whitman; Whitman
FS-10-1970-801 VV
FS-10-1970-901.....Whitman; Whitman
FS-10-1970D-801..................VV; VV
FS-10-1970D-802..................VV; VV
FS-10-1970D-901...Whitman; Whitman
FS-10-1970S-501........................ VV
FS-10-1971D-501...................... Wiles
FS-10-1975S-501........................ VV
FS-10-1975S-502.................... PCGS
FS-10-1982-501a ....NGC
FS-10-1982-501b......................NGC
FS-10-1983D-501........................ VV
FS-10-1983S-501........................ VV
FS-10-1985P ....Whitman; Whitman
FS-10-1986P..........Whitman; Whitman
FS-10-1987P..........Whitman; Whitman
FS-10-2004D-401......................Fivaz
FS-10-2015-801.............Tanner Scott

Twenty-Cent Pieces

FS-20-1875S-301......................NGC
FS-20-1875S-302......................NGC
FS-20-1876-801........................ SBG
FS-20-1876CC-101................HA, HA

Quarter Dollars

FS-25-1822-901.................. Whitman
FS-25-1825-301.................. Whitman
FS-25-1825-302.................. Whitman
FS-25-1825-303..... Whitman; Whitman
FS-25-1828-901.................. Whitman
FS-25-1831-301........................NGC
FS-25-1833-901........................NGC
FS-25-1834-901........................NGC
FS-25-1840o-501 ....NGC
FS-25-1841o-101 ....NGC; Briggs
FS-25-1843o-501 ....NGC
FS-25-1845-301........................NGC
FS-25-1847-301 ....NGC
FS-25-1847-302/801 .... NGC; NGC
FS-25-1850-301.........................NGC
FS-25-1853-301...............Fivaz; Fivaz
FS-25-1853-1301.....................Briggs
FS-25-1853o-501 ....NGC
FS-25-1854o-501 ....NGC
FS-25-1855-101.......................Fortin
FS-25-1856-301.........................NGC
FS-25-1856-401........................... HA
FS-25-1856S-501.......................NGC
FS-25-1857-401................... Whitman
FS-25-1857-901 ....NGC
FS-25-1857o-301 .... PCGS
FS-25-1857o-302 .... Whitman
FS-25-1858-901...........Steven Feltner
FS-25-1861-101.......................Fortin
FS-25-1861-901........Fivaz; SBG; SBG
FS-25-1863-301.................. Whitman
FS-25-1872-301.................. Whitman
FS-25-1872-302.................. Whitman
FS-25-1872-401.......................Fortin
FS-25-1875-301.................. Whitman
FS-25-1876-302 .... Whitman
FS-25-1876-303 .... Whitman
FS-25-1876-304.........................NGC
FS-25-1876-305...................... PCGS
FS-25-1876-306.........................NGC
FS-25-1876-307.................. Whitman
FS-25-1876S-301.................... PCGS
FS-25-1876S-302............... Whitman
FS-25-1876CC-101.................. PCGS
FS-25-1876CC-301...................NGC
FS-25-1877CC-301...................NGC
FS-25-1877S-501.......................NGC
FS-25-1891-301.........................NGC
FS-25-1892-101.................. Whitman
FS-25-1892o-301 .... Whitman
FS-25-1892o-401/901 .... Whitman
FS-25-1892S-501.......................NGC
FS-25-1897S-501 ... James Wooldridge
FS-25-1899 .... Whitman
FS-25-1902o-301 .... Whitman
FS-25-1907D-301............. NGC; NGC
FS-25-1907S-501................ Whitman
FS-25-1908D-301............... Whitman
FS-25-1909-S-501............... Whitman
FS-25-1914D-101 .... PCGS
FS-25-1916D-501 ....NGC
FS-25c-1917D-801 VV
FS 25-1917S-401 ....Rick DeSanctis
FS-25-1918S-101.......................NGC
FS-25-1920-401.................. Whitman
FS-25-1920S-401................ Whitman
1924-S counterfeit...... Lawson, Lawson, Lawson
FS-25-1928S-501..................... PCGS
FS-25-1928S-502......................... VV
FS-25-1929S-401..................... PCGS

FS-25-1930-401 ..Ron Pope; Ron Pope
FS-25-1932-101 .... Whitman
FS-25-1934-101 ....NGC
FS-25-1934-401 ......Fivaz; Wiles; Wiles
FS-25-1934D-501 ... Whitman; Whitman
FS-25-1935-101 .... Whitman
FS-25-1936-101 ....NGC
FS-25-1937-101 .... NGC; NGC
FS-25-1937D-501 VV
FS-25-1939D-501 .... Whitman
FS-25-1939S-101 .... NGC; NGC
FS-25-1940D-101 VV
FS-25-1940D-501 ....NGC; VV
FS-25-1940D-502 .... Whitman
FS-25-1941-101 ....NGC
FS-25-1941-102 ....VV; VV; VV
FS-25-1941-103 .... Whitman
FS-25-1941-801 ....NGC
FS-25-1941D-101 .... Whitman
FS-25-1941D-801 ....VV; VV
FS-25-1941S-501 .... Whitman
FS-25-1941S-503 .... Whitman
FS-25-1941S-801 .... Sean Craig
FS-25-1942-101 .... NGC; NGC
FS-25-1942-801 .... NGC; NGC
FS-25-1942-802 ....VV; VV
FS-25-1942-803 ....NGC
FS-25-1942D-101 .... NGC; NGC
FS-25-1942D-801 .... NGC; NGC
FS-25-1942S-501 .... Sean Craig
FS-25-1943-101 VV
FS-25-1943-102 ....NGC
FS-25-1943-103 .... NGC; NGC
FS-25-1943D-101 ....NGC
FS-25-1943S-101 .....NGC; NGC; NGC
FS-25-1943S-401 .... Whitman
FS-25-1943S-501 .... Whitman
FS-25-1943S-502 .... Whitman
FS-25-1943S-503 ....NGC; VV
FS-25-1944-101 ....NGC
FS-25-1944D-101 ...... VV; VV; VV; VV
FS-25-1944S-101 .... VV; VV; NGC
FS-25-1945-101 VV
FS-25-1945S-102 ....PCGS
FS-25-1945S-501 .... Whitman
FS-25-1946-101/801 ....VV; VV
FS-25-1946-102/802 ....PCGS
FS-25-1946D-501 ....NGC
FS-25-1946S-501 ....NGC
FS-25-1947-101 VV
FS-25-1947-901 .... DM Rare Coins
FS-25-1947S-501/101 VV
FS-25-1947S-502 VV
FS-25-1948S-501 ....PCGS; VV
FS-25-1948S-901 .... DM Rare Coins
FS-25-1949D-501 ....PCGS
FS-25-1949D-601 ....NGC; Fivaz
FS-25-1950-801 ....NGC
FS-25-1950D-501 ....NGC
FS-25-1950D-801 ...... VV; VV; VV; VV
FS-25-1950D-802 VV
FS-25-1950D-601 ....NGC
FS-25-1950S-801 .....NGC; NGC; NGC; Whitman
FS-25-1950S-501 ....NGC; VV
FS-25-1950S-601 .... Whitman
FS-25-1951D-501 ....PCGS; VV
FS-25-1951S-501 .... DM Rare Coins
FS-25-1952-901 .... Whitman
FS-25-1952-902/101 .... Whitman
FS-25-1952D-101 VV
FS-25-1952D-501 .... Whitman
FS-25-1952S-501 VV
FS-25-1952S-502 ....NGC
FS-25-1953-101 . NGC; NGC; Whitman
FS-25c-1953-901 ....NGC; Whitman
FS-25-1953D-801 .... NGC; NGC
FS-25-1953D-501 VV
FS-25-1953D-601 VV
FS-25-1956-101 VV
FS-25-1956-701 .... Whitman
FS-25-1956D-501 ....NGC
FS-25-1957D-901 .... Whitman
FS-25-1957D-902 .... Whitman
FS-25-1959-101 ....NGC
FS-25-1959-102 ....VV; VV
FS-25-1959D-501 ....PCGS; VV
FS-25-1960-801 ....NGC
FS-25-1961-101 ....NGC
FS-25-1961D-501 ....VV; VV
FS-25-1961D-502 ....NGC
FS-25-1961D-503 VV
FS-25-1962-101 ....NGC
FS-25-1962D-501 ....VV; VV
FS-25-1963-101 .... Whitman
FS-25-1963-102/803 .... Whitman
FS-25-1963-103 .... Whitman
FS-25-1963-801 VV
FS-25-1963-901a .... Whitman
FS-25-1963-802 VV
FS-25-1963D-101VV; VV; VV; VV; VV; VV
FS-25-1964-801 ....VV; VV
FS-25-1964-802 ....VV; VV
FS-25-1964-803 .... Whitman
FS-25-1964-804 ....VV; VV
FS-25-1964D-101 ....NGC
FS-25-1964D-501 .... NGC; Lawson
FS-25-1964D-503 VV
FS-25-1964D-801 ....VV; VV
FS-25-1964D-901 ......NGC; VV; VV; VV
FS-25-1964D-902 ....PCGS; Lawson
FS-25-1965-101 ....VV; VV; VV
FS-25-1965-102 ....VV; VV
FS-25-1966-801 ....VV; VV; VV
FS-25-1967-101 ....VV; VV; VV
FS-25-1967-801 ....VV; VV
FS-25-1968D-801 VV
FS-25-1968S-101 ....VV; VV; VV
FS-25-1968S-501 ....NGC
FS-25-1968S-801 ....VV; VV
FS-25-1968S-901 ....Gallego; Gallego
FS-25-1968S-902 ....Gallego; Gallego
FS-25-1969D-501 ....VV; VV
FS-25-1969D-502 .... Wiles
FS-25-1969S-101 VV
FS-25-1969S-501/102 VV
FS-25-1970D-101 ....VV; VV; VV
FS-25-1970D-102 ....VV; VV
FS-25-1970S-801 ....Wiles; Wiles
FS-25-1971D-801 ....VV; VV
FS-25-1976D-101 .. Wiles; Wiles; Wiles
FS-25-1976D-102 ....VV; VV
FS-25-1983-901 .... Whitman
FS-25-1989-501 .... Whitman
FS-25-1989D-501 VV
FS-25-1990S-101 .... Wiles; VV; VV
FS-25-1994-501 .... Whitman
FS-25-1995S-101 ....VV; VV; VV
FS-25-2004D-901 .... Whitman
FS-25-2004D-902 .... Whitman
FS-25-2005P-MN-803 .... Whitman
FS-25-2005P-MN-805 .... Whitman
FS-25-2005S-KS-901 ....NGC; Whitman
FS-25-2007P-WY-801 .... Whitman
FS-25-2007P-WY-802 .... Whitman
FS-25-2009P-DC-801 .... PCGS; VV
FS-25-2009P-DC-802 ....PCGS; VV
FS-25-2009D-DC-801 ....PCGS; VV

Images on page 250 are credited to: (first column, top to bottom)—Tanner Scott, Whitman, and Sandy Peters; (second column, top to bottom)—Siramet (eBay), Siramet, Siramet, and Whitman.

All images in the appendices are from the Whitman Publishing archives, except for the photograph on page 266, which is courtesy of Gutesa via Shutterstock.

Photographs of Washington quarter design alterations are courtesy of José Gallego.

All other photographs are from the Whitman Publishing archives.

INDEX

CONECA

New Member Application / Renewal Form

Today's Date: _____/_____/_____

Membership Type: _____ Adult Annual Member - $25
_____ Young Numismatist (under 18) - $10

Mailing Options: _____ U.S. bulk rate - No extra charge
_____ First Class or Outside the U.S.A. - $12.50 additional

Total: _____ Amount Due

Name: ______________________________

Address: ______________________________

City: ____________________ State: ______

Zip +4 Code: ______________________

Phone: ______________ Email: ______________________________

Recommended by: *The Cherrypickers' Guide*

Comments/Interests:

____

____

Send application and check/money order (payable to CONECA) to:

c/o Maria Rickert-Kittell, Membership
PO Box 223
Armada MI 48005-0223

Your membership is subject to approval by the Membership Committee and subject to the rules and regulations set forth in the CONECA Constitution and By-Laws.

A PDF version of the CONECA membership application, which includes 2-year and life memembership options, as well as more options for alternate delivery of the ErrorScope *publication, is available at conecaonline.org.*

"Buy the Book Before the Coin!"

Whitman Publishing offers books for every collector.

The best way to enjoy your hobby (and profit from your investment) is to learn as much as possible, especially from recognized experts in the field. Whether you collect classic U.S. coins, world coins, ancients, medals, tokens, or paper money, Whitman Publishing has the perfect books to add to your library. The guide books pictured above are just a few from the Bowers Series. The entire Whitman catalog is online at Whitman.com.

Books in the Bowers Series cover these topics and more!

Morgan Silver Dollars
Double Eagle Gold Coins
United States Type Coins
Modern United States Proof Coin Sets
Shield and Liberty Head Nickels
Flying Eagle and Indian Head Cents
Washington Quarters
Buffalo and Jefferson Nickels
Lincoln Cents
United States Commemorative Coins
United States Tokens and Medals
Gold Dollars
Peace Dollars
The Official Red Book®
Franklin and Kennedy Half Dollars
Civil War Tokens
Hard Times Tokens
Mercury Dimes, Standing Liberty Quarters, and Liberty Walking Half Dollars
Half Cents and Large Cents
Barber Silver Coins
Liberty Seated Silver Coins
Modern United States Dollar Coins
The United States Mint
Gold Eagle Coins
Continental Currency and Coins
Quarter Eagle Gold Coins
American Silver Eagles

Authors in the Bowers Series include Q. David Bowers, Rick Snow, Rick Tomaska, Roger W. Burdette, David W. Lange, Katherine Jaeger, Frank J. Colletti, Joshua McMorrow-Hernandez, and other hobby favorites.

Whitman Publishing books, folders, albums, and other hobby products are available online, and at local hobby retailers, coin shops, and book stores nationwide.
For information, call toll free, 1-866-546-2995, or email customerservice@Whitman.com

SAVE $10 ON MEMBERSHIP

Revel in the fun, the history and the allure of coin collecting in the pages of *The Numismatist*, the hobby's premier monthly magazine. Enjoy webinars, videos, blogs, podcasts, counterfeit detection resources, and virtual exhibits from the Money Museum. Plus, receive free admission to our annual shows, exclusive member discounts, and so much more – all for as little as $20.

IN THE AMERICAN NUMISMATIC ASSOCIATION

Call **800-514-2646** or visit

MONEY.ORG/JOIN

(BE SURE TO ENTER DISCOUNT CODE **RED24** AT CHECKOUT)

Offer limited to collectors who have not been members of the American Numismatic Association in the previous 12 months. Gold membership (magazine delivered online) $20; Platinum membership (magazine delivered by mail + digital access) $36.

Offer expires **12/31/2023.**

AMERICAN NUMISMATIC ASSOCIATION

We Are Always Looking to Buy Coins

If you have any coins you want to sell, regardless of the size of your collection, please give us a call! Here's why you should consider Northeast Numismatics when selling your coins:

Top Prices Paid

We try to pay top dollar for any coin offered to us, and immediately pay for anything we purchase.

Hassle-free and Timely

Regardless of the quantity, we will give you an offer on your coins quickly, and will immediately return any coins you decide not to sell.

Solid Reputation

Northeast Numismatics has been in business for over 50 years, serving thousands of collectors, investors, and dealers. You can have confidence in the fact that you'll be treated fairly and professionally.

No Shipping Costs Involved

We will send you a prepaid FedEx invoice and box, so there's no cost to send us your coins. Contact us for details.

If you'd like to discuss selling your coins, please contact Tom Caldwell or Chris Clements. Both can be reached toll-free at 800-449-2646. Or you can reach them via email: tom@northeastcoin.com or chris@northeastcoin.com. You can also find us on the web at

www.northeastcoin.com.

Northeast Numismatics, Inc.
100 Main Street, Suite 330 • Concord, MA 01742
800-449-2646

GreatCollections®

Certified Coin and Paper Money Auctions

More Cherrypicker Varieties are sold by GreatCollections than any other major auction house!

1958 Lincoln Cent DDO
PCGS MS-65 RD CAC (Ex. Blay)

$1,136,250.00

1919 Mercury Dime DDO FS-101
NGC AU-55 CAC

$23,062.50

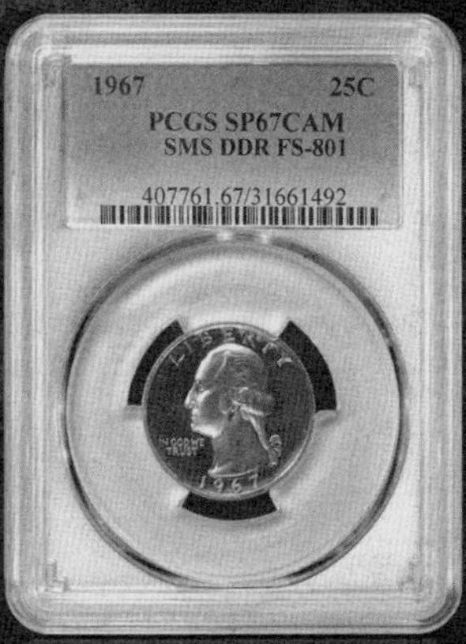

1967 Washington Quarter SMS DDR FS-801
PCGS Specimen-67 CAMEO

$11,753.50

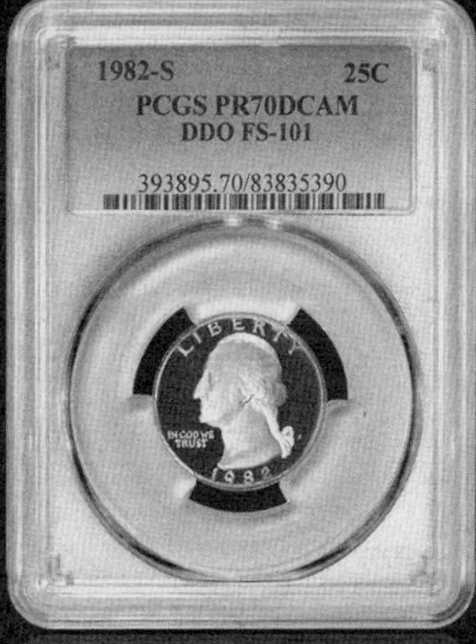

1982-S Washington Quarter DDO FS-101
PCGS Proof-70 DCAM

$6,435.00

Whether buying or selling, use **GreatCollections.com**

©2023 GreatCollections Auctions • 17500 Red Hill Avenue, Suite 160, Irvine CA 92614 • Tel: 1.800.44.COINS

PARADIME COINS

SIGN UP TODAY @
www.ParadimeCoins.com/subscribe
For your First Shots at New Purchases

www.ParadimeCoins.com

INFO@PARADIMECOINS.COM

PCGS NGC CAC TOP POP TONED SEATED GOLD

LBRC

Larry Briggs Rare Coins
P.O. Box 187
Lima, Ohio 45802

Only A Few Can Claim "Best"!

Contact LBRC today for the ultimate selection of Early Coppers and Bust Type coins.

Larry places emphasis on Seated Rare Date and stocks an extraordinary selection of Error and Variety coins in all types and denominations. With over 50 years of expertise Larry can provide you the hardest to find merchandise.

Larry is a teacher, researcher, author, and authenticator. He is an expert in grading, errors and varieties, and counterfeit coins.

Visit us at trade shows and view our great selections for yourself.

Larry is one of the few...
"Best In The Industry"!

Civil War
Store Card
Medals/Tokens
Colonials

Half Cents
Large Cents
Small Cents
Seated/Bust

Morgan/Peace
Gold
Error/Varieties

and every Seated series, concentrating on rare coins.

All Major Vams

Visit with Larry Briggs On The Bourse at Shows Across The U.S.

http: Larrybriggsrarecoins.com

email: lbrc@bright.net

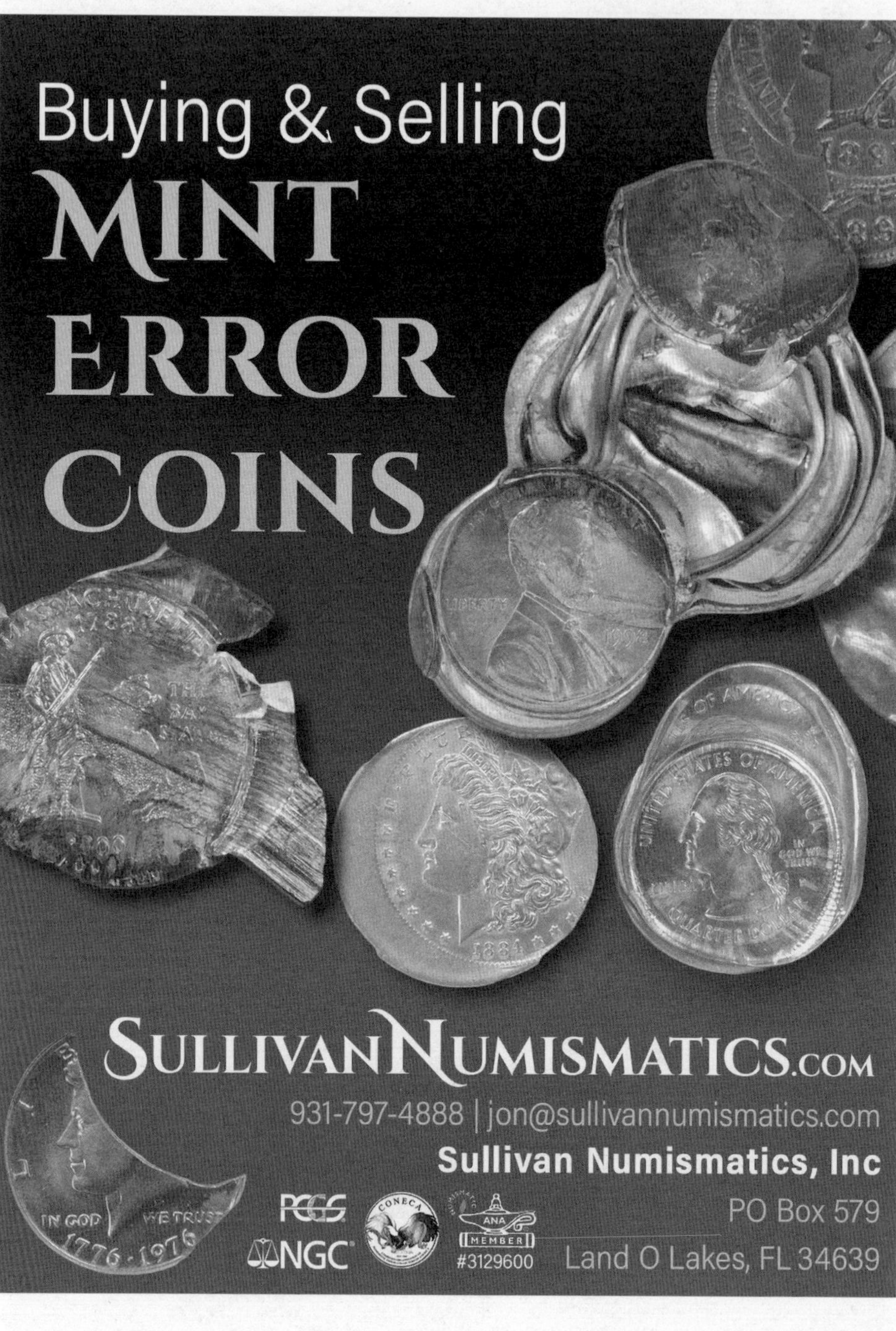

Buying & Selling
MINT ERROR COINS
SULLIVANNUMISMATICS.COM
931-797-4888 | jon@sullivannumismatics.com
Sullivan Numismatics, Inc
PO Box 579
Land O Lakes, FL 34639
PCGS
NGC
CONECA
ANA MEMBER
#3129600

Steinmetz is Buying & Selling
All Gold & Silver - *Call for Quotes!*

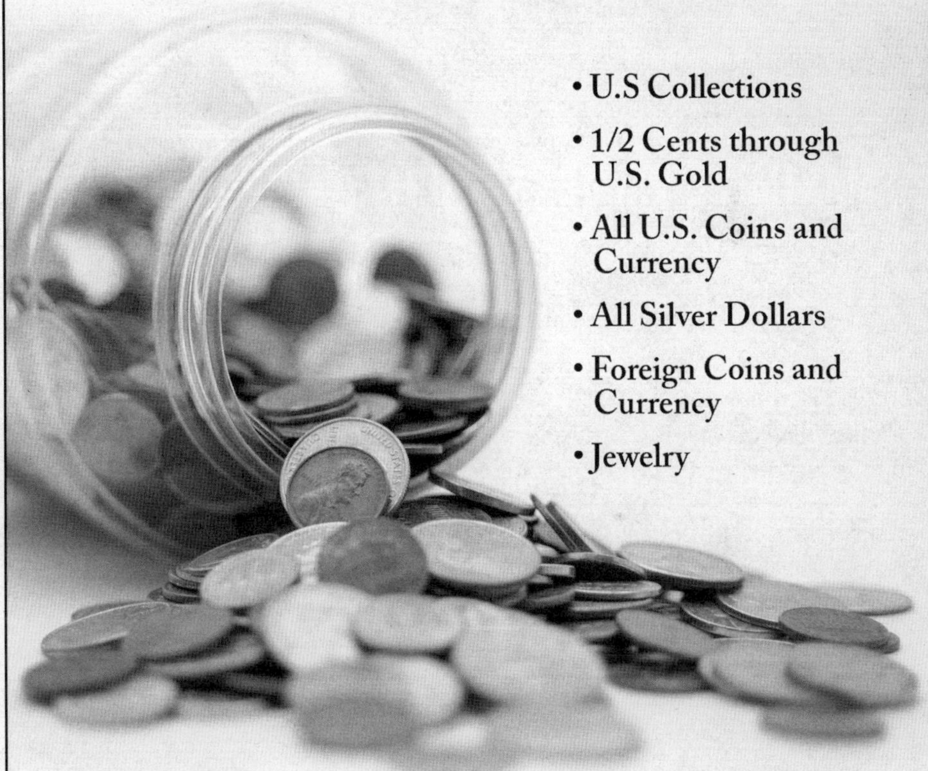

- U.S Collections
- 1/2 Cents through U.S. Gold
- All U.S. Coins and Currency
- All Silver Dollars
- Foreign Coins and Currency
- Jewelry

Free Appraisals - We Will Travel

LANCASTER
Dennis E. Steinmetz
dsteinco@aol.com
350 Centerville Rd.
717-299-1211 or **800-334-3903**

YORK
Michael Steinmetz
michael@steinetzcoins.com
2861 E. Prospect Rd. (Rts. 24 & 124)
717-757-6980 or **866-967-2646**

www.steinmetzcoins.com

THE STANDARD FOR THE RARE COIN INDUSTRY

HAVE YOUR COINS GRADED & ENCAPSULATED BY THE MOST TRUSTED BRAND IN THE INDUSTRY

GET STARTED PCGS.COM

MAXIMIZE VALUE, SECURITY AND LIQUIDITY

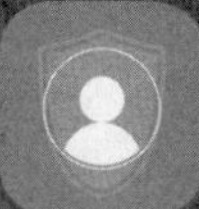

JOIN THE LARGEST COIN COMMUNITY & BENEFIT FROM OUR LIBRARY OF FREE NUMISMATIC APPS / RESOURCES

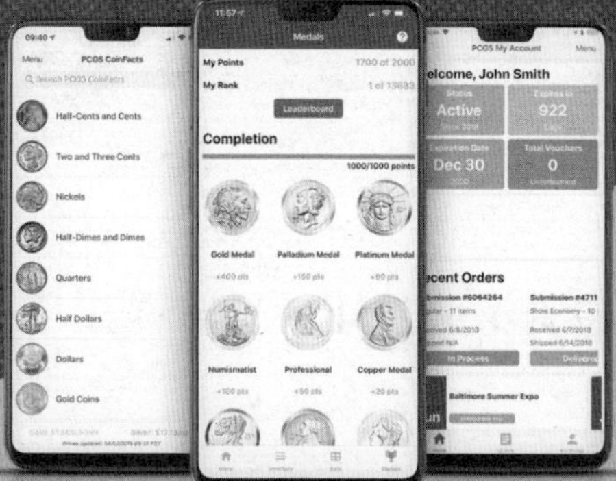

PCGS.COM/APPS

©2020 Professional Coin Grading Service · A Division of Collectors Universe, Inc · NASDAQ:CLCT 909307
info@PCGS.com · 800-447-8848 · @PCGScoin

The NGC VarietyPlus® Program

1936-S/S FS-501 Five Cents

NGC's popular VarietyPlus program attributes more than 18,000 of the most sought-after US and world coin die varieties. VarietyPlus not only attributes the variety on the NGC certification label, but also provides a free online catalog with high-resolution images, diagnostic tips, reference information and more.

Learn more at NGCcoin.com/varietyplus

U.S. COIN AUCTIONS

What is Your Collection Worth?

1942/1 Mercury Dime
FS-101, MS67+ PCGS
Realized $90,000

2004-D Wisconsin State Quarter
FS-5902, Extra Leaf Low, MS67 PCGS
Realized $6,000

1943-S Quarter, MS66+ PCGS CAC
FS-101, Doubled Die Obverse
Realized $9,400

1856-S/S Quarter, VF30 PCGS
FS-501, Large Over Small S
Realized $3,055

1829 Dime, Fine 12 PCGS CAC
FS-301, Curl Base 2
Realized $10,800

1873 Arrows Dime, AU58 PCGS CAC
FS-101, Doubled Die Obverse
Realized $12,000

For a free appraisal, or to consign to an upcoming auction, contact a Heritage Consignment Director today. 800-835-6000

HERITAGE
AUCTIONS
THE WORLD'S LARGEST
NUMISMATIC AUCTIONEER

DALLAS | NEW YORK | BEVERLY HILLS | CHICAGO | PALM BEACH
LONDON | PARIS | GENEVA | BRUSSELS | AMSTERDAM | HONG KONG

Paul R. Minshull #16591. BP 20%; see HA.com 72471